The Process of
Social Organization

The Process of
Social Organization

Marvin E. Olsen
Indiana University

HOLT, RINEHART AND WINSTON
New York / Chicago / San Francisco
Atlanta / Dallas / Montreal / Toronto / London

preface

For many students, both beginning and advanced, the field of sociology is a chaotic jumble of unrelated or contradictory ideas, concepts, and propositions. They are confronted with a vast array of terms such as "social interaction," "social organization," "culture," "social system," and "institution," each perhaps meaningful by itself but none fitting together to form a logically consistent and unified analytical framework with which to examine social life. Study of specific topical areas—such as the family or race relations or stratification—often proves rewarding and challenging to students, but all too often they fail to understand or appreciate the common phenomenal and conceptual core that pervades all these topics and binds together the field of sociology.

This intellectual fragmentation and confusion among students reflects the multiplicity of perspectives and approaches abounding among sociologists today. When large numbers of professionals in a field disagree on the meanings of basic concepts, or do not fully synthesize these concepts into a unified whole, it is no wonder that students turn away from that discipline in dismay. They may be willing to forgive sociology's lack of methodological rigor or theoretical definitiveness, but not what appears to be conceptual chaos.

The underlying premise of this book is that sociology is ultimately concerned with a fundamental phenomenal reality—the process of social organization—which can be studied from a single encompassing analytical perspective incorporating the major concepts in sociology. The explicit purpose of the book is to present the basic concepts and theories of social organization as coherently and comprehensively as possible, within this overall analytical perspective.

Two major themes pervade the book: *process* and *social organization*. The continual stressing of these analytical perspectives gives the work whatever overall unity it possesses. Above all, I conceive of social reality as a continual ongoing process of activity or becoming. Dynamic processes, not static objects, are the ultimate essence of human life. Social order grows out of the constant patterning of social interactions and relationships, and all social structures must be seen as particular instances of ongoing processes.

The second pervasive theme is that of social organization. The unique concern of sociology, I argue, is with social processes and phenomena that transcend the individual personality. Social organization, in all its various forms, always has an existence and properties that are not reducible to characteristics of its individual members. The whole is more than the sum of its component parts and can only be understood and explained as an entity in itself. I use "social organization" as a generic term, referring to all processes and instances of organized social life, and not in the narrower sense of "formal associations." The study of social organization must, of course, take into account individuals' actions and interactions, for it is through these processes that organization arises. But interpersonal phenomena are not, in themselves, the primary focus of the sociologist concerned with social organization. They are, I would suggest, the proper objects of study for social psychologists. In the opposite direction, cultural phenomena, such as values, norms, and technology, are relevant for social organization only to the extent that they reflect or influence ordered social life.

This is not a textbook in the usual sense. No attempt is made to discuss extensively either empirical generalizations or the research on which they are based, and many topics usually included in introductory texts (such as the family, religion, education, race relations, or criminology) are omitted here. Nor is it a theoretical treatise, since it does not attempt to set forth, develop, or test any specific theories. Its purpose, instead, is to provide the student of sociology with a systematic introduction to the fundamental concepts and ideas necessary for examining and analyzing the process and forms of social organization, so that he may have a relatively firm foundation on which to base his further studies. Its intended use is as a supplement to whatever standard text or additional readings an instructor chooses to assign.

I have not attempted here the infinitely more demanding task of constructing a systematic general theory that would incorporate all sociological concepts into a set of interrelated propositions. The creation of
such theories must remain the ultimate goal of sociology, but that
endeavor is still considerably beyond our abilities.

I make no claim of being either eclectic or definitive in this work.
Many sociologists may not fully agree with all that I have said here,
and undoubtedly other authors would have treated many of these ideas
somewhat differently. To achieve logical coherence and consistency,
however, one must employ a dominant unifying theme, which in turn
largely dictates one's selection and use of more specific conceptualizations. Although I have judiciously attempted to keep the discussion
as close as possible to the main stream of contemporary sociological
thought, to maintain uniformity and continuity it has been necessary to
treat certain ideas in a manner that may seem slightly unconventional
to some readers. The intended effect of these alterations is not idiosyn-
crasy, but rather clarification and redirection of conceptual thinking in
sociology. The intellectual venture undertaken in this book is far from
completion; scientific analysis, like social life itself, is a continual process of
development. But perhaps the best means of enlarging one's own thinking
is to put one's ideas down on paper and then invite one's colleagues
to evaluate and criticize them.

The viewpoint presented here was developed in the course of my
lectures to introductory sociology students at The University of Michigan
and Indiana University during the past several years. Although the
book is thus essentially designed for beginning students, it attempts to
demand somewhat more of the reader than do many standard introductory texts. Hopefully, therefore, it will also prove challenging to
upperclassmen and to graduate students.

My intellectual debt to Alfred North Whitehead and the other
developers of process philosophy is fully apparent. The substantive
ideas developed here are drawn from extremely diverse sources, but
four names deserve particular mention: the teachings of Guy E. Swanson
and Amos H. Hawley, and the writings of Émile Durkheim and
Talcott Parsons. Needless to say, they are in no way responsible for this
book, and some of them might even be surprised to find their names
linked in this manner, but their influences on my thinking are inexorably
interwoven throughout this work.

I also express my deep gratitude to all those persons who have
unselfishly contributed to this book through their innumerable suggestions, criticisms, and encouragement: to James Moulton, who first
prompted me to begin this project; to Professors Guy E. Swanson,

Paul E. Mott, Walter Buckley, Don C. Gibbons, J. Eugene Haas, and Richard L. Simpson, who critically read earlier versions of the manuscript and offered countless ideas for improvement; to my wife, Katherine, for her unlimited confidence and encouragement; to Betty Beedie, who diligently typed the manuscript; and to all my students who have served as critical audiences for my thinking.

Finally, a special word of appreciation is due to Professors John H. Burma and Thomas E. Lasswell, who first awakened in me a vision of "the sociological imagination."

M.E.O.

BLOOMINGTON, INDIANA

FEBRUARY 1968

contents

The Process of
Social Organization

CHAPTER 1

The Phenomenon
of Social Organization

"The actual world is a process. . . ." Thus Alfred North Whitehead stated the fundamental principle of process philosophy. "The flux of things is one ultimate generalization around which we must weave our philosophical system." Every phenomenon of which man is aware—from galaxies to electrons, from human beings to amoebae, from societies to families, from philosophies to nursery rhymes—exists in a state of continual "becoming," which Whitehead describes as "a creative advance into novelty."[1] As expressed by Wilmon Henry Sheldon, there are "no fixed entities, no ultimate terms; a thing, a being, even being *qua* being, is not what it is but what it is going to be. Transition, a pure relation, is the ultimate fact. . . ."[2] In short, reality is process, and process is reality.

The dynamic nature of our existence frequently escapes our attention, primarily because of our perceptual and conceptual limitations. These limitations are not insurmountable, however. Not long ago most men believed that the earth stood still (presumably at the center of the universe), while the sun revolved around it. Today, as the result of scientific research in astronomy, we know that we inhabit a spinning globe which continually circles the sun as the entire solar system revolves around the core of a

---

[1] Alfred North Whitehead, *Process and Reality* (New York: The Macmillan Company, 1929), pp. 33, 317, 42.
[2] Wilmon Henry Sheldon, *God and Polarity* (New Haven, Conn.: Yale University Press, 1954), p. 542.

galaxy which is hurtling through space at unimaginable speeds—even though we still appear to be motionless. Biological science, meanwhile, demonstrates the marvelous complexity of the continual life cycle of all living organisms, from creation through growth and adaptation to death. More recently, psychology has begun to understand some of the processes involved in the development of the human mind and the emergence of mature personalities.

Social Reality and Social Organization

If this conception of reality as a continual ongoing process applies to the physical, biological, and psychological realms of existence, must it not also be relevant to human social life? Are not all of our relationships with one another, as well as all the patterns of social order and cultural ideas that emerge from these interactions, constantly fluctuating and developing? In short, is not social life essentially a dynamic process of becoming? This is a metaphysical proposition, and hence can never be proved (or disproved), but our present knowledge unquestionably points in this direction. Underlying our discussion in this book, therefore, is the fundamental thesis that social organization is an ongoing process. As a result, social life is always characterized by contingencies, probabilities, and unknowns. Although many of the concepts and terms comprising modern sociology—and hence also this book—are static (or structural) in nature, they must not divert us from our fundamental view of social life as a dynamic process.

Compounding the complexity of social reality, in addition to its ever-changing nature, is the vast web of social organization that pervades all human life. There are some three billion people in the world today, most of whom interact with many other individuals every day. Out of these billions of daily interactions arise countless millions of continuing social relationships, from which emerge millions of families, groups, associations, and communities, which in turn comprise the several hundred societies that today constitute human civilization.

These two fundamental ideas of process and organization unite in the realization that *social organization is a dynamic process.* As a result of this process, social life becomes ordered and meaningful for its participants, although never static. That is, *social organization is the process of bringing order and meaning into human social life.*

Let us explore further this notion of order. Order is not a static phenomenon, but a dynamic pattern or regularity among the events comprising a given situation. This pattern must persist with relative stability for some minimal period, depending upon the situation. Automobiles on a highway are in continual motion relative to one another, but their movements are ordered as long as they all remain on the right-hand side of the highway.

Order may be produced in many different ways: through atomic attraction and repulsion, through physical forces, through ecological effects ("balance of nature"), through psychological drives, or through interpersonal interaction and communication. All of these factors affect human life, but most social order is the result of interaction and communication. As individuals influence each other and exchange information, they frequently adjust their activities to one another, introduce regularity and predictability into their relationships, and begin to share common ideas. Through this process of social organization they bring order and meaning into their common social life.

The process of social organization necessarily involves at least two interacting persons, but it is not a characteristic of either of them as individual personalities. It arises, rather, through their interaction and communication, as social order emerges from recurrent social relationships, and as the participants create a shared body of cultural ideas. Put more formally, *social organization is the process of merging social actors into ordered social relationships, which become infused with cultural ideas.*

Let us bring these concepts back down to ground level. When John first accidently bumps into Mary on the sidewalk on the way to class, this is a random encounter. As they recognize each other and begin to talk, interaction and communication begin to occur. If they henceforth meet each other periodically at this same place and each time stop to talk, we might say that a social relationship is forming. To the extent that they go out of their way to meet each other, wait for each other at a designated spot, and perhaps extend this relationship into other activities such as dating, patterns of social order have been created. Out of this relationship, finally, will emerge a sharing of ideas (and perhaps also of objects symbolizing these ideas), giving their relationship a common meaning to both Mary and John. Thus the process of social organization develops.

A couple such as John and Mary represent perhaps the simplest type of social organization, but the same basic process may be observed wherever human relationships become ordered and meaningful. Since it is a generic process, social organization may assume or produce unlimited specific forms, such as families, friendship groups, communities of all sizes, voluntary associations (from the AAA to zoological clubs), businesses and industries of every imaginable kind, social classes, mobs, economic market networks, governments, total societies, and international confederations. In short, all aspects of human social life involve the fundamental process of social organization. Thomas Hobbes' classic description of "presocial" human life—as "solitary, poor, nasty, brutish, and short"—is now recognized as poetic fiction, but it provides a dramatic suggestion of what human life might be like if man were not capable of creating social organization.

Students of the social sciences are sometimes confused by the fact that the same term—social organization—is used to designate both the process by which social relationships become ordered and also the specific outcomes or products of this process. "Social organization," in other words, may refer either to actions and processes, or to objects and entities. Thus we might first describe the process of organizing a new business and then refer to this business as a type of organization. There is a crucial semantic reason for this double meaning of "social organization." The entities that we call "social organizations" are always results or outcomes of the underlying process of social organization; they are specific forms of an ongoing process. Furthermore, the social entities that emerge from this process are themselves constantly changing. Use of the term "social organization" as both process and entity should remind us that social reality, no matter how it may be structured at any given instant, is forever undergoing a process of becoming.

Levels of Analysis

To be aware that social organization occurs is one thing; to study and comprehend this process is quite another task. As a point of departure, we note that human life can be analyzed from several different perspectives. All of human existence must ultimately be conceptualized as a single, unified whole, since all aspects of the ongoing process of reality are to some extent interrelated. Because of the extreme complexity of human life, however, our minds must ordinarily view it from one perspective at a time. Four distinct and basic outlooks on human life are commonly used by all of us: organic, psychological, social, and cultural perspectives.

With an *organic perspective* one focuses on the biological features of human life, so that *the individual is viewed primarily as an organism.* Medical practice is perhaps the clearest example of this perspective; part of a physician's training involves learning to treat a body solely as a biological organism, not as a unique person. An organic perspective may also prevail in sexual attraction, or when we study such things as the process of heredity or man's ability to survive in space.

With a *psychological perspective* one focuses on the mental characteristics of human life, so that *the individual is viewed primarily as a self-*

conscious mind or personality. This perspective predominates in such problems as teaching a child to read, administering psychotherapy to a mentally ill person, becoming acquainted with a new friend, or testing an employee's aptitude for promotion to a supervisory job.

With a *social perspective* one focuses on the interpersonal aspects of human life, so that *the individual is viewed primarily as a member of some social relationship*. Activities such as maintaining a marriage, implementing a community recreation program, operating a business, or running a government are appropriately viewed from this perspective.

With a *cultural perspective* one focuses on the symbolic meanings in human life, so that *the individual is viewed primarily as a carrier of shared cultural ideas*. This perspective comes into play, for instance, when we observe people criticizing the literary qualities of a book, expounding religious beliefs, perpetuating the myth of Santa Claus, or attempting to increase scientific knowledge.

All four of these perspectives on human life are fabrications, in the sense that they are intellectual abstractions imposed upon ongoing processes of reality by human observers. Nonetheless, the distinctions between them are not entirely arbitrary. The simple observation that these four perspectives on human life have been used by mankind throughout history should suggest that each of them has some basis in reality. If this is so, then they should also provide foundations for different types of analysis of human life. That is, the use of each perspective suggests a different set of questions to be asked, problems to be investigated, and theoretical explanations to be formulated.

These four types of analysis have been developed as scientists concerned with studying man have divided human life into a number of specialized disciplines, each of which focuses primarily on one basic perspective. As a result, there are four fundamentally different ways of studying, analyzing, and explaining human life. Some disciplines associated with each type of analysis are listed in Table 1–1. This chart is incomplete in that it ignores the tendency of each discipline to "spill over" into other types of analysis. Psychology, for example, takes account of physiological and social influences on the personality. We have also ignored the many interdisciplinary fields that attempt to bridge adjacent types of analysis, such as physiological psychology, social psychology, and sociocultural studies of art, religion, knowledge. Finally, history cannot be identified with any particular level of analysis, since it is not so much a separate discipline as a special type of inquiry—essentially a concern with describing specific past events—which may be applied to any substantive area, from philosophy to politics to personalities.

The chart nevertheless clearly emphasizes one important point about

TABLE 1-1

Types of Analysis of Human Life and Associated Academic Disciplines

Type of Analysis	Academic Disciplines
Cultural	Philosophy, linguistics, ethnology, law, literature
Social	Sociology, economics, political science, social anthropology
Personality	Psychology, psychoanalysis
Organic	Biology, medicine, physical anthropology

the social sciences. All of these disciplines—sociology, economics, political science, social anthropology, as well as related interdisciplinary fields—share a single analytic perspective. All of them are concerned with describing and explaining ordered social relationships, whatever their particular substantive concerns. In fact sociologists, economists, and political scientists are finding it increasingly difficult to distinguish one field from another as their disciplines become more sophisticated, and the major difference now between sociologists and social anthropologists is that the latter normally restrict themselves to studying nonliterate or "premodern" societies.

Thus far we have sought only to distinguish among the organic, psychological, social, and cultural perspectives on human life. Let us now observe that these four types of analysis represent increasing degrees of separation or independence from the physical world. It is not that social or cultural perspectives are necessarily more complex or conceptually abstract than are organic and psychological perspectives. The point is that social and cultural life are somewhat less directly related to, and constrained by, physical existence than are organic and psychological phenomena. To reflect this ordered sequence we shall refer to these perspectives as "levels" of analysis.

To the extent that the four levels of analysis are grounded in reality, and thus represent different kinds of real phenomena, they are interrelated in three ways: by emergence, independence, and interpenetration.

The concept of *emergence* refers to the observation that *each succeedingly higher level of phenomena develops out of the level immediately preceding it, and is always dependent to some extent on all lower levels.* More specifically: (a) personalities develop only in conjunction with organic life, and cannot survive if the organism dies; (b) social relationships occur only when two or more personalities interact, and cease to exist when all of their members withdraw either psychologically or physically; and (c) cultures are outgrowths of social activities, and become mere relics when the social entities that created them or the individuals who carry them disappear.

The concept of *independence* refers to the observation that *each level of phenomena, although emergent from those below it, nevertheless, possesses some degree of autonomy.* Phenomena at each level have characteristics uniquely their own that are not fully determined by the lower levels. It is impossible to explain any given level solely in terms of those below it; the properties of the prior phenomena do not sufficiently explain the emergent phenomena. A personality is something more than just an acting organism, a group is something more than just several interacting personalities, and a culture is something more than just a symbolic reflection of its society.

The concept of *interpenetration* refers to the observation that *each succeedingly higher level, by virtue of its partial independence, can and frequently does influence the lower levels from which it emerged, even though it could not exist without them.* In other words, influences between levels of phenomena are always reciprocal. Personality tensions cause stomach ulcers, while poor health often affects one's personality. Communities exercise many constraints upon the actions of their members, as well as providing for their biological welfare, while at the same time the sustenance needs and personality characteristics of individuals continually affect the nature and scope of community activities. And at the cultural level, beliefs and ideas can shape societies, change personalities, and even produce martyrs, while concurrently such cultural phenomena always reflect the social life, personality structures, and organic characteristics of their proponents.

The Discipline of Sociology

Although social life emerges from the organic and personality levels, we have argued that it has characteristics of its own that cannot be explained by biological or psychological principles. The social sciences—economics, political science, social anthropology, and sociology—are all expressly concerned with the study of social processes as real phenomena. All of them seek to discover uniquely social principles that will help us understand, explain, and predict social life in all its various manifestations. But if these different social sciences all focus on the social level of analysis, what is distinctive about sociology? How might we describe this discipline and distinguish it from the other social sciences?

To some extent sociology has tended to become the residual category of the social sciences, absorbing whatever substantive areas were not already claimed by the older disciplines of economics and political science. Thus we find sociologists studying such diverse phenomena as the family, communities, voluntary associations, race relations, social stratification, crime, bureaucracies, and mass communications.

One traditional way of giving sociology some intellectual unity is to take a "social-problems" approach. Sociology is then seen primarily as seeking solutions to the social problems besetting contemporary societies —from juvenile delinquency to international tensions. And in fact the findings of sociology, as well as those of all the other social sciences, may be applied to practical affairs whenever they are relevant. But to define sociology solely in such terms is to forget that it is a pure science, concerned with increasing our knowledge about human social life. It is not itself a form of applied social engineering.

Another way of imposing coherence upon sociology is to conceive of it as virtually synonymous with social psychology. Sociology is then described as the study of individual social behavior or of interpersonal interaction. Such areas of study are perfectly legitimate and very important, but they ignore the whole realm of social organization. The name we give to the discipline that studies social organization is irrelevant, and it might just as well be "organology" as "sociology," except for the weight of tradition. To all of the founders of this field—Auguste Comte, Herbert Spencer, Emile Durkheim, and Max Weber, to mention a few—the fundamental and unique concern of sociology was with social organization. Actions of individuals were incidental except insofar as they contributed to broader social processes.

Contemporary sociologists are increasingly realizing that their discipline has a unique scientific task—one that cuts across all the specialized subfields of sociology as well as all the other social sciences, that goes far beyond the social-problems approach in intellectual depth, and that clearly distinguishes sociology from social psychology. This unique task of sociology is to describe empirically and to explain theoretically the process of social organization wherever and whenever it occurs. Sociology thus becomes the fundamental source of concepts and theories for whatever substantive phenomena social scientists choose to study.

For the purposes of this book, therefore, *sociology is the scientific study of the process and forms of social organization.*[3] There are two key terms in this definition: "scientific study" and "social organization." We

---

[3] This conception of sociology does not imply that sociologists should not study either social-psychological phenomena (such as individuals' attitudes and actions) or sociocultural phenomena (art, religion, law, science, and so on). But these sociologists must reailze that they are working in interdisciplinary areas across levels of analysis, and their theories and research must take account of both perspectives involved.

have already glanced at the concept of "social organization," and most of the rest of this book examines various aspects of that process. In the following chapter, though, we shall digress briefly to consider the meaning of "scientific study."

Beyond its scientific goal of describing and explaining the process of social organization, sociology also accepts a broader, more humanistic challenge. The discipline offers its students, and seeks to develop within them, a new way of looking at, thinking about, and acting toward social life. C. Wright Mills termed this perspective "the sociological imagination" and described it as "the quality of mind that seems most dramatically to promise an understanding of the intimate realities of ourselves in connection with larger social realities. It is not merely one quality of mind among the contemporary range of cultural sensibilities—it is *the* quality whose wider and more adroit use offers the promise that all such sensibilities—and in fact, human reason itself—will come to play a greater role in human affairs."[4]

[4] C. Wright Mills, *The Sociological Imagination* (New York: Oxford University Press, 1959), p. 15.

RECOMMENDED READING

BERGER, PETER L., *Invitation to Sociology*, chaps. 1–2 (Garden City, N.Y.: Doubleday Anchor Books, 1963).
A presentation and elaboration of the sociological perspective from a humanistic point of view.

INKELES, ALEX, *What is Sociology?*, chaps. 1–2 (Englewood Cliffs, N.J.: Prentice-Hall Foundations of Modern Sociology Series, 1964).
An inclusive introduction to the discipline of sociology, plus a discussion of its basic theoretical concerns.

MILLS, C. WRIGHT, *The Sociological Imagination*, chap. 1 (New York: Oxford University Press, 1959; available in paperback as a Grove Press Evergreen Book).
A statement of the role of sociology in understanding, criticizing, and shaping contemporary society.

SIMPSON, GEORGE, *Man in Society* (New York: Random House paperback, 1954).
A broad overview of the social sciences, emphasizing their interrelations and common characteristics, as well as the particular concerns of sociology.

CHAPTER 2

The Study of
Social Organization

We have repeatedly called sociology a social science and we have defined
it as the scientific study of social organization, but we have yet to specify
what science is. Physicists measure electric currents, biologists dissect
frogs, psychologists administer intelligence tests, economists chart the
growth of the Gross National Product, linguists decipher ancient codes—
and all of these activities are labeled "science." What features do they all
share in common?

Although many people associate the idea of "science" with particular
fields of inquiry, such as physics or chemistry, or with specific research
techniques, such as laboratory experiments or space probes, these conceptions are not accurate. It is generally agreed today that *science is a means
of acquiring knowledge that is potentially applicable to all phenomena*.
It is not what one studies, the research techniques used, or the amount of
knowledge acquired, but rather the manner in which knowledge is acquired that makes one's work scientific. In the words of Karl Pearson,
"The unity of all science consists alone in its methods, not in its material."[1]

[1] Karl Pearson, *The Grammar of Science* (London: Adam and Charles Black, 1900), p. 12.

The Scientific Process

The process and method of science pervade the contemporary world, and we easily forget that science is only one of many ways in which men have sought knowledge—and a relatively new one at that. How does science differ from other means of acquiring knowledge, such as literary and artistic inspiration, philosophical and religious insight, or logical deduction? *Science can be described in terms of two fundamental characteristics: theory and research.*

The goal of the scientific process is always to explain rationally the phenomena being studied. Such explanation may involve the establishment of cause-and-effect sequences of events, it may specify in detail how a process occurs, or it may indicate the consequences of a given process for other related phenomena. All scientific explanation, regardless of its particular nature, is achieved through the construction of *theories,* or sets of logically consistent and interrelated concepts and propositions that outline relationships among various aspects or properties of the phenomena being studied. The idea that the earth and the moon remain at a relatively uniform distance from each other because of the opposing forces of gravity and centrifugal force is an example of a theory in astronomy. The idea that as a society becomes larger and more complex its component parts must increase in functional interdependence if it is to remain unified is an example of a theory in sociology.

Theories are intellectual creations and hence must be abstracted from the phenomena which they attempt to explain. In one sense, then, a theory is but a representation of the ongoing process of reality. Theories do not exist until men create them. Once a theory has been formulated, however, it is just as "real" and at least as important to its creators as are physical objects or biological organisms. Theories are intellectual abstractions created to explain existing phenomena, but these ideas may in turn be used to modify the conditions that originally suggested them.

If the scientific process were to end with theory construction, as it did in the physical sciences until the seventeenth century and in the social sciences until the twentieth century, there would still be nothing unique about it. Neither "natural philosophy" nor "social philosophy" became a science until it incorporated a second crucial feature: *empirical research.* The scientist must always ask: "What is the evidence for this theory?" and then proceed to examine the adequacy of the theory against the facts of the empirical world. Only after a theory has withstood the assaults of several well-designed empirical tests can we begin to have confidence in its ability to explain the phenomena being studied.

Ideally, the acquisition of scientific knowledge should follow a single path: (a) some phenomenon, series of events, or problem is seen to exist; (b) a theory is proposed to explain one or more aspects of this phenomenon, based on whatever is known about it and whatever critical insights or educated guesses the theorist can suggest; (c) several specific, testable hypotheses are logically derived from the more general theory; (d) these hypotheses are tested in a series of appropriate, unbiased, and independent empirical studies, and are shown to be either valid or invalid; and finally (e) on the basis of these findings the theory is either tentatively accepted (pending the future discovery of disconfirming evidence) or rejected. It may be noted in passing that only hypotheses derived from a theory are examined in empirical research; the theory itself cannot be directly tested and hence can never in a final sense be proved or disproved. Some theories, however, are much "better" than others in the extent or adequacy with which they explain phenomena, and when dealing with practical problems we often (out of necessity) treat a theory for which considerable supporting evidence exists as if its validity were proven.

In practice the ideal sequence of steps is frequently modified, although the basic procedure cannot be ignored if the endeavor is to remain scientific. The working relationship between theory and research is normally reciprocal, rather than one-way, with each one influencing the other. Research data affect theories in several ways: theories are purposefully formulated to take into account existing knowledge, old theories are revised in the light of recently acquired information, and the invention of new research techniques often provides novel perspectives that in turn suggest new theories. These kinds of intellectual cross-fertilization between theory and research can be highly stimulating to a science, and need not be discouraged as long as they do not get out of hand. Only when research is used solely to support dogmatically propounded theory does science cease to exist. The history of science includes many a zealot who accepted the facts that supported his pet theory and ignored all other data, but this practice is less prevalent today.

A more critical problem for contemporary science—especially social science—lies in the tendency to ignore theory. To make their work "totally scientific" and to erase armchair speculative philosophy from their disciplines, many social scientists during the early decades of this century refused to have anything to do with theory. This position, which was largely a response to the fierce opposition the social sciences encountered in their efforts to become intellectually respectable, is understandable but nonetheless woefully one-sided.

Contrary to much popular thinking, the simple gathering of empirical facts can never be the final goal of science. Facts, taken by themselves without reference to any theory, are worthless to science since they do not explain themselves. Of what scientific benefit, for example, might it be to know that a particular beach contained 6,937,025,114 grains of sand, or that a given individual spoke 18 times during the course of a PTA meeting? Knowledge of specific facts may enable us to test theoretical hypotheses or deal with practical problems, but such knowledge does not increase our scientific understanding of ourselves or our world. In short, in the scientific process the gathering of data through empirical research is always a means to the end of attaining systematic theory.

Empirical research is often linked to theory through *empirical generalizations*. A generalization summarizes two or more empirical facts about a given phenomenon or class of similar phenomena, so as to provide an encompassing yet concise description of reality. The statement that an acid and a base when combined always produce a salt is a generalization from chemistry, while the statement that forgetting is most rapid immediately after learning and thereafter proceeds at a much slower rate is a generalization from psychology. Like theories, empirical generalizations are intellectually abstracted from the phenomena to which they refer, but unlike theories they merely describe these phenomena and do not explain them. Neither of the above examples tells "how" or "why"; both simply tell "what" happens in certain situations. They are valuable pieces of information, but they are not theories.

Conceptually, then, descriptive generalizations are quite distinct from explanatory theories. Nevertheless, in practice the two often become intertwined, with theories being formulated to explain verified generalizations and generalizations forming much of the content of theories. From the point of view of theory construction, this is desirable since it keeps one's theories relevant to empirical phenomena. The danger lies in the temptation to treat empirical generalizations as if they were theoretical explanations, and to forget that they are only the building blocks of theories.

The term "laws" is also frequently encountered in scientific literature, especially in the natural sciences. Although this word carries many connotations, scientific laws are either theories or empirical generalizations for which considerable supporting evidence exists. The point at which a theory or generalization becomes a scientific law is rather arbitrary, although a useful bench mark is the absence of any disconfirming evidence. We do not normally designate a piece of scientific knowledge as a law as long as there is any indication that it might not be totally valid. The theory of gravitational attraction, for example, is often termed a law, while the observation that considerable social stratification exists in all industrialized societies remains at best a crude empirical generalization.

Science, like all other aspects of human life, is a continual, ongoing process. The explanatory theories that constitute the heart of any branch of science are constantly being created, modified, or rejected. We must therefore conceptualize both empirical facts and scientific theories as dynamic processes moving through time.

To the extent that adequate theoretical explanations of existing phenomena are achieved in the manner discussed here, science is being used to increase man's knowledge. Such knowledge may in turn be used for the prediction and control of future events, but these steps take us from the realm of science into engineering, or the application of scientific knowledge to the solution of practical problems.

The Scientific Method

Intellectual endeavors are scientific if they attempt to explain phenomena through the creation of logical theories substantiated by empirical research. To label a piece of work as science indicates nothing about its quality, however. Some scientific efforts are mediocre at best, while others exemplify the highest ideals of the scientific method. As in all professions, scientists over the years have developed a set of well-established standards for the creation of theory and the conduct of research. All scientists are expected, both by their colleagues and also by the larger public, to adhere to these standards, and sanctions are applied to those who do not. *These normative standards, which describe how all scientific endeavors are to be carried out, together define what is usually called "the scientific method."*

Some of these standards for scientific work concern actions or procedures that should or should not be performed. Books on research methods go into these topics at great lengths, and we need not elaborate them here. These procedural standards include, for instance, recording and communicating all techniques employed, attempting to hold constant or to control all nonrelevant factors in research situations, and avoiding the falsification of research to make it compatible with one's theory.

A second category of scientific standards consists of orientations that should be held by all scientists. The most commonly mentioned of these attitudes are objectivity, skepticism, neutrality, relativism, and humility.[2]

Objectivity is the attempt to free one's theories and research from all traces of personal or subjective bias, such as preferences and desires, predispositions and beliefs, prejudices and loyalties. The difficulties inherent in maintaining objectivity have long been recognized—indeed, Francis

---

[2] The following discussion of these attitudes is drawn largely from Robert Bierstedt, *The Social Order* (New York: McGraw-Hill, Inc., 1963), pp. 17–22.

Bacon's sixteenth-century description of the Idols of the Tribe, Cave, Market Place, and Theater has never been surpassed—but contemporary science is still far from overcoming them. Deliberate falsification of data is relatively rare today, but probably no research is totally devoid of unintentional biases, which creep in without the scientist's knowledge and despite his best intentions. To counter these subtle biases, scientists place strong emphasis on independent repetitions of studies, since the most adequate test of objectivity is agreement among a number of qualified scientists working independently of each other. To make possible such replication a science must have a standardized technical vocabulary, and all procedures employed by its practitioners must be reported in detail.

Skepticism has been described as "a willingness, if not indeed an eagerness, to question everything before accepting it, and especially those things for which there is insufficient evidence."[3] This spirit of skepticism distinguishes the true scientist from the idle speculator. Although both may be curious about why something happens and both may propose theories to explain the event in question, the scientist will not accept any theoretical explanation—even tentatively—until it has been adequately substantiated by empirical evidence.

Neutrality means that the scientist, in his professional role, should take no moral, ethical, or value positions. Science should be value-free. As a member of his community and his society the scientist will, of course, hold many political, religious, social, and other values. Furthermore, his selection of questions to investigate is often guided by values and ethical concerns; he studies problems that he feels are important. Finally, he may utilize his scientific knowledge in attempting to achieve whatever goals he believes desirable. But in his professional work as a scientist seeking new knowledge, he must temporarily put aside all such value positions and attempt to be ethically neutral. Science is concerned only with explaining what is, not with prescribing what should be. Science may be used to discover new or more effective means of achieving desired goals, but it cannot formulate or select goals or the values on which they rest.

Relativism is the willingness to discard old ideas or theories as more adequate or complete knowledge becomes available. In science there is no absolute, universal, final truth. Man's knowledge about his world and himself is continually changing, and the scientist must always be willing to reject today what he accepted yesterday. "Science, in other words, has no notions so sacred, no propositions so privileged, no truths so absolute that they are not subject to change when new evidence arises to challenge them."[4] This relativistic conception of truth gives scientific work an in-

---

[3] Bierstedt, p. 21.
[4] Bierstedt, p. 20.

valuable asset: a built-in self-correction process that never permits knowledge to become distorted or obsolete for too long.

Humility, finally, has only recently become dominant within many scientific disciplines. Not too many centuries ago an educated man could personally possess virtually all existing scientific knowledge, which often resulted in a marked degree of self-pride. In fact, as late as the middle of the nineteenth century Auguste Comte believed that the scientific pinnacle had been attained in the creation of sociology, of which he believed he knew all there was to know, and which he proposed should form the basis of a revolutionary new religion, with Comte as its first and principal prophet. What wiser persons have long known, and what more of us discover every day, is that as knowledge slowly expands, so does our awareness of all the questions remaining unanswered. In the words of Will Durant: "Education is a progressive discovery of our own ignorance."[5]

Prerequisites for Social Science

In principle, the process and method of science can be used to study any phenomenon—stars, electricity, cell growth, personality disorders, community power structures, or religious beliefs—as long as this phenomenon meets three fundamental requirements: observability, regularity, and variability. One means of deciding whether science is applicable to social phenomena is to determine whether social life satisfies these basic prerequisites.

First, *the phenomenon must be observable by human senses.* It may be observable directly, as in the cases of rock formations and chemical reactions, or only indirectly through its effects, as in the case of gravity or neuroses or social stratification, or through what other people tell us, as in the case of migraine headaches or group norms and ethical values. Sensory observability is necessary so that the phenomenon can be measured and/or described by those seeking to study it. Sometimes highly sophisticated and complex tools must be developed before a phenomenon can be observed and measured—subatomic particles, for example, cannot be examined without high-energy accelerators and bubble chambers—but if the phenomenon is at least potentially observable there is no absolute reason why it cannot be scientifically studied. In short, the scientific method can be applied to any real phenomenon. Science may not be able to study ghosts, but it can examine people's beliefs about ghosts!

Second, *the phenomenon to be studied must exhibit some regularities.* If it were completely random and capricious, it would be impossible to

---

[5] Quoted in *Time Magazine,* August 13, 1965, p. 48.

describe and measure it, let alone formulate enduring theories about it. We are able to study magnetism because the earth's magnetic forces are ordered in certain ways, we can study biological inheritance because of regularities in gene transmission, and we can study human families because family life everywhere exhibits many uniformities. The existence of regularities in any phenomenon being studied is at first merely assumed by the scientist. As his knowledge of this phenomenon increases, however, he can subject these assumptions to empirical tests and determine the extent of their validity.

The third prerequisite is that *the phenomenon must evidence at least some variability*. These variations may exist among different manifestations of the phenomenon at a given time, or among successive states of the phenomenon over time, or both. But scientific inquiry is impossible without a minimal amount of variation. Electricity could not be studied if electrons never altered their positions—and in fact was not extensively studied until physicists realized that this did occur. Human learning could not be examined if people were born possessing an identical fixed amount of knowledge and never learned anything else. Nor could the process of urbanization be investigated if all people lived in cities and never moved.

Not only must the phenomenon being studied exhibit variation, but the scientist must also incorporate this variation within his research and theories. More pointedly, it is impossible to explain the advent or dynamics of any phenomenon on the basis of static or fixed entities. Assuming, for example, that the average level of human intelligence has not changed significantly during the past several hundred years, it is senseless to attribute the rise of industrial manufacturing to increasing intelligence. The causes of this phenomenon must be sought among other concurrently changing processes.

Human social life meets all three of these prerequisites for scientific study. People's actions and interactions are directly observable, and their attitudes, values, ideas, and expectations may be ascertained by asking about them, by determining their effects on actions, and by examining them in spoken and written forms. The assumption that regularities do exist in social life also seems quite reasonable. Experience has no doubt convinced us all that many aspects of human life are ordered and predictable. To take a mundane example, the probability is extremely high (though not absolute) that whoever you are, regardless of age, race, sex, religion, or any other characteristic, if you live in the United States and are over three years old, you will not venture outside your home tomorrow morning without some type of clothing on at least part of your body. This illustration brings out an aspect of the assumption of regularity that is often overlooked: such regularity need not be complete. Science can proceed on the assumption of ordered probabilities, and in fact most social science (and increasingly physical and biological science also) operates almost entirely in terms of probabilities.

Finally, variability is clearly ubiquitous in social life. Indeed, the social scientist is often confronted with so much variation that he finds it difficult to determine which variables are relevant to his present concern and which are not.

It would seem, therefore, that the endeavors of social science are fully warranted. Given the observability, regularity, and variability of human social existence, social scientists should be able to skeptically observe social phenomena, objectively formulate empirical generalizations, create value-free theories, modify and improve these theories on the basis of empirical research, and thus slowly but steadily increase our understanding of the process of social organization. Whether or not we are capable of realizing this challenge is another question, but at least the effort is justifiable—and could prove highly rewarding.

In sum, *social science attempts to use the scientific process and method to study and explain observable uniformities and variations in social processes and forms.*

Limitations of the Social Sciences

The intellectual challenge facing social science is plainly evident—but it is also evident, even to the beginning student, that these disciplines thus far have barely begun to accomplish this task. Why have the social sciences realized so little of their vast potential? An adequate answer would require a thorough review of the course of intellectual history, which would take us far afield. Two observations, however, may offer a partial explanation.

First, *the social sciences are all relatively new in relation to the physical sciences.* Sociology, for instance, is no more than one hundred years old, and the vast bulk of existing sociological work has been done within only the past thirty or forty years. This is hardly enough time in which to develop a totally new field of scientific endeavor.

Second, *the social sciences suffer from several severe limitations in their atempts to use the scientific process and method.* Although these difficulties are not unknown in the physical sciences, they are generally less severe there.

The most critical of these problems is the difficulty of maintaining objectivity and neutrality. The physicist studying the effects of air pressure is not nearly as susceptible to subtle subjective biases or prevailing values as is the sociologist studying the stratification pattern of his own community. The sociologist studies phenomena in which he is frequently an involved participant, and toward which he holds personal attitudes and values. To detach oneself sufficiently from one's subject matter to maintain scientific objectivity and neutrality is a most demanding requirement and perhaps can never be fully realized. The best the social scientist can do is to avoid conscious biases and to state openly his relevant personal values, so that others may try to compensate for them. This is far from a perfect procedure—although fortunately, given sufficient time, "the world bites back" to correct many of these weaknesses.

Another handicap to social science is the sheer complexity of its subject matter. At this point in the development of sociology we cannot even begin to fathom, let alone describe or explain, the totality of all social processes and forms that comprise a society such as our own. Whenever we do attempt to explain some phenomenon, we almost invariably discover that it has not one cause and one effect, but rather a multitude of both causes and effects, all interrelated and reciprocal.

The social sciences are also prevented by ethical considerations, as well as by simple lack of resources, from performing many of the kinds of controlled experiments used in the physical sciences. For instance, we cannot deliberately foment a revolution in order to observe its internal dynamics, nor can we place a bureaucracy in a laboratory and manipulate its structure at will. And even if such procedures were technically feasible, most social scientists would have strong ethical reservations about using them. How far should a sociologist intrude into other people's lives in the name of science? Chemicals and guinea pigs do not object to being used as subjects for experiments, but the use of human subjects does pose numerous ethical problems. As a result of this lack of experimental control, the best explanation a social scientist can often give of any phenomenon is that "such and such factors would affect it in such and such ways for such and such reasons *if* all else were held constant"—which never actually occurs.

The final handicap to social science comes from the larger public, which often resists or even represses its work. The phenomena that the social sciences study are often extremely important to everyone involved, and within any population there will be some people who are quite satisfied with the present situation and prefer to remain in ignorance concerning it rather than take the chance of disturbing the *status quo* by studying it. And if social scientific knowledge is discovered and made available, it is not infrequently hotly denounced by persons seeking to protect their cherished traditional beliefs or their vested interests in existing social patterns. In a few avid sentences, Robert Merton has aptly described the difficulties encountered by sociologists in gaining public acceptance of their work:

Should the sociologist's systematic inquiry only confirm what has been widely assumed . . . he will, of course, be charged with "laboring the obvious." He becomes tagged as a bore, telling only what everybody knows. Should investigation find that widely held social beliefs are untrue . . . he is a heretic, questioning value-laden verities. If he ventures to examine socially implausible ideas that turn out to be untrue, he is a fool, wasting efforts on a line of inquiry not worth pursuing in the first place. And finally, if he should turn up some implausible truths, he must be prepared to find himself regarded as a charlatan, claiming as knowledge what is patently false. Instances of each of these alternatives have occurred in the history of many sciences, but they would seem especially apt to occur in a discipline, such as sociology, that deals with matters about which men have firm opinions presumably grounded in their own experiences.[6]

We now realize that it is pointless to debate whether or not sociology is a science, since the argument turns entirely on one's definitions of terms. Two concluding observations seem justified, however: First, in terms of its ultimate goals and standards of inquiry, sociology is as scientific as any discipline—especially one dealing with social life—can realistically hope to become. Second, in terms of its ability to explain social phenomena through empirically verified theories, sociology is still far from being a mature science, although it is constantly striving in this direction.

[6] Robert K. Merton, "Notes on Problem-Finding in Sociology," in Merton, et al., eds., Sociology Today (New York: Basic Books, Inc., 1959), pp. xv–xvi.

RECOMMENDED READING

CHINOY, ELY, Sociological Perspective, chap. 1 (New York: Random House paperback, 1954).
A discussion of the nature and use of concepts in sociological analysis.
DE GRAZIA, ALFRED, "The Hatred of New Social Science," American Behavioral Scientist, vol. 5 (1961), pp. 5–13.
A speculative account of the factors hindering public acceptance of social science, and a defense of its value.
INKELES, ALEX, What is Sociology?, chap. 7 (Englewood Cliffs, N.J.: Prentice-Hall Foundations of Modern Sociology Series, 1964).
A brief but comprehensive examination of the major problems involved in the application of the scientific method to sociological analysis.
STOUFFER, SAMUEL A., "Some Observations on Study Design," The American Journal of Sociology, vol. 55 (January 1950), pp. 335–361.
These observations pertain to the use of the controlled experimental method in social science.

CHAPTER 3

The Setting of Social Organization

Psychologists studying the process of perception frequently employ as an experimental stimulus a drawing of two opposing facial profiles whose noses do not quite touch each other. Or at least it seems to be two faces—until one stares at it for a moment. Then suddenly the space between the profiles becomes a bird bath, while the faces dissolve to mere background. The point demonstrated here is that any phenomenon may be perceived either as an object to be observed or as background to some other phenomenon. This problem of distinguishing between object and background is as pervasive in the study of social life as it is in psychological experiments. We must, therefore, begin our exploration of the process of social organization by briefly examining the setting in which it occurs. Once the relevant background factors have been identified, we should then be able to maintain a clear focus on social organization itself.

Social organization cannot occur in a vacuum. This process is only part of the totality of ongoing existence and can be understood only in relation to its setting. The sociologist must therefore always be aware of, and take into account, the many diverse factors that form the background for social life. Four such factors are especially crucial, for they directly limit and shape all social organization. These are the natural environment, population, the human being, and material technology. None of these is itself part of social organization, nor do they fully determine its functioning or structure, but together they form the main parameters for all organized social life. All four can also be viewed as prerequisites for the process of social organization. *By themselves these factors are not sufficient to create social organization, nor do they directly constitute it, but without them there could be no social life.* Figuratively speaking, they are the four sides of the frame that bounds the moving picture of social reality.

The Natural Environment

The most basic of these background conditions is the natural environment—the earth on which we live, as well as the surrounding universe. We know that human life is utterly dependent on a particular mixture of gases, certain specific elements and chemical combinations, and a very limited range of temperature variation. The flow of human activities, and even our conception of time, are shaped and regulated by the rotation, tilt, and movement of the earth, the results of which are days, seasons, and years.

The natural environment also provides human societies and other forms of social organization with many vital resources necessary for survival and the achievement of common goals. (A "resource" is anything that a person or an organization uses in the course of his or its activities as a means of attaining some goal.) All societies draw on the natural environment for such obvious resources as food and water, minerals and chemicals, building materials and fuels. Solar energy, climate, electricity, and even time may also be viewed as natural resources for human societies.

Although the more extreme forms of geographical determinism are no longer accepted by most social scientists as offering useful theoretical explanations of social life, we sometimes forget or minimize our dependence on the natural environment. It is easy to see the ways in which the social organizations of Eskimos or desert tribes are shaped by the natural environment. But have not the technological advances of "civilization" largely eradicated these influences? To some extent, yes. Modern technology is enabling man to harness, control, and exploit the natural environment and its resources more effectively than ever before. Nevertheless, a severe earthquake or hurricane quickly reminds us of our inescapable dependence on nature. And imagine the consequences for all human societies of just a moderate decline in annual rainfall or a slight change of thirty degrees in mean annual temperature. Furthermore, to the extent that we do manage to control nature, our societies must be organized to make this control possible—we must have weather bureaus, agriculture departments, flood control programs, and the like. From a broader perspective, then, our question must be answered negatively. Mankind's attempts to create social organization are always inescapably influenced by the natural environment.

Population

The second fundamental requirement for social organization is the existence of a population of people. By itself, a population is nothing but a statistical category; it has no organization of any kind. It does, however, provide the "raw material" for the creation of social organization, since organizations are always composed of relationships among a population of people. Social organization arises when a population acts collectively in an environment to achieve goals of some kind.

In a fundamental sense, social organization is always a property of populations, not of single individuals. As population phenomena, social organizations are highly influenced by the characteristics of the populations that comprise them. A number of sociologists, beginning with Émile Durkheim,[1] have argued that population size is the main factor in determining the organizational complexity of a society. Other social scientists consider additional variables equally important, but no one would deny that the size of an organization's population is a crucial determinant of its social structure and functioning. A community with a million inhabitants will never achieve the personal intimacy of a village with a dozen families, but it is able to support a vast array of specialized activities far beyond the capabilities of the village. Apart from absolute size, the rate at which a population is growing or declining may also have multiple ramifications for social organization—witness the endless problems in education, housing, transportation, and recreation programs being encountered in the United States today as the result of rapid population growth. And on a broader scale, many experts agree that most nonindustrial societies will be unable to raise their standards of living unless they first curb their present population "explosions."

Although size is undoubtedly the most critical population characteristic for social organization, other factors are also important. For instance, societies differ markedly in their age distributions, and a predominantly "young" society faces problems quite different from those encountered by "aging" societies. The racial composition of a society may likewise influence many aspects of its social life—if the members of the society believe race to be socially important. Finally, serious imbalances in the sex ratio

---

[1] Émile Durkheim, *The Division of Labor in Society,* trans. George Simpson (New York: The Free Press, a division of The Macmillan Company, 1933).

of a population will disrupt patterns of family organization and may contribute to many kinds of social problems.

The personality characteristics of individuals, on the other hand, are largely irrelevant as long as one maintains an organizational perspective. From this point of view, families are patricentric, matricentric, or equalitarian no matter what persons comprise them, associations are centralized or decentralized regardless of their individual members, social classes are open or closed in spite of people's attitudes toward social mobility, and even the assassination of a president cannot destroy a well-organized government. In sum, the process of social organization can be described and explained without utilizing psychological or personality variables, but population characteristics can never be ignored.

The Human Being

The third factor in the setting of social organization is the human being, especially his mind. The sociologist must make several assumptions about human beings as biological and psychological entities—or more precisely, as biological and psychological processes. Social organization develops out of the actions of individuals and could not exist if people did not possess certain characteristics.

The most important of these assumptions about man is that he is inexorably dependent upon other persons (and hence collectively interdependent) for the satisfaction of a wide variety of imperative biological, emotional, and cognitive needs. All societies must first of all provide some organized means whereby their members can obtain food, shelter, clothing, and other necessities for physical survival. The manner in which the economy of a society functions to perform this task may affect many other aspects of social life. Man's sex drive, meanwhile, underlies all forms of family organization. Beyond these primary biological needs, the human being possesses a host of emotional desires (such as for response and acceptance) and cognitive motivations (such as for information, new experiences, and creativity). In all of these cases, the individual normally turns to his fellow creatures either as sources of need fulfillment or as companions in his efforts to achieve gratification. In fact, psychologists and social psychologists have amassed considerable evidence to support the contention that the entire process of personality formation, organization, and growth is totally dependent on social interaction with others. Left entirely to itself, a human baby will never become anything more than a helpless animal—if it even manages to survive—while total isolation can produce psychosis in an adult.

Sociologists also assume that the human beings who participate in social organization possess at least a minimum amount of intelligence (they can learn and solve problems) and that they are capable of symbolization and symbolic communication (they can think and communicate in abstract symbols). It is possible to have organized collective life based on common instincts, as in ant colonies and beehives, but virtually all human interaction clearly involves symbol manipulation and communication. And even when symbols are not being immediately utilized—as during a fist-fight or when boys watch a pretty girl walk down the street—it is likely that the situation will have symbolic meaning for the participants. As a result of their ability to symbolize, human beings can relate to and take into consideration each other's minds as well as overt behaviors, and thus modify their own thoughts and actions on the basis of what they believe and discover other persons to be thinking or feeling.

Another assumption sociologists make about human beings is that they are normally motivated to achieve a wide variety of goals, ranging from mere survival to full maximization of their lives. Beyond the basic demands of survival, no attempt is made to prescribe the exact nature of these goals or to define "maximization of life." Those decisions are made by the participant individuals. But the sociologist must assume that all people normally seek desired goals and expend effort to achieve these goals. Notice the word "normally" in this statement. It is certainly true that at times some individuals do not seek goals, or do not even wish to live. But to the extent that they withdraw from social life in these ways they no longer contribute to the process of social organization. Sociologists are constantly on guard against the charge of imputing teleology, or intended purposes, to social organizations. Only minded individuals can have purposes and goals; there is no such thing as a "group mind." However, the members of any organization can share common goals, which they seek to attain through their joint actions and which become identified with that organization. For convenience sociologists often use the phrase, "organizational goals," but this is merely a shorthand way of saying "goals shared and jointly sought by the members of a social organization, which in turn become identified with that organization." With this understanding, sociologists assume that social organizations normally seek to survive and to attain some goals, just as do individuals. Again, no attempt is made to specify in advance the nature of any organization's goals beyond mere survival. All other organizational goals must remain problematic, to be empirically determined.

The crucial point concerning all of these human characteristics is that they are taken for granted in the study of social organization. They are given constants, or parameters, for the study of organization, but they are not themselves variables to be investigated or explained. Put more directly, from the point of view of social organization all individuals are assumed to meet the requirement of dependence, symbolization, and motivation, and hence are interchangeable. The particular nature of an individual's personality is not relevant for studying the functioning or structures of organizations to which he belongs. In reality, of course, individuals' personality characteristics do sometimes influence social organization, especially if these people occupy key positions. But these kinds of individual variations must be treated as random fluctuations by sociologists if they are to form theories applicable to many or all instances of social organization.[2]

Material Technology

The fourth factor underlying social organization is material technology. This term refers to all of the knowledge possessed by a population of people concerning the use of physical objects and forces. Such knowledge might include techniques for obtaining natural resources, preparing food, constructing shelters, making tools, manufacturing desired goods from safety pins to automobiles, curing diseases, utilizing forces such as magnetism or electricity, synthesizing chemical compounds to produce new products such as plastics, smashing atoms, and so on. The range of material technology is unlimited, from the most primitive tools to yet undreamed-of means of conquering space. All of these techniques nevertheless share the common feature of enabling men to deal with and more effectively utilize the world in which they live.

The creation of social organization does not depend on the possession of material technology beyond that required for physical survival. Primitive socieities have existed without even a knowledge of fire-making, and the internal combustion engine is certainly not a prerequisite for organized social life. The technological knowledge utilized by a population does, however, have tremendous consequences for the social organization it creates. Revolutionary turning points in human societies have been marked, for instance, by the development of knowledge about grain cultivation, which made possible settled communities, about steam engines, which introduced widespread industrialization, and about public sanita-

---

[2] It is important here to distinguish between a description of an organization for the purpose of understanding that particular organization, and an analysis of an organization for the purpose of testing general theoretical hypotheses. In the first case the investigator would seek to determine the ways in which individual members affected the organization; in the second he would focus entirely on social processes and ignore individual variations.

tion and rapid transportation, which are necessary for large-scale urbanization. Today we are witnessing the manifold ramifications of electronic communications and air travel, as our world steadily "shrinks" and becomes increasingly interdependent. And as for tomorrow, we can only speculate about the possible dynamic social effects of atomic energy and space travel. Material technology is always inseparably linked with social organization, as both cause and consequence of ongoing social processes. Technology does not unequivocally shape social organization, but its effects cannot be escaped.

In summary, these four vital factors comprising the setting of all social organization—the natural environment, population, the human being, and material technology—always severely influence organized social life. At the same time, *established social organization repeatedly affects all of these background factors in a continual reciprocal process.* For instance, an organized program of agricultural planning can greatly increase a society's food supply, a birth-control program may have pronounced effects on the birth rate of a society and eventually on its total population size, an extensive program of mass education will markedly influence the goals sought by individuals, and the creation of organized research programs often leads to major technological discoveries. Once again we are led to the conclusion that social organization is inextricably intertwined with the larger setting in which it exists.

The Social Environment

One more paramount item remains in the setting of all social organization. Any given instance of organized social life occurs against a background consisting not only of the four factors discussed above, but also of innumerable other organizations. A political party, to take one simple example, must constantly compete with other associations for the commitment of its members, must depend on the economy to produce enough surplus wealth to support nonproductive political activities, must formulate programs to deal with an unending stream of community and national problems, must compete with one or more other parties for control of the government, and must even take the interests of other societies into account in the formulation of its major policies. Endless bonds of interdependency thus unite all aspects of social life.

If either individuals or organizations are to survive over time or to achieve whatever goals they seek, they are almost inevitably forced to turn to others in their social environment. The resulting social interdependency can be either positive, as when federal, state, and local governments cooperate in welfare programs, or negative, as when the construction of a new highway is blocked by the protests of a homeowners' association. Whatever its specific nature, interdependency confronts us throughout all spheres of social life. As further illustrations of this interdependency within the social environment, consider such phenomena as families entrusting the education of their children to schools, businesses and labor unions negotiating new contracts, suburbs relying on the central metropolis for their economic livelihoods as well as many municipal services, or wealthy nations acting on the belief that their own welfare ultimately depends on the success of remote underdeveloped societies in raising their standards of living.

In short, *individuals and organizations almost always exist and act within a complex social environment.* Surrounding virtually every social phenomenon is a vast web of organized social life, which somehow must be dealt with or taken into account. Man cannot and does not live alone!

In this chapter we have taken a brief look at the major features in the setting of all social organization. The natural environment, population characteristics, qualities of the human being, accumulated material technology, and the interdependent social environment do not fully determine the exact ways in which men organize their collective actions, but their influences can never be escaped. In the next two chapters we shall confront directly the dynamics of social organization: social interaction, social ordering, and the creation of culture.[3]

[3] Although cultural and social phenomena constitute separate "levels of analysis," the total process of human social organization involves many (but not all) cultural ideas as well as social interaction and ordering. Cultural values and norms, for instance, are integral aspects of all social organization, whereas material technology remains an external parameter.

RECOMMENDED READING

Brown, Harrison, *The Challenge of Man's Future* (New York: The Viking Press, Inc., 1956).
Effects of the natural environment, material technology, and population size upon human societies, both primitive and modern, are lucidly discussed, with emphasis on contemporary crises in these realms.
Cottrell, W. F., "Death by Dieselization: A Case Study in the Reaction to Technological Change," *American Sociological Review*, vol. 16 (June 1951), pp. 358–365. (Also Bobbs-Merrill reprint S-53.)
Describes and analyzes the widespread disruptive effects on a small com-

munity caused by a technological change that destroyed the community's major economic base.

DAVIS, KINGSLEY, "Final Note on a Case of Extreme Isolation," *The American Journal of Sociology*, vol. 52 (March 1947), pp. 432–437. (Also Bobbs-Merrill reprint S-63.)
Descriptions of two different girls who were severely isolated during the first several years of their lives, neither of whom developed normal symbolization capabilities.

HAWLEY, AMOS H., "World Urbanization: Trends and Prospects," in Ronald Freedman, ed., *Population: The Vital Revolution*, chap. 5 (Garden City, N.Y.: Doubleday Anchor Books, 1964).
Demonstrates and examines the close relationship existing between the rates of population growth and urbanization in many societies.

MEGGERS, BETTY J., "Environmental Limitations on the Development of Culture," *American Anthropologist*, vol. 56 (October 1954), pp. 801–824. (Also Bobbs-Merrill reprint S-189.)
A summary of current knowledge concerning the effects of the natural environment upon social life.

CHAPTER 4

The Creation of Social Organization: Social Order

Thus far we have been concerned primarily with laying the groundwork necessary for understanding the process of social organization. We have described social reality as an ongoing dynamic process which is continually being created, we have seen that organized social life can be studied scientifically, and we have discovered that all social organization is continually influenced by the setting in which it occurs. But as yet we do not know what constitutes social organization, or how it is created. What is the nature of this universal social process, how does it develop, and what does it involve?

In this and the next chapter we shall attempt to answer these fundamental questions. In doing so, we shall be achieving the first objective of this book: providing a basic conceptualization of the generic process of social organization.

Two words of caution are necessary at the outset, however. First, we shall be talking here in general terms about all instances of social organization, from the smallest and simplest friendship group to the largest and most complex society. Our focus will be on the process of social organization itself, not on the innumerable specific forms it assumes. In our everyday affairs we are normally much more interested in the specifics of the organizations with which we deal than with any common characteristics they might possess. We shop at a particular store, for instance, because we like its goods or prices or service; we are not concerned about the many organizational similarities between this and all other stores. As sociologists attempting to analyze and explain social life, however, we must seek to identify the most general and fundamental characteristics of all social organization.

Second, we must also remember that the process of social organization may be either unpurposeful and unplanned or purposeful and planned. Descriptions of this process often give the impression that all social organization is purposefully and rationally created for the attainment of specified goals. In actuality, most social organization throughout human history has been relatively, if not totally, unpurposeful and unplanned. One of the most significant features of modern societies, however, is the extent to which men are trying today to rationalize and plan their organized social life.

We take a moment now to map the conceptual labyrinth ahead. We shall begin by exploring the basic process of social interaction among social actors, as well as several crucial features of the social relationships that result from such interactions. As social relationships become increasingly patterned and recurrent, social life begins to evidence predictable regularities. Thus social order emerges from social interaction. These patterns of social order exhibit numerous characteristics that are not properties of the individuals comprising them. Although social order is continually being created and changed, observers constantly isolate specific instances of this process and describe the structural forms they display. Social ordering and social structure therefore refer to two complementary ways of analyzing social life; the first perspective stresses dynamic processes while the second emphasizes static forms. Finally, collective social life always gives rise to shared symbolic ideas, which become associated with established social arrangements. Thus culture emerges from social ordering. Cultural ideas such as values, norms, rules, and beliefs in turn influence and help to perpetuate patterns of social order. This overall process is social organization.

Social Interaction

Since the creation of all social organization is initiated through social interaction, we begin our conceptual exploration with this process. The participants in any social interaction are termed *social actors*. Why not simply speak of them as individuals? In many cases social actors are persons, but organizations may also participate in interaction as actors. A government, for instance, may enter into a contract with a construction firm to build a new highway. True, this contract must be negotiated by individuals, but these persons are here acting only as representatives of their respective organizations, not as autonomous actors. It is the government that agrees to provide the necessary funds and the construction company that agrees to build the highway, not the individuals who sign the contract. We therefore need a term such as "social actor" to refer both to individuals and to organizations. In short, *social actors may be either individual persons or social organizations acting as units.*

Social actors, as the name implies, perform actions. When the actions of one actor in some way affect another actor (or actors), social interaction takes place. (Notice that no social interaction transpires if the intended recipient totally ignores these actions, so that they produce no discernible cognitive or behavioral results.) Since most interactions involve the transmission of ideas, many sociologists use the terms "interaction" and "communication" almost synonymously. In some situations, though, this usage stretches the meaning of communication beyond its usual denotation, as when a thief picks the pocket of an unsuspecting victim, or when one army stages a military attack upon another. We shall therefore employ only the broader term, "interaction," keeping in mind that most social interaction necessarily involves at least some communication of ideas.[1] Put more formally, *social interaction occurs whenever one social actor affects the thoughts or actions of another social actor in some manner.*

Social interaction sometimes moves in only one direction, as when a television commercial persuades a viewer to try a new brand of soap. Usually, though, it is reciprocal, with each participating actor affecting the other parties involved. Regardless of whether or not it is reciprocated, social interaction can occur between any number of actors and with all degrees of complexity. A casual two-person conversation is an instance of social interaction, but so is an agreement among dozens of nations to jointly lower tariffs on international trade.

All interactions fall at some point on a scale ranging from totally instrumental to totally expressive. Actions are called instrumental if they are merely means to some other end, as when a store clerk sells merchandise to a customer, or when several community agencies join forces in a fund-

---

[1] To distinguish between interactions that involve communication and those that do not, sociologists sometimes speak of the former as "symbolic interactions" and the latter as "behavioral interactions." In behavioral interaction each actor relates only to the overt behaviors of the other participants, while in symbolic interaction the participants try to take account of each other's meanings as well as acts. Most social interaction combines these two types in various degrees, though sociologists would point to symbolic interaction as the dominant feature of human social intercourse. Interactions among animals are thought to occur almost exclusively on the behavioral level, although an interesting case is posed by animals such as chimpanzees and porpoises, which apparently can communicate at least rudimentary symbols.

raising drive. Expressive actions are valued for their own sake, as in a back-yard chat with the neighbors or in a ballet performance. Many interactions are predominantly either instrumental or expressive, but others, such as competitive games and sports, are designed to produce both instrumental goal attainment and expressive enjoyment simultaneously. This procedure of classifying social interaction in terms of its major purpose is used extensively by sociologists, but one must keep in mind that instrumentality and expressiveness are only the extremes of a continuum that contains innumerable intermediate points.

Social Relationships

Some social interactions are one-time affairs, while others are repeated so sporadically that no continuity develops. Many other interactions, however, are renewed time after time in a fairly similar manner. Occasional dates grow into a "steady" routine, the members of a hobby club gather periodically to share their mutual concerns, sporadic sales between a manufacturer and a retail store evolve into a standing arrangement, and wartime alliances between nations lead to permanent treaties. When social interactions are repeated or perpetuated in this manner, we often speak of this process as the development of social relationships. *A social relationship is a case of enduring social interaction.* There is no definitive point at which repeated interaction becomes a social relationship, so that the nature of the situation being analyzed largely determines which term is used. Nevertheless, this concept of ongoing, relatively enduring social relationships does provide an extremely useful way of describing much social interaction.

Why do social actors put forth the efforts necessary to create social relationships? The underlying causes are almost as diverse as the specific kinds of relationships established. For analytical purposes, though, we can classify these causal factors into several broad categories. The most common of these include:

1. Personal satisfaction. Individuals may develop an enduring relationship because they provide some kind of psychological gratification for one another. They find that they enjoy each other's company, and hence they seek to perpetuate their friendship, companionship, love, or whatever else attracts them to each other personally.

2. Common interests and goals. Regardless of whether or not social actors particularly care for each other, mutual interests and concerns may bring them together and provide the basis for a continuing relationship. In turn, they may more or less purposefully agree to cooperate with each

other in order to achieve a mutual goal. "Politics makes strange bed-fellows," says the old adage. Whereas personal-attractive relationships often provide a relatively clear example of expressive social interaction, goal-directed relationships are primarily instrumental.

3. Expectations and obligations. Social actors may feel expectations and obligations toward each other and as a result maintain a social relationship, even though they do not particularly like each other or share similar interests and goals. These social relationships might be based on long-standing traditions, as in the fealty bond between feudal lord and peasant. They might be derived from ethical, moral, or religious beliefs, as in the professional obligation of physician to patient, the responsibility that a parent feels toward his children, or the religious dictum to "love your neighbor as yourself." They might also be essentially legal in nature, as expressed in a formal contract or specified in law. Needless to say, these various kinds of social expectations and obligations are not mutually exclusive.

4. Mutual interdependence. We have noted that all social life is to some extent interdependent, so that every social relationship occurs within a complex social environment. Interdependence is not only a result of previously established relationships but is also a causal force producing additional bonds among actors. Interdependency is most evident in economic activities, in which a chain of reciprocal relationships often exists from producers of raw materials to manufacturers to transporters to wholesalers to retailers to customers. Governmental programs such as public housing, mental health services, water conservation, and highway construction are all collective responses to interdependent needs of communities, states, and the nation as a whole. From a broader perspective, all facets of contemporary societies display increasing specialization of activities, thus creating broadening spheres of interdependency, which in turn necessitate the development and perpetuation of social relationships. Unlike the relatively self-sufficient primitive, modern man could not survive long by himself. How many of us could provide all of our own food, clothing, housing, and other necessities of life, especially in an unfavorable natural environment? Without doubt, interdependency is the predominant basis for social relationships—and hence for social organization—in modern society.

5. Force. Outright physical coercion does not account for many continuing social relationships, outside of prisons and other custodial institutions. It is plainly evident on the international scene, though, and a totalitarian police state relies heavily on coercive techniques. Coercion is only the crudest of many types of force, however. Much more common is the exercise of force through compensations and deprivations. The most

obvious medium for exercising these pressures in our society is money, as in paying wages for work, offering of "incentives," raising and lowering of prices, or imposing fines. But compensations and deprivations take many other forms: providing or withdrawing opportunities for interaction and communication, facilitating or hindering the attainment of goals, or administering symbolic sanctions. The most subtle kind of force, finally, is that based on the possession of expert knowledge and/or persuasive ability, ranging from that of the primitive "medicine man" to the contemporary "technical expert" or "manager of public relations."

These five categories of causal factors leading to the development of social relationships are distinguished for analytical purposes only. Although one type of factor might be most evident in a particular situation, virtually all real relationships incorporate more than one—and often all—of these factors in various degrees. There are no simple, single-factor causal explanations of human social life!

Once such causal factors are present, through what process are continuing relationships actually created? The answer takes us to the heart of the process of social organization and also demonstrates why social phenomena have a reality apart from their component social actors. The process of establishing social relationships involves a profound change in the actions of the participating actors. Normally, though not inevitably, it also leads to a change in their orientations, or ways of thinking and feeling. Let us first explore the change in actions and then turn to orientations.

Prior to the creation of a particular social relationship the actors concerned are acting as independent, autonomous elements in respect to this situation. They may, of course, be participating members of other relationships among themselves or with additional actors, but they are autonomous elements among themselves in reference to the relationship being created. This statement is actually a tautology, since obviously actors cannot be members of a relationship before it has been established. The underlying idea is not redundant, however. When they are first initiating a social relationship, the involved actors are always acting independently of each other—again in reference to the emerging social bond. For terminological convenience we say they are acting as *social elements* in reference to this relationship.

Once an even rudimentary relationship has been created among social actors, however, their actions are to some extent altered. The participants must now act as committed, involved members of the larger social unit they have established. At least some of the time they must carry out the duties and responsibilities of membership. When they do this, we say that they are acting as *social parts* of the relationship. If they do not act as responsible parts, the relationship will soon disintegrate. If no one is willing to serve as chairman of the new neighborhood clean-up committee, the neighborhood will undoubtedly remain dirty. On the world scene, when even a few nations refuse to pay their dues to the United Nations, the entire organization is severely weakened.

The essential point here is that social actors act differently when participating as responsible parts of a relationship than they do when acting as autonomous social elements.[2] Membership in an established social relationship affects the actions of the participating actors. And if something has discernible consequences, it must surely exist—hence the argument that social relationships are real phenomena, even though we cannot directly observe them. The extent and nature of these action changes are variables that sociologists often investigate.

Perhaps the clearest example of this transition of social actors from elements to parts is a marriage. Each person must independently pledge that "I will" form this bond, and either one is free to halt the process by refusing to commit himself. (The reasons why people initiate this relationship are not directly relevant here. Regardless of whether the underlying causal factors are attraction, goal seeking, obligations, interdependence, or force, the result is a marriage.) Once the commitment is made, however, each person is expected to "love, honor, and cherish" the other "till death do us part"—and to the best of its ability the larger community will see to it that these responsibilities are fulfilled. Skeptics and cynics may endlessly argue the relative benefits and disadvantages of marriage, but there is no denying that married life is different from bachelorhood.

Although the distinction between acting as a social element and as a social part is most clearly seen in the initial creation of a social relationship, it applies to all social life. In any situation, social actors may be acting either as elements or as parts in reference to a given relationship. Even when an actor is not considered by others to be a member of a relationship, he may nevertheless act as if he were a part of it. On the other hand, an actor considered to be a member of the relationship may at times act toward it as if he were an independent element. On the individual level, a person is acting as an element when he says, "Let's join forces and cooperate on this job," but as a part when he says, "It's my duty as supervisor to distribute this work among all of us." On the organizational level, two railroads exploring the possibilities of a corporate merger are acting as elements on this occasion, but they would be participating as parts of a larger transportation network when they coordinated their time schedules with those of connecting railroads. As these examples suggest, any social actor may act as either an element or a part, depending on the situation.

[2] I am indebted to Guy E. Swanson for these concepts of "elements" and "parts" in reference to social relationships.

Indeed, it might even be hypothesized that all social actors are always acting simultaneously as both elements and parts, though in widely varying degrees.

The concepts of "elements" and "parts" are analogous to terms used in chemistry. By themselves, chemical elements—sodium and chlorine, for instance—exhibit characteristics peculiarly their own, by which each can be separately identified. This condition holds true even if elements are mixed together, as long as there is no chemical reaction between them. Through a process of chemical interaction, however, the elements can join to form an entirely new substance—in this case, salt. The elements of sodium and chlorine have now both lost their individual identities and characteristics, and have instead become parts of a more inclusive chemical compound, which has properties not belonging to either of its component parts by themselves. In an emergent process such as this, the original elements are transformed into parts of a new entity. The analogy between chemicals and social actors is not perfect, since social relationships are rarely as thoroughly unified as are chemical compounds, with the result that actors are constantly alternating between the actions of elements and of parts.[3] Nevertheless, it does help us to visualize the essential features of this process.

In summary of these concepts of social elements and parts, *social actors are elements to the extent that they participate in a particular social situation as relatively independent units, autonomously determining their own actions toward others. Social actors are parts to the extent that they participate as members of a larger social relationship or organization, with their actions being determined by the demands of that relationship.*

We noted earlier that the process of creating social relationships normally involves changes in the orientations (thoughts and feelings) of the actors, as well as in their actions. In most cases these two kinds of change are interwoven, each reinforcing the other. A change of orientation is not imperative for the establishment of a relationship, however. A social relationship can be created as long as the participants sometimes act as committed parts, regardless of whether or not their thoughts and feelings are altered.

The concepts used to describe this process of change are *self orientations* versus *collective orientations*. These are actually the end points of an analytical continuum, and any social actor's orientations may fall anywhere along the scale in a given situation. Although participation in a social relationship often involves some shift from self to collective orientations, participants may display a preponderance of either type or a bal-

---

[3] This difference between chemicals and social actors illustrates one way in which social science is more complex than physical science.

anced mixture of both. *Self orientations are characterized by expedient calculations of the costs involved and the benefits to be gained through participation in a relationship,* so that the actor is primarily interested in his own individual welfare. *Collective orientations are characterized by moral*[4] *concerns with the obligations and responsibilities of participation in a relationship,* so that the actor is primarily interested in the common welfare of all.[5]

Robert MacIver has expressed the crucial importance of this distinction between self and collectivity orientations:

> The problem of human society everywhere is the adjustment of the ego interest and the group interest. This is the problem not merely of social order but of every social relationship. . . . Every human organization of every kind, whether it be a family, a business, a state, or a church of God, finds some way of reconciling the interest of the individual and the interest of the whole. This fact is the primary condition of the remarkably complex structure of civilized society.[6]

These two fundamental dimensions of all social life—acting as elements or parts in reference to a relationship, and holding self or collective orientations toward that relationship—are similar but not identical phenomena. The obvious parallel is that social actors who act as relatively independent elements tend to be self-oriented, while actors who participate as relatively involved parts of a relationship tend to be collectively oriented. In the great majority of cases this is what occurs. Social actors enter into new relationships as elements with expedient orientations because they believe that the relationship will benefit them in some way, while at other times they carry out their responsibilities as parts of established relationships because of their moral orientations toward the common welfare. A social relationship is unquestionably strengthened to the extent that its members do adopt collective orientations toward that relationship.

---

[4] The term "moral" is used here in its broadest sense.

[5] The self-collectivity dimension of social relations is often confused with the instrumental-expressive dimension of social interaction, but the two variables are conceptually distinct. Two members of a city council, interacting for the wholly instrumental purpose of deciding where to build a new park, might relate to each other with either self orientations ("Which location would most benefit my own constituents, or perhaps my own wallet?") or collective orientations ("Which location would most benefit the entire community?"). Similarly, if they were debating each other for the sheer expressive pleasure of matching wits, they might also hold either self orientations ("How can I counter his last point, so as to have the final word?") or collective orientations ("How can I respond to his last point, so that we will better understand each other?").

[6] Robert M. MacIver, *The Web of Government,* rev. ed. (New York: The Free Press, a division of The Macmillan Company, 1965), p. 310.

In some social situations, however, these two dimensions do not neatly coincide. A number of actors, for instance, can come together as independent elements in the creation of a social relationship as a result of their common collective orientations toward some larger social object. Americans living in a foreign country frequently band together in their own little "U.S. colony," even though they may be total strangers to each other. On the other hand, actors can participate as integral parts of a social relationship because they believe it will directly benefit them. A college student might despise fraternity life but nevertheless carry out all his duties as a loyal member of the house, as a means of establishing social contacts that could prove useful to him later in life.

Objectively measuring degrees of element-part activity and self-collective orientations in any actual social relationship is an exceedingly challenging task, which sociologists have not yet mastered. These two sets of concepts are both fundamental to contemporary social theory, even though no single theoretical scheme adequately incorporates them both. Most theories of social relationships tend to focus on social actors either as self-oriented elements or as collectively oriented parts, but do not attempt to separate these basic variables or to combine all four concepts into a unified theory. As an unfortunate consequence, the theories based on these two conceptual frameworks are often radically different. Theories utilizing an "expedient-element" framework tend to see all cases of enduring social interaction as exchange relationships, in which each participant contributes something to the others, and in return receives something he desires or values. Of particular importance to these theories are questions of resource procurement, techniques of bargaining and compromise, power differentials among participants, and the process of social conflict. In contrast, theories utilizing a "moral-part" framework tend to view all social relationships in terms of mutual obligations, in which each member assumes certain social responsibilities, as a result of which everyone benefits. Crucial questions for these theories involve assignment of actors to duties, the teaching and sharing of common social concerns, techniques of cooperation, and the process of strengthening or perpetuating social relationships.[7] The sharp contrasts between these two bodies of social theory

---

[7] Contemporary theorists using an expediency orientation include George C. Homans, *Social Behavior: Its Elementary Forms* (New York, Harcourt, Brace & World, Inc., 1961), Peter M. Blau, *Exchange and Power in Social Life* (New York: John Wiley & Sons, Inc., 1964), and Ralph Dahrendorf, *Class and Class Conflict in Industrial Society* (Stanford, Calif.: Stanford University Press, 1959). Notable theorists using a moral orientation include Émile Durkheim, *Moral Education* (New York: The Free Press, 1961), Charles H. Cooley, Social Organization (New York: Charles Scribner's Sons, 1922), and Talcott Parsons, *The Social System* (New York: The Free Press, a division of The Macmillan Company, 1951).

frequently confuse and exasperate students of sociology, but the opportunities they present for a new theoretical synthesis may also prove highly challenging.

Social Order

Social relationships provide the threads of social life, but separate threads do not by themselves constitute a fabric. Countless ongoing relationships of numerous hues and textures must be endlessly interwoven in complex patterns to create the continually flowing material of social organization. Sociologists use the term *social ordering* to refer to this process, in which social relationships become arranged into multidimensional patterns that are relatively stable over time. The observed regularities and uniformities in social life that result from this process are called *social order*. The absence of social order is sometimes called *social anarchy*. Neither complete anarchy nor absolute order ever occurs in real life, of course; rather we are forever experiencing varying degrees of order and disorder. Social ordering is never a static condition, but always a dynamic process of fluctuation and variation.

Illustrations of social ordering can be drawn from all areas of human life. To cite a few common examples: (a) most adults live together in pairs consisting of one member of each sex, and year after year share countless daily activities with their partner; (b) store clerks smoothly carry out numerous exchange transactions with streams of customers, most of whom are total strangers to them; (c) expressway traffic flows primarily into a city between seven and ten o'clock in the morning, but out of the city between three and six o'clock in the evening; (d) the members of a bridge club gather at a specified location every Monday evening at eight o'clock, and then engage in predictable and ritualized interactions; (e) members of audiences at lectures remain quietly seated, rather than running about or shouting to each other; (f) children usually progress through school at the rate of one grade per year, so that if they complete college they do not enter the labor market until after age 21; (g) in most communities, stores and offices tend to be located in some areas, factories in other areas, and residences in still different areas; (h) we deposit a letter in a mailbox with confidence that it will reach its destination fairly quickly, regardless of where it is going or what information it contains; (i) individuals who violate legal statutes are judged and punished through established, impersonal procedures, rather than by the persons whom they have harmed; (j) millions of people in the United States participate in a nationwide involuntary medical care program as the result of decisions reached by a few hundred legislators; and (k) scores of nations cooperate with each other in highly complicated financial and trade arrangements.

In sum, *social order emerges as ongoing relationships become inter-woven into relatively stable and hence predictable arrangements.* Stated differently, *social order arises as the interactions of social actors become recurrent through time and complexly patterned.*

We argued in the first chapter that social order not only emerges through the interactions of persons behaving as social actors, but also exists independently of its creators. Can we now substantiate this argument? On what grounds are we justified in saying that patterns of social order are "real" phenomena that can be objectively studied apart from their component members? Is not social order just a conceptual abstraction derived from generalizations about the behaviors of individual people?

Although this question raises some fundamental philosophical issues, most sociologists would contend that *patterns of social order exhibit numerous properties that are not characteristics of their individual members.* Any given occurrence of social order possesses, to some degree, such properties as complexity and formalness, stability, rate of change, power relations among its component parts, functional requirements that must be satisfied if it is to continue existing or operating, and integration or cohesion. All of these properties are qualitatively distinct from the personality characteristics of the individuals who create or perpetuate that social order. Knowing the personality profiles of Tom, Dick, Harry, Bill, and Bob tells us nothing about the basketball team they comprise—nothing about the duties of the various positions on the team, the coordination of their ball handling, their stability as a team under pressure, their rate of improvement during the season, or their overall ability to win basketball games.

If features such as these are not inherent in individual members, then they must be properties of overall patterns of social order. Carrying this line of reasoning one step further, if a phenomenon exhibits properties that are distinctly its own, then it must have existence of its own. It must be something more than just interacting components. In other words, *patterns of social order possess a unity that is always greater than the sum of their component parts.* Émile Durkheim eloquently expressed this idea:

A whole is not identical with the sum of its parts. It is something different, and its properties differ from those of its component parts. . . . By reason of this principle, society is not a mere sum of individuals. Rather, the system formed by their association represents a specific reality which has its own characteristics. . . . We must seek the explanation of social life in the nature of society itself.[8]

[8] Émile Durkheim, *The Rules of Sociological Method,* trans. Sarah A. Solovay and John H. Mueller (New York: The Free Press, a division of The Macmillan Company, 1933), pp. 102–103.

We reiterate that social actors who are responsible parts of a larger social entity act (and often think) differently from actors who are presently autonomous social elements. From a process perspective we might add that *acting differently means being different*. *Actors acting as parts of social relationships create patterns of social order that become realities distinct from these individual actors*. Social order exists not in the actors themselves, but in the uniformities of recurrent social interaction that transpire among the actors through time. As a consequence, social order can and must be empirically investigated and theoretically explained as an objective social reality.

Durkheim's illustration of the fallacy of reductionist thinking, or trying to explain a social phenomenon solely in terms of its component parts, is also worth noting:

It will be said that, since the only elements making up society are individuals, the first origins of sociological phenomena cannot but be psychological. In reasoning thus, it can be established just as easily that organic phenomena may be explained by inorganic phenomena. It is very certain that there are in the living cell only molecules of crude matter. But these molecules are in contact with one another, and this association is the cause of the new phenomena which characterize life, the very germ of which cannot possibly be found in any of the separate elements.[9]

To assert the independence of patterns of social order from their constituent members is easier than to demonstrate objectively this independence. Since social order, like gravity, cannot be directly observed by human senses, we must ascertain its existence through its effects on other phenomena, just as the effects of gravity are demonstrated by a falling apple. The consequences of the existence of social order can be witnessed both in individuals' actions and in cultural ideas.

On the indivdual level, Durkheim's concepts of *exteriority* and *constraint* provide two classic illustrations of the effects of social order.[10] The exteriority of social order to individuals is seen in the fact that its patterns may continue to exist over time despite changes, or even a complete turnover, in its membership. Anything short of total simultaneous withdrawal by all members will not necessarily destroy a group, a community, or a society. In fact, many organizations—of which a university is an excellent example—establish ordered procedures for the departure of old members and the acquisition and training of new members. Podunk University continues to exist and operate despite a complete turnover of students every few years, as well as a turnover of faculty members that differs only in the slightly longer length of its cycle. As a result of the relatively stable

[9] Durkheim, p. 102.
[10] Durkheim, chap. 1.

persistence of social order through time, individuals must treat these patterns of relationships as external to themselves. Social order is already there when the individual comes onto the scene, and he has no choice but to recognize its existence and to take account of its demands. He may conform to these demands, deviate from them, or attempt to change them, but he cannot ignore them.

The constraints of established social order, then, are seen in the ways in which it influences individuals' actions. These patterned social arrangements limit or obstruct some kinds of behavior and simultaneously provide opportunities for other kinds. Most members of an underdeveloped agricultural society cannot obtain a college education no matter how intelligent they may be, because their society does not have adequate economic surpluses to build schools, train teachers, or free students from productive labor for four years. They are not, however, forced to ride a commuter train in and out of a city for two hours every day. In the United States, on the other hand, it is quite difficult for a child from a well-to-do family to avoid college, no matter how unintelligent (within normalcy) he may be, because of the strong social pressures from all directions that push him to enroll. Nor can he easily escape dependence upon the automobile as a major means of transportation. In a more direct manner, individuals are punished for doing some things (such as stealing), rewarded for doing some things (such as selling a company's product), punished for not doing other things (such as not paying income taxes), and rewarded for not doing some things they might wish to do (as in the award of a military decoration for defending a position rather than retreating under heavy fire). Finally, individuals are often provided with entire ready-made sets of actions, or roles, which they simply act out with little or no individual modifications—as illustrated by American dating rituals.

On the cultural level, ordered social life will often, over time, influence common values, beliefs, traditions, norms, and other ideas. Widespread practice of racial discrimination and segregation will result in cultural beliefs and traditions that justify and support these actions, while extensive equal-status interaction across racial lines will produce strong values and norms favoring racial equality. Even more striking is the finding that, among numerous primitive peoples, religious monotheism is more likely to occur in societies containing three or more levels of sovereign organization (such as families, communities, and tribes) than in societies that lack this degree of social complexity.[11] An empirical correlation of this sort does not prove either causation or direction of influence, but it does indicate that patterns of social order and shared cultural ideas tend to covary with one another.

[11] Guy E. Swanson, *The Birth of the Gods* (Ann Arbor, Mich.: University of Michigan Press, 1960), chap. 3.

These various arguments and illustrations concerning the reality of social order and its partial independence from its constituent members are not totally conclusive. But they are strong enough to convince most social scientitsts that exclusive reliance on the psychological level of analysis is not adequate to explain organized social life. At the same time, we must understand that this independence of social order is always partial, never complete. *Individual personalities and patterns of social order always interpenetrate each other's existence and functioning.* On the one hand, social order must ultimately be created by, and expressed through, the behaviors of individual persons. The ways in which people act as members of social relationships will determine the shape of their common social existence. On the other hand, apart from ordered social life, man remains only a biological organism that never becomes human. The human personality is almost entirely the result of participation in social life, and personality organization must be continually supported and reinforced through social interaction.

Summarizing at this point, we have seen that social order emerges as the interactions of social actors become perpetuated in social relationships, which in turn become interwoven into ongoing patterns of observable regularities. These patterns of social order exhibit their own unique properties, are real phenomena in that they produce discernible consequences, and thus are said to possess a unity that is greater than the sum of their component parts. Individual personalities and social order are both partially autonomous processes, but these two levels of human existence inevitably interpenetrate and mutually influence each other.

Social Structure

Thus far we have avoided the problem of how to describe and analyze the dynamic, flowing patterns of social order. This task is not facilitated by the English language, since the nouns that provide the subjects of most of our sentences refer primarily to static objects, not to ongoing processes. Yet obviously we all do think and talk about various kinds of social ordering every day. How do we do this? The answer is quite simple, but it necessarily involves a perceptual and conceptual distortion of social reality. Because we are accustomed to thinking and speaking about static objects, we transpose the ongoing processes of social ordering into unchanging structural descriptions. We accomplish this by temporarily "freezing" dynamic social processes and then reporting the forms seen to exist among their component parts. Our mental and verbal accounts of social order refer only to isolated static instances of what is in reality a continually flowing process. These static pictures of social order are descriptions of *social structure*.[12]

An important distinction must be noted here. Social order is often stable but never static. That is, the basic features of a particular arrangement of social relationships may persist for some time, but these patterns exist among ongoing relationships, which in one way or another are always varying. The social relationships that comprise a community, for instance, vary from day to day, yet the community as a social organization remains relatively stable through the years. Stability is never inevitable, since the numerous disruptive forces besetting any organization continually threaten its stability and frequently result in significant social changes in the organization. Nevertheless, a minimum amount of stability must prevail if the organization is to endure.

A depicted social structure, in contrast, is always a static, unvarying configuration of social relationships. We use this motionless structural terminology as a convenient means of describing and analyzing the dynamic processes of social life. We must not forget, however, that *any particular description of social structure is a perceptual and conceptual abstraction from social reality.*

Various kinds of charts and diagrams often supplement verbal sketches of social structures. We are all familiar, for instance, with the "organizational chart" that adorns the walls of executive offices. The neatly drawn boxes and arrows indicate which vice president supervises which divisional superintendents, who in turn supervise various departmental managers, and so on down to the lowest ranking file clerk or maintenance man. Such charts never portray the total social structure of the organization, but they are useful for showing the basic, formal skeleton of the organizational structure. Sociologists have devised other types of charts, commonly called sociograms, to depict the patterns of friendships and other relatively personal social relationships that exist in all organizations. Sociograms can also be used to diagram communication channels ("Who communicates with whom?"), flow of influence ("Who influences whom?"), and all other types of social relationships.

A very subtle conceptual problem, which has pervaded our initial discussion of social structure, must now be brought into the open. On the one hand, social order exists whenever social interactions become patterned and recurrent. As an ongoing process, social ordering is always occurring. Hence the reality of social order is not dependent upon its being consciously recognized or reported. On the other hand, we have thus far

---

[12] Much of the conceptualization of social structure presented in this section is taken from S. F. Nadel's *The Theory of Social Structure* (New York: The Free Press, a division of The Macmillan Company, 1957).

carefully referred only to descriptions of social structure, not to structure itself. These structural descriptions, we noted, are always perceptual and conceptual abstractions from social reality, formed by participants or outside observers. The student of philosophy will recognize this conceptual distinction between "real existence" and "perceptions and conceptions" as having an ancient lineage, and as having been imbedded in contemporary science via Kant's ideas of "noumena" and "phenomena."

To avoid becoming sidetracked into this philosophical debate, let us here simply note that social scientists constantly strive to make their structural statements as congruent as possible with existing patterns of social order. They seek to do this not only by following the guidelines of scientific methodology, but also by deriving their descriptions of social structure from many different observations of social order. Instead of merely observing and recording a single instance of the process of social ordering at one point in time, the sociologist will (or at least should) study several different instances of this process at successive time periods, to insure that the forms he is reporting are relatively stable through time. Hopefully, then, his analyses of social ordering will be more accurate than the casual impressions of one-time spectators.

To repeat, patterns of social order exist whether or not they are recognized, while descriptions of social structure are always created by human observers. But what is social structure itself? Unfortunately, we cannot give an unequivocal answer, since there is no consensus on the meaning of this concept. Many social scientists use the term social structure as a synonym for social order, in reference to existing patterned regularities in social life. The major drawback of this usage is that it robs the process of social ordering of its dynamic qualities and turns social order into a static, "frozen" object. Other social scientists prefer to use social-structural terminology only in reference to abstracted descriptions of social order, as a means of emphasizing the distortions of reality that are inherent in all structural statements. Perhaps the best we can do here is to suggest a compromise conception, in which "social structure" refers to an arrangement or configuration of social activities that is seen to exist over some period of time and that is believed to depict underlying patterns of social order. A social structure thus incorporates the major recurrent features of many specific instances of social order. In short, *social structure is patterned social order as we observe it.*

Perhaps an analogy and a diagram will help to clarify this concept of social structure. For the analogy, imagine the human mind to be a continuously operating motion picture camera. Let us focus this camera on a specific instance of social interaction—say a man and a woman in conversation, with the man reaching out his hand toward the woman. The camera records a continuous stream of still pictures of the ongoing interaction. No one of these pictures tells us very much about the nature of the social relationship being expressed through these actions, any more than an organizational chart or a sociogram depicts dynamic social processes. Whatever patterns of social order these two people have created—whether it be a marriage or a business arrangement or a play production—existed as a dynamic process before the picture was snapped, and will continue into the future. Nevertheless, to observe and record this flowing process we must temporarily "freeze" it and isolate one particular instant in time. The resulting picture is thus a totally static and highly distorted representation of social life.

The camera takes more than one snapshot, however. From a succession of still pictures taken through time we can construct an image of the dynamic social order being created in this situation. We can now see that the woman is the man's secretary, and that he is in the process of giving her instructions for the day's work. Note, though, that the "real" nature of this social relationship must still be inferred from a series of static perceptions or pictures. We "see" and can describe to others a social structure consisting of an employer and a subordinate employee, but this is a mental conception abstracted from a series of specific instances of social interaction. We believe this structural description to be an accurate portrayal of the social order existing through time in this situation, but we can never be certain that we have avoided all perceptual and conceptual distortion. Furthermore, any account of social structure must be arbitrarily delineated. By focusing on just these two people and ignoring others who might be standing in the background, our portrayal of this social-structural arrangement additionally distorts social reality.

The diagram in Figure 4-1 is another attempt to illustrate this same conception of social structure as an observed configuration derived from several observations of social order. The flowing lines represent ongoing social interactions and relationships, which exist through time. At first they are totally random, but at a later time patterns of social order emerge. The cross-sectional slices indicate observations of instances of these social processes made at four different points in time. (In the lower part of the diagram these slices have been turned sideways to display their contents.) The first two observations, being totally different, provide no basis for inferring the presence of social structure. But the latter two similar observations do enable us to identify a persistent structural form, which we hope is a relatively accurate portrayal of the existing patterns of social order.

How much similarity or stability over time must we perceive in our observations of social processes before we can conceive of the existence of social structure? This is an empirical question that social scientists cannot

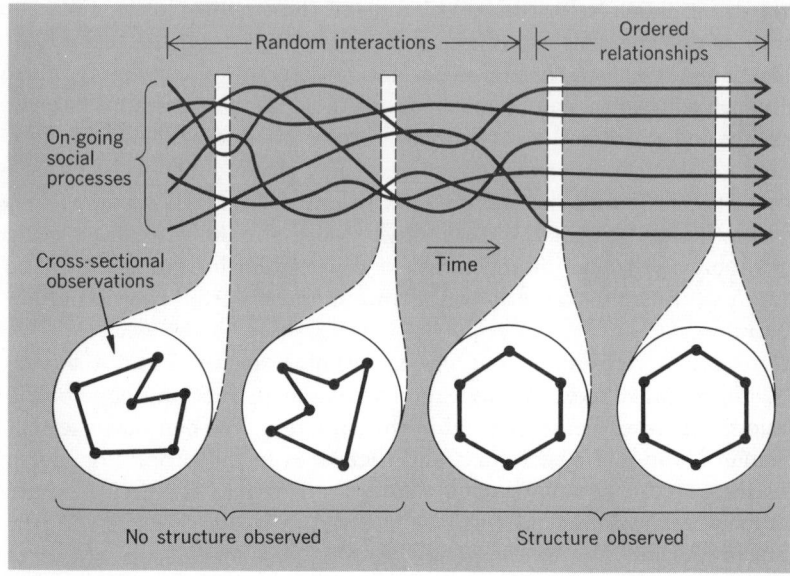

FIGURE 4–1. Diagram of the perception and conception of social structure.

yet answer, although we can suggest two broad generalizations. First, the degree of stability over time necessary for the observation of any type of structure is an entirely arbitrary consequence of human mental abilities. We think of a stone as having a static structure only because we cannot perceive the constant exchange of atoms between it and the surrounding environment as it is slowly worn down by natural forces. Our memories, aided by photographs, do enable us to remember that the tall oak tree in front of our house was once a tiny seedling, but nevertheless we still tend to think of it as a stable entity rather than as a dynamic process. Individual personalities are somewhat easier to perceive as changing phenomena—especially in children—but we will still tolerate only a limited amount of variation. We expect personalities to remain relatively stable from day to day, and we label as mentally ill those who do not. On the other side of the fence, why do we not see hurricanes, light rays, chemical reactions, or atomic explosions as stable structures? Sensitive mechanical instruments may be capable of "freezing" and recording these processes as static phenomena, but human minds lack these perceptual and cognitive capabilities.

The second generalization is that sensitivity to the existence of social order differs among individuals. Furthermore, it is possible to train people

—and this is part of the education of a social scientist—to increase their awareness of social order, and hence their ability to perceive and conceptualize social structure. All of us would undoubtedly agree that a marching band or a university classroom or a business corporation possesses enough social order to warrant describing its social structure. But can we speak of the social structure of a simple conversation, a cocktail party, or a lynch mob? Most of us would probably see these phenomena as being far too transient to have an observable social structure. Yet sociologists have studied the social order existing in each of these situations, and have in each case been able to describe one or more social structures.

In summary, we have conceptualized social structure as a specific configuration derived from observations of many instances of social order. This conceptualization makes structure an outgrowth of process. Instead of thinking of a person (noun) doing something (verb), as the English language forces us to do, we should more accurately think of actions (verbs) as constituting a personality (noun). Similarly, we should speak of patterned and recurrent interactions among social actors as creating structured social organizations, rather than of social organizations as static objects that carry out activities. That we do not normally think in these process terms is partly a result of the way in which our minds have learned to operate. Our normal manner of thinking, however, does reflect the paradoxical fact (to be elaborated in Chapter 6) that once organizations have been created through the actions of social actors, these dynamic social entities do themselves participate as social actors in further processes of social organization.

At first glance, this whole argument that structure results from process, rather than vice versa, may seem highly academic. Of what importance is it for the actual operation of society? As a theory of social structure it may interest only social scientists, but as a broad perspective from which to view all social life it has manifold consequences. The essential feature of this perspective is that no social organization—from a friendship clique to the United States—is a fixed entity that, once created, continues to function perpetually until some outside force destroys it. Social reality is quite the opposite. All social organizations must be continually recreated through the ordering of interactions and the sharing of ideas among their members. As a result, social organizations are always undergoing modifications, change, and growth or decline. In short, social organizations exist in a constant process of becoming. This situation has two major consequences for human endeavors: On the one hand, we can never rest contented in the belief that once we have established some cherished organization we can henceforth reap its benefits with only minimum housekeeping efforts. The perpetuation of social order and organization demands endless attention and labor. On the other hand, though, we need never be helplessly and rigidly tied to the practices and traditions of the past. Social organizations can be endlessly flexible; hence they always remain open to further improvement.

We have thus far explored the concepts of social interaction, social relationships, social ordering, and social structure. If human beings were not capable of symbolization and the communication of symbolized ideas, our journey would end here. Because we are concerned about people rather than ants, however, we must now push on to an exploration of the phenomenon of culture.

RECOMMENDED READING

DURKHEIM, ÉMILE, The Rules of Sociological Method, trans. Sarah A. Solovay and John H. Mueller, chap. 5 (New York: The Free Press, a division of The Macmillan Company, 1938).
The classic statement of the reality of social phenomena apart from their constituent individuals.

FEIBLEMAN, JAMES, AND JULIUS W. FRIEND, "The Structure and Function of Organization," Philosophical Review, vol. 54 (1945), pp. 19–44.
The general process of organization is analyzed from a logical and philosophical perspective.

HOMANS, GEORGE, The Human Group, chap. 3, "The Bank Wiring Observation Room." (New York: Harcourt, Brace & World, Inc., 1950). (Also Bobbs-Merrill reprint S-123.)
A detailed description and illustration of the creation of social order in a factory work crew.

NADEL, S. F., The Theory of Social Structure, esp. chaps. 1, 6, and 7 (New York: The Free Press, a division of The Macmillan Company, 1957).
A demanding but rewarding theoretical discussion of social structure, as seen from a process viewpoint.

PARSONS, TALCOTT, AND EDWARD SHILS, eds., Toward a General Theory of Action, chap. 1 (New York: Harper & Row, Publishers, 1962).
The personal, social, and cultural levels of organization are contrasted and interrelated in this statement by a number of social and behavioral scientists.

WARRINER, CHARLES K., "Groups are Real," American Sociological Review, vol. 21 (October 1956), pp. 549–554.
An argument for the reality of groups and organizations, as opposed to nominalistic, neonominalistic, and interactionist perspectives on social organization.

WEBER, MAX, The Theory of Social and Economic Organization, trans. A. M. Henderson and Talcott Parsons, ed. Talcott Parsons, pp. 112–120 (New York: The Free Press, a division of The Macmillan Company, 1947).

A classic statement of the concepts of social action, interaction, and relationships.

WHYTE, WILLIAM F., "The Social Structure of the Restaurant," *The American Journal of Sociology,* vol. 54 (January 1949), pp. 302–310. (Also Bobbs-Merrill reprint S-314.)

The concept of social structure is clearly illustrated in this study of a small association.

CHAPTER 5

The Creation of Social Organization: Culture

Man's superior brain has enabled him to become master of all other forms of life on earth. Unlike most lower animals, he can develop ideas as well as conditioned reactions, manipulate these ideas in the process of thinking, and create abstract concepts and generalizations. But this ability to learn and think affects man's social life only as he shares his ideas with others through symbolic communication. It is the accumulation of bodies of shared ideas that gives human social organization its unique qualities.

Emergence of Culture

As individuals interact with each other in recurrent social relationships to form patterns of social order, they generate ideas about these collective endeavors which they share with their fellow participants. As they communicate about common activities, exchange attitudes, values, and beliefs, develop common standards of action, and adopt similar ways of doing things, they create a *culture*. In short, *cultural ideas emerge from shared social life*. These cultural ideas in turn become associated with particular patterns of social order. If one seeks to become a member of an ongoing social organization, he must not only engage in established relationships but must also acquire its associated cultural ideas. This does not mean that all members of a given social organization necessarily think alike, but over time these participants will come to share a body of common ideas.

A few examples will illustrate this idea of cultural emergence. The development of capitalism as a form of economic order led to the creation of a "business ideology" and laissez-faire philosophies of government; mounting use of automobiles prompted the development of traffic codes; and the activities of the League of Nations provided a base of social technology that proved useful in the establishment of the United Nations.

Cultural ideas, therefore, largely reflect and express their underlying patterns of social order. Although discrepancies often exist between ideas and practices, these differences cannot become too great without imposing severe strains and conflicts on both the social order and its accompanying culture. As a consequence of the emergence of cultural ideas from collective social life, patterns of social order gain unity, stability through time, and functional effectiveness in achieving goals.

We have previously argued that patterns of social order display properties not inherent in their constituent members, and possess a unity greater than the sum of their component parts. Social order, then, occurs independently of the personalities of the individuals who comprise it. We now suggest that *cultural ideas are also real phenomena, which can exist apart from the social orders in which they are created.*

The partial independence of culture from social order can be illustrated in several ways. First, cultural ideas frequently survive, at least in libraries and museums if not in most people's memories, long after the society that generated them has ceased to exist. The cultures of ancient Greece and Egypt, for instance, are well known to historians today. Second, cultures may remain virtually unchanged over time, despite drastic alterations in the underlying patterns of social order. The ideal of monogamous marriage is as strong today in the United States as it was two hundred years ago, despite the many changes in family living introduced by industrialization and urbanization. Third, cultural ideas developed in one society may spread to all corners of the globe, as Roman legal principles have done and as English and American concepts of democracy are presently doing. Fourth, and most important, cultural values, beliefs, and other ideas continually influence the patterns of social order from which they emerged. Social ordering—together with the personalities of individual participants—is constantly shaped, constrained, and changed by its associated culture. A prominent current example of this phenomenon is the current attempt to resolve the "American dilemma" by bringing interracial practices into accord with the value of human equality. Another example is the translation of the goal of "promoting the general welfare" into specific programs to combat poverty, disease, and ignorance.

Despite this partial autonomy of cultural ideas and the many influences they exert upon social life, *patterns of social order and their attendant cultures always thoroughly interpenetrate each other*. All organized human life has both social and cultural components. Although it is often necessary to separate these realms for scientific analysis, this procedure unavoidably distorts the process of social organization. Cultural ideas divorced from ongoing social relationships—such as the religious beliefs of the Aztec Indians—are of no direct relevance for existing social life. Similarly, social ordering without associated cultural ideas remains rudimentary, as in the mating and herding patterns of many animals. (The "social" life of ants and bees might appear to contradict this statement, but it is entirely determined by heredity, not culture.)

In sum, all human social organization is infused with cultural ideas, so that social ordering and culture each extensively influence the other. The process of social organization invariably incorporates both the ordering of social relationships and the creation of associated cultural ideas.

Concept of Culture

Thus far we have been content to describe culture as shared ideas, but a more direct confrontation with this concept is now called for. "Culture" is one of the most widely used and controversial concepts in social science. It has been defined in hundreds of ways. Most of the controversy, broadly speaking, has revolved around the differences between "anthropological" and "sociological" conceptions of culture. Anthropologists have usually restricted their field studies to primitive societies, small and simple enough to allow these investigators to examine personality, social, and symbolic phenomena simultaneously. Their concern was with the total "way of life" of a society; they ignored differences between what we have termed "levels of analysis" and gave "culture" an extremely broad meaning. This perspective was reinforced as many early social scientists tried to demonstrate that all human activities, no matter how strange or exotic, were learned, not inherited. The inclusive anthropological concept of culture provided a useful means of describing all nonbiological, or "superorganic," aspects of human life—from pottery-making to courtship practices to religious beliefs.

Many pioneer sociologists borrowed this anthropological conception of culture as "the total way of life of a people" and rather uncritically applied it to all behavioral, social, and symbolic phenomena. As a consequence the terms "social organization," "social order," and "culture" came to be used almost interchangeably in sociological literature.

Within the past few years, however, increasing numbers of sociologists (as well as some anthropologists) have begun to differentiate more precisely between "social" and "cultural" phenomena.[1] The contemporary, more limited concept of culture refers only to bodies of ideas that are shared by a number of people. As we have already seen, cultural ideas are an integral aspect of the total process of social organization, along with patterns of social order, but they do not constitute the entire process. In more formal terms, *a culture is a relatively unified set of shared ideas that is associated with one or more patterns of social order within the process of social organization.* Note that this definition does not specify the particular content of any given culture, how unified it actually is, or how closely it reflects the underlying social order. These are all problematic variables to be empirically studied.

A subtle distinction remains to be made between cultural ideas and specific actions and objects. It is not uncommon for social scientists to mix these terms, as in speaking of the cultural "trait" of gift-giving. Usually this is done merely for convenience of expression, but in this case it does confuse the cultural idea that one ought to give gifts on certain occasions with the social interactions through which the gifts are actually exchanged and with the material objects involved. This particular instance of social interaction might be a direct outgrowth of a cultural norm requiring gift-giving, and the giver might hope that his gift will serve as a token of his concern for the other person, but the cultural idea is not identical with either the social interaction or the physical object.

At the same time, though, it is culture that gives meaning to both actions and objects. If someone kills another person under one set of conditions, it is culturally defined as murder and the killer is severely punished. But if the same act is performed under a different set of conditions, the killer is honored as a war hero. Similarly, we go to archeological museums to view the artifacts of ancient civilizations (or to museums of science and industry to view our own artifacts), but the beads and pottery (or computers and nuclear reactors) we examine there have no meaning to us unless we understand the cultural ideas they represent.

In short, social actions and material objects often symbolize cultural ideas, while culture gives meaning to actions and objects. Although these phenomena are interwoven, for analytical purposes we restrict the concept of culture to shared ideas. The meanings cultural ideas give to particular forms of social life must then be investigated by the social scientist.

Cultural ideas are not distributed randomly among all people. They tend, instead, to be organized into relatively consistent and interrelated

---

[1] A. L. Kroeber and Talcott Parsons, "The Concepts of Culture and of Social Systems," *American Sociological Review,* vol. 23 (October 1958), pp. 582–583.

sets, so that it is possible to speak of cultural organization as a parallel process to social and personality organization. Organized sets of cultural ideas—usually referred to simply as cultures—are normally associated with particular patterns of social order. That is, each social organization possesses a distinctive culture of its own. Unless an organization has always been extremely isolated from all other human life—an exceedingly rare occurrence—its culture will of course share numerous ideas with many other cultures. The culture of a given family, for example, may incorporate ideas derived from the cultures of other families, from its community, from its church, from its social class, and from its society.

Nevertheless, the culture associated with each organization will possess a few ideas peculiar to it that distinguish it from all other cultures. Continuing the above example, each family will have its own customs and traditions, its own values, and its own special ways of doing things. More important than these few original ideas, however, is the fact that each culture is distinct in the arrangement of its component ideas. Although the values of the Smith family culture may be almost identical to those of the Brown family, the two families may be quite different in the priority rankings they assign to these values. Both families may believe that unselfish cooperation is desirable, but the Smiths may stress it much more than the Browns.

For clarity of communication, many sociologists use the single word "culture" only in relation to societies. The sets of cultural ideas associated with all occurrences of social order within a society are then called "subcultures." Thus we would speak of the culture of the United States but of the subculture of a community or a corporation or a delinquent gang or a hobby club. Societal cultures are rarely unique, since they often share common values, norms, languages, or other traits. Nevertheless, the culture of a society will normally dominate all subcultures within it, so that smaller organizations within a society will have only limited freedom in selecting, modifying, arranging, or rejecting ideas from the societal culture. For the most part, all subcultures will conform to and reflect the culture of their encompassing society. Subcultures that become too divergent from the larger societal culture are frequently labeled as "deviant," and efforts are made to change, restrict, or destroy them so as to maintain the stability and unity of the total society.

In contrast, societal cultures often differ radically, especially if these societies are relatively isolated from each other. One society's greatest virtue is another society's worst sin. In the United States we look with abhorrence upon parents who coldly murder their own children, but in other societies infanticide and religious child sacrifices have been praised as the highest tribute parents could pay toward the common welfare and

the pleasure of the gods. Any particular cultural idea—but especially social values—can be understood and analyzed only in relation to the entire
culture and social setting in which it exists. Ethnocentrism, which is the
judging of another culture's ideas by one's own values, is a devasting
destroyer of objective scientific analysis.

Despite wide cultural variability among the world's societies, many
cultural ideas are shared by most, if not all, societal cultures. The incest
"taboo" is the most commonly cited illustration of a cultural universal, although it must be realized that the definition of what acts constitute incest
does differ among societies. To the best of our knowledge, all societal
cultures also contain values and norms pertaining to marriage and parent-
hood, personal and public property, public responsibilities of individuals,
crime, art, and religion.[2] The specific contents of such universal cultural
traits differ from one society to another, but these types of ideas are
common to all men.

Components of Culture

Any kind of idea—from knowledge of fire-making to a philosophical
principle—may be included within a culture or subculture. Not all such
cultural ideas are directly incorporated within the process of social organization, however. Many shared ideas—including literature, artistic and
esthetic concepts, religious beliefs, scientific knowledge, material technology,[3] and language—are not integral parts of this process, though they
often do extensively influence social life. We will be concerned here only
with the four types of cultural ideas inherent in the process of social organization: *social values, social beliefs, social standards,* and *social technology.* These are the components of culture that become infused into patterns of social order, thereby completing the social organization process.
Let us examine these four socially relevant aspects of culture in greater
detail.

*Social values are shared agreements among the members of a social
organization as to what is desirable or undesirable in social life.* They are
the common conceptions that people generate (as a result of their

---

[2] George Peter Murdock, "The Common Denominator of Cultures," in Ralph
Linton, ed., *The Science of Man in the World Crisis* (New York: Columbia University
Press, 1944), pp. 123–142.
[3] Earlier we treated material technology as one of the factors comprising the
setting in which social organization occurs. All technological information is part of
culture, but material technology (as opposed to social technology) does not directly
enter into the process of social organization.

collective social activities) as to what is good or bad, important or unimportant, and commendable or deplorable in social life. Social values differ from values held by individuals in that they are shared among most (or all) members of an organization, are identified with the organization, and become infused into the patterns of social order comprising that organization. As an illustration we cite James Vander Zanden's suggested list of the major value configurations in American society:

1. Materialism. Americans are prone to evaluate things in material and monetary terms. . . . We tend to get quite excited about things as opposed to ideas, people, and aesthetic creations.
2. Success. . . . Part of the American faith is that "There is always another chance" and that "If at first you do not succeed, try, try again." If we ourselves cannot succeed, then we have the prospect for vicarious achievement through our children.
3. Work and Activity. . . . Work and activity are exalted in their own right; they are not merely means by which success may be realized; in and of themselves they are valued as worthwhile.
4. Progress. A belief in the perfectibility of society, man, and the world has been a kind of driving force in American history. . . . Americans tend to equate "the new" with "the best."
5. Rationality. Americans almost universally place faith in the rational approach to life. We continuously search out more "reasonable," "time-saving," and "effort-saving" ways of doing things.
6. Democracy. "Democracy" has become almost synonymous with "the American way of life." . . . We extol the Declaration of Independence with its insistence that "all men are created equal" and "governments [derive] their just power from the consent of the governed."
7. Humanitarianism. . . . Philanthropy and voluntary charity have been a characteristic note of America. More recently, more attention has been given to numerous programs for social welfare, with government playing an active role.[4]

Social values take many diverse forms. Some are narrowly focused into specific goals for social action (such as giving everyone a high school education), others are broader and more abstract ideals for social life (such as democratic government and individual equality), while others are pervasive "world views" or ways of thinking that underlie all social organization (such as the idea that society exists for the benefit of man, not vice versa). Another distinction widely utilized by sociologists is that between ideological and utopian values.[5] Ideologies are sets of values that explain, justify, and support existing social arrangements, such as the idea of separation of church and state, or the American business creed of "rugged individualism." Utopias are sets of values that evaluate, criticize,

[4] James W. Vander Zanden, Sociology: A Systematic Approach (New York: The Ronald Press Company, 1965), pp. 67–69.
[5] Karl Mannheim, Ideology and Utopia (New York: Harcourt, Brace & World, Inc., 1936).

and change existing social orders, such as the ideas of racial equality or political democracy. Over time, an idea that once served as a utopia for social change frequently becomes an established ideology supporting the *status quo*.

Social beliefs are shared ideas concerning the nature of man and his social life. Of crucial importance in the contemporary world, for instance, are the widely held beliefs that a child's biological parents are the persons best suited to rear him, that most individuals are capable of judging right from wrong and so can be held accountable for their actions, that persons with light skins are superior to those with dark skins, and that there is a divine purpose behind human affairs. Such beliefs may be either logical or illogical, scientifically accurate or inaccurate, naive or sophisticated. In all cases, however, their effects on social life can be immense.

Social standards are shared agreements among the members of a social organization regarding acceptable and unacceptable actions. These standards tell individuals what they should and should not do as members of that organization. Social standards are classified broadly as *norms* and *rules*.

Norms are standards containing some degree of morality, which are observed because they are thought to be "right" and hence "ought" to be followed, regardless of their usefulness or effectiveness. Our culture, for example, teaches us that it is wrong to steal or to directly insult people or to purposely keep others waiting, and that it is right to thank a person who has helped us, to be faithful to one's spouse, and to respect private property belonging to others. Norms vary extensively in the importance that people attach to them and the rigor with which they are enforced. Sociologists sometimes use the term *folkways* to refer to norms that specify appropriate but not mandatory actions and that are enforced interpersonally rather than through collective action. Manners, customs, traditions, fashions, and fads are various types of folkways. *Mores*, on the other hand, are norms that the members of an organization feel are extremely important for the common welfare and that are enforced by specially designated agents of the organization. Military codes of honor, constitutional bills of rights, and religious commandments are all mores.

Unlike norms, *social rules contain no moral implications*. These standards of action are more or less purposefully and rationally established as a means of attaining some goal, and they are usually followed for purely expedient reasons. To play chess, one must abide by the established rules of the game; to receive unemployment compensation one must meet certain criteria set by the state; to be eligible for promotion in the military one must have completed a certain amount of time in grade. Like norms, though, rules also vary widely in the extent to which conformity is expected and in techniques of enforcement. Rules have a tendency to shift into norms over time; the longer a rule has been established and observed, the more likely people are to think that "this is the way things ought to be done."

Both rules and norms can be codified into laws and enforced by the power of the state, although in most societies the majority of the folkways never become laws. The social standards that people view as crucial to their way of life are most likely to be made into laws, but there is no necessary relationship between the social importance of a standard and its legal status. Many states still require a year's residence before one can vote in a presidential election, while no state in this country legally prevents a family from adding to the population explosion by having fifteen children.

The prescriptions and proscriptions of social norms and rules establish socially expected standards for social action, but in practice there may be considerable disjunction between these standards and actual behaviors. A social value may say "Love thy neighbor as thyself," the accepted norm may be "Treat your neighbor in a polite and civil manner," while our actions may vary from having an affair with our neighbor's wife to throwing stones through the windows of a neighbor who is of a different race.

Social technology refers to knowledge about the technical aspects of social organization—how to establish, maintain, and operate this process. Included would be such knowledge as how to manage a monetary system, the procedures for operating a mayor-council form of city government, Robert's Rules of Order, the techniques of conducting a jury trial, the idea of the corporate form of business organization, and the methods of operating a university on the trimester plan. Most of humanity's social technology has been accumulated through a long process of trial and error, although very slowly we are learning to transform the theories and findings of social science into applied social engineering. Technological knowledge about the process of social organization, like material technology, tends to accumulate at a continually increasing rate: the more knowledge a society has, the more likely it is to acquire new information through innovation. Material technology, however, is presently growing considerably faster than social technology, which causes numerous social problems.

Summary: The Creation of Social Organization

Our exploratory journey through the process of creating social organization is now at an end. Many features of this process, as well as properties of the organizations it produces, remain to be examined in later chapters. At this point, though, we should have gained at least a working familiarity with the basic concepts of the social organizational process. Let us now briefly recapitulate these major ideas.

The creation of social organization takes place within a setting imposed by the natural environment, population characteristics, properties of the human being, material technology, and the social environment. As a result of a wide variety of causal factors, social actors (either individuals or organizations) interact with each other and influence each other's actions and thoughts. Enduring social relationships arise as these interactions are perpetuated through time. Whereas social actors enter any given social relations as relatively autonomous elements in respect to that relationship, as they become participants in the relationship they must at times act as relatively committed parts of this larger phenomenon. Social actors engaged in social relationships can hold either self orientations (stressing expedient exchange) or collective orientations (stressing moral obligations), but membership in a relationship frequently produces some shift from self to collective orientations.

Social ordering emerges as these social interactions and relationships evidence predictable regularities or arrangements. Social order thus consists of patterned and recurrent social interactions that maintain their uniformities with some degree of stability over time. These patterns of social order display properties of their own that are not inherent in the constituent members. As a result, they possess a unity greater than the sum of their component parts, which gives them an existence of their own. They are exterior to individual personalities and they constrain or influence the actions of their members. At the same time, individual personalities and patterns of social order always interpenetrate each other, so that neither can exist entirely apart from the other.

As a means of describing and analyzing social order, we are forced by the limitations of our own minds to "freeze" these ongoing processes into static pictures. By combining many such instances of social order, we are able to abstract conceptions of social structure, or specific observed patterns of social order.

Shared cultural ideas in turn emerge from social ordering, as the participants communicate with each other about their joint activities and create common ideas of how social life should and can be organized. A unique set of cultural ideas tends to become associated with each social organization, so that most or all of its members eventually share its culture. Of special importance for the process of social organization are the aspects of culture we call social values, beliefs, standards, and technology. Culture, like social order, evidences distinctive properties that give it existence and reality of its own. The culture of an organization will therefore always influence and shape, as well as reflect, its underlying patterns of social order. Nevertheless, culture and social order inevitably interpenetrate each other, as do personalities and social order, so that all three aspects of social life become fused into the overall process of social organization.

In sum, *the process of social organization occurs as social actors interact in patterned and recurrent relationships to create social ordering, which in turn becomes infused with cultural ideas.* Social organization thus centers on patterns of social order, but also incorporates portions of both individual personalities and cultures. Figure 5-1 depicts the process of social organization in terms of these three interpenetrating aspects. The diagram is necessarily rather structural, but it does indicate the flow of time and hence by implication the dynamism of this process.

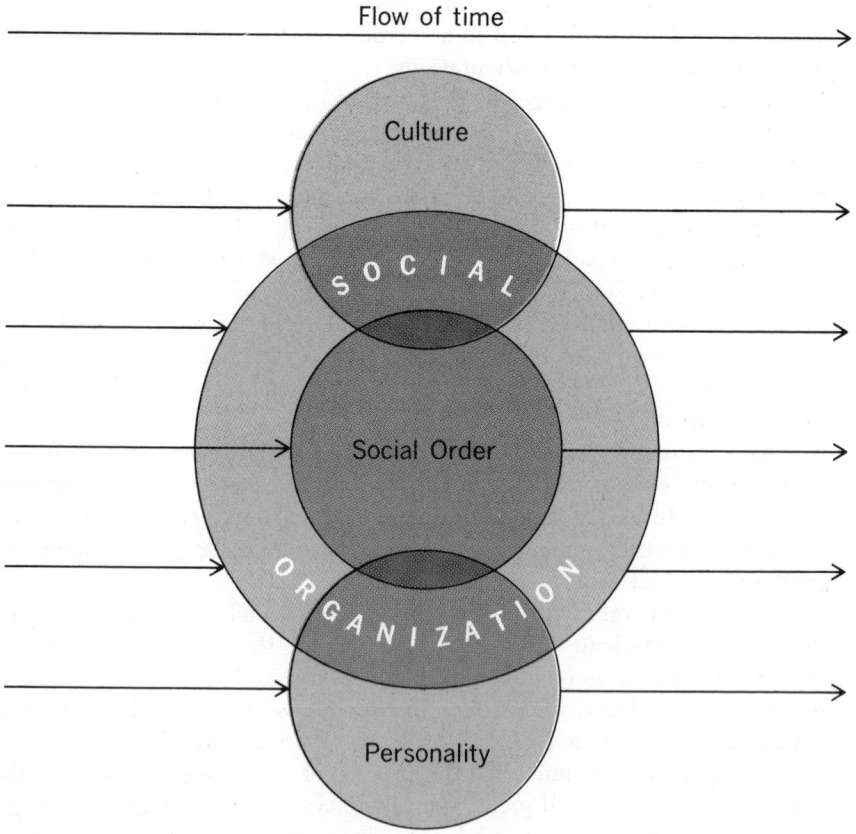

FIGURE 5–1. Interpenetration of personality, social order, and culture in the process of social organization.

The crucial idea here is that through the process of organization—whether it be on the psychological, social, or cultural level—the whole becomes more than the mere sum of its parts. By virtue of its organization, the emergent phenomenon exists as a real entity in and of itself. Whitehead saw this principle of emergent organization as the basis of all existence: "The ultimate metaphysical principle is the advance from disjunction to conjunction, creating a novel entity other than the entities given in disjunction. . . . The many become one, and are increased by one."[6]

[6] Alfred North Whitehead, *Process and Reality* (New York: The Macmillan Company, 1929), p. 32.

RECOMMENDED READING

KLUCKHOHN, CLYDE, *Mirror for Man,* chap. 2 (New York: McGraw-Hill, Inc., 1949).
The concept of culture is elaborated, illustrated, and analyzed in nontechnical language.
KROEBER, A. L., AND TALCOTT PARSONS, "The Concepts of Culture and of Social Systems," *American Sociological Review,* vol. 23 (October 1958), pp. 582–583.
A brief statement clarifying the conceptual distinction between social and cultural phenomena.
LIPSET, SEYMOUR MARTIN, "The Value Patterns of Democracy: A Case Study in Comparative Analysis," *American Sociological Review,* vol. 28 (August 1963), pp. 515–531.
American culture is analyzed in terms of its major dimensions and contrasted with the cultures of England, Canada, and Australia.
MINER, HORACE, "Body Ritual Among the Nacirema," *American Anthropologist,* vol. 58 (June 1956), pp. 503–507. (Also Bobbs-Merrill reprint S-185.)
The expression of "exotic" cultural ideas through daily rituals is illustrated in this anthropological account of a contemporary society.
WILLIAMS, ROBIN, *American Society: A Sociological Interpretation,* rev. ed., chap. 11 (New York: Alfred A. Knopf, 1960).
A discussion of the major values in American culture.
YINGER, J. MILTON, "Contraculture and Subculture," *American Sociological Review,* vol. 25 (October 1960), pp. 625–635.
The concepts of subculture and contraculture are distinguished and described.

CHAPTER 6

Social Organizations as Entities

Our discussion of social organization has thus far been largely (and somewhat self-consciously) expressed in terms of dynamic processes. But we have mentioned that social organizations are also objects or entities. We all talk about such phenomena as communities, businesses, churches, clubs, schools, governments, and societies as real social entities. Indeed, through the legal procedure of incorporation any organization may acquire, in the eyes of the law, all the rights and obligations of individuals. What, then, is this thing we call Regional City—General Products Company—First United Church—our gang—the upper class—the economy—the United States?

We are now concerned with social organizations as delineated social objects. More specifically, in this chapter we shall examine several aspects of all social organizations: the ways in which an organization is distinguished from its social environment, some general characteristics of organizations, functional requirements of organizations, and relationships between an organization and its component subunits. This discussion will pertain to all kinds of organizations, from small groups through total societies. In the following chapter we shall examine several different types of social organizations.

Delineation of Social Organizations

What is a social organization? In more precise terms, how is any specific organizational entity delineated from its social environment? Let us approach this question negatively, by first eliminating several sociologically inadequate conceptions of organizations.

Most social organizations possess land, buildings, or other forms of property, and we often loosely think of the organization in terms of its physical artifacts. But any social organization is quite clearly much more than just physical property, since organizations frequently gain and lose property without significantly changing themselves. When the First National Bank moves into its new building it remains the same bank. Almost all organizations also possess a distinctive name or title by which they are identified. Again a moment's reflection should convince us that the name is not the organization itself, but only a verbal symbol that stands for the organization in communication. After the Plainville Community Service and Recreation Association has shortened its name to Plainville Civic Association, it is still the same organization. A change of name sometimes indicates an alteration in an organization, but the name itself means nothing.

"Of course a social organization is not physical property or a name," we might argue. "But can't we describe an organization as a number of individuals who have joined together to carry out common activities. For example, isn't a university actually a collection of students, faculty, and administrators who are jointly engaged in the tasks of acquiring and disseminating knowledge?" This conception of social organization as a number of interacting individuals is extremely common, but sociologically it is inadequate. An organization must have members in order to exist, but these individual members do not, in and of themselves, constitute the organization. Any social organization can over time experience a complete turnover of membership and yet remain the same entity.[1] In fact, if the organization is to last longer than the human lifespan, it must change members. Whether it be the Thursday Afternoon Ladies' Knitting Club or the United States, its membership is constantly changing, without any necessary changes in the organization itself. Social organization is created as people interact, but the organizations that emerge through this process cannot be equated with any particular individuals.

[1] The one possible exception to this generalization is the nuclear family of husband, wife, and children, but even here at least some members can change without destroying the family. And if we conceive of the Jones family as a social phenomenon continuing over several generations, rather than just a single marriage, then the generalization is still fully applicable.

If social organizations do not consist of property, names, or specific people, then what is an organization? As an ongoing process, we have described social organization as the merging of social actors into patterned and recurrent social orders which become infused with cultural ideas. But how do selected portions of this process become delineated into specific organizations that can be named, own property, gain members, and carry out activities? Delineation of social organizations as entities—which is itself a continual process—is accomplished primarily through the development of boundaries, structural stability, and a unique culture.

The first, and perhaps most crucial, step in the process of delineating an organization is to establish *boundaries* around it. The phenomena comprising it must be distinguished in some way from other ongoing activities, so as to separate the organization from its social environment. There must be some basis for saying: "This is part of the organization, but that is not," or "He belongs to the group, but she does not," or "Our association sponsors these activities, but not those." Some organizational boundaries are totally arbitrary, as in the case of the imaginary line running down the middle of a street that separates a city from its adjoining suburb. Usually, though, some basis for identifying organizational boundaries does exist in the underlying patterns of social organization—such as who attends meetings and who doesn't, or who shares our values and who doesn't. Such existing "breaks" in ongoing interactional and cultural processes are in turn often clarified and strengthened through shared conceptualizations of membership and boundary lines.[2]

Because of our human perception of time, boundaries of physical and biological objects usually appear to be fairly definite. The rate of exchange between the object and its surrounding environment is slower than our ability to perceive change, so that its boundaries seem to be well defined and quite permanent over time. We all agree without argument where a table stops and a chair begins. Boundaries of social organizations (and also personalities), however, tend to be considerably less sharp and stable to our senses. Consequently, organizational boundaries are frequently either vague and blurred or else based largely on arbitrary definitions.

For example, the boundaries of the typical American family would appear to be very definite: a single family consists of a married couple and their minor, unmarried children. In any given family, though, this generalization can be difficult to apply. What about a grandparent who

---

[2] Whether or not participants are self-consciously aware of what they are doing when they create these boundaries is not crucial for our concern here, although this factor obviously affects the strength and viability of any actual boundaries.

lives with the family, or an unmarried adult son or daughter still living at home, or a foster child for whom the parents care? In many cases these people would be included within the family, but in some situations the family members (or the sociologist) might exclude them. As another example, some churches count as members all persons living in their area who were ever baptized in that faith, regardless of the present convictions or actions of these people. Other churches count as members only individuals who have formally requested membership and who are currently active in the church. Universities, meanwhile, are frequently perplexed by the problem of how to treat "nonstudents" who attend classes and other campus events without ever registering as students. And how does one define the boundaries of a community, with people moving in and out every day? Legally, one might have to reside within the city limits for thirty to sixty days before he is eligible to vote in local elections, but from a broader perspective the person is a participating member of the community from the first day he lives there, regardless of whether his dwelling is inside or outside the city limits.

The difficulties inherent in trying to establish rigid boundaries are especially apparent in regard to societies. Disputes over physical borders have led to innumerable international conferences, conflicts, or even wars throughout human history. International relations also force most societies to establish rather arbitrary definitions of citizenship. The United States is quite inclusive in this respect, granting citizenship to all persons born within the geographical limits of the country or its territories. Residents of American Samoa are citizens of the United States, as are children born in this country to parents who are themselves aliens. Needless to say, nations differ widely in their legal prescriptions for citizenship.

A few common types of organizational boundaries are described below, although this list is far from complete:

(1) Formal membership rosters, on which the names of all members of the organization are listed. Formal membership status is frequently contingent upon some action by the individual, such as paying dues, professing a certain belief, or undergoing an initiation ritual.

(2) Interpersonal identification of members with each other, as in the case of most small friendship groups. One becomes a member of such a group when he is tacitly accepted by the other members.

(3) Geographical location, or physical presence in a specified area such as a neighborhood or a community.

(4) Self-identification by a person with an organization, as employed by some political parties and religious bodies.

(5) Limitations on social relationships, based on observations or prescriptions concerning who interacts with whom in what ways on a regular basis.

(6) Willingness to defend the organization against disruptive forces —"If you're with us, stand and fight for us."

(7) Shared cultural values and norms, as in the case of ethnic classes and professional associations.

These types of organizational boundaries are not mutually exclusive, and many organizations use several of them simultaneously or under differing conditions. But all of them do serve to delineate the organization from its environment.

The second step in delineating organizations as concrete entities involves the maintenance of *structural stability*. We have observed that patterns of social order may remain relatively stable through time, despite continual alterations in their component interactions and relationships. Ideally, sociology should be able to specify which features of any given organization must persist if its social order is to remain stable, and which features may vary without disrupting these essential patterns. If a government replaces a constitutional monarch with an elected president, for instance, has its basic social order been changed? What if the powers of the presidency are slowly expanded in relation to the legislature? Unfortunately, we cannot make such precise determinations at the present time, so that the operational definition of "stability" remains quite arbitrary.

We can, however, add two additional notions about stability to our previous conceptualization. One is the observation that stability is often achieved through constant change, not in spite of it. Strong resistance to change in the social order of an organization might result in lengthy persistence, as occurs in many primitive societies, which frequently endure practically unaltered for hundreds of years. But if such a society encounters disruptive social forces too powerful for it to resist—such as economic pressures from Western societies—its inability to change with shifting conditions will likely mean its destruction. The more highly interrelated an organization is with its social environment, the more frequently it must change in many small ways if it is to preserve its fundamental patterns of social order. The United States is often said to be a very stable society, since it has experienced almost two hundred years of uninterrupted democratic government, yet certainly this society has been anything but unchanging during that period of time.

The other notion is that relative stability must exist in the total configuration of an organization—that is, in most or all of its component patterns of social order—if it is to be delineated as a social entity. Its basic form and essential features can be differentiated from the social environment only if the overall structure of the organization persists for some minimal time. Persistence of only one or a few of the relationships occurring within an organization usually will not give stability to the entire organization. In short, organizational entities display some degree of overall structural stability through time.

The third and last step in the delineation of an organizational entity is the creation of a *unique culture* associated with that organization. The concept of cultural uniqueness, whether in terms of the content or the arrangement of its component ideas, was discussed in the previous chapter, and need not be elaborated here. The main point is that any organization tends over time to acquire a culture that differs in some way from the cultures of all other organizations, even though it may share many specific ideas with numerous other cultures, and even though it may only be a "subsubsubculture" within a total societal culture. Once an organization has developed a unique set of cultural values, goals, norms, rules, and other ideas, the presence of this culture further delineates that organization from all other social phenomena.

To the extent that the delineation process described here does occur, social organizations will exist as distinct entities. In other words, *the objects we call social organizations are delineated outcomes of the ongoing process of social organization*. Social reality is always a flowing process, but portions of it frequently become bounded and display structural stability and a unique culture, and hence constitute social entities. Another way of expressing this same concept is to say that *a social organization is a relatively bounded and stable occurrence of social order, together with an associated culture*.

Social organizations are real phenomena, regardless of whether anyone recognizes their existence. But recognition of an organization by its members will profoundly affect the ways in which they act toward it. For instance, a number of people might have been living close to each other, interacting with each other, and sharing a common culture for a long time—and thus have created a social organization we would call a community. However, until they perceive this organization as an existing entity, a "community" as such will not exist for them. Because they are not aware of their membership in a common social unit, they will not strive to perpetuate or change that organization or to generate collective orientations toward it. Once they perceive the existence of a "community" (regardless of what they call it), however, this organization will become as real to them as their physical environment. They will speak of it as "their community," they will pay taxes to the community rather than to the individual who stamps their tax receipts, and the community as a whole will likely act to establish schools, a police department, a recreation program, or whatever other collective activities are seen as necessary for the common welfare.

Characteristics of Social Organizations

Given a delineated (and perceived) social organization, the sociologist frequently begins his analysis by describing its structure. Many structural characteristics are, of course, peculiar to the organization being examined; nevertheless, most organizational structures can be evaluated in terms of several fairly standard dimensions, three of which we consider in this section. Very likely the sociologist will also try to record at least the more salient features of the culture of the organization he studies. Through further analysis he may then seek to understand various dynamic processes occurring in the organization, relationships among its component subparts, and links between it and other organizations in its social environment. These concerns will be explored later in this chapter and in subsequent chapters.

The three structural variables mentioned here—size, complexity, and formalness—by no means exhaust all possible dimensions of structural analysis, but they are perhaps the most basic. First of all, any organization can be described in terms of its *size*. This is not always as easy as it sounds. What do we mean by the "size" of an organization? The most obvious criterion is number of individual members. Taking a "head count" is not too difficult in smaller organizations—provided, of course, that we have succeeded in accurately identifying the organizational boundaries and hence defining membership. In larger organizations such as societies, even this elementary measurement often becomes quite demanding. Thousands of man-hours of work and millions of dollars are expended for each census of the United States, and population figures for nations such as China and India are still only educated guesses.

In many cases a count of members (however defined) is adequate for the question at hand, but in other situations a more sophisticated measure is required. When studying a special-interest voluntary association such as a PTA, for instance, we often need to determine degrees of participation. Some persons will be officially enrolled in the association but have nothing else to do with it, others will attend meetings only sporadically, still others will be active participants in all activities of the association, and a few persons will be deeply involved through occupancy of leadership positions. Which of these participation criteria provides the most representative picture of the organization, and how are they to be measured? Such considerations further complicate the task of determining organizational size.

Other criteria beyond mere number of members or participants might also be used. Business corporations, for example, are frequently compared in terms of their total economic assets, the size of their gross profits, and similar monetary factors. Hospitals and other service organizations that deal with large numbers of nonmember clients are perhaps most meaningfully evaluated in terms of the extent and nature of services provided. Or we may seek to determine the size of an organization by ascertaining the number of component subparts it contains or the total scope of its activities.

Clearly, even such an apparently simple task as determining organizational size may pose numerous conceptual and operational problems for the social scientist. But one important generalization is quite apparent: *the size of an organization has extensive consequences for most of its other characteristics and activities.* Although this statement may sound obvious, there have been very few theoretical writings or empirical studies dealing with the effects of organizational size.[3] In general, increasing size appears to produce greater internal complexity—that is, development of many subparts with specialized activities, extensive internal interaction and communication, and pressures for overall coordination of activities—but the specific nature of this structural growth depends on many additional factors. At the same time, as organizational size increases, interactions among members often tend to become more formalized, or impersonal and routinized. Finally, increasing size also offers the possibility—though does not guarantee—that the scope and effectiveness of the organization's goal-seeking activities may expand, owing to availability of additional resources, functional specialization among subparts, overall efficiency of operation, and similar factors. In sum, size may be only the first of numerous dimensions along which organizations are analyzed, but it always remains crucial.

The second major characteristic of all social organizations is degree

---

[3] Three exceptions are the following studies: Theodore R. Anderson and Seymour Warkov, "Organizational Size and Functional Complexity: A Study of Administration in Hospitals," *American Sociological Review*, vol. 26 (February 1961), pp. 23–28; Mason Haire, "Biological Models and Empirical Histories of the Growth of Organizations," in his *Modern Organizational Theory* (New York: John Wiley & Sons, Inc., 1959), pp. 272–306; and Fredric W. Terrien and Donald L. Mills, "The Effects of Changing Size upon the Internal Structure of Organizations," *American Sociological Review*, vol. 20 (February 1955), pp. 11–13. Thirteen general propositions concerning the effects of size on other aspects of an organization have been proposed by Paul E. Mott, *The Organization of Society* (Englewood Cliffs, N.J.: Prentice-Hall, Inc., 1965).

of structural *complexity*. As just noted, increasing complexity tends to be an outgrowth of expanding organizational size, although these two dimensions are never perfectly correlated, because of the effects of other compounding factors. For an organization to be described as relatively complex, its patterns of social order must be numerous and interrelated and it must contain many diverse subunits. Families, friendship cliques, and other small groups are never described as complex organizations. But large size alone is not enough, since if all the parts of an organization were similar and relatively unrelated to each other, the organization would still not be considered complex. Such would be the case, for instance, in a typical communitywide association of butchers (or bakers or barbers). Even though two hundred butcher shops belong to the organization, all of them are more or less alike, each is fairly independent of the others, and there is no full-time executive staff with its own unique tasks. The social structure of a complex organization is just what the term implies—complex and complicated. It contains many subparts, each with its own distinctive patterns of social order, all of which are interdependent in their activities, and all of which are responsible to some type of central unit.

Most relatively complex organizations also tend to be hierarchically arranged, with several levels of successively diminishing authority spreading downward from the elite positions at the apex of the structure. So pervasive is this arrangement that many social scientists use as a working definition of complexity the presence of three or more levels of authority in an organization. To anticipate a later chapter, however, we note here that a rigid hierarchy is not inevitable in all complex organizations. Relatively decentralized organizations largely avoid this structural pattern.

In short, *complexity refers to the degree to which the component parts of a large organizational structure are both diverse and interdependent.* Government bureaus, large businesses, universities, labor unions, cities, and modern societies are all common illustrations of extremely complex social organizations. Indeed, one of the most pervasive trends in contemporary social life is the growing size and complexity of most forms of social organization.

The third basic structural characteristic of all organizations, degree of *formality*, is related to both size and complexity. Although it is not inevitable, there is a marked tendency for organizations to increase in formality as they grow in size and complexity, since a certain amount of standardization and predictability is necessary to keep a large, complex organization operating smoothly. In a relatively formalized social structure, such as an army chain of command, many of the interactions between members and between component subunits are prescribed in advance. Social actors are restricted in their selection of interaction partners, and they cannot freely vary the nature of these interactions. In contrast, an informal social structure, such as the ties of personal friendships uniting the members of a small clique, is characterized by fluidity and spontaneity. Social actors have relatively wide freedom to create and modify social interactions as they please. In other words, *formality refers to the degree to which interactions comprising the social order of an organization are specified in advance and rigidly prescribed.*

Although formality and informality thus constitute the opposite poles of an analytical dimension, any given organization will normally display various combinations of both characteristics simultaneously. That is, all organizations will have some degree of formal ordering and some degree of informal ordering. Different organizations stress these two types of structures in varying degrees—a hobby club perhaps giving predominance to informal relationships, and a steel mill stressing the formal arrangement of jobs in the company—but the two types are not mutually exclusive. An elaborate set of informal relationships may, in fact, exist alongside (and be interwoven with) the most formalized patterns of social order that men can devise—as seen, for example, in military units. We might even postulate that the creation of a highly formalized social structure necessitates the development of a strong complementary web of informal relationships if the organization is to operate effectively or remain stable.

These organizational characteristics of size, complexity, and formality are usually thought of as essentially structural in nature, since measurements and analyses of them are taken from structural descriptions of organizations. In marked contrast are such ubiquitous dynamic processes as conflict and change, integration, power exertion, and stratification. Although these phenomena are sometimes also described in static structural terms—as when we speak of the "class structure" as a community—to be properly understood they must be viewed and analyzed as ongoing social processes occurring within all social organizations. Because each of these organizational processes involves numerous variables and complicated trains of events, we shall defer examination of them until later chapters.

Organizational Requirements

We mentioned in the previous chapter that as organizational entities develop through the general process of social organization, they acquire properties of their own and interact as social actors with other organizations. Basic structural characteristics such as size, complexity, and formalness, as well as more dynamic operational processes, all illustrate such organizational properties and actions. Another instance of this same phenomenon is seen in the numerous *functional requirements*[4] that all organizations must satisfy if they are to survive, remain stable and unified, and achieve whatever goals they seek. That is, *social organizations must perform certain activities and/or meet certain conditions*—or else become either partially or totally disorganized.

The term "organizational needs" is a frequently used synonym for this same idea, although for some readers it conveys too many biological overtones. These functional requirements are not inherent in the organization in any anthropomorphic sense, but neither are they inherent in any particular individual members—except insofar as the members act as responsible parts of the organization and thus recognize the existence of these requirements. Organizational functional requirements are located in the relationships between an organization and its natural and social environments, and in the relationships among its component subunits. They must therefore be satisfied through various kinds of organizational actions.

A number of social theorists have suggested lists of basic organizational requirements, among which the following are common themes:[5]

1. Maintenance of the population, through either reproduction or recruitment.
2. Provision for the training and/or socialization of members of the organization.
3. Promotion of communication and interaction among members and parts of the organization.

---

[4] "Functional" here refers to the overall operation of a social organization. This generic use of "functional" must not be confused with the specific analytical technique called "functional analysis," which is discussed in a later chapter.

[5] These items are summarized from the following works: David F. Aberle, *et al.,* "The Functional Prerequisites of a Society," *Ethics,* vol. 60 (January 1950), pp. 110–111; John Bennett and Melvin M. Tumin, *Social Life: Structure and Function* (New York: Alfred A. Knopf, 1948), p. 168; Theodore Caplow, *Principles of Organization* (New York: Harcourt, Brace & World, Inc., 1964), pp. 121–124; Kingsley Davis, *Human Society* (New York: The Macmillan Company, 1948), pp. 28–31; and Talcott Parsons, Robert F. Bales, and Edward A. Shils, *Working Papers in the Theory of Action* (New York: The Free Press, a division of The Macmillan Company, 1953), chaps. 3–5. Parsons and his collaborators have suggested that all of these functional requirements can be classified into four categories, which they call "adaptation," "goal attainment," "integration," and "latency." Adaptation is the manipulation and utilization of the external natural and social environments to procure necessary resources and to dispose of organizational "products." Goal attainment is the coordination and direction of organizational activities toward the attainment of whatever goals the organization seeks. Integration is the interrelating and solidifying of subparts so as to promote overall organizational unity. Latency involves both the maintenance of basic organizational values and norms, and also the socialization and training of individual actors to perform necessary activities (role requirements) for the organization. For an introductory discussion of this scheme, see Edward C. Devereux, Jr., "Parsons' Sociological Theory," in Max Black, ed., *The Social Theories of Talcott Parsons* (Englewood Cliffs, N.J.: Prentice-Hall, Inc., 1961), pp. 53–63.

4. Establishment of a division of labor through specialization of tasks, activities, duties, and responsibilities.
5. Assignment of social actors to necessary roles, or tasks, activities, duties, and responsibilities.
6. Ordering of relationships among the component parts of the organization.
7. Sharing of common social values among the members, including agreement on organizational goals.
8. Establishment of a common, consistent, and adequate set of social norms and rules.
9. Procurement of necessary resources from the natural and social environments.
10. Development of methods for organizational decision-making.
11. Coordination of organizational activities so as to achieve organizational goals.
12. Provision for the allocation to members of the benefits of organizational activities.
13. Protection of the organization against external threats and stresses.
14. Control of deviant and disruptive actions by organizational members.
15. Creation of procedures for managing or resolving conflicts within the organization.
16. Promotion of organizational unity or integration.
17. Development of procedures for changing the organization.

Undoubtedly this list is far from complete, but it does illustrate the range of functional requirements that all social organizations face at one time or another.

Organizational requirements can be divided analytically into two broad categories, although in practice the two types merge imperceptibly. *Survival requirements,* or functional imperatives, must be satisfied by all organizations if they are to exist for any length of time. They are basic to the process of social organization. *Operational requirements,* or functional requisites, must be satisfied if an organization is to operate effectively and attain its goals. Some kinds of operational requirements are common to all social organizations, while others are determined by the actions and goals of specific organizations at particular times. Unfortunately, we lack adequate criteria for even tentatively classifying organizational requirements as either "survival" or "operational."[6]

Many, if not all, organizational requirements can normally be met in more than one way, through different courses of organizational action. As an illustration, a society can procure new members through the birth of children to present members, through immigration of persons from other societies, or by waging war to conquer additional people. Sociol-

---

[6] For a discussion of the distinction between survival and operational requirements of organizations, see Amitai Etzoini, "Two Approaches to Organizational Analysis: A Critique and a Suggestion," *Administrative Science Quarterly,* vol. 5 (September 1960), pp. 257–278.

ogists speak of these diverse means of satisfying a given functional requirement as "functional alternatives," "functional equivalents," or "functional substitutes."[7] This phenomenon tends to give an organization considerable flexibility. In most cases survival and operational requirements do not rigidly determine either the actions or the structure of the organization—though they may influence and limit organizational forms and activities.

If the survival and operational requirements of an organization are not met, it will experience either partial or total disorganization. This process need not occur immediately, however. The organization may be able temporary to weather problems or obstacles, and many requirements can be dealt with rather intermittently. Once an adequate set of norms and rules has been adopted or devised, for instance, the organization may be able to rely on these standards of action for some time, with only occasional minor modifications. Over a period of time, nevertheless, unsatisfied functional requirements will begin to generate tensions and to disrupt the organization. The resulting process of social disorganization is essentially the reverse of the process of social organization. Social relationships will not be perpetuated, patterns of social order will break down, common cultural ideas will be rejected, boundaries will be destroyed, and the organization will lose stability and unity. Eventually the organization as an entity will cease to exist.

Failure to satisfy functional requirements is only one of several possible causes of social disorganization, and there is no set sequence or timetable through which this process invariably occurs, but the overall process of disorganization is frequently witnessed in all spheres of social life—from broken marriages to the "fall" of empires.

Organizational Subunits

We now shift our attention from the organization as a whole to its component subunits. Organizations and individuals are similar in that they can both interact as social actors with other social objects. But there is a crucial difference between these two kinds of social actors. Whereas the sociologist usually treats the individual as a single unified entity, this is not true of organizations. Most social organizations contain a number of subunits, each of which normally possesses some degree of autonomy, and which can therefore be examined as an organization in its own right. Furthermore, most "whole organizations" are simultaneously parts of

---

[7] Robert K. Merton, *Social Theory and Social Structure*, rev. ed. (New York: The Free Press, a division of The Macmillan Company, 1957), chap. 1.

larger social units. Consequently, whether a given organization is studied as a separate entity or as a part of a more encompassing whole is largely an arbitrary decision of the researcher, depending on the problem under investigation. For analytical purposes, he temporarily treats a given social object as a whole organization, and then examines its component subunits as parts of this more inclusive entity.

Two conditions normally exist among the subunits of any organization, though in varying degrees in different organizations and at different times within the same organization. These are functional specialization and functional autonomy.

On the one hand, in any organization more complex than a simple friendship group there will be some degree of *functional specialization*, or *division of labor*, among the subunits. The various subunits (and sub-subunits, and so on) will tend to become specialized in their activities, so that they perform different kinds of activities. To the extent that these specialized functions mesh with each other and contribute to the overall functioning of the larger organization, it will become strongly unified. In any case, however, each subunit will tend to lose self-sufficiency as it increasingly performs one or a few specialized activities, so that if left to itself it could not long survive. It relinquishes to other subunits the responsibility for satisfying most of its survival requirements and hence becomes highly interdependent upon them. In return, by concentrating all of its actions on the activities it can perform most effectively, it gains functional efficiency.

Not all the departments in an automobile factory build cars, for instance. Some concentrate on production, while others specialize in advertising, marketing, finance, research, or administration. Nor does specialization stop at this level. Within the production department, one section makes bodies (one of its shops producing doors, another seats, and so on), a second section makes engines, and a third makes transmissions. This kind of minute task specialization, extending clear down to the individual worker, is one of the keys to the high efficiency of modern industry—as well as most other types of complex organizations—but it also creates many critical problems of overall coordination among the diverse subunits and of personal satisfaction among individual members.

On the other hand, the subunits of most organizations also normally possess some degree of *functional autonomy*, or limited ability to act independently of the larger organization.[8] Each subunit will evidence its own unique patterns of social order and cultural ideas. The larger organi-

---

[8] This concept of functional autonomy has been extensively discussed by Alvin Gouldner, "Reciprocity and Autonomy in Functional Theory," in Llewellyn Gross, ed., *Symposium on Sociological Theory* (New York: Harper & Row, Publishers, 1959), pp. 241–270.

zation may attempt to limit and control the functional autonomy of its component parts to a considerable degree, so as to acquire overall stability and unity. In anything less than a completely totalitarian organization, however, this control can only be partial, leaving the subunits with some latitude to act on their own. It is usually to the long-run benefit of the whole organization to grant its component parts considerable leeway within broadly specified limits, for this greatly increases the flexibility of the organization and its ability to deal with changing circumstances— even though this procedure does multiply the short-run administrative and coordination problems of the larger organization.

Considering the automobile company again, the sales department specializes solely in the marketing of cars which it does not itself produce, but it might still be given (or assume) considerable freedom to devise advertisements and grant dealer franchises with only minimal supervision by higher executives. Degree of subunit functional autonomy varies widely among different organizations and even among various subunits of the same organization. As a general proposition, it has been suggested that the process through which the larger organization is created may influence the relative autonomy of its component parts. If the larger organization is established through the merging of what were once relatively independent units, these units often retain more functional autonomy than do subunits that are initiated by a more inclusive organization.[9]

From a theoretical viewpoint, these two conditions of functional specialization and autonomy are mutually contradictory, since as a subunit becomes increasingly specialized it must relinquish self-sufficiency. In actual practice, though, the two conditions usually coexist to some degree; each specialized subunit will evidence some amount of functional autonomy. This is not an accidental outcome of poor organization, but rather an attempt to gain the functional advantages of both conditions simultaneously. However, since both conditions raise numerous problems of communication, coordination, and control for the organization as a whole, they both contribute to a pervasive tendency toward administrative centralization, which we shall encounter in a later chapter.

As the extent and scope of functional autonomy increase or decrease among the subunits comprising an organization, one of two opposing processes may become predominant. To the degree that subunits gain functional autonomy, *segmentation* frequently occurs, though this is not inevitable. In contrast, as subunits lose functional autonomy—due to such factors as control by the larger organization, functional specializa-

---

[9] Seymour M. Lipset, *Political Man* (New York: Doubleday & Company, Inc., 1963), chap. 12.

tion, or acceptance of a more inclusive culture—*institutionalization* often occurs.[10] These concepts are simply a convenient way of applying the distinctions between element-part actions and self-collectivity orientations to organizational subunits. That is, *relatively segmented units of an organization act primarily as autonomous elements with self orientations,* seeking their own goals in as expedient a manner as possible. In contrast, *relatively institutionalized units act primarily as committed parts with collective orientations,* seeking to meet the functional requirements of the encompassing organization and to contribute to the attainment of collective goals.

These two processes—segmentation and institutionalization—are mutually incompatible, since an increase in one leads to a corresponding decrease in the other. Both, however, can occur simultaneously among various subunits of the same organization or even within one subunit at different times. We must also guard against subjective bias toward one or the other of these processes. Neither of them is exclusively beneficial or detrimental for any social organization. Both are vital for organizational survival and functional operation, although an excessively strong movement in either direction can harm any organization.[11] Let us examine both of them in greater detail.

The concept of segmentation was first used by Durkheim to describe societies composed of communities and other organizations (such as clans) that are all relatively similar to each other.[12] Because of this similarity, segmented units of an organization are not highly specialized or interdependent; each can exist and act with relative autonomy. They will continue to be subunits of a more encompassing organization as long as they at least periodically interact with each other in patterned ways and share a common culture. But they also retain the capacity to function autonomously whenever such actions are expedient or necessary. In addition, they often possess relatively distinct cultures of their own, or cultural autonomy. As these subunits become increasingly segmented,

[10] "Institution" is frequently used in sociology to mean merely patterns of social order and/or cultural ideas that are strongly established, widely accepted, and relatively stable over time. This conceptualization lacks preciseness, however, and in practice often becomes too vague to be meaningful.

[11] Segmentation should not be equated with disintegration, and institutionalization with integration, as is sometimes done. Excessive segmentation will cause disintegration, while a certain amount of institutionalization is necessary for integration. But within limits the degree of segmentation or institutionalization of subunits can vary without disturbing the overall integration of the organization. This variable of segmentation and institutionalization refers to relationships of subunits to the larger organization, whereas integration or disintegration is a property of the organization as a whole.

[12] Émile Durkheim, *The Division of Labor in Society,* trans. George Simpson (New York: The Free Press, a division of the Macmillan Company, 1933), p. 175.

their relationships with the larger organization may move in several possible directions:

(1) The subunit seeks to influence the larger organization, and perhaps eventually dominate it.

(2) The larger organization seeks to regain tighter control over the subunit, leading to increased conflict.

(3) The subunit and the whole maintain an uneasy "truce," while continually trying to influence or change each other.

(4) The unit completely severs its ties with the parent organization and becomes wholly autonomous in relation to it.

In a relatively segmented organization, in which many or most of the constituent subunits possess much functional autonomy, internal conflict and balancing of power are critical social processes. As each subunit acts to protect its own interests and attain its own goals, it will almost inevitably come into conflict with other subunits. The larger organization will therefore constantly be threatened with disintegration if it cannot cope with these pervasive conflicts. If such conflicts cannot be permanently resolved—as often they cannot—stability must then be obtained through the balancing of power among contending subunits. The threat or overt exercise of power is met with one or more countervailing pressures from other units, with the results that each unit respects the interests of the other units and at least minimal overall stability is maintained. The twentieth-century international scene, with its alternating periods of open warfare followed by peace based on a delicate balance of power, is a clear example of this kind of situation. Another example would be the relationships among tribes in many contemporary African nations. The overriding concern of a relatively segmented organization is therefore the management of tensions and conflicts and the maintenance of approximate power equality among all its subunits. Out of the process of segmentation, however, can come social changes that may be of great benefit to the larger organization, enabling it to adapt to shifting environmental pressures.

In the process of institutionalization, the subunits of an organization become oriented toward the total organization and away from their own particular interests. They accept responsibilities of membership in the larger entity, share its values, norms, and other cultural ideas, act to fulfill its functional requirements, and contribute to the attainment of whatever goals this organization seeks. "When an [organization] serves public rather than merely private interests, and does so in an accepted, orderly and enduring way, it may be called an 'institution.'"[13] Because

---

[13] Leonard Broom and Philip Selznick, *Sociology: A Text with Adapted Readings,* 3rd ed. (New York, Harper & Row, Publishers, 1963), p. 32. These writers use the

the various subunits often concentrate their efforts on different organizational requirements, they tend to become functionally specialized: a division of labor occurs among them. The result of such specialization is interdependence, so that the subunits lose much of their functional autonomy and become highly dependent upon each other and the whole organization. Loss of functional autonomy can occur without functional specialization, however. Judicious use of power—in the form of force or authority—by the larger organization to control its subunits, for instance, can effectively limit or destroy their ability to act independently or to survive outside the organization.

Institutionalization can occur in any kind of organization, though we most commonly observe it on the societal and community levels. In a society, for instance, we often speak of the political, economic, legal, educational, communicative, and other functional networks as constituting the major institutions—that is, institutionalized subunits—of that society to the extent that they act to meet societal survival and operational requirements and share in the societal culture. In a community, specific associations such as schools, churches, hospitals, the fire department, the city council, and the chamber of commerce frequently become the central institutions. Although it is not commonly done in sociology, we could carry this line of reasoning further and point to groups such as grievance committees or accounting departments as being institutionalized parts of business associations, and to student councils and athletic teams as institutionalized parts of universities. In short, any social phenomenon becomes an institutionalized subpart of a larger organization to the extent that it supports and contributes to overall patterns of social order and cultural ideas. To the extent that highly institutionalized subunits act to fulfill functional requirements and achieve goals for the larger organization, this organization will tend to become viable, effective, and cohesive.

In organizations in which the institutionalization of subunits is relatively high, the critical social processes are promotion of overall unity and collective goal attainment. To the extent that the component units are functionally specialized, there is a continuing demand for unified coordination of their interrelationships. If the larger organization is relying on power to control its subunits, it must constantly exert force or authority to maintain internal order. Given overall coordination and stability in the organization, plus the satisfaction of its functional requirements

---

term "association" rather than "organization," but the institutionalization of associations is only one instance of this general process. Some writers apply the idea of institutionalization to values and norms rather than to organizations, but to the extent that organizations embody cultural phenomena, this conception becomes merely a special case of the more general process.

through the actions of responsible parts, the organization then can direct most of its acivities toward the goals it collectively seeks. The various academic departments within a college, for example, are highly institutionalized subunits that have limited functional autonomy because of their extensive specialization and interdependence; hence their activities must be coordinated by the offices of various deans if they are to cooperate in the common endeavor of educating students. On the societal level, most established churches in the United States act as firmly institutionalized parts of the total society, accepting its values, performing the necessary functions of upholding societal norms and socializing children, and increasingly contributing in a relatively coordinated manner to the realization of such societal goals as improving race relations and eliminating poverty.[14] The overriding concern of an organization with a high degree of institutionalization among its subunits is therefore the coordination of internal relationships and the directing of organizational activities toward collective goals. Nevertheless, if the subunits of an organization become too highly institutionalized, the organization can become rigid and incapable of changing to meet new problems and conditions.

In sum, the two processes of segmentation and institutionalization are always occurring in all organizations; neither of them is a static condition. Both can have beneficial consequences for societies and other organizations, although either one can be harmful if carried to extremes. The relative degrees of institutionalization and segmentation within an organization must therefore be taken into account in all efforts to study the functioning of that organization.

In this chapter we have looked at several aspects of all social organizations: the process of delineating an organization from its social environment; the basic characteristics of size, complexity, and formalness; the survival and operational requirements of organizations; and various kinds of relationships between an organization and its subunits. More precise analysis of any given social organization requires that we first determine what type of organization it is. Our next task, therefore, is to construct a broad typology within which all organizations can be classified. This task will be taken up in the next chapter.

---

[14] Religions that reject this process of institutionalization by continual opposition to established patterns of social life are commonly termed "sects" by sociologists, to distinguish them from "churches."

RECOMMENDED READING

ABERLE, DAVID F., et al., "The Functional Prerequisites of a Society," Ethics, vol. 60 (January 1950), pp. 100–111. (Also Bobbs-Merrill reprint S-1.) An attempt to specify a number of important functional imperatives, or survival needs, of social organizations.

ANDERSON, THEODORE R., AND SEYMOUR WARKOV, "Organizational Size and Functional Complexity: A Study of Administration in Hospitals," American Sociological Review, vol. 26 (February 1961), pp. 23–28. (Also Bobbs-Merrill reprint S-2.) A report of an empirical study dealing with relationships between organizational complexity and various measures of organizational size.

CAPLOW, THEODORE, Principles of Organization, chaps. 1 and 2 (New York: Harcourt, Brace & World, Inc., 1964). Several basic characteristics of most social organizations are examined and elaborated in the introductory chapters of this theoretically oriented textbook.

GOULDNER, ALVIN, "Reciprocity and Autonomy in Functional Theory," in Llewellyn Gross, ed., Symposium on Sociological Theory, pp. 241–270 (New York: Harper & Row, Publishers, 1959). The processes of functional autonomy and functional reciprocity among the parts of a social organization are extensively examined and analyzed.

HAIRE, MASON, "Biological Models and Empirical Histories of the Growth of Organizations," in Mason Haire, ed., Modern Organization Theory, chap. 10 (New York: John Wiley & Sons, Inc., 1959). (Also Bobbs-Merrill reprint S-109.) An exploration of the usefulness of biological models and historical data for explaining and predicting growth in organizational size and complexity.

CHAPTER 7

Types of Social Organizations

All of the sciences—physical, biological, psychological, and social—frequently find it useful to classify phenomena into categories comprising a typology. Early typologies tend to be quite *ad hoc* and imprecise. As a science develops, though, it seeks to derive its classifications from established theoretical principles and empirical generalizations. A refined typology of this sort is usually called a taxonomy.

Sociology at present has nothing approaching a rigorous taxonomy—nor even a single, unanimously accepted typology by which all social organizations might be classified for descriptive purposes. It is obvious that there are many different kinds of organizations, but the construction of a rigorously defined and exhaustive typology is proving to be extremely difficult. Needless to say, this lack of a standard typology produces many semantic problems, as well as conceptual and analytical confusion.

This chapter continues our previous focus on organizations as delineated social entities. Our specific purpose here is to sketch a tentative typology of all social organizations, as a means of demonstrating the wide variety of forms that the process of social organization displays. This classificatory scheme is quite crude and must be viewed as simply an outline for further work along these lines. It consists only of major types—or what might be analogous to phyla in biology—and no attempt is made (with one exception) to further subdivide these categories into more narrowly defined subtypes. Furthermore, although the major types of organizations discussed here are relatively distinct, they are not mutually exclusive. In short, this is only a first approximation to a working typology, and is in no sense a final sociological taxonomy.

Nevertheless, this classificatory scheme should serve the student of social organization as a heuristic tool for descriptive and analytical purposes. It does not tell us anything about real organizations, but it can help us to observe and study social phenomena by providing a conceptual outline within which to work. In addition, it alerts us to look for similarities among organizations falling within the same category and for variations among organizations in different categories. It is not the only typology currently being used in sociology, but it does have the advantage of being more extensive than any of the others.[1]

Our proposed typology consists of ten categories: populations, aggregations, classes, groups, families, communities, associations, networks, societies, and confederations. The first and last of these are rather peripheral to our concern with social organization, however. The first type—populations—is not actually a kind of organization at all, but is merely the setting in which organization occurs. The last type—confederations—is only minimally developed in today's world. The various types are presented below in rough order of increasing organizational complexity,[2] although this arrangement will not necessarily apply to any single organization. A particular "extended" family might be more complexly organized than the small business association that it owns and operates, but such "inversions" are the exception, not the rule. The ranking of communities as less complex than associations is perhaps the most arbitrary feature of this arrangement, since New York City is clearly much more complex than a grocery store. However, when communities and associations of approximately equal size are compared, associations usually tend

---

[1] This typology includes most kinds of organizations commonly identified and studied by contemporary sociologists. It is, in effect, a composite of numerous other, less extensive typologies. A few broad categories, such as "secondary groups" and "multibonded groups," have been omitted on the grounds that they are so inclusive as to be analytically useless. Also omitted are social entities that are purely political in nature, such as townships, counties, and the like.

[2] As discussed in the previous chapter, organizational complexity is determined by such factors as the number of subunits contained within the organization, the degree to which these subunits are functionally specialized and hence interdependent, and the extent to which overall organizational activities are coordinated or controlled by a central unit. In general, complexity tends to increase with size, but not invariably. A social class is usually larger than a family, but classes precede families in this typology, on the argument that classes usually evidence less complex social ordering and culture than do most families. However, classes do sometimes create quite complex associations as a means of achieving their collective goals.

to have the more complex social structure—and this tendency appears to be increasing.[3]

The brief typological descriptions that follow are intended only to convey the essential idea underlying each category. Extensive explorations and analyses of each type and its various subtypes are beyond our present concern. The formal definitions given for each category are only proposals, not definitive statements. The purpose of a definition is solely to convey an idea as precisely and concisely as possible, and the specific words comprising that definition are not only arbitrary but also totally unimportant in themselves.

With this warning in mind, let us proceed to examine our typology of social organizations.

Populations

Individuals are often classified by social scientists into various categories, based on common characteristics, actions, ideas, or other criteria. There are endless possibilities, such as: (a) men and women; (b) single, married, separated, divorced, or widowed; (c) urban, suburban, and rural residents; (d) "liberals" and "conservatives"; (e) Protestants, Catholics, and Jews; (f) manual versus nonmanual workers; (g) Republicans, Democrats, and Independents; (h) grammar school graduates, high school graduates, and college graduates; (i) "inner-directed" versus "other-directed" persons. The term "aggregate" is sometimes employed in reference to all of the persons in any given category, since this word means a sum or total of discrete entities. For both technical and semantic reasons, though, the term "population" is preferable.[4]

The important point here is that the "members" of a population do not necessarily interact, form patterns of social order, or share a common culture. (If they do carry out these processes, they cease to be merely a population.) They are placed together in a common category by an outside observer on the basis of criteria he designates, not through their own social interactions. In short, a population is not, in and of itself, an organization. Nevertheless, identifiable populations are very important social phenomena, both for the creation of social organization and for sociolog-

---

[3] One reason why communities perhaps appear to be more complexly organized than they really are is that we often think of the community in terms of its formal government—which technically speaking is an association within the community.

[4] Technically, "aggregate" connotes the existence of something more than the sum of a number of items, whereas "population" clearly means just a counting of people (or other objects) who are in some way socially identifiable. Semantically, "aggregate" is easily confused with "aggregation."

ical analysis. As we saw in Chapter 3, a population of people provides the setting in which social organization occurs. Organization, we said, is in one sense a population phenomenon. By identifying populations that evidence several common characteristics, social scientists can often discover potential or developing social organizations. This category of populations is therefore included within our typology as a means of distinguishing populations of individuals from types of established social organizations and at the same time stressing the relevance of population phenomena for social life and social science.

Formally defined, *a population is a category of unorganized individuals that is identified by an observer on the basis of one or more common characteristics.*

Aggregations

Collective phenomena such as crowds, mobs, publics, and audiences are examples of aggregations. These phenomena are, in effect, populations of people who interact only transiently and temporarily with each other, so that the resulting patterns of social order and shared culture are highly ephemeral. Nonetheless, they do evidence some minimal amount of social organization. Because of their ephemeral nature, and also because most of them have relatively few effects upon established patterns of social life, these phenomena have not been extensively studied by social scientists as a form of social organization. They cannot be totally dismissed from the study of social organization, however, since they provide unusual insights into the processes by which organization is created, and also because they occasionally produce extensive social change.

Students of these phenomena, both in sociology and psychology, have commonly referred to them as "collective behavior." To the extent that these scientists have been concerned largely with the behaviors of individuals within such collectivities, this term has been appropriate. When we consider the collectivity as a social entity, however, we need a new generic organizational term. We shall use the name "aggregation," which means "a collected but relatively unorganized whole."[5] More precisely, *an aggregation is a social organization that is relatively spontaneous in origin, temporary in duration, and minimally ordered.*

[5] The word "collectivity" might at first seem a more logical choice, but this term is frequently used as a synonym for associations or for all social organizations. Such phenomena as riots, fads, panics, crazes, and revolutions are also commonly included under the heading of "collective behavior," but these are forms of social activity, not delineated social organizations.

Classes

When loosely unified social organizations become somewhat more stable through time than aggregations, when they exercise some amount of social power, and when they can act collectively to achieve shared goals, we call them social classes. Class is one of the most ambiguous concepts in sociology, and almost everyone gives it a slightly different meaning. It is usually associated with the phenomenon of social stratification, but in practice it refers sometimes to purely economic conditions, sometimes to social prestige and deference, sometimes to social power, sometimes to people who share common interests and values, sometimes to populations of individuals who frequently interact, sometimes to abstract statistical categories, and frequently to several of these ideas in combination.

We shall apply the concept of class directly to social stratification in a later chapter; here we limit ourselves to elaborating its most general meaning. Expanding upon an idea developed by Ralf Dahrendorf,[6] we suggest that *a class is a loosely ordered and unified social organization based on the similar power, privileges, and prestige of its members.* A class exists, that is, when persons who occupy approximately similar positions within the allocative (or stratification) process of a society, community, or other encompassing organization begin to interact in ordered and perpetuated patterns and to develop a unique culture. The common interests and social conditions of these people lead them to organize themselves in some manner for the collective attainment of shared goals. These attempts will often lead them into conflict with competing classes and other organizations, so that the use of power becomes a pervasive aspect of class activities. Little internal differentiation of partially autonomous subunits occurs within a class.

This conceptualization of social class is broad enough to include the various classes within a feudal type of society (such as serfs, peasants, artisans, nobility), the castes of modern India, the three "estates" of pre-revolutionary France, Marxian conceptions of class (such as bourgeoisie and proletariat), whatever social classes exist in the contemporary United States (such as a "power elite" or an "upper-middle class" or the "socially dispossessed"), and perhaps even such collectivities as college students or Negroes.[7] Whether or not these phenomena actually constitute organized

[6] Ralf Dahrendorf, *Class and Class Conflict in Industrial Society* (Stanford, Calif.: Stanford University Press, 1959), chap. 5.

[7] To the extent that these people do constitute social classes, such classes must not be confused with associations of more limited purpose such as the National Student Association or the National Association for the Advancement of Colored People.

social classes is always a problematic question. To qualify as organizations, they must evidence some patterns of social order and a distinctive culture; otherwise they remain simply unorganized populations. Under these criteria, a stratum of individuals with similar socioeconomic status (based on such criteria as occupation, education, and income) who did not interact with each other in any ordered manner would not constitute a class.

Following the ideas of Max Weber,[8] most sociologists have either explicitly or implicitly conceived of classes as being based ultimately on economic factors. Only recently have we begun to think of classes in the broader context of power suggested here.[9] To the extent that economic power dominates a society, it will form the primary basis of all classes. But as other forms of social power—such as legal authority or technical knowledge—grow in functional importance within the society, they provide new foundations for different social classes.

Groups

For many social scientists the word "group" is synonymous with social organization—or at least with all organizations smaller in size than a total society. The term also has a more restricted and precise meaning, which we use to designate this fourth category in our typology of social organizations.

Groups are almost always smaller in number of members than are classes. However, most groups do tend to be more tightly unified than classes, and sometimes they also display at least rudimentary structural differentiation into partially autonomous subunits. Such unification and internal ordering are outgrowths of the strong interpersonal bonds that normally join the members of a group—ties largely (though not exclusively) based on personal identification of the members with each other. That is, *a group is a social organization whose members know and identify with each other personally as individuals.*

This diverse category includes such phenomena as friendship cliques, work crews, neighborhood *Kaffeeklatsch* gatherings, teenage gangs, sports teams, juries, discussion groups, and committees of all kinds. The interpersonal identification that is characteristic of all groups is immensely aided by small size and frequent interaction among members, although neither of these factors is absolutely necessary for the creation of a group. Finally, groups can exist either as relatively autonomous social entities, as in the

[8] Max Weber, "Class, Status, and Party," in H. H. Gerth and C. W. Mills, *From Max Weber: Essays in Sociology* (New York: Oxford University Press, 1946), chap. 7.
[9] Dahrendorf, chap. 5. See also Gerhard E. Lenski, *Power and Privilege* (New York: McGraw-Hill, Inc., 1966).

case of a neighborhood gathering, or as parts of larger organizations, as in the case of committees.

Some groups, such as friendship cliques or youth gangs, are frequently described by sociologists as "primary groups."[10] The interactions among the members of these groups are especially personal and intimate, and the interpersonal bonds are extremely strong. Technically, we should speak of "primary relations" rather than "primary groups," since "primariness" is a variable that exists to some extent in all groups and also in more complex organizations. Groups vary, that is, in the degree to which the relationships among their members are "primary" in nature. Nevertheless, the concept of "primary group" does provide a convenient means of designating those groups in which the interpersonal relationships are especially close, so that the members tend to respond to each other's total personalities.

Families

Can there be any ambiguity as to what constitutes a family? We certainly know what a family is—or do we? Does this type of social organization include just two spouses and their children, or must we also take into account uncles and aunts, cousins, grandparents, "in-laws," and nieces and nephews? Some peoples might say yes, but others no. The point here is that the meaning of "family," and hence its boundaries, are culturally determined and differ widely from one society to another (and often even within a single society). In one society the biological father of a child acts as its male parent, while in another society the mother's brother assumes this duty. In a third society a marriage consists of one male and several females, while in another several males may marry one female.

Despite these diverse variations, the idea of kinship (however defined) is present in all known societies. Some version of the family as a type of social organization exists everywhere. In its most universal conception, *a family is a social group that is further characterized by ties of kinship among all its members.* In other words, a family is united by either biological or marital kinship bonds among its members, as well as by interpersonal identification. These additional ties normally give the family more stability and unity than exists in nonkinship groups.

Sociologists also usually include families under the heading of "primary groups," but once again the degree of intimacy or "primariness" in family social relationships varies considerably from society to society, and

---

[10] Charles H. Cooley, *Social Organization* (New York: The Free Press, a division of The Macmillan Company, 1956), chap. 3.

even from one family to another. The fact that several people are related and live together is no guarantee that they will relate intimately to each other.

Communities

Although the family as a social entity can sometimes be relatively self-sufficient, most families do not live by themselves, isolated from all others. For many reasons, ranging from economic interdependence to shared cultural values, families normally band together to form communities.[11] The community, rather than the family, then becomes the social setting for most everyday economic, political, religious, educational, recreational, and similar activities. As communities become larger and more complex, other types of organizations often are established within the community to perform these various activities. Nevertheless, the community as a whole remains the social unit within which all such social functions usually take place. In brief, *a community is a social organization that is territorially localized and through which its members satisfy most of their daily needs and deal with most of their common problems.*[12]

In modern societies, communities are never totally self-sufficient, as they may be in very primitive societies. But normally they are more self-contained, in terms of the range of needs satisfied and services rendered, than are any other types of social organization except societies. Communities vary widely in size and complexity, from "Crossroads Junction" to New York City, but this diversity should not obscure their many similarities. The fact that communities always occupy a definite geographical area has given rise to a proliferation of sociological studies of community spatial patterns, although it should be borne in mind that the requirement

[11] When the family is viewed as a subunit of the community in this sense, individuals living alone are often treated as families, by the U.S. Census as well as by sociologists. It should also be noted that in very primitive societies a community may be composed of a single extended family, or clan.

[12] This definition is adapted from Amos H. Hawley, *Human Ecology* (New York: The Ronald Press Company, 1950), pp. 257–258. The concept of community is sometimes used in sociology in quite a different sense, as when we speak of "the intellectual community" or "the business community." Often this is just a convenient means of referring to an identifiable but completely unorganized population of individuals. Sometimes, though, this population will develop enduring patterns of social order and a shared culture—as might be true of a "business community." The emerging organization should then be referred to as a social class, as we have defined this term. Finally, some writers also speak of "supernational communities" or "international communities"—primarily to emphasize that societies are today becoming increasingly interdependent, so that the territorial setting in which one lives his life is slowly becomng the entire world.

of spatial location does not exclude nomadic communities as long as they retain their organization as they move about.

As a final point, the sociological concept of community must be distinguished from the legal term "city." Most of the activities of almost all communities extend beyond the legal city limits to include suburbs and other immediately surrounding areas. In some cases, though, a community may be smaller than its legal city, as in the case of a relatively self-contained immigrant settlement or ghetto. There is no definite point at which the community as a social organization ends and its surrounding hinterland begins, so that when studying large communities many sociologists prefer to use such units as the "Standard Metropolitan Statistical Area" as defined by the U.S. Census Bureau, or the even broader concept of "metropolitan region."

Associations

As social life becomes increasingly complex, with social actors pursuing a widening variety of goals through collective action, they create various kinds of relatively specialized organizations. Each of these organizations is limited in its range of activities, focusing on only one or a few aspects of social life. Its goals are restricted to its area(s) of particular concern and competence, and most or all of its actions are aimed in these directions. This functional specialization tends to deprive these organizations of operational self-sufficiency so that they become highly interdependent. The generic name for all such specialized organizations is associations. *An association is a social organization that is more or less purposefully created for the attainment of relatively specific and limited goals.* In contemporary societies this is by far the broadest and most inclusive type of social organization.

The goals sought by associations, and hence their organizational characteristics, vary almost infinitely. As examples of the more common subtypes of associations we might cite the following: governmental departments, agencies, and legislatures; factories and industries of all kinds; retail, wholesale, and service businesses, ranging from drug stores to construction companies; schools, colleges, and other educational organizations; churches, denominations, and similar religious bodies; labor unions and occupational and professional associations; fraternal and service organizations; legal and financial firms; special-interest associations, from antique collectors to zoology enthusiasts; civic, charitable, and welfare agencies; communication and transportation concerns; political parties and lobbies; social and recreational associations; military services and units; hospitals, clinics, and related health organizations; libraries, museums, orchestras, theaters, and other literary and artistic bodies; scientific laboratories and institutes; producer and consumer cooperatives; civil rights and similar ethnic associations; coercive organizations such as police and prisons; and patriotic and veterans associations. These examples only skim the surface of the multitude of different kinds of associations that exist in a society such as the United States, and undoubtedly many important subtypes have been omitted, but they do illustrate the scope of the concept of association.

Associations range in size from a two-man partnership to General Motors Corporation or the United States Government. Increasingly, however, they are tending to become not only large, but also highly complex and formally organized. There are numerous exceptions, but this dominant trend is clear in modern society. As a result, the claim is sometimes made that large, formal, complex associations are relatively new phenomena in human affairs. In an absolute sense this is not true, since some types of complex associations, such as armies, have existed since the beginning of recorded history. But in a relative sense, the predominance of such associations in all facets of social life is one of the most significant features of contemporary societies.

We have not attempted, in constructing this typology of social organizations, to break down any of the other categories into subtypes. Because of the wide variety of different kinds of associations, however, it may prove useful (for illustrative purposes only) to briefly describe one such scheme here. Peter Blau and Richard Scott have suggested that all associations can be divided into four subcategories on the basis of who benefits from the attainment of their dominant goals.[13] Embodied in each of these four subcategories of associations is a distinctive kind of organizational problem that is the primary concern of all associations in that category.

(1) Business associations. Includes all associations whose dominant goal is benefiting their owners by making money, such as industries, stores, construction and repair concerns, communication and transportation companies, and all other private businesses. The distinctive organizational problem is promoting operating efficiency, since the association must operate efficiently if it is to show a profit.

(2) Mutual benefit associations. Includes all associations whose

---

[13] Peter Blau and Richard C. Scott, *Formal Organizations* (San Francisco: Chandler Publishing Company, 1962), pp. 45–67. For a formal taxonomy of associations based on many different dimensions, see J. Eugene Haas, Richard H. Hall, and Norman J. Johnson, "Towards an Empirically Derived Taxonomy of Organizations," in Raymond U. Bowers, ed., *Studies on Behavior in Organizations* (Athens, Ga.: University of Georgia Press, 1966), chap. 8.

dominant goal is benefiting their members in some way, such as occupational and professional associations, labor unions, political parties, literary and artistic bodies, civil rights associations, social and recreational organizations, special-interest associations, and churches. The distinctive organizational problem is maintaining internal democratic control by the members over activities of the association, so that it will directly benefit them.

(3) Service associations. Includes all associations whose dominant goal is providing services of some kind to clients, such as schools and colleges, hospitals, charitable and welfare agencies, law firms, police departments, and prisons. The distinctive organizational problem is preventing exploitation of the relatively dependent clients—or in other words, maintaining professional operating standards in the association.

(4) Commonweal associations. Includes all associations whose dominant goal is serving an entire community or society, such as governmental organizations of all kinds, military units, public health services, scientific institutes, and libraries and museums. The distinctive organizational problem is maintaining external (or public) democratic control over the association's activities, to insure that it always benefits the common welfare.

Networks

Functionally interdependent groups, families, communities, and associations must interact with each other within extensive networks of patterned relationships if they are to satisfy their survival and operational requirements, coordinate joint activities, and achieve common goals. In the past, the setting for most such complementary exchange relationships has been the local community, within whose confines more specialized groups and associations normally functioned. These arrangements are altered, however, as associations grow in size and span several communities or an entire society, and as means of transportation and communication increasingly link together all communities within a society. This process of expansion beyond the local community leads to the growth of organized functional networks.

Included within this category are such phenomena as political networks (including national and local governments, as well as related organizations such as political parties and pressure groups—all of which are sometimes referred to as the "polity" of a society); educational networks (public and private schools, colleges and universities, some aspects of the mass media, and technical training programs); economic networks (either the total economy of a society, including factories, distributors, stores, and service establishments, or specialized sectors of the economy such as agriculture or heavy industry); legal networks (composed of courts, law firms, police departments, prisons, and similar activities); religious networks, (churches and synagogues, seminaries, religious orders, and so on); military networks (the various armed services and the local militia); communication networks (television and radio stations, newspapers, magazine and book publishers, and movie producers); socialization networks (families, nursery schools, youth groups, parts of the mass media, and many other related activities); and medical networks (clinics, hospitals, laboratories, public health services, and other medical facilities).

The term "network," as used in this discussion, was first suggested by S. F. Nadel, who stressed that all of the social relationships comprising a social network are to some degree interrelated.[14] Activities or changes in one part of such a network will therefore have effects throughout many other parts of the network. Notice that any given network will often include several different kinds of associations and groups, and sometimes also families, classes, and communities. Concurrently, one specific kind of group or association may fit into two or more different networks, according to its various activities. Thus schools are part of the socialization as well as the educational network of our society; families perform educational and religious as well as socialization actions; governmental agencies may become involved in economic, educational, and legal, as well as political events; and the mass media frequently become engaged in all these networks. The unifying feature of any given network, regardless of which or how many other organizations it incorporates, is its focus on a particular kind of activity or set of related activities. All the various parts of a network are involved in some manner with a single social process—be it economic, political, legal, educational, religious, communicative, or socializing. Finally, since most functional networks are societywide in the scope of their activities, networks are usually described as the major subsectors of a society.

Formally defined, *a network is a functionally specialized social organization that links together numerous associations, groups, and other types of organizations throughout a society, all of which are interrelated through their concern with a common set of activities.*

---

[14] S. F. Nadel, *The Theory of Social Structure* (New York: The Free Press, a division of The Macmillan Company, 1957), pp. 16–17. Sociologists often refer to networks as social institutions, since they are highly institutionalized subparts of society. This usage is confusing, though, since the process of institutionalization can occur in any organization, and is not limited to networks.

Societies

Societies are the most inclusive, complex, and dominant type of social organization in today's world. Most other organizations exist within the confines of a society, all aspects of human social life are encompassed by a society, and to a large extent the way in which a society functions will influence all the patterns of social order and subcultures that comprise it. In recent years the term "society" has come into wide popular usage, and most people probably have some vague conception of its meaning. For social-scientific purposes, however, we must give this vitally important concept a precise and unambiguous interpretation. The following definition is directed toward that goal: *A society is a broadly inclusive social organization that possesses both functional and cultural autonomy and that dominates all other types of organization.*[15]

The ideas of societal functional and cultural autonomy require some elaboration. Functional autonomy can be demonstrated in several different ways. First, most social relationships occur within the boundaries of a society, with only a small minority of all relationships involving actors from different societies—and in these latter cases the society retains control over their continuation. Second, a society is relatively self-sufficient, or independent of other societies. Self-sufficiency does not mean that a society provides all of its necessary resources or satisfies all the needs of its members, but rather that it establishes the social procedures and mechanisms by which all resources are procured and all needs are satisfied. Third, a society possesses functional autonomy in decision-making. It is the ultimate legitimate decision-making organization for all its members, and hence it has sovereignty over all decisions concerning them. Fourth, the functional autonomy of a society is shown by the fact that it is the supreme organization to which its members give loyalty and which they defend against disruptive external and internal forces.

A society possesses cultural autonomy in that all of its members share a common, distinctive, and unique culture. Any number of specific traits of this culture may be shared with other societies, including technical and scientific knowledge, customs and traditions, language, and norms and values. At the same time, many subparts of a society may hold numerous cultural ideas of their own that are not shared throughout the whole society. Nevertheless, the common culture of the total society—and especially its dominant social values and norms—forms a distinctive and unified set of ideas that is unique to that society.

As an illustration of this phenomenon of societal functional and cul-

---

[15] This definition is adapted from Ronald Freedman, *et al.*, *Principles of Sociology*, rev. ed. (New York: Holt, Rinehart and Winston, Inc., 1956), p. 78.

tural autonomy, consider Canada. Even though its economy is heavily dominated by United States businesses and its people are constantly bombarded by American culture via the mass media, it vigorously maintains its own political and economic independence and distinctive norms and values. The contemporary divided societies of Germany, Korea, and Vietnam provide especially interesting cases for sociology. Originally, each was a relatively unified single society (or part of a larger society, as in the case of Vietnam). The erection of political barriers, however, has split in half almost all of their functional and cultural ties, so that realistically each half now forms a relatively separate society.

Like communities, societies have historically been located within a defined territorial area, and some theorists include the requirement of spatial unity in their definitions of a society. As long as communication and transportation facilities were severely limited, spatial unity was a requisite for functional and cultural autonomy. Given the technological developments of the twentieth century, however, this necessity no longer exists. We have already discarded the idea that a society must be territorially contiguous; witness Alaska and Hawaii or the two halves of Pakistan. And in the not too distant future, space travel and space stations may permanently obliterate the spatial unity of many societies.

The terms "state" and "nation" are frequently used interchangeably with "society," but technically each has a different meaning. A state is a specifically defined political entity, centering around a government. It is, in effect, a political network, or polity. In many instances the boundaries of a state are conterminous with those of its total society; the state is then the whole society as viewed from a purely political perspective. In Africa, though, most political states still contain several relatively autonomous native societies, while the separate states of the United States are clearly not societies (although the United States as a whole is simultaneously a state and a society). In short a state is a political unit, while a society is a considerably more inclusive social organization, of which its government is only one aspect. A nation, in the contemporary sense of the word, exists when a political state coincides with a total society and when the polity is the dominant social network within the society. In other words, a nation is the particular kind of society that happens to be prevalent in today's world. Indeed, because all major contemporary societies are also nations, it is difficult for us to realize that this is not a theoretical imperative. Historically, however, societies have not always been nations—as demonstrated by military and early colonial empires, in which a single political unit spanned many separate societies. Conceivably, too, a society might exist in which the religious, educational, or some other major network was the dominant sphere of power.

Confederations

Some day the entire world may constitute a single society, organized as an international federation. Such an organization would be infinitely more inclusive and complex than any single nation, and would constitute a logical final category in our typology of social organizations. As yet, however, this category of international federations is more a potentiality than a reality. No existing international organization begins to compete with national societies in inclusiveness, complexity, or power. In fact, only a few of them—most notably the European Economic Community (the "Common Market")—possess any political sovereignty above that of their member nations.

Because true international federations do not yet exist, our present discussion is limited to international confederations. *A confederation is a loosely organized combination of relatively autonomous societies who cooperate in some joint activities without relinquishing their separate sovereignties.* Confederations are considerably less complex than societies (and even many communities and associations), so that by listing them as the final category in our typology we are violating our underlying principle of increasing organizational complexity. We do this, however, on the grounds that presently existing confederations may eventually evolve into true international federations—which would form a logical final category.

Examples of contemporary international confederations are the United Nations, UNESCO, the World Health Organization, the Organization of American States, the European Free Trade Association, the North Atlantic Treaty Organization, the Nordic Council, and the Latin American Free Trade Association.[16] The significant feature of all such organizations is that their members are nations, not individuals or other types of organizations.[17] They are, in effect, essentially just stable relationships among national governments. Whether or not confederations such as these will eventually provide the framework for the creation of new, international federations is a question that only the future can answer.

In conclusion, it must be reiterated that the definitions of these various types of social organizations, and indeed the whole typology itself, are entirely arbitrary. This classificatory scheme is presented not as a finished

---

[16] The European Economic Community is at present primarily an international confederation, but even the limited amount of political sovereignty it possesses gives it some characteristics of a true international federation.

[17] Many associations today cross national boundaries to become international in scope. However, the limited ranges of activities of all such international associations, plus the fact that they are composed of individuals or private associations, disqualifies them as confederations.

taxonomy of all social organizations, but merely as a heuristic device for describing and illustrating the vast range of different kinds of social organizations that exist in the contemporary world.

The Web of Organizations

The various types of social organizations we have examined in this chapter rarely exist side by side as separate and wholly unrelated entities, like books randomly placed on a bookshelf. Almost universally, *organizations overlap and interlock with each other, forming a gigantic social web, the totality of which is human social life.* Societies, because of their relative self-sufficiency, come closer than any other type of existing social organization to fitting the bookshelf analogy. But even here, nascent international confederations do bind societies together to some extent. All other types of social organizations exist today within the confines of enveloping societies. They cannot escape the pervasive influences of their society, and in a legal sense they owe their very existence to the larger society. Networks, in turn, normally encompass portions of numerous associations, communities, groups, and even families. Going still further down the line, associations and classes frequently cut across scores of communities and other organizations, while a community often contains hundreds or thousands of associations, groups, families, and aggregations. Groups, finally, are normally found within almost all other types of organizations.

This interlocking web of social organizations is bound together in two different ways. First, individuals are almost invariably members of more than one organization. The typical person in a contemporary society is probably a member of a family, several small groups, a church, a labor union or business or professional association, a community, possibly a class, sometimes an aggregation, at least sporadically most of the major social networks, and always his society. Through such overlapping memberships, the activities of all the organizations comprising a society become interrelated and at least partially coordinated. Second, the organizations themselves crosscut and overlap each other in their actions. To take a simple example, a business concern influences many families through the work schedules and pay rates of its employees, many friendship cliques and committees are formed within the business, this organization must deal with labor unions, a chamber of commerce, and other associations, it pays taxes to the local community as well as to the federal government, the manner in which it is organized may contribute to the formation of "working" and "management" social classes, it plays an active part in maintaining the economic network of the society, it may rely heavily on business contracts from the national government, and in times of crisis it is called upon to help defend the society by carrying its burden of the national defense effort.

Just as individuals can participate in social life as either elements or parts, so *social organizations can be seen either as relatively autonomous social elements or as parts of some larger and more inclusive social organization.* A hospital, for example, may be viewed both as a relatively independent association (as when it provides various medical services, assigns doctors and nurses to duty shifts, or sets fees for patients) and as an integral part of the medical network of the community and the society (as when it cooperates with other hospitals, clinics, and public health services to control communicable diseases or deal with a natural disaster). The hospital, in turn, is composed of many smaller organizations, such as medical service teams, shifts of nurses, laboratories, and kitchens. These are usually thought of as subunits of the total hospital, but normally they do possess limited amounts of functional autonomy. It should be evident that all social organizations are always simultaneously elements and parts; this distinction is merely a matter of degree and focus.

The utility of these concepts of elements and parts, as applied to social organizations, is that they alert the sociologist to several critical tensions or pressures that normally exist in virtually all organizations. Because the actions and demands of independent elements are different from those of involved parts, organizations often experience both centrifugal and centripetal forces in relation to both their constituent subunits and larger organizations of which they are a part.

On the one hand, social organizations generally attempt to increase their functional autonomy in relation to more inclusive organizational entities, so as to maximize their chances of obtaining whatever goals they seek. They also attempt to keep their own subparts relatively dependent on them (or institutionalized), so as to prevent tensions and disruptions and thus insure their own continued survival. Since organizations at all levels of size and complexity are simultaneously pushing in both these directions, stress and conflict are inherent in all social organizations.

On the other hand, these pressures are limited by counterforces, which also occur in almost all organizations. The push toward increasing functional autonomy is mitigated by functional interdependency. To the extent that any organization is interdependent upon other organizations, it must join with them in creating and maintaining more inclusive and unifying patterns of social order and cultural ideas, thus taking on responsibilities as a part of a larger social entity. The push toward increased control over subunits, meanwhile, is mitigated by the need for functional flexibility. If an organization is to remain flexible and adaptable, and thus retain its stability over time, it must allow its own parts a certain amount of autonomy so that they can deal with constantly changing situations and demands.[18] The most basic operational requirement for all social organizations, therefore, is to establish a working balance among these opposing pressures toward simultaneous segmentation and institutionalization in both upward and downward directions.

These ideas of centrifugal and centripetal forces in organizations, leading to segmentation and institutionalization at various organizational levels, can be illustrated with an everyday example. Consider a department store that is part of a nationwide chain of stores. Although many of the activities of this store will be guided by policies of the parent chain, the store managers will very likely seek to exercise as much autonomy as possible in their daily operations—such as hiring clerks or planning sales. At the same time, they will attempt to maintain relatively tight control over each of the separate departments in the store, to insure that similar accounting and sales procedures are used in all the departments. Meanwhile, each department supervisor experiences much the same types of pressures on his level of organization—seeking autonomy in relation to the total store and control over individual clerks. Because of the specialized nature of each department, however, it is functionally dependent on many other departments and hence is limited in the degree of autonomy it can obtain. The hardware department, for instance, is not capable of delivering purchases or billing charge customers. Similarly, the store as a whole cannot operate entirely independently of the larger chain to which it belongs, since it depends upon specialized units of that company for bulk purchasing of goods, preparation of sales catalogs, training of management personnel, and many similar functions. Both the chain and the store will benefit, though, by granting their respective subunits at least moderate amounts of functional autonomy, so as to encourage initiative, flexibility, and adaptability at all organizational levels.

We might summarize this entire discussion of various types of social organizations by saying that *despite the untold number of specific organizations that arise from the continual ongoing process of social organization, all of these organizations are to some extent interwoven with each other to form a single dynamic whole.* To paraphrase John Donne: "No social organization is an island unto itself."

Thus far our discussion of social organization (a general process) and social organizations (specific entities) has focused almost entirely on what

[18] These ideas are developed at some length by Alvin Gouldner in "Reciprocity and Autonomy in Functional Theory," in Llewellyn Gross, ed., *Symposium on Sociological Theory* (New York: Harper & Row, Publishers, 1959), pp. 241–270.

sociologists sometimes call the "macro" level of analysis. That is, we have been looking at social organization as a phenomenon in and of itself. But what about the individuals who comprise any organization? Obviously, we cannot gain a complete understanding of organized social life without investigating the ways in which individuals take part in social organization. Since we could not examine all aspects of social life at once, we had to gain an appreciation of the nature of social organization before we could ask how individuals fit into this process. We can now rectify our omission, however, and in the next two chapters we turn to the topics of individual participation in, and preservation of, social organization.

RECOMMENDED READING

BLAU, PETER, *Formal Organizations*, pp. 2–8 (San Francisco: Chandler Publishing Company, 1962).
An introductory discussion of the major features of formal associations.

FARIS, ELLSWORTH, "The Primary Group: Essence and Accident," *The American Journal of Sociology*, vol. 38 (July 1932), pp. 41–50. (Also Bobbs-Merrill reprint S-81.)
A reanalysis of Cooley's "primary group" concept, pointing out that the essence of the "primary group" is the existence of social relationships that are highly personal.

HAWLEY, AMOS H., *Human Ecology*, pp. 222–233 (New York: The Ronald Press Company, 1950).
Examines the structural and functional differences between the polar types of "dependent" and "independent" communities.

LINTON, RALPH, *The Cultural Background of Personality*, pp. 15–19 (New York: Appleton-Century-Crofts, 1943). Reprinted as "Society" in John F. Cuber and Peggy B. Harroff, eds., *Readings in Sociology*, pp. 226–228 (New York: Appleton-Century-Crofts, 1962).
A brief enumeration of the common characteristics of all societies.

McIVER, ROBERT M., *Community: A Sociological Study*, pp. 22–28 (New York: The Macmillan Company, 1928). Reprinted as "Community and Association" in Edgar A. Schuler, *et al.*, eds., *Readings in Sociology*, 3rd ed., pp. 515–525 (New York: Thomas Y. Crowell Company, 1967).
A classic discussion of the differences between societies, states, communities, and associations as types of social organizations.

SPIRO, MELFORD, "Is the Family Universal?," *American Anthropologist*, vol. 56 (October 1954), pp. 839–846. (Also Bobbs-Merrill reprint S-276.)
Describes the ways in which Israeli *kibbutz* perform many functions that are usually associated exclusively with the family.

CHAPTER 8

Participation in Social Organization

The process of social organization, as we have seen, incorporates social interactions and relationships, patterns of social order, and shared cultural ideas. Actions of individual persons, insofar as they behave as autonomous personalities, are not directly relevant here. To the extent that people behave idiosyncratically, in terms of personal motives, goals, and meanings, and without regard for existing social orders or cultures, they do not contribute to social organization.

Whenever individuals interact with others through time, however, they become participants in the process of social organization. They may either create new relationships or join previously existing patterns of social order. In both cases they begin to change at least some of their actions from those of a relatively independent social element to those of a relatively involved social part. The more extensive this shift in their actions, the more deeply involved they become in social organization.

The process of interpersonal social interaction, in and of itself, is of direct concern to the social psychologist rather than the sociologist studying social organization. Social psychologists investigate the ways in which individuals, as relatively autonomous actors, initiate and carry out social interactions and are in turn affected by these interactions. As even rudimentary relationships are created in this manner, these relationships will exhibit properties of their own that distinguish them from the participating actors. But social psychologists focus primarily on the actions and atti-

103

tudes of the individual actors within these relationships, not on the relationships or emerging patterns of social order. The student of social organization, in contrast, will be more concerned with the ways in which individual participants contribute to or influence the social organizations to which they belong. From this organizational perspective, actions of individuals are purely incidental, except insofar as these persons participate as parts of social organization.

To bridge this academic gap between sociology and social psychology, we focus in this chapter on the process of social role enactment. The concept of social roles is the major analytical tool used by social scientists in their attempts to explain the ways in which individuals participate in all forms of social life.

Social Roles

For social roles to exist there must first be some amount of social organization. Roles are component parts of social organizations and cannot exist apart from patterns of social order and cultures. *Roles are, in effect, the smallest subunits of all social organizations.*[1] Individuals enact roles and thus become involved in social ordering, but the individual himself is not a subunit of any organization. A given person is often a member of numerous different organizations, so that he cannot simultaneously be a structural subunit of all of them. But the roles he enacts within an organization belong exclusively to that social entity and hence constitute its smallest subunits. To fill a social role, therefore, a person must at least temporarily act as an integral part of some social organization. Whether or not he is considered a member of the organization while acting in this manner depends on the prevailing criteria for membership. It is possible, for instance, to enact the role of worshipper at a church service without being a formal member of that church.

Role enactment necessitates involvement in organized social life, but participation does not necessarily entail role enactment. It is safe to say that many of the participants in an organization must frequently fulfill

---

[1] This conception of roles as parts of established organizations directly contradicts some current social theories, which see social organization as being created through the enactment of previously existing roles. These theories often define all instances of social interaction as social roles, and hence fail to distinguish between individuals acting as autonomous elements and as parts of social organizations. Or, if they do distinguish between social elements and parts, they classify all nonrole activities as "deviant behavior." See Talcott Parsons, *The Social System* (New York: The Free Press, a division of The Macmillan Company, 1951), chap. 7.

organizational roles if that organization is to attain goals or even survive. But any individual might, at any given time, interact with others as either an element or a part. As a relatively autonomous element, his actions would be determined largely by his own motivations, interests, and goals. As a relatively involved part, his actions would be shaped to some extent by expectations and demands of the larger organization. Only in the latter situation would he be enacting a social role in the organization. He might well retain membership in the organization while acting as an element—so long as he did nothing that would lead others to deprive him of membership—but he would not then be fulfilling an organizational role. *To enact a social role a person must act as a relatively involved part of an established social organization.*

Let us illustrate this idea with an everyday example. Suppose that John Doe works for an insurance company. While explaining the provisions of a policy to a customer, he is enacting the role of salesman within this organization. The things he says and does are highly—though not totally—determined by the rules and operating procedures of the company. At other times he might also fulfill additional roles in the organization, as when he presided over a meeting of the sales staff. While eating lunch with several friends in the company cafeteria he would still be participating in the activities of the organization, but in this situation he might well act primarily as an autonomous element in relation to the company (provided he did not carry on business over lunch). And he definitely would not be enacting an organizational role if he stayed after the closing hour to embezzle company funds.

The process of role enactment is analogous on the individual level to the process of institutionalization among larger subunits of an organization. In the process of institutionalization, as in the enactment of social roles, component parts of an organization relinquish at least some functional autonomy and become interdependent upon each other and the total organization, they often (though not always) function to satisfy survival or operational requirements of the organization, and they share in the common culture of the organization. The two processes are indeed so similar that we often speak of institutionalized subparts of an organization as carrying out organizational roles, and of socially responsible roles as being institutionalized.

The distinction made here between actions of relatively autonomous personalities (that is, acting as an element) and enactment of organizational roles (acting as a part) should not be confused with three other previously mentioned dimensions of social interaction: (a) self versus collectivity orientations toward social relationships, since people can fulfill social roles for either expedient or moral reasons; (b) instrumental versus expressive actions, since role enactment can serve as either a means to some other goal or as an end itself; and (c) primary versus impersonal social interaction, since, for example, many of the intimacies of courtship are socially prescribed in the role of suitor, while casual conversation between two strangers waiting at a bus stop is highly impersonal even though neither of them is presently enacting a social role.

Social roles exist within all types of social organizations, from the smallest and most informal group to the largest and most complex society. For example: a friendship clique might include the role of initiator, who suggests activities for the group; a family usually provides for such roles as disciplinarian, cook, and income-producer; an association may contain a wide variety of roles, from chief executive to foreman to janitor; a mob frequently follows its leaders; social classes sometimes create the role of spokesman to present and defend their interests; community roles vary from those of the mayor to the "town gossip"; social networks rely upon the fulfillment of communication and coordination roles to keep their interrelated activities operating smoothly; and societal roles are as important as those of a prime minister or congressman, as demanding as that of a soldier in combat, or as nebulous as that of a voter or taxpayer.

Social Positions

We have thus far conceived of social roles as dynamic processes, but they can also be viewed from a more static or structural perspective. *Any location within a social structure, or observed pattern of social order, is termed a social position.* Associated with each position is a set (often more than one) of related roles that the incumbent of the position is expected to enact. The concepts of roles and positions thus provide complementary means of analyzing what is essentially the same phenomenon—the former emphasizing dynamic activities and the latter, static arrangements.

A process orientation to social life suggests, however, that to identify a given social position we must perceptually and conceptually "freeze" ongoing role activities and single out the structural point at which a set of roles being enacted by an individual converge.[2] For example, the position of "store manager" represents the juncture of such roles as "direct supervisor of department heads," "second-line supervisor of store clerks," "coordinator of store activities," and "representative of the store in community affairs." The position of "chairman of the entertainment committee" is

___

[2] For an elaboration of this position, see J. Eugene Haas, "Role, Position, and Social Organization: A Conceptual Formulation," *The Midwest Sociologist*, vol. 19 (December 1956), p. 34.

derived from the convergence of the roles of "coordinator of committee activities," "member of the executive council," and "subordinate of the association president." The position of "State Governor" is identified by such roles as "chief administrator of the state government," "chief executive of the state," "employer of all state employees," and so on. Both dynamic roles and structural positions are real social phenomena; they are simply different aspects of the process of participation in social organization.

There are two significant differences between roles and positions, however. First, because a social position is an identified location within a social structure, it is seen as existing whether or not anyone is presently occupying it. This is not always true of roles. The positions of store manager, chairman of the entertainment committee, and state governor will all be recognized by members of their respective organizations during the interim period after one incumbent leaves and before another is selected. Some roles, in contrast, are not anticipated and must be enacted by an individual before they will be recognized as existing. Such unformalized and transient roles as "confidant to the President," "sparkplug of the athletic team," or "mediator of family quarrels" do not constitute social positions. Another distinction between positions and roles is that positions are often more institutionalized, so that they are governed by a wider range of social norms.[3]

Components of Roles

Just as social organization always consists of both social ordering and culture, so social roles—the smallest units of any organization—always contain the twin components of overt action patterns and cognitive expectations. *Cognitive expectations prescribe and proscribe actions and attitudes for the persons enacting a given role.* These role expectations are of three different types: cultural, situational, and personal.[4] Cultural expectations are contained in the culture of the organization of which the role is a part. They are, in effect, the social norms and rules that apply specifically to this role. Situational expectations are held by the other people, or role partners, with whom the role is enacted in a given situation.

[3] William J. Goode, "Norm Commitment and Conformity to Role-Status Obligations," *The American Journal of Sociology*, vol. 66 (November 1960), pp. 246–258.
[4] This categorization scheme is derived from S. Stanley Sargent, "Conceptions of Role and Ego in Contemporary Psychology," in Muzafer Sherif and John H. Roherer, eds., *Social Psychology at the Crossroads* (New York: Harper & Row, 1951), pp. 355–370.

These role partners (such as a physician's nurses and patients, the lawyers and defendants in a judge's court, or one's spouse and children) derive some of their expectations for the role from their common culture, but they also create some of them especially for the situations in which they encounter the role.[5] Personal expectations are those which the enactor holds for himself in this role. Again, some of his expectations are learned from his culture and some from his immediate role partners, but others may be uniquely his own.

The more encompassing, precise, and rigid the cultural expectations pertaining to a role, the less opportunity the individual has to shape the role to fit the immediate situation and his own personal expectations. Thus, for instance, the Roman Catholic Church minutely defines almost everything a priest does when celebrating a Mass. In contrast, the doctrine of academic freedom grants the university professor great leeway—though not unrestricted license—to say whatever he wants in the classroom. An organization loses some immediate control over the way its roles are enacted if its cultural expectations provide only broad outlines and general guidelines, so that role actors and their partners are given wide latitude to shape the details of each role to fit the demands of the immediate situation and their own expectations. Both the organization and the individual can benefit from such an arrangement, however. Because role actors can alter their actions to deal with the various contingencies that arise in different situations and at different times, the organization as a whole gains flexibility, adaptability, and hence stability. At the same time, these individuals are encouraged to become creative in their social actions, to be concerned for the expectations and desires of others, and to assume responsible orientations toward the social organizations in which they participate.

Cognitive expectations tell a person what he should and should not do in a role, but *a social role is not actually fulfilled until individuals express these expectations in overt patterns of action and interaction.* The carrying out of role actions should not be viewed as a mere exercise in behavioral conformity to preordained expectations, however. Role acting is a creative social process, in the course of which existing expectations are often altered and new ones established. It is through role acting that roles are actually created.[6] A role actor is always devising a performance for his

[5] The idea of situational role expectations is similar to the widely used sociological concept of "definition of the situation." The major difference between the two concepts is that "definitions of situations" frequently apply to several different roles simultaneously, if they all occur in one social situation.

[6] This idea of role acting as a creative process rather than as a mere behavioral conformity has been insightfully discussed by Ralph Turner in "Role Taking: Process versus Conformity," in Arnold Rose, ed., *Human Behavior and Social Processes* (Boston: Houghton Mifflin Company, 1962), pp. 20–40.

role partners on the basis of his own goals, his partners' expectations, cultural norms and rules, and the demands of the immediate situation.[7]

No matter how minutely cognitive expectations may be defined, they can never anticipate and specify actions for every contingency. Hence every role enactment is a creative performance. Some roles give the individual much more room for social creativity than do others, of course. But considerable skill in social interaction is necessary to bring any role to life. As Shakespeare noted long ago: "All the world's a stage, / And all the men and women merely players."

Unfortunately, considerable terminological ambiguity has crept into sociology concerning the process of role enactment. There are at least three distinct forms of this phenomenon.[8] *Role acting* is the basic process of assuming a social role, accepting expectations for it, and shaping one's actions in terms of it. A role actor, that is, seriously fulfills a social role in interaction with others. *Role playing*, on the other hand, is not "for real." It occurs when children "play at" being firemen or mothers, and also when adults pretend to assume roles that they do not normally occupy. Sometimes, of course, it is hard to tell whether a person is seriously acting a role or only pretending to play it, and fraudulent role acting is not a rare occurrence. *Role taking*, finally, is the mental activity of temporarily putting onself in another person's role so as to better understand and predict his attitudes and actions. Empathetic skill in mentally "taking the role of the other" is an extremely valuable asset to anyone engaging in social interaction, and we all do it in many of our daily encounters.

We can now formulate a more precise conceptualization of social roles that takes into account both their cognitive and behavioral components. *A social role is an interrelated set of expectations and actions that is an integral part of some social organization.*

Role Enactment

The various social roles that individuals enact as they participate in organized social life are acquired in one of two ways: by ascription or by achievement. *Ascribed roles are assigned to individuals because of one or more social characteristics they possess.* The most fundamental of these ascriptive criteria are age and sex, although factors such as race, religion,

---

[7] The most provocative analyst of this process is Erving Goffman. See his *The Presentation of Self in Everyday Life* (Garden City, N.Y.: Doubleday Anchor Books, 1959), and numerous other writings.

[8] The following three concepts are taken from Walter Coutu, although the terms used here are not his: "Role-Playing versus Role Taking: An Appeal for Clarification," *American Sociological Review*, vol. 16 (April 1951), pp. 180–187.

family background, and socioeconomic status are also often used as bases for assigning roles to individuals. Under most circumstances it is extremely difficult, if not impossible, for a person to acquire an ascribed role without possessing the requisite social characteristics. Our society does not allow persons below a specified age (usually 21) to vote as citizens no matter how mature they may be, and it will not tolerate a homosexual male who attempts to assume the role of "wife" to another man. On the other hand, if one possesses a certain characteristic, the accompanying role (or roles) cannot easily be escaped. The son of a peasant in a feudal society has little freedom of choice in selecting most of his social roles, but neither does the son of the reigning king. In the contemporary United States, essentially the same process often occurs in the assignment of many occupational and related roles. The social fate of the child of an illiterate Negro tenant farmer is broadly (though not fully) predetermined, but so is the future career of the child of a wealthy, college-educated business executive.

Achieved roles are gained by individuals on the basis of demonstrated capability or performance. In this case, the person must satisfy certain socially prescribed criteria before he is awarded the role, and he will likely lose the role if he fails to fulfill its requirements. Sometimes the criteria for achieving a certain role are precisely defined. To become a United States Senator, one must receive a plurality of all votes cast in a senatorial election, and to become a lawyer, one must pass state bar examinations. Quite often, though, such criteria are specified only vaguely, if at all. What does one do to achieve the roles of "top influential" in a community or "office wit" at one's job? As a broad generalization, it is noteworthy that the number and variety of acheived roles are constantly expanding in modern societies as organized social life becomes increasingly complex. Illustrations of achieved roles abound in contemporary societies: member of a football team, vice president of a business corporation, spouse, bridge partner, chairman of a committee, city attorney, foreman of a construction crew, deacon of a church, commander of a military unit, or college student.

The more important roles in most societies throughout human history have normally been ascribed rather than achieved. In this manner it was assured that these vital roles were always filled, while open conflict for the roles was kept to a minimum and the society remained stable. A monarchy does not face the succession crises that periodically occur in societies with elected governments. Open competition for those societal roles which carry considerable amounts of social power is a relatively recent development—and even today it is still quite rare in many traditional societies. The shifting of socially vital roles from ascription to achievement places unprecedented demands on an organization for collective social sophistication and maturity, and can produce serious social problems—as many modernizing societies in today's world are discovering. In the long run, though, open role achievement not only increases individual freedom by allowing persons to acquire and enact those roles for which they are most qualified and which they personally desire, but it can also benefit the larger organization by channeling the most competent people available into crucial roles and by encouraging these persons to perform to the best of their abilities.

In actual social life, the processes of role ascription and achievement are often combined. Many social roles occur in sets, so that if a person fulfills one role he is also expected to enact other associated roles. Many businesses expect their executives to participate in community civic activities and to display certain status symbols, the holder of a military commission is expected to act as a "gentleman" as well as an officer, a minister's wife might also be required to head the Sunday School and the Women's Alliance of her husband's church, a person convicted of a felony is commonly denied the citizen's right to vote and may even be refused a job once he is free, and professors are normally expected to engage in research as well as teach. In all of these examples the original role is achieved, but the other roles comprising the total set are ascribed to the person on the basis of the original role.

As individuals participate in numerous different social activities and organizations, they commonly acquire and learn to enact many diverse social roles. A single person often possesses a "repertoire" of several dozen ascribed or achieved roles, which he enacts at different occasions and in different settings. Quite obviously, he cannot fulfill all of these roles simultaneously. As he enters each new social situation, he selects (either consciously or unconsciously) from his repertoire the role that is most appropriate. As the situation changes, he may later discard this role and shift to another. Meanwhile, most or all of the other social roles he might potentially be enacting will remain temporarily dormant. In short, *at any given time only a few of an individual's entire repertoire of possible roles are salient for him.*

A man at home enacting the role of father with his children is not presently enacting his other roles of office manager, political party worker, bowling-team member, or volunteer fireman. These roles are not salient for him at the moment. Nevertheless, he can quickly shift roles if his employer should phone him or if he hears the town fire siren. In general, the more immediate a particular organization is in a person's life, the more salient will be his role(s) in that organization. Thus family and occupational roles are highly salient for most people much of the time, while the role of church member may become salient only once a week, and the role of citizen of one's nation might become important only sporadically at election time.

This phenomenon of differential role saliency enables individuals to fulfill many diverse roles in various types of organizations at different times, even though these roles may not be fully compatible with each other. To the extent that such incompatible roles are kept segregated from each other, they will not come into conflict. The man who arranges to spend Monday, Wednesday, and Friday evenings with his wife and Tuesday, Thursday, and Saturday evenings with his mistress has turned a potentially explosive situation into one that is relatively peaceful and rewarding—at least for him.

Differential saliency of one's various roles also provides opportunities for individuals to act at least occasionally as relatively autonomous personalities. If a person finds himself in a social situation for which no existing roles are relevant or salient, he is free to act "on his own" as a social element—and perhaps to initiate the creation of new social organizations. In contrast, a member of a tightly controlled traditional or totalitarian society is constantly confronted with a few rigidly prescribed roles that pervade his entire life, so that he has little opportunity for autonomous action. The existence of a large number of competing and limited social roles, from which a person can pick and choose, is therefore one means of providing for freedom of action in social life. Complete freedom will not result from the total elimination of all social roles, however. Absence of social organization, and hence of all roles, produces social anarchy, not freedom. Participation in social organization through the enactment of social roles often provides the individual with opportunities and benefits that would be totally unavailable if he were to act alone. To mention one obvious example, the industrial complex that provides Americans with unprecedented personal wealth can operate successfully only through the combined efforts of millions of responsible workers.

Consequences of Roles

We encounter social roles—both our own and those of other actors—whenever we participate in social organization. Roles vary considerably, as we have already seen, in the manner in which they are acquired, in the nature and content of their expectations, in the ways in which they are enacted, and in their relative saliency at any given time. But as a general phenomenon, they pervade all organized social life. What, then, are the consequences of social roles for both individuals and organizations?

Social roles have two major consequences for individuals. First, *roles provide guidelines for our social actions*. If one is acquainted with the main expectations for a certain role, he can fairly easily "step into" this role—the analogy to a suit of clothing is intentional—and carry it out. Much fruitless and possibly embarrassing trial-and-error searching for appropriate actions is thereby avoided. Although you have never before eaten in a particular restaurant, you are able to walk in, order a meal, eat it, pay your bill, leave a tip, and walk out, all without the slightest hesitancy or worry about what to do next. The setting is novel, but the role is not; you have enacted this role of a restaurant customer many times before, and you are thoroughly familiar with its expectations and actions.

Second, *roles give regularity and predictability to our social interactions*. In addition to telling us how to act, social roles aid us in anticipating and predicting the actions of others with whom we interact. Once we determine the role another person is enacting, and presuming that we already know something about this role, we then can predict with a fair amount of accuracy (though never total certainty) what he will do and how he will react to our actions. On the bases of these anticipations, we then modify our own actions to take account of what we expect him to do. The salesman in a clothing store is a total stranger to the person who comes in to buy a new suit, but even before any communication takes place between them, this customer will have a rather detailed idea of what the salesman will do and say. From the salesman's point of view, the role of the customer is only slightly less predictable, and with experience he will learn to categorize most customers into one of a few standard types or roles. For all participants, then, social interaction through role enactment becomes a continual process of interweaving one's own role expectations and actions with one's anticipations of others' expectations and actions.

The enactment of social roles also has several consequences for the organizations in which these roles occur. *To the extent that the roles comprising a social organization are adequately fulfilled, that organization will gain in overall stability and unity.* Its patterns of social order will be regularized, interrelated, and perpetuated over time. In addition, *adequate enactment of vital organizational roles contributes to the satisfaction of that organization's functional requirements.* If the membership chairman of an association adequately performs his duties, for instance, recruitment of new members will not become a serious problem for the organization. Not all activities within an organization—and hence not all roles—will necessarily contribute to the satisfaction of organizational requirements. Some roles (such as that of a gangster in the community) can even have serious detrimental consequences for social organization. But the survival and operational requirements of an organization are much more likely to be satisfied through the enactment of socially responsible roles than through the random actions of relatively autonomous and self-oriented individuals.

Role Conflict

As social organization grows in size, scope, and complexity, individual participants are called upon to enact an ever widening and increasingly diversified repertoire of social roles. A direct outgrowth of these demands is role conflict, which almost all members of contemporary societies experience at one time or another. Most role conflicts can be classified as one of two basic types. *Interrole conflict, or role incompatibility, occurs when a person is called upon to enact two or more incompatible roles simultaneously.* A common example is the plight of the educated woman who experiences social pressures to have a career and also be a wife and mother. *Intrarole conflict, or role inconsistency, occurs when an individual and one or more of his role partners hold incompatible expectations for a single role.* The student who does not believe in cheating but is pressured by his friends to use a "crib sheet" on a forthcoming examination experiences this kind of role conflict. One type of role conflict can, and often does, lead to the other type, either sequentially or in combination.

Role conflict is produced by any number of different social situations, of which the following are only a few illustrations: (a) membership in two or more organizations that make incompatible role demands on an individual—such as a club that encourages drinking and a church that discourages it; (b) convergence over time of two or more roles that were originally separated and enacted by different people, but which are now expected of the same person—as in the situation of competing wife and career roles; (c) inconsistency among the major values of an organization's culture, or between its values and its expectations for certain roles—as when the norms hold that killing is wrong but the soldier is told to shoot the enemy; (d) the necessity of enacting the same role to different sets of role partners who hold conflicting expectations for the role—such as the social worker who must deal with clients seeking help ranging from money to psychotherapy; and (e) cultural expectations for a role that have not kept abreast of changing demands being made upon that role—as in the case of a university president who is nominally a scholar but actually mainly a fund raiser.

If role conflict is so prevalent in our lives, why are we not all "nervous wrecks" from trying to deal with overdemanding and impossible role expectations? The apparent answer is that most people learn to utilize a wide variety of "coping mechanisms," or social and psychological techniques for managing or resolving role conflicts. An examination of these various social-psychological processes is outside the purview of this book, but several excellent analyses are available for the interested reader.[9]

In brief summary, both dynamic social roles and structural social positions are parts of larger, established social organizations. It is through the enactment of roles and the filling of positions that individuals actively participate in social organizations. The expectations and actions which comprise a social role provide guidelines and predictability for one's social interactions. At the same time, role enactment contributes to the process of social organization. Social organizations could not exist if necessary roles were not adequately fulfilled by individuals acting as responsible parts of those larger entities. Role enactment can create problems, however, since total involvement in minutely predefined roles leaves the person with few opportunities for individual creativity, and ultimately produces social organization that is rigid and incapable of change. A fundamental challenge inherent in social life, therefore, is to create social organization that provides opportunities for meaningful individual action within social roles whose enactment is rewarding to both the actor and the total organization.

What does an organization do to insure that its component roles will be adequately enacted, and also to deal with actions by individual participants that are detrimental to the welfare of the organization? This question leads us into a consideration of the process of social control, which we shall undertake in the next chapter.

[9] See the following: J. W. Getzels and E. G. Guba, "Role, Role Conflict, and Effectiveness," *American Sociological Review*, vol. 19 (April 1954), pp. 164–175; Neal C. Gross, Ward S. Mason, and Alexander W. McEachern, *Explorations in Role Analysis* (New York: John Wiley & Sons, Inc., 1958), chaps. 15–17; Robert K. Merton, *Social Theory and Socal Structure*, rev. ed. (New York: The Free Press, a division of The Macmillan Company, 1957), pp. 368–384; and Jackson Toby, "Some Variables in Role Conflict Analysis," *Social Forces*, vol. 30 (1952), pp. 323–327.

RECOMMENDED READING

BALES, ROBERT F., "Task Roles and Social Roles in Problem-Solving Groups," in Eleanor E. Maccoby, Theodore M. Newcomb, and Eugene L. Hartley, eds., *Readings in Social Psychology*, 3d ed., pp. 437–447 (New York: Holt, Rinehart and Winston, Inc., 1958).

This classic study distinguishes two basic types of leadership roles that tend to develop in many organizations.

GOFFMAN, ERVING, *Presentation of Self in Everyday Life* (Garden City, N.Y.: Doubleday Anchor Books, 1959).

An analysis of the various processes and problems involved in role enactment.

GROSS, NEAL, ALEXANDER W. MCEACHERN, AND WARD S. MASON, "Role Conflict and Its Resolution," in Maccoby, *et al.*, *Readings in Social Psychology*, pp. 447–459.

A field study of alternative ways in which persons subject to role conflict tend to resolve it.

LIEBERMAN, SEYMOUR, "The Effects of Changes in Roles on the Attitudes of Role Occupants," *Human Relations*, vol. 9 (1950), pp. 385–403. Reprinted in Neil J. Smelser and William T. Smelser, *Personality and Social Systems*, pp. 264–279 (New York: John Wiley & Sons, Inc., 1963).

A field study of the extent to which role changes affect a person's attitudes and thus produce social control.

TURNER, RALPH H., "Role Taking: Process versus Conformity," in Arnold Rose, ed., *Human Behavior and Social Processes*, pp. 20–40 (Boston: Houghton Mifflin Company, 1962).

Argues that role enactment is a dynamic and continual process of creation, not just behavioral conformity to preexisting expectations.

CHAPTER 9

Preservation of Social Organization

The task of preserving social organization would be considerably simplified if individuals willingly and adequately fulfilled all necessary organizational roles, if social actors never experienced role conflict, if various social and psychological pressures did not lead persons to commit "deviant actions," and if the subunits of an organization were totally institutionalized so that their activities never conflicted with each other. These conditions are never realized in actual social life, however—and perhaps fortunately so, since a perfectly ordered utopian world might be a very dull place in which to reside.[1] Given the dynamic and imperfectly ordered nature of social life, the preservation and perpetuation of established social organization remains a continual problematic concern for both participants and observing social scientists. How are patterns of social order and shared cultural ideas maintained through time despite a continual flow of personnel, conflicts among social actors, constant variations and alterations in role expectations and actions, and differing demands placed upon social actors by the various organizations in which they participate?

[1] This theme has been elaborated by Ralph Dahrendorf in "Out of Utopia: Toward a Reorientation of Sociological Analysis," *The American Journal of Sociology*, vol. 64 (September 1958), pp. 115–127.

Social Control

The answer to the question above can be stated concisely, though its many specifications, manifestations, and implications can only be suggested here. *Social actors perpetuate social organization because of the social controls exerted upon them in social life.* All social actors—both individuals and organizations—are constantly subjected to various kinds of controls, so that the process of social control occurs throughout organized social life. We shall here be concerned only with organizational controls upon individual actions. The broader question of how organizations influence and control each other falls under the heading of social power, to be explored in Chapter 12.

Social controls on individual behavior often are imposed upon the individual by himself, as well as by other actors, but nevertheless they always represent the demands and pressures of organized social life. Social norms, rules, laws, and role expectations provide prescriptive and proscriptive standards for participation in social organization, as well as criteria by which social actions are judged. They do not enforce themselves, however. Social controls must be exercised by all organizations to insure that participating actors abide by established standards of action, enact appropriate social roles, fulfill social responsibilities as organizational parts, and thus preserve social order and culture. Because all social organization is perpetuated through this control processes, *social control is inherent in organized social life.*

The absolute necessity of social control in all organizations does not imply, however, that the process of social organization demands absolute and total conformity to arbitrarily imposed standards by all participants. Some organizations—such as concentration camps, highly traditional communities, or totalitarian societies—might attempt to enforce total behavioral conformity, but the vast majority of organizations do not.

In the first place, the norms, rules, and role expectations of the organization need not be arbitrarily imposed or rigidly upheld. To the extent that rationality is applied to the process of social organization, the standards of action that evolve may greatly facilitate the attainment of the goals the members of the organization are seeking through their collective activities. Similarly, these standards can be modified, changed, or totally rejected by the members if "democratic" decision-making procedures have been established, if individuals and subunits possess some degree of functional autonomy, and if the standards are viewed as secular (or man-made) guidelines rather than as sacred (or divinely inspired) imperatives.

Second, total conformity of all actions to established social standards is never necessary for the maintenance or operation of social organization. In fact, despite the predictions of George Orwell's *1984* and Aldous Huxley's *Brave New World*, it is highly doubtful if total conformity could ever be achieved in any real organization. Most organizations normally attempt to influence or control only the activities that are vital to their welfare, so that these demands commonly pertain to only a limited portion of any person's whole life. Various types of organizations usually seek to control different kinds of actions, so that an activity that is extensively controlled in one organization—such as personal friendships among members—is often left to individual discretion in another organization. In the long run, moreover, total social control is almost always destructive of social organization, since existing organizations can never be changed or new ones developed if people are not sometimes free to innovate and create novel patterns of social order or cultural ideas.

Third, standards for social action need not be rigidly prescribed. As we saw in the case of role expectations, many organizational standards provide only broad outlines and general guidelines, leaving considerable latitude for individual and situational modification and elaboration. In addition, organizations frequently provide alternative standards for a given activity or situation, from which individual participants are free to select the ones most appropriate to their activities.

Fourth, the word "control" unfortunately carries many invidious connotations for some people, which lead them to protest against "conformity." As an aid to maintaining analytical neutrality, these people might prefer a term with a more acceptable image, such as "social responsibility." Although in practice some social control is unquestionably aimed at achieving behavioral conformity as an end in itself, this is not inevitable and it does not explain the whole process of social control. In a broader sense, the purpose of social control is to encourage individuals to act as responsible participants in social organization, so that these organizations will be perpetuated and will be able to achieve whatever goals they seek. From this perspective, social control is only a necessary means to a more fundamental end. If, in any given organization, social controls do promote socially responsible actions by individual participants, the resulting viable social organization can provide these persons with opportunities and benefits—and hence personal freedom—that would be unattainable outside of organized social life. Social control in some areas of life— such as the enforcement of public health measures or the prevention of crime—can increase the total amount of personal freedom available to all individuals in a society.

Finally, the specific techniques through which social control is effected need not include overt coercion. Indeed, coercion is a relatively inadequate technique, and often is invoked only as a last resort when the individual is unwilling (or unable) to respond to any other form of control. Although coercion can produce beneficial results for an organization, especially if applied carefully and sparingly, it is perhaps the least effective means of achieving social responsibility in most situations over any period of time.

For analytical purposes, control techniques are commonly classified as internal or external, although these are but two sides of the same basic process. *Internal social control is exercised by the individual over himself*, because of his own desires to abide by established social standards and expectations. It is voluntary in the sense that no one else directly compels the person to act the way he does. It is still social control, however, since the individual must have learned from the culture of the organization both the standards to which he is conforming and the desire or motivation to conform. Internal social control is inseparably linked with the broader process of socialization, which we shall examine before elaborating the various techniques of internal control.

External social control is exercised over an individual by a social organization, through other persons acting as its agents. The organization exerts pressures on the individual or the situation in which he acts, so as to influence his actions. This kind of social control is often described as involuntary, as opposed to voluntary internal control, although even here an element of choice remains. A person always has the option of leaving an organization (by resigning, emigrating, or dying) if he does not wish to abide by its demands—although in many cases such a choice might not even be considered by the individual.

Socialization

Internal social control depends upon the individual's having knowledge of the relevant culture and some degree of personal maturity. In other words, it presumes a previous process of socialization. *Socialization is the total process in which an individual develops a human personality and learns to be a social actor.* Thus socialization can be viewed from two different analytical perspectives: we may emphasize the development of the personality as it matures in childhood and throughout adult life, or we may emphasize the learning of those capabilities necessary for participation in organized social life.

The process of socialization, in both its "personality-formation" and "social-learning" aspects, is frequently thought of as occurring primarily in childhood, but this is a gross oversimplification. Certainly childhood, and especially the first few years, is an especially critical period in a person's life, for it is during this time that he acquires basic personality characteristics and learns many fundamental interaction skills—one of the most important of which is language. Nevertheless, the socialization process never ends with adolescence, but rather continues throughout a person's entire life. Our personalities are continually developing and changing, and whenever we enter into new social relationships or organizations we must learn appropriate patterns of interaction and cultural ideas. In fact, for the sociologist concerned with studying social organization, adult socialization activities are often of greater relevance than is childhood socialization. We must therefore keep in mind throughout the following discussion that this entire socialization process applies to all persons at all times.

The study of socialization spans the academic disciplines of psychology, social psychology, and sociology, although it is a central concern of the social psychologist. Psychologists and psychologically oriented social psychologists tend to focus primarily on the "personality-formation" aspects of socialization. They inquire into such questions as how the newborn baby learns to communicate with others, how the child forms images of himself, how the person is influenced by various socialization agents such as parents, siblings, friends, schools, and churches, and how the total personality grows, becomes organized, and maintains its unity. These phenomena are of vital significance, for both practical and scientific reasons, but they fall outside our present concern. As a basic generalization, though, we note that an individual's personality is largely a product of his social environment, as acquired through social interaction.

Sociologists and sociologically oriented social psychologists, meanwhile, tend to focus more on the "social-learning" aspects of socialization. The crucial problems for these investigators center on the processes of learning cultural norms and rules, acquiring social-interaction skills, becoming familiar with various role expectations and techniques of role acting, developing collective social orientations, and related phenomena. Much of one's social learning takes place within "primary groups" such as the family and peer group, which is why social scientists point to these organizations as the major agents of socialization. During childhood, when the individual is first acquiring social capabilities, almost all of his activities center in intimate "primary groups." Later in life, social learning also occurs in larger and more complex organizations, but again it is among one's immediate acquaintances within these organizations that most socialization actually transpires.

Our present knowledge about the dynamics of social learning is fragmentary, although what we do know suggests that it occurs primarily through social reinforcement within interaction situations. When we first enter a social situation for which we are totally unprepared—and to some extent whenever we initiate interaction in any situation—we tend to act in a rather random, trial-and-error fashion, trying first one action and then another. If other persons are present, we can imitate their actions, assuming that what is appropriate for them also applies to us—which is frequently open to doubt. Our task is also made easier if someone else tells us what to do, either verbally or in writing. In this case, though, we must decide whether or not our instructor is competent, whether he represents the other participants for whom he speaks, and whether the instructions are congruent with what is actually being done at the present time. In short, we necessarily remain in a state of some uncertainty until other persons begin responding to our actions.

Once we do receive responses from other actors, however, we gain a basis for evaluating our own actions. Some of the things we do will likely be disapproved by others, and we will be discouraged from doing them again. Other things we do will be at least accepted by others, giving us some leeway in deciding whether or not to repeat them. Finally, still other things we do will be approved by others, and we will be encouraged to continue them. Many crucial variables are left unexplained in this brief outline, including one's ability to interpret correctly the responses of others, one's receptivity to reactions from others, and the nature and strength of approving and disapproving responses. Nevertheless, it does suggest that social learning is essentially similar to all other forms of learning, in which the nature and degree of reinforcement received by the individual in response to his actions are the crucial factors determining what and how much he learns. The unique features of social learning are simply that we learn social capabilities (rather than purely cognitive information, emotional associations, or motor skills) and that the significant respondents are almost always other social actors with whom we are engaged in ongoing social interaction.

The "personality-formation" and "social-learning" perspectives on socialization suggest that this process has a dual outcome: the simultaneous development of both personal autonomy and social responsibility. We often uncritically think of these two goals as contradictory. After all, if one accepts social responsibilities does he not surrender at least a portion of his personal autonomy? In some settings, yes, but not always. The assumption of social responsibility can also lead to greater personality development and hence increased personal autonomy. To cite a common example, marriage (which certainly entails numerous responsibilities) sometimes does become an unbearable prison for an individual, but it can also provide him with opportunities for personal growth and satisfaction that are not normally available to a bachelor. The development of individual maturity and the creation of social organization are never inherently incompatible—though they can become so. They can, and frequently do, both increase together, with each reinforcing the other. The fundamental paradox of socialization lies in the fact that through this process the individual simultaneously develops a mature and relatively autonomous personality, and also learns to become a responsible and involved part of organized social life.

Numerous and diverse theories have been offered to explain this socialization paradox, and we cannot outline all of them here. One does merit our attention, however, because of its pervasive influence on many sociologists. George Herbert Mead used the idea of "taking the role of the other" to explain the dynamics underlying all socialization.[2] A few highlights of his theory follow. Socialization begins when an individual (ego) realizes that his actions are causing other persons (alters) to respond to him, and that these responses have consequences for him. As ego not only becomes self-consciously aware of the consequences of his actions, so that they have meaning for him, but also attributes this same conscious awareness to others, he will then attempt to anticipate the meanings that others give to his actions. In other words, during interaction, ego temporarily puts himself in the place of alter, views himself through alter's eyes, and tries to determine how he would interpret and respond to his own actions if he were alter. It is as if he continually asked himself, "What would I think and do in this situation if I were him and were receiving this action?" This process Mead called "taking the role of the other." As ego temporarily puts himself in the place of alter, he will then be able to view himself and his actions as others see him, from a partially objective rather than a wholly subjective viewpoint. On the basis of countless "external" perceptions of himself through the eyes of others, he forms self-conceptions, or generalized pictures of himself as seen by others. These self-conceptions in turn become fused, over time, into a fundamental self-identity around which his entire personality is organized. Thus his innermost self—which Mead called the "I"—as well as his overall personality structure are largely shaped through social interaction (or "symbolic interaction," in Mead's terminology).

At the same time, this process of "taking the role of the other" also contributes to a person's social learning. It enables him to anticipate alter's probable responses to his intended actions before he overtly acts. He can then determine or modify his own actions on the basis of these anticipated

<hr />

[2] George Herbert Mead, *Mind, Self and Society* (Chicago: University of Chicago Press, 1934).

responses. One's anticipation of alter's responses is, of course, never perfect. But over time this process contributes immensely to the individual's learning of social capabilities—the result of which Mead called the "me," or the ways in which the person responds to others. In sum, both the "I" and the "me"—both personal autonomy and social responsibility—are direct outgrowths of meaningful social interaction.

Internal Social Control

Once a person has undergone some socialization—the amount necessary depends on the situation and the individual—he becomes capable of exercising internal control over his own actions. This type of social control occurs in three principal ways, which we shall describe as internalization, identification, and compliance.[3]

Internalization occurs as social norms (including cultural role expectations) are accepted by the individual as his own personal standards of action. These norms and role expectations are not just learned, but are incorporated by the individual into his personality. He then abides by them not because of external forces or rational decisions, but because his own mind and total personality compel him to. If he should violate a deeply internalized norm, he would feel guilty regardless of whether or not anyone else knew of his actions, and he would likely punish himself severely.

Norm internalization is largely an unconscious process. We are not usually aware of doing it and hence rarely realize the extent to which our "own" standards are actually learned from the cultures in which we participate. Most people would probably be surprised, if not shocked, to discover the degree to which their "self-discipline" is actually a reflection and expression of deeply internalized social norms. For instance, many of us probably believe quite strongly that killing is morally wrong, and thus find it difficult to realize that we would have no scruples against it if we lived in a society that encouraged killing. The fact that our moral inhibition is actually an internalized social norm can be easily demonstrated, however. If an individual is placed in an organization whose culture does encourage killing under certain conditions—such as an army in battle—he will then very likely come to feel that killing is permissible or even desirable in this situation.

[3] The latter two terms are not wholly standardized in sociology, and various synonyms are frequently employed, but the underlying concepts are widely accepted. These particular terms are adapted from Herbert C. Kelman, "Compliance, Identification, and Internalization: Three Processes of Attitude Change," *Journal of Conflict Resolution*, vol. 2 (March 1958), pp. 51–60. See also his "Processes of Opinion Change," *Public Opinion Quarterly*, vol. 25 (Spring 1961), pp. 57–78.

Social scientists presently know very little about how or why the process of internalization occurs, although many speculative theories have been suggested. One of the most fascinating events in the history of social thought was the convergence of the work of Émile Durkheim, George Herbert Mead, and Sigmund Freud upon the crucial importance of internalization for social life. Durkheim, a sociologist, Mead, a social psychologist, and Freud, a psychologist, came from different intellectual backgrounds, worked independently, and had little or no knowledge of each other. Yet at approximately the same time (the early years of the twentieth century) each of them developed theoretical viewpoints that emphasized norm internalization.[4] They used different terminology— Durkheim spoke of the "collective conscience" becoming manifest within individuals, Mead discussed the incorporation of "the generalized other" within the self, while Freud examined the effects of the "superego" upon the personality—and their resulting theories differed in numerous substantive respects. But to a remarkable extent they all saw social life as resting primarily on voluntary conformity by individuals to social standards that had been incorporated into their personalities.

Since we are already familiar with some of the thinking of George Herbert Mead, let us examine briefly his idea of "the generalized other." As an individual temporarily "takes the role of the other" and sees himself through another person's eyes, he develops conceptions of what this person expects of him. At first, these conceptions are closely tied to particular individuals, as the young child becomes aware of "what mother expects of me," "what brother expects of me," and "what teacher expects of me." Mead called this the "play" stage, since the child is largely "playing" at the roles of specific others as they relate to himself. Over time, though, the expectations of all those persons with whom one interacts in a given situation become fused into a single conception of what is expected of him by others in this social setting. Mead referred to this as the "game" stage, since the child is now learning to participate in organized games or group activities. Eventually, as the individual matures, these various situationally relevant standards of action tend to merge into a single generalized conception of what all other people—an amorphous "they"—expect one to do. Mead used the term "the generalized other" to describe this third stage.[5] At each stage of this process, the individual not only learns the expecta-

---

[4] For discussions of this convergence, see: Talcott Parsons, "The Superego and the Theory of Social Systems," in Parsons, *et al.*, *Working Papers in the Theory of Action* (New York: The Free Press, a division of The Macmillan Company, 1953), chap. 1; and Guy E. Swanson, "Mead and Freud: Their Relevance for Social Psychology," *Sociometry*, vol. 24 (December 1961), pp. 319–339.

[5] It is interesting to note that contemporary "situational ethics" questions the desirability of this third stage, and argues that the expectations and standards applied to any given activity should be derived only from that particular situation.

tions of others, but also incorporates them into the self-conceptions he forms of himself, so that they become not just what others—another person, other participants in a game, or "they"—expect of me, but what I expect of myself, because of my own self-images and self-identity. In this way, social norms become internalized within the individual.

A second kind of internal social control results from psychological identification by an individual with a social organization. *As a consequence of identification, an individual often accepts the social standards of an organization because of his desire to establish a relationship with that organization.* These social standards do not become internalized, but the individual voluntarily and willingly accepts them and abides by them because they are part of the organization with which he identifies. Once a person has psychologically identified himself with a social organization, no external pressures are necessary to induce him to conform to its standards of actions. The college freshman who modifies his appearance and behavior in an attempt to replicate the upperclass fraternity men whom he admires is responding to this kind of social control. So is the store proprietor who becomes more conservative in his political opinions and votes a straight Republican ticket because of his identification with "the business community." A third example would be the recent immigrant to a society who conspicuously adopts all the customs and traditions of his neighbors because "this is the way we do things in my new country." Over time, strong identification with an organization can lead to internalization of its norms, but the processes are analytically distinct.

Social control resulting from identification can occur regardless of whether or not the individual actually belongs to an organization. In fact, this phenomenon is especially common among nonmembers who are seeking membership by demonstrating their acceptance of organizational norms and rules. Sociologists frequently use the concept of "reference group" for an organization by whose standards an individual abides as a result of identification, regardless of whether or not he is actually a member of that organization.[6] The manual worker who accepts the "middle class" as a reference group will often conform more rigorously to "middle-class" norms than will business and professional persons.

---

[6] The reader interested in recent writings on reference-group theory might consult the following: Robert K. Merton and Alice S. Rossi, "Contributions to the Theory of Reference Group Behavior," in Merton's *Social Theory and Social Structure,* rev. ed. (New York: The Free Press, a division of The Macmillan Company, 1957), chap. 8; Muzafer Sherif, "The Concept of Reference Group in Human Relations," in Muzafer Sherif and M. O. Wilson, eds., *Group Relations at the Crossroads* (New York: Harper & Row, Publishers, 1953), pp. 203–231; and Tamotsu Shibutani, "Reference Groups and Social Control," in Arnold Rose, ed., *Human Behavior and Social Processes* (Boston: Houghton Mifflin Company, 1962), pp. 128–147.

Internal social control also takes the form of compliance resulting from expedient or utilitarian considerations. *Compliance occurs when an individual abides by the social standards of an organization in hopes of benefiting from this conformity.* That is, he expects to gain rewards or escape punishments because of his actions. He does not internalize the organizational standards, nor does he accept them because they are part of an organization with which he identifies. In this case, voluntary compliance is based on more-or-less rational calculations of expediency. The individual decides that, for one reason or another, it is in his interests to conform. A motorist follows posted speed limits to avoid the possibility of receiving a speeding ticket, an employee takes on extra duties and works overtime in hopes of being promoted, and some college students study only to attain satisfactory grades.

This phenomenon of compliance is clearly related to social sanctioning (directly applying rewards and punishments), which is discussed in the next section. The distinction between compliance and sanctioning lies in the fact that rewards and punishments are not actually necessary for compliance. The individual's actions are controlled by the anticipation of rewards and punishments, regardless of whether or not he ever receives them. Compliance based on calculated expediency is particularly important in producing conformity to rules, in comparison with norms, since rules are not internalized and are not always accepted as a result of identification.

External Social Control

In the process of external social control, overt pressures are exerted by an organization as a means of inducing behavioral conformity among individuals. These pressures can be aimed either at the social situation in which the person acts or at the individual himself. The first procedure is described as indirect external control, or social manipulation, while the second constitutes direct external control, or social sanctioning.[7]

Social manipulation controls individuals' actions indirectly by altering the social settings in which they act. No direct pressures are brought to bear upon the person. Instead, the patterns of social order in which he participates are shaped in such a way that some potential actions are possible while others are not. It is extremely unlikely, for instance, that an individual will ever become a professional criminal if he never has any

---

[7] I am indebted to Albert J. Reiss, Jr., for the conceptual distinction between indirect and direct external control, as derived from Karl Mannheim, *Man and Society in an Age of Reconstruction* (New York: Harcourt, Brace & World, Inc., 1940).

contacts with criminals and hence encounters no opportunities to become acquainted with their way of life or occupational skills. In another direction, one reason why many parents send their daughters to college, and perhaps also encourage them to join the "right" sorority, is to provide them with opportunities for meeting suitable potential husbands. Finally, one of the principal reasons why so many Negroes in the United States are poor, uneducated, unskilled, live in slums, and evidence "lower-class" behavior is precisely that the white community has for generations denied them the opportunities to gain an adequate education, secure better jobs, live in desirable neighborhoods, or learn "middle-class" values and norms.

Besides the opening and closing of "doors" to possible social activities, social manipulation can also be accomplished by changes in the structure of an existing organization. A clear example of this type of social control occurred in a sociological experiment dealing with resistance to change.[8] The purpose of the study was to discover how new production techniques might be introduced into a small factory without arousing hostility and resistance among the workers. The employees were divided into a number of small groups, some of which were allowed to discuss (under the direction of a management representative) the various work problems they were encountering and possible ways of resolving these difficulties. Discussion continued in these groups until all the members arrived at a solution that was acceptable to management—until they "voluntarily" decided to make the changes that management desired. Other groups of workers were simply informed of the changes to be made, without any opportunity for discussion. Measurements taken after the changes had been introduced revealed that productivity was considerably higher (and dissatisfaction lower) in the groups that had "participated" in the process of decision-making. As this case suggests, "human-relations management" as practiced in many organizations can easily be converted into subtle social manipulation.

One other important technique of social manipulation involves purposeful structuring of the socialization process through which individuals learn organizational norms and rules. The final effect of this procedure is to determine the social bases of internal control, but it must begin with modifications in external social conditions. By bringing "socially and culturally deprived" children into a Head Start Program, we hope to prepare them to benefit more fully from later schooling. The Army teaches its norms of military discipline to new recruits by temporarily cutting them off from virtually all outside social relationships and subjecting them to constant demands and duties. On a more extensive plane, twentieth-cen-

[8] Lester Coch and John R. P. French, Jr., "Overcoming Resistance to Change," in Eleanor Maccoby, et al., eds., Readings in Social Psychology, 3rd ed. (New York: Holt, Rinehart and Winston, Inc., 1958), pp. 233–250.

tury totalitarian nations have experimented with controlled socialization techniques such as state-operated nurseries, political propaganda combined with educational instruction, and official youth organizations for children of all ages.

Social sanctioning is the process of directly administering rewards and punishments to individuals as a means of obtaining conformity to organizational standards. An endless variety of sanctions is employed in organized social life, from the simplest and most informal compliments and criticisms to the most formal and elaborate rituals of bestowing knighthood or executing a death sentence. Social sanctioning may be interpersonal, such as praising or ostracizing a person, it may be organizational, as in promotions or demotions to new positions, it may be economic, as in levying fines or giving bonuses, it may be symbolic, as in awarding a citation or censuring an individual, or it may be physical, as when a person is placed in jail or given a key to the executive lunchroom. In general, the more immediate and personal a sanction, the more effective it will be in producing social control.

Despite the widespread use of all kinds of social sanctions throughout social life, formal sanctioning is perhaps the least adequate means of effecting social control. Three inherent problems can be briefly mentioned. One is that of surveillance. How can an organization possibly watch all of its members all the time, so as to detect every instance in which sanctioning is necessary or appropriate? A second problem is that of administration. Punishments tend to produce only minimally acceptable behavior, never total commitment, while rewards can be used only sparingly if they are not to lose all effectiveness by becoming "rights" rather than "privileges." Third is the problem of reinforcement. No matter how severely a person is sanctioned, it will have little ultimate effect on his actions if the larger social environment does not support and reinforce the intent of the sanction. If a person emerges from jail as a local hero, it is doubtful that the confinement will influence his future actions in the desired direction.

For the reasons just mentioned, most organizations rely primarily on means of control other than formal sanctioning, and reserve formal sanctions for only the more seriously beneficial or disruptive types of actions, using them either as supplements or as last resorts when all other methods fail.

Deviant Actions and Social Disorganization

We have tacitly assumed that the purpose of social control activities is to obtain whatever kinds of behavioral conformity are necessary to preserve established social organization. In short, social control is used to encourage desired actions and to discourage or prevent "deviant actions." But what constitutes "deviant action"? Are there any definite criteria by which all "deviant actions" can be identified or classified? The answer is "no." Any action by any actor might in some situations be considered deviant. Deviancy is culturally defined, so that actions that the members of one organization or subculture condemn and seek to control might be praised and rewarded by the members of another organization or subculture.[9]

The greatest variations in definitions of deviancy usually occur among societies with widely divergent cultures. In the United States we would react with horror if someone butchered a stranger from another community, boiled the victim, and then called in his neighbors to share the feast. Yet there are still tribes in New Guinea that consider such actions highly praiseworthy. Differing definitions of deviancy can also be found within societies, however. Gambling is a crime in most parts of the United States, but not in Nevada. A man who deserts his family is severely criticized by most "middle-class" persons, but this action is commonly condoned among many "lower-class" people. And the relaxed standards for sexual behavior that are accepted by an increasing number of young people today still dismay their elders. The point to be stressed is that whatever constitutes "deviant action" within any given social organization is determined by its prevailing culture, not by any absolute criteria. Hence "social problems" are always relevant to a given social setting and time.

Whether or not the particular actions that a given organization defines as deviant and attempts to control are actually detrimental to the welfare of that organization is a problematic question open to investigation. But the fact that a particular "deviant action" has no objectively harmful consequences for an organization will not prevent its becoming the object of social control measures if the culture of that organization defines it as deviant. In other words, no matter how effectively an organization controls its members, the exercise of social control never automatically guarantees the preservation of social organization. The crucial factor is whether or not social control operates to encourage those actions which benefit the organization and to prevent those actions which actually do have harmful consequences.

One final point concerning "deviant actions" remains to be noted. Such actions cannot be equated with the broader process of social disorganization. Widespread and prolonged "deviant" activity does at times

---

[9] The fact that the definition of deviancy is always relative to the organization in which it occurs does not rule out the possibility that some actions might be inherently "immoral" when judged by extrahuman or divine principles. But this question is outside the purview of social science.

lead to the disruption or destruction of existing social organizations, but only under certain conditions. "Deviant action" will produce social disorganization—or the breakdown of the total process of social organization —only if: (a) such actions are practiced by large numbers of people over a considerable time, rather than being sporadic actions by isolated individuals; (b) actions defined as deviant are actually detrimental in some way to existing patterns of social order or cultural ideas; (c) these actions are not effectively controlled by the organization; and (d) the organization is already so weakly unified that it cannot absorb or manage whatever conflicts arise as a result of these "deviant actions."

In short, social disorganization is a considerably broader and more complex phenomenon than is "deviant action" by individuals. Furthermore, uncontrolled "deviant" activity is only one possible cause of social disorganization. Patterns of social order and cultural ideas can also be destroyed by such phenomena as conquest by another organization, drastic changes in the natural environment, rapid decline or growth of population, unmanageable technological innovations (such as atomic weapons), unresolved conflicts among the various subunits of the organization, breakdown of internal communications, sharp differences in basic values among organizational subunits, or failure to satisfy any of the other requirements necessary for organizational survival. In fact, "deviant actions" are often not so much a cause of social disorganization as a consequence of this process.

Social organization cannot be preserved for long if social controls— either internal or external—are not exercised in some manner. But the perpetuation of social organization is ultimately dependent upon the adequacy of all the various processes contributing to the creation of organization in social life.

In conclusion, we reiterate the fundamental idea that social control need never be a purely repressive process designed to enforce behavioral conformity for its own sake. Rather, it is through the process of social control that individual participants in social organizations are encouraged to act in socially responsible ways so as to perpetuate these organizations and contribute to the achievement of common goals. Through such organized social activities individuals can gain opportunities and benefits that are unattainable by individual action. Meaningful personal autonomy ultimately results from the assumption of collective responsibilities in organized social life.[10]

---

[10] For a further discussion of this general thesis, see Marvin E. Olsen, "The Mature Society: Personal Autonomy and Social Responsibility," *Michigan Quarterly Review*, vol. 3 (July 1964), pp. 148–159.

At this point we have at last completed our exploration of the basic concepts used by sociologists in their studies of the process and forms of social organization. We have examined the setting in which social organization occurs, the creation of social relationships and patterns of social order, the emergence of shared cultural ideas, numerous features of delineated social entities, various differing types of social organizations, the ways in which individuals participate in social organization through the enactment of social roles, and the social control procedures that contribute to the preservation of social organization. We are now prepared to investigate several fundamental processes that occur within virtually all organizations: social conflict and change, social integration or unification, exertion of social power, and social allocation or stratification.

RECOMMENDED READING

ASCH, S. E., "Effects of Group Pressure upon the Modification and Distortion of Judgments," in Eleanor E. Maccoby, Theodore M. Newcomb, and Eugene L. Hartley, eds., *Readings in Social Psychology*, 3rd ed., pp. 174–183 (New York: Holt, Rinehart and Winston, Inc., 1958).
A classic laboratory example of the ability of group pressures to influence an individual's thoughts and actions.
BERGER, PETER, *Invitation to Sociology*, chaps. 4–5 (Garden City, N.Y.: Doubleday Anchor Books, 1963).
The processes of social control and role enactment are presented and illustrated in a highly readable manner.
COCH, LESTER, AND JOHN R. P. FRENCH, JR., "Overcoming Resistance to Change," in Maccoby, *et al.*, *Readings in Social Psychology*, pp. 233–250. (Also Bobbs-Merrill reprint S-45.)
An experimental study of the use of organizational manipulation as a means of social control.
MEAD, GEORGE HERBERT, *Mind, Self and Society*, pt. III, secs. 20, 22, 27, and pt. IV, sec. 33 (Chicago: University of Chicago Press, 1934).
Highlights of Mead's theory of social organization through social control based on the internalization of the "generalized other" into the "me" of the self.
SCHEIN, EDGAR H., "The Chinese Indoctrination Program for Prisoners of War: A Study of Attempted 'Brainwashing,'" in Maccoby, *et al.*, *Readings in Social Psychology*, pp. 311–334.
The process of "brainwashing" is analyzed as an example of intensive social control.
SHIBUTANI, TAMOTSU, "Reference Groups and Social Control," in Arnold Rose, ed., *Human Behavior and Social Processes*, pp. 128–147 (Boston: Houghton Mifflin Company, 1962).
A discussion of the concept of reference groups and the ways in which this phenomenon produces social control.

CHAPTER 10

The Processes of Social Conflict and Change

The processes to be examined in these next four chapters are perhaps of equal importance for social organization. They all occur, in varying degrees, throughout almost every area of social life, with manifold consequences for the organizations in which they exist. From the perspective of our overall process conception of social organization, however, the phenomena of conflict and change appear to be somewhat more fundamental than the others. If social reality is in fact an ongoing dynamic process, then conflict and change are ubiquitous throughout social life. Our concern here is to gain a basic understanding of both of these processes, not to determine their empirical frequencies, but even the most casual observation of contemporary social life suggest that they are indeed pervasive phenomena. No aspect of social organization is so totally insulated from its surrounding environment that it never encounters external stresses, nor so perfectly ordered that it never experiences internal strains. Disruptive forces are thus constantly impinging upon all social organization from diverse sources. The results are perpetual social conflict and change.

Conflict and change are distinct processes with many different characteristics, and part of our present concern is to conceptualize the essential nature of each. In actual social life, however, they are often interwoven, so that their effects are reciprocal. Neither phenomenon is an imperative cause or consequence of the other, so that either one can exist by itself, but in fact they often occur together and share many common

133

features. For this reason we consider them jointly in a single chapter. We shall also investigate various sources of these processes, two broad theoretical perspectives commonly employed by sociologists to explain them, and several aspects of their management or control.

Nature of Social Conflict

Our common-sense notion of social conflict would probably be of two (or more) actors seeking the same goal, such as two suitors vying for a woman's favors or several lobby groups trying to influence the outcome of a legislative proposal. Further thought readily suggests the possibility of conflicting actors seeking mutually incompatible goals, as when a labor union demands higher wages for its members from a business concern that is trying to hold down mounting production costs. A third possibility would be a single organization beset by internal disputes, as when some congregations of a nationally organized church wish to promote active social change while other congregations prefer to emphasize traditional rituals and services. Another common example of social conflict is role incompatibility and inconsistency, which we have already described. Going still further, we could also point to conflict arising among organizations as they seek to attract and hold members, antagonisms centering on inconsistencies between organizational ideals and actual practices, or attempts by one organization to influence or destroy other organizations. In short, *conflict can arise in any social situation in which two or more actors interact.* This broad proposition excludes intra-individual psychological conflict, but encompasses all social encounters.

It may be noted that some of the conflicts above are located within one organization, whereas others involve relationships between two or more organizations. This distinction between intra- and interorganizational conflict depends entirely on the perspective of the observer. A strike, for instance, can be described either as conflict between a union and a company or as conflict within the economic network of a society.

In this discussion we shall use the term "conflict" in its broadest meaning, to include all of the foregoing examples. In general, *conflict occurs whenever there is discord or opposition between two or more actors within the process of social organization.* Conflict is thus a generic process that contains several subtypes, including competition (orderly pursuit by actors of a prescribed goal), aggression (attempts by one actor to harm or destroy another), hostility (if it is openly expressed between actors), and cleavages (splits among actors or factions of an organization).

Reflected in these subtypes of conflict are several theoretical dimensions along which most instances of social conflict can be classified:[1]

(1) Instrumental versus expressive conflict. Instrumental conflict is marked by opposing practices or goals, whereas expressive conflict results from desires for tension release, from hostile feelings, or from ignorance and error. In other words, instrumental conflict is a means to some other end, whereas expressive conflict is an end in itself.

(2) Inherent versus induced conflict. Inherent conflict arises from irreconcilable differences in a given situation, while induced conflict is "artificially" or purposefully created as a means of gaining other goals—such as prestige among one's supporters.

(3) Ideological versus operational conflict. When a conflict concerns basic values it tends to become ideological in nature, or a question of "right" and "wrong." When a conflict is over operational procedures for obtaining common goals, it is a practical question of "effectiveness" and "ineffectiveness."

(4) Direct versus indirect conflict. Direct conflict involves immediate confrontation among the contesting actors, as in a debate, whereas indirect conflict is mediated through one or more third parties, as in many court cases.

(5) Institutionalized versus noninstitutionalized conflict. The former pole of this continuum is characterized by explicit rules and control procedures designed to keep the conflict within limits and of some benefit to all those involved. The latter end of the continuum is random, unpredictable, and uncontrolled by any larger organizational unit.

Social conflict also normally varies along several different empirical dimensions, the more common of which include: frequency (how often does it occur?), scope (how many actors or what parts of an organization are involved?), intensity (how committed are the participants to the conflict?), duration (how long does it last?), and expression (through what specific activities does it occur?). Any instance of social conflict can be described in terms of all of these variables, but over time such characteristics often change.

Although there is a common tendency to equate conflict with the breakdown of social organization, *conflict is neither identical to nor indicative of social disorganization.* This generalization is supported by two significant observations. First, social conflict frequently exhibits consider-

---

[1] These theoretical dimensions of conflict are summarized by Raymond W. Mack and Richard C. Snyder in "The Analysis of Social Conflict—Toward an Overview and Synthesis," *Journal of Conflict Resolution,* vol. 1 (June 1957), pp. 212–248. These authors derived the dimensions from several other writings.

able patterning or ordering (especially when it is relatively instrumental, practical, and institutionalized), and thus constitutes an established social relationship. In other words, conflict can itself become a type of social ordering within the process of social organization. One researcher, for instance, has identified several distinct stages through which most community controversies pass before they are resolved.[2] Second, conflict can, under certain conditions, promote increased unification or integration of social organization. We shall explore this idea more extensively in the following chapter.

By way of summarizing the essential nature of social conflict, we paraphrase five propositions that Raymond Mack and Richard Snyder suggest as the fundamental properties of all conflict phenomena and situations.[3]

(1) Conflict requires at least two actors (individuals or organizations), since it is by definition an interaction relationship.

(2) Conflict arises from some kind of "scarcity," or desired but limited resources, activities, positions, or goals.

(3) Conflict actions are designed to limit, thwart, destroy, control, or otherwise influence another actor, and a conflict relationship is one in which the actors can gain only at each other's relative expense.

(4) Conflict requires interaction among actors in which their actions and counteractions are mutually opposed.

(5) Conflict relations always involve attempts to acquire or exercise social power.

Nature of Social Change

We have stressed that social conflict and change are intertwined in social life, so that neither process can be fully understood apart from the other. Conflict often produces changes in social organization, conflict frequently accompanies change and becomes an integral part of this process, and change in one area of social life can in turn stimulate additional conflict in other related activities. Social change cannot be equated with social conflict, however, for they are separate processes.

Conflicts among opposing actors normally introduce some amount of discord into existing patterns of social order and shared cultural ideas. As a result, conflict tends to produce variations in social activities. Whether or not these variations have lasting consequences for social organization

---

[2] James Coleman, *Community Conflict* (New York: The Free Press, a division of The Macmillan Compan, 1957), pp. 10–14.

[3] Mack and Snyder, "The Analysis of Social Conflict."

depends on the nature, intensity, resolution, and other features of the conflict situation. In contrast, social change has fairly broad and permanent effects on organized social life. A hobby club debating whether to modify its requirements for membership and expand its scope of activities is engaged in conflict, which might dominate several meetings. Only if the proposal is adopted and carried out is the group actually changed, though, since if it is defeated the club will presumably continue as before (unless, of course, the dissenting members resign and the group collapses). A community conflict centering on whether to construct a new city park results in community change only if the park is actually built and the public recreation program is altered to make use of it. On the national level, a political battle over whether to lower income taxes is not itself a societal change (though it might be a novel activity for the legislature), but the decision on this issue could have untold ramifications throughout the economy and ultimately the entire society.

These illustrations suggest that *we are here conceiving of social change as a relatively extensive and enduring reordering and/or redefining of the process of social organization.* This conception of social change is based on rather arbitrary criteria, however. On the one hand, our underlying process orientation toward social life implies that ongoing social organization is continually fluctuating and varying. From this viewpoint, organization and change are synonymous. On the other hand, sometimes this dynamic process of social organization is noticeably and lastingly shifted or modified in some way. These critical alterations in organized social life are what we normally think of as social changes. But when does a ceaseless process of variation become an identifiable instance of significant social change? Quite obviously there is no sharp dividing line, so that what one calls "social change" is actually an arbitrary decision made by a participant or an outside observer. A particular alteration becomes "social change" when it appears to be relatively extensive and enduring in relation to what has previously occurred in this area of social life. The sociologist usually resolves this dilemma by stating, "For purposes of this study, I shall consider X to be a change, but not Y." When analyzing the operations of a welfare agency, for example, he might treat a temporary modification in the intake interview procedure as a routine variation in work patterns, and focus his attention primarily on broad changes in the authority structure of this organization resulting from the appointment of a new director. In other words, the total social setting and the particular problem under investigation jointly determine what is "fluctuation" and what is "change" in a given situation. As involved participants in ongoing social life, all of us frequently make similar decisions about change and nonchange, although perhaps in a somewhat less conscious manner.

Some changes enter social life so slowly and imperceptibly that we remain unaware of them until after they have fully transpired. This is not the usual case, however, since *most social changes are preceded by conflicts within an organization, and are in turn resisted by forces seeking to prevent change.* An outbreak of open conflict is not imperative for social change, but conflict frequently does promote change. Once people have created workable social organizations within the ongoing processes of social life, they understandably wish to perpetuate these existing patterns of social order and shared cultural ideas. Established social organization can be preserved without keeping it rigid and unchanging, but quite frequently this is what does occur. Although Newton's law of inertia is not inherent in organized social life, people frequently act as if it were. In such situations, conflict is necessary to upset or disrupt established practices before extensive change can take place.

Conflict often promotes social change, but it never automatically results in permanent changes. Social change is only one of a number of possible consequences of disruptive conflicts. Other frequent outcomes of conflict are avoidance or suppression of the conflict situation, standing "agreements to disagree" that quiet the conflict but do not resolve it, compromise solutions that effectively maintain the *status quo,* individual "deviant actions," random fluctuations that have no cumulative effect on the organization, or temporary social adjustments that are discarded after the conflict abates. Only if there is some kind of relatively permanent and extensive alteration in the organization as a result of this conflict can we say that social change has occurred.

A proposed or attempted alteration in social ordering or culture will in turn often generate additional conflict. Resistance to social change is extremely common in social life. Such factors as vested interests in the *status quo,* opposing values and goals, apparent deficiencies and inadequacies in the proposed alteration, perceived intolerable consequences, and sheer human inertia commonly give rise to opposing forces that may succeed in limiting or blocking social change. And even well established changes are often resisted for long periods of time. Thus conflict is a consequence as well as a cause of social change. The ultimate fate of any social change may be said to hang in the balance between the forces producing it and those opposing it.

Resistance to change is sometimes explained in terms of psychological phenomena such as fear of the unknown, reluctance to try something new, or a "closed mind." From an organizational perspective, though, resistance can be seen as an outgrowth of social processes rather than as individual perversity. Members of an organization normally value the social order and shared culture they have created and maintained, because of the

benefits derived from their collective activities. It is not surprising, therefore, that at least some of them will see any given change as destruction
of beneficial organization, not improvement of it. For instance, opposition
to new programs of the federal government and advocacy of increased
power for communities and states within the United States is often explained as "conservative reluctance to change." This political position can
also be interpreted, however, as a defense of traditional American governmental principles. We tend to forget that two hundred years ago this same
position was described as liberal, not conservative, because of its insistence
on local self-determination.

Another factor affecting the degree to which social change is resisted
is the extent to which the values and norms of an organization have become secularized. In many "premodern" societies the dominant cultural
values and norms are viewed as more-or-less sacred commandments,
either given to man by some extrahuman power or else sanctified by
countless generations of belief and practice. People in these societies
commonly find it unthinkable even to question their cultural values or
social practices, let alone change them. Needless to say, such conditions
obstruct all attempts to "modernize" these societies. Sacred outlooks and
beliefs are by no means absent in contemporary "modern" societies, but
they are slowly giving way to secular perspectives on social life. Social
values and norms are increasingly seen as man-made, heuristic guides to
organized social living, and hence open to change whenever necessary
or desirable.

Once a change is introduced into one part of an organization, the
further question remains of how extensively it will influence other parts.
On the one hand, *to the extent that the various subunits of the organization are interrelated and institutionalized, a change in any one part will
tend to have ramifications throughout other parts or the whole organization.* An initial alteration, that is, can set off a chain reaction, or snowball-
ing, of further changes. For example, the introduction of new production
procedures into a factory may alter existing work groups, which in
turn leads to worker demands for union control over job assignments,
which causes the union to grow in size and strength, which forces management to revise many of its policies and programs, which ultimately
changes the structure and functioning of the whole organization. On the
other hand, *to the extent that the various subunits of the organization are
segmented and functionally autonomous, a change in any one part remains isolated in that part.* It will produce few or no corresponding
changes in other parts of the organization. Sometimes this situation will
create no difficulties for the overall organization. At other times, though,
as this one changing part becomes increasingly divergent from the rest

of the organization, serious social problems erupt. An illustration of this phenomenon is seen in many developing nations, in which the military officers become better educated, more "Westernized," and more politically sophisticated than the rest of the people in the society. The frequent outcome of such disparity is a military *coup d'état.*

Another important factor determining the spread of change from one subunit throughout an entire organization is the amount of social power exercised by the part that first changes. In general, *the more powerful the subunit of an organization that initiates a change, the greater will be the effects of this alteration on other parts of the organization.* In contemporary societies, for example, social changes introduced by the national government or by dominant economic concerns (such as major industries or banks) normally produce many more derivative changes throughout the entire society than do alterations initiated by churches or by special-interest associations. From a broader perspective, sociologists often argue that the fundamental processes of industrialization, urbanization, and bureaucratization are drastically affecting all other realms of contemporary societies, including the family, education, religion, race relations, mass communications, and social stratification.

Sources of Conflict and Change

Whenever any events or forces disturb, limit, oppose, sever, destroy, or otherwise disrupt ongoing processes of social organization, conflicts or changes are likely to occur. A complete cataloging and analysis of all possible sources of social conflict and change would be far beyond the scope of this discussion. We can, though, outline and illustrate the more important types. For analytical purposes, *all sources of conflict and change can be divided into two broad categories: (a) sources external to an organization, or stresses; and (b) sources internal to an organization, or strains.*[4] Stresses and strains acting on an organization produce tensions and disruptions within the ongoing process of social organization. These tensions and disruptions do not necessarily lead to conflict or change, since they are often resolved or suppressed in some manner before their presence becomes significant for the organization. In many cases, however, underlying tensions and disruptions do grow into conflicts as they are brought into the open and as involved actors take sides in the controversy and thus

---

[4] Much of the following discussion of sources of social conflict and change is adapted from Wilbert Moore, "A Reconsideration of Theories of Social Change," *American Sociological Review,* vol. 25 (December 1960), pp. 810–818. See also his *Social Change* (Englewood Cliffs, N.J.: Prentice-Hall, Inc., 1963), chaps. 1, 4.

oppose one another. In still other cases, tensions and disruptions caused by stresses and strains eventually result in relatively permanent and extensive social changes.

Let us first examine several sources of external stresses. Because stresses originate outside of a given social organization, they do not automatically produce tensions and disruptions within the organization. Stresses affect the organization only to the extent that they actually influence it in some manner. A famine in China, for instance, would probably have no immediate effects upon the United States. However, if as a result of this famine China should seek to purchase large shipments of grain from the United States, a widespread controversy might be set off in this country, and some of our laws might even be changed. Other types of stresses, meanwhile, have more direct effects upon social organization, producing immediate social tensions and disruptions which in turn often lead to conflicts or changes. Rapid population growth provides an example. The addition of thirty million people to the population of the United States every ten years (which has been the approximate rate for the past several decades) creates countless problems for this society, since communities, schools, transportation and communication networks, governmental programs, business concerns, and many other social activities must all constantly expand.

The major sources of external stresses are the four factors comprising the setting of all social organization—the natural environment, population, the human being, and material technology—plus the social environment within which an organization exists. Stresses from all five of these sources are constantly impinging upon virtually every social organization. Let us briefly examine each of them.

Any major change in the natural environment will have consequences throughout almost all social organization. Climatic alterations, depletion of vital natural resources, natural disasters, disease epidemics, and even a heat spell or a heavy snowfall all exert countless pressures upon organized social life. Apart from such "crisis" situations, stresses also arise from the fact that most natural phenomena (including space, time, and human energy) are necessarily limited in availability and hence must be rationed in use. Scientific discoveries have given us partial control over many natural forces, but their effects upon social organization will not be totally eliminated in the foreseeable future.

The effects of variations in population size and composition upon social organization have already been illustrated in Chapter 3 and need not be repeated here. Nevertheless, *one specific kind of population stress —the "demographic transition"—deserves special mention,* because of its increasing seriousness for many societies throughout the world. Until quite recently, all societies have experienced both high death and high birth rates, which combined to keep their populations stable. With the introduction of better diets, public sanitation practices, and modern medicine, however, the death rate invariably declines—often quite drastically. For some time after that the birth rate often remains high, because of traditional beliefs and values regarding childbearing and ignorance concerning methods of birth control. The result is a population "explosion," as more and more people are born but fewer and fewer die. When and if the birth rate also declines, the population will again be stabilized. Until that happens, however, the society is faced with a multitude of social pressures and problems that can become virtually unresolvable. The best efforts of such a society to raise its standard of living through industrialization may go to naught, as population increase far exceeds economic development.

Personality variations among individuals normally do not directly affect social organizations, unless these individuals occupy positions of extreme power or strategic functional importance. In a collective sense, though, *characteristics of the human being that are vital for the creation of social organization—such as basic needs, intelligence, symbolization ability, and motivations for survival and goal attainment—do vary among populations, and hence can place strains upon any organization.* Of these basic characteristics of the human being, level of intellectual development has perhaps the broadest consequences for social conflict and change. Changes in the overall level of intellectual development of the members of an organization, including amount of knowledge possessed, critical reasoning abilities, and intellectual sophistication, can induce manifold tensions and disruptions. Amount of formal education, which is the best single indicator of intellectual development, is related to a vast range of social and cultural phenomena, and any marked shifts in the educational attainments of the members of an organization will have consequences for many aspects of their collective activities.

The most readily apparent source of external stresses upon social organizations is material technology. Every major advance in material technology, from fire-making to atomic fission, has disrupted established patterns of social life in some way. A prominent example is the automobile, which has altered vast portions of American society in the past two generations, including suburbanization trends, courtship practices, friendship ties, recreation activities, economic markets, and governmental jurisdictions. Electronic communications have had equally far-reaching consequences for contemporary societies. One sociologist has compiled a list of 150 social changes in American society resulting from the invention of the radio,[5] and a similar list for television might be much longer.

[5] William F. Ogburn, *Recent Social Trends* (New York: McGraw-Hill, Inc., 1933), pp. 153–156.

A challenging topic for study—about which we know very little—is why innovation (invention and discovery) occurs when it does. One suggestive approach to this question is William Ogburn's theory of cultural accumulation.[6] He points out that innovation cannot take place until the necessary background knowledge, or cultural base, has been accumulated. Since any innovation is essentially an outgrowth or new synthesis of previously existing information, this contributory knowledge must first exist. Once the necessary cultural base for a particular innovation has been developed, however, it is only a matter of time until that innovation occurs. Ogburn attempted to substantiate his theory by studying simultaneous inventions. Numerous inventions have been made at approximately the same time by two or more persons who worked independently of each other but who presumably shared the same cultural base of information. To cite a few examples: the printing press was invented by Coster in 1423 and by Gutenberg in 1443, photography was developed by both Daguerre and Talbot in 1839, and the telegraph was invented by Henry in 1831 and by Morse, Cooke-Wheatstone, and Steinheil, all in 1837. Ogburn's theory is not wholly adequate, since in effect it simply says that innovations occur because other innovations have previously occurred and been retained in the culture, but it does shed some light on an otherwise largely unexplored topic.[7]

No organization—except for the most isolated of primitive tribes—itself creates most of the material technology it uses. Diffusion, or the spreading of ideas and objects from one organization to another, has occurred throughout human history, although faster and further today than ever before. As a consequence, most social organizations are constantly bombarded with new technology. These ideas and objects may be ignored, rejected, altered, or adopted, but in any case they place stresses upon an organization and hence often produce conflict and change. A family quarrels over whether or not to buy a color television set, a school reorganizes its curriculum to incorporate teaching machines, a community encounters severe economic problems when hundreds of its workers are replaced by automatic machines, and a small nation suddenly finds itself listened to in the United Nations after it has acquired atomic weapons from its allies. In short, as material technology is created and then diffused throughout the world, few organizations can escape the stresses that it introduces.

The social environment of any organization includes all other organizations with which it comes into contact. *As an organization acts to*

[6] William F. Ogburn, *Social Change* (New York: The Viking Press, Inc., 1922), chap. 5, 6.

[7] For a more psychologically oriented discussion of innovation, see Richard T. LaPiere, *Social Change* (New York: McGraw-Hill, Inc., 1965), especially chap. 4.

perpetuate itself and achieve its goals, it must continually take account of limits, demands, and restrictions imposed by its social environment. An organization will have to compete with other organizations for members or resources, it will have to deal with demands and activities of these other organizations, it may have to abide by policies and laws imposed upon it by them, it will have to adjust to changes in their activities, and it often depends upon them for the attainment of whatever goals it seeks. All of these forces act as stresses upon the organization, creating numerous tensions and disruptions which often lead to conflict or change. Mankind may be slowly reducing the influences of the natural environment upon social life, but modern communication and transportation are continually increasing social interdependence and hence the size and complexity of the social environment with which any organization must contend.

Consider, for example, a small, "independent" retail store. This business relies upon several wholesalers for the goods it sells. It must abide by numerous federal, state, and local laws. It may be pressured by labor unions to handle only union-made items, by churches to remain closed on Sunday, or by ethnic associations to hire clerks with certain ethnic characteristics. It utilizes newspapers and other communication media for advertising. And it will remain in business only as long as members of the community patronize it.

Internal strains constitute the second category of sources of conflict and change. Because strains originate within a social organization, they will inevitably produce disruptions and tensions in that organization. They represent disjunctions, fissures, and ruptures occurring in the organization itself, and hence cannot be ignored or escaped. All organizations continuously experience many diverse kinds of internal strains. For this reason social theorists often speak of social conflict and change as immanent and universal within social organization.[8] The first major spokesman for this point of view was Karl Marx, who argued that human history tends to follow a dialectic process.[9] From a dialectic perspective any given social situation (a thesis) contains the seeds of, and eventually gives birth to, a fundamentally different and opposing social situation (an antithesis), which then conflicts with the original situation until a third set of social conditions (a synthesis) emerges that incorporates and unifies all previously existing conditions into a totally new (and presumably superior) type of social organization. We do not have to accept a rigid dialectic perspective—which most Western theorists today reject—to appreciate the

[8] Pitirim A. Sorokin, *Social and Cultural Dynamics* (Boston: Porter Sargent, 1957), chap. 38.

[9] T. B. Bottomore and Maximilien Rubel, *Karl Marx: Selected Writings in Sociology and Social Philosophy* (London: C. A. Watts & Co., Ltd., 1956).

supreme importance Marx attached to perpetual conflict and dynamic change within man's social life.

The major sources of internal strains can conveniently be classified into three main subcategories: individual, cultural, and functional (or operational) disjunctions.

Disjunctions between individual actions and established patterns of social order take many forms, all of which frequently result in organizational strains. First of all, most individuals at least sometimes act as relatively independent elements seeking their own personal goals, rather than as responsible parts of social organizations. As long as the other persons with whom this individual interacts do not expect him to act as a member of a common organization, no strains need arise. But if these interaction partners are acting as members of an organization and also expect our individual to responsibly carry out a role as part of that organization, strains will be generated.

"Deviant actions"—from simple violations of customs to serious crimes—are another source of social strain within this first subcategory. Sociologists commonly attribute such actions to weak or ineffectual social control procedures. Lack of adequate social sanctions within an organization, for instance, unquestionably gives rise to numerous strains, as when a police force is unable to control a riot or a factory cannot prevent substandard work. We must, however, avoid carrying this thinking to its extreme by assuming that all "social problems" and "deviant actions" are due simply to poor techniques of external social control. Most organizations make no attempt to impose total social conformity upon their members—if that were even possible. Limited social control can have many beneficial consequences for social organization, despite attendant strains, by allowing members to exercise a certain amount of initiative and creativity in their actions, thus keeping the organization flexible.

The benefits for organizations of limited demands upon individual members are especially evident in the process of role enactment. As we have already seen, open competition for roles, a wide range of available roles, and nonspecific role expectations all tend to promote organizational flexibility and operational effectiveness as well as freedom of individual action. Beyond these features of role enactment, some organizations are more or less purposefully arranged to promote individual choice and variation in role actions, as in political elections and economic markets within Western societies. But to gain these benefits an organization must bear the price of a certain amount of social strain.

Disjunctions between cultural ideas and patterns of social order are caused by discrepancies or changes within the culture of an organization, which then produce strains throughout the organization. Two or more sets of sharply disparate social values, for example, might be contained within the same culture. Examples would be religious demands for moral virtues versus secular concerns with "having a good time," or traditional ideas of thrift, hard work, and self-reliance versus contemporary emphasis on cooperation as a "member of the team." To the extent that such sets of values are irreconcilable, social strains are bound to occur.

Social conflict can erupt within an organization if the norms and rules being observed are not congruent with basic values. As an illustration, the values of a community might unequivocally hold that drinking, gambling, and other such "vices" are morally wrong, while at the same time many residents might covertly accept the norm that these activities are perfectly acceptable as long as they are done in private. Similarly, the government of a community might loudly deplore "creeping influences" of the national government, but simultaneously argue that participation in a federally sponsored urban renewal program is in keeping with long-standing traditions of community improvement.

The norms and rules of an organization also frequently contain internal inconsistencies that place strains on the organization. The by-laws of a labor union, for example, might state that no discrimination will be practiced against members because of race, religion, or nationality, but also stipulate that all new applicants must be personally recommended by a present member, almost all of whom are white, Anglo-Saxon Protestants. Or consider a family whose norms simultaneously prescribe joint decision-making on all major issues but proscribe the wife from having any say about what job her husband takes.

Just as changes in material technology often disrupt organizations, so innovation or diffusion of social technology will commonly introduce social strains. One well-known illustration makes this point evident: Henry Ford pioneered industrial mass-production techniques as a means of building cars inexpensively, but the rapid diffusion of his idea throughout most other industries also introduced such far-reaching consequences as loss of meaning in work, elimination of small handicraft producers, creation of complex and highly centralized business concerns, growth of industrial labor unions, and governmental programs to regulate mass production.

Finally, it hardly needs to be pointed out that actual social practices in all organizations at best only approximate cultural ideals, and often diverge widely from them. The Soviet Union expounds ideals of economic equality for all, but actually evidences at least as much economic stratification as other industrialized societies, while the United States believes in full political democracy but systematically prohibits several million people from voting because of overt residency and covert racial restrictions. On the local level, there is in most communities a marked correlation between a family's socio-economic status and the quality of education its children receive, despite our insistence on the importance of free and equal education for all. To a degree, "imperfections" such as these are probably inevitable in social life. Nevertheless, such disparities between cultural ideals and actual social practices invariably create strains within social organization and frequently lead to social conflicts or changes.

Functional (or operational) strains in social organization arise within patterns of social order, as a consequence of their structures and modes of functioning. Most of these strains center around one (or more) of four situations that occur in all organizations: incomplete fulfillment of organizational requirements, differences in activities and power of partially autonomous subunits, allocation of organizational benefits, and demands for centralized coordination and control.

a A brief review of the list of typical social requirements facing all organizations (given in Chapter 4) should convince us that these requirements can become overwhelming. No social organization can simultaneously satisfy all of its survival and operational requirements. It must assign some kind of priority ranking to its functional requirements, focusing its activities on the critical ones and at least temporarily deemphasizing or ignoring others. Laboratory studies of small groups have indicated that they tend to progress through a fairly standardized series of phases or stages, each of which emphasizes one specific type of functional requirement.[10] The point here is that priority ranking of organizational requirements and phase movements among various types of requirements will invariably introduce strains into social organization. And we must add that organizations often fail to satisfy functional requirements even when they are receiving priority attention.

b The component subunits of any social entity will usually have some degree of functional autonomy apart from the total organization. The very fact that they can act at times as relatively autonomous social elements is enough to ensure that strains will emerge within the organization. To the extent that subunits do act to gain their own self-oriented goals and hence compete with each other in their activities, rather than working for the welfare of the organization as a whole, tensions and disruptions will multiply. This type of social strain becomes particularly acute when power differentials develop among the various component units as a result of unequal resources, size, control over communication, or operational effectiveness. Power differentials often lead to such phenomena as domination, exploitation, coalition formation, and open "warfare," all of which further disrupt the encompassing organization.

[10] R. F. Bales and F. L. Strodtbeck, "Phases in Group Problem-Solving," *The Journal of Abnormal and Social Psychology,* vol. 46 (1951), pp. 485–495.

c. Another related process is allocation, or the distributing of the benefits of organizational activities among subunits. Leaving aside the strains engendered when one or a few dominant parts commandeer most of the benefits for themselves, there is the inevitable dispute between "fair" and "equal" distribution. The parts that are larger or that contribute more toward organizational operations will often demand "fair" distribution of benefits (rewards based on size or activities performed), while smaller or less involved parts will commonly demand "equal" distribution (rewards the same to all parts). Furthermore, whenever some parts of the organization feel that they are being systematically deprived of their just rewards, they are likely to demand alterations in the allocation process, either through peaceful changes (the "haves" share more with the "have nots") or through violence (the "have nots" forcibly take from the "haves"). The process of allocating organizational benefits to subunits will thus almost unavoidably disrupt social organization to some extent.

d. The last of these operational problems within all organizations stems from the functional necessity for some degree of overall direction, coordination, and control. To the extent that the subunits of an organization are functionally specialized, they tend to become interdependent upon each other and hence interact within complex exchange networks. To promote and maintain these interdependent relationships, the organization must exercise some centralized control if it is not to disintegrate. Pressures will mount for it to establish procedural rules and laws, enforce them, and settle problems among subunits. Nevertheless, development of centralized coordination and control procedures necessarily imposes restrictions upon the subunits and requires them to surrender at least some power and functional autonomy to the larger organization. They may vigorously resist such moves toward increased centralization, especially when these appear to be in excess of what is functionally imperative for the survival of the total organization. Such a situation clearly invites the appearance of strains, conflicts, and changes within an organization.

In summary, the various sources of social stresses and strains discussed in this section are listed in Table 10-1. We note again that tensions and disruptions—and often also conflicts and changes—are ubiquitous throughout all organized social life, as the result of both constant external stresses and inevitable internal strains. In the words of Ralf Dahrendorf: "The notion that wherever there is social life there is conflict may be unpleasant and disturbing. Nevertheless, it is indispensable to our understanding of social problems. . . . Not the presence but the absence of conflict is surprising and abnormal."[11]

[11] Ralf Dahrendorf, "Out of Utopia: Toward Reorientation of Sociological Analysis," *The American Journal of Sociology*, vol. 64 (September 1958), pp. 115–127.

TABLE 10–1
Sources of Social Conflict

I. External Stresses

    1. The natural environment
    2. Population changes and imbalances
    3. Human characteristics, especially level of intellectual development
    4. Innovation and diffusion of material technology
    5. The social environment surrounding an organization

II. Internal Strains

    1. Disjunction between individual actions and social order
       a. Individuals acting as elements when expected to act as parts
       b. Individual "deviant behavior"
       c. Assignment and enactment of social roles

    2. Disjunction between culture and social order
       a. Sets of disparate social values
       b. Incongruencies between basic values and norms and rules
       c. Inconsistencies among norms and rules
       d. Innovation and diffusion of social technology
       e. Discrepancies between cultural ideals and actual social practices

    3. Disjunctions within the social order of an organization
       a. Disregard or inadequate fulfillment of organizational needs
       b. Differences in activities and power among partially autonomous subunits
       c. Allocation of the benefits of organizational functioning
       d. Necessity for centralized coordination and control

Theories of Conflict and Change

Given ever-present stresses and strains acting upon social organizations to produce tensions and disruptions, our next problem is to construct a theoretical explanation of the process through which these stresses and strains lead to open conflict and especially to relatively permanent organizational change. Unfortunately, sociology does not yet have a general theory to predict the probable outcomes of any given conflict, or to explain why social change occurs in one situation but not in another. Even more sophisticated would be a theory indicating the process through which social conflict leads to various kinds of social change.[12] From a broader

[12] Some attempts have been made to discover social conditions and forces leading to political revolutions. See James C. Davies, "Toward a Theory of Revolution," *American Sociological Review*, vol. 27 (February 1962), pp. 5–19.

viewpoint, though, we can identify two kinds of theorizing, or "schools of theoretical thought," in contemporary sociology concerning social conflict and change. Neither of these constitutes a general theory, but both do offer useful insights. We shall call them the "adjustment" and "power" perspectives on conflict and change.

The adjustment perspective stresses the functional requirements that all organizations must satisfy if they are to persist through time and attain collective goals. Of particular importance, for both survival and operational reasons, are certain "key features" that determine the basic nature of an organization and influence or shape most of its activities. These key features vary among organizations and over time within an organization, but they frequently include such characteristics as organizational boundaries, internal patterns of social order, overall organizational unity, centralized decision-making procedures, or major cultural values. The key features of an organization need not remain static, and in fact are often dynamic processes that change through time, but whatever happens to them will have manifold consequences for the entire organization.

Beginning with this empirical observation, the adjustment perspective goes on to suggest that *whenever stresses or strains seriously threaten the key features of an organization—whatever they might be—the organization will very likely initiate compensatory actions to counter these disruptions, in an attempt to preserve its key features.* These compensatory activities sometimes successfully nullify or resolve the stresses and strains before they affect the organization's key features, while at other times they fail in this task. In either case, *considerable conflict is almost invariably created within the organization or between it and its environment, and widespread changes are likely to occur throughout the organization.* If these compensatory activities successfully defend the threatened key features, then whatever changes do occur will be confined to other, less crucial organizational characteristics or activities. In other words, the major outlines and key features of the organization are protected against disruptive stresses and strains, but as a direct consequence of continual changes *within* the organization. To the extent that the organization successfully practices such adjustive maneuvers, it survives through time as a relatively stable social entity and functions effectively to obtain whatever goals it seeks.

There are limits, however, beyond which adjustive or counterbalancing activities and changes cannot go if the organization as a whole is to be maintained in its present form. When disruptive stresses and strains or their resulting conflicts are so severe and prolonged that compensatory mechanisms cannot cope with them, the key organizational features being protected will themselves be altered or destroyed. The entire organization then changes; there is change *of* the organization rather than just within the organization. The nature and extent of this total organizational change will depend on numerous factors, such as the strength of the disruptive forces, the particular key features affected, the degree to which various organizational subunits are institutionalized, and the previously existing overall unity and stability of the organization.

This distinction between change "within" and "of" organizations is admittedly arbitrary, depending on which features of the organization are taken to be crucial and which merely peripheral, and on how much variation can occur in a key feature before it is considered to have changed, but the distinction is useful for certain analytical purposes. In either situation, nevertheless, *social conflict and change are seen as the results of a process of constant adjustment by an organization to disruptive stresses and strains that threaten its key features.* From this perspective, conflict and change represent a perpetual process of social reorganization.[13]

A radically different conception of social conflict and change is held by theorists who stress the crucial importance of power in social organization. This perspective also begins with an empirical observation concerning the activities of all organizations, and then proceeds to explain conflict and change as an outgrowth of these activities. The component subunits of an organization virtually always possess some amount of functional autonomy, or ability to act independently of the larger organization. At times, therefore, they will tend to act as self-oriented elements, rather than as collectively oriented parts. They will temporarily seek to deal with their own internal problems and to achieve their own goals, rather than contribute to the functioning of the encompassing organization.

At this point the power perspective steps in to explain the creation of social conflict and change. *To the extent that organizational subunits act as elements rather than as parts, their activities will necessarily create conflicts within the organization*—for two reasons. First, they will remain interdependent upon, and interrelated with, many other organizational subunits, with whom they must contend. These other subunits will therefore obstruct and limit any unit attempting to act independently, at least partially thwarting its activities. Second, the larger organization usually expects this subunit to continue acting as a responsible part rather than as an autonomous element. Consequently, it will exert various forms of social power upon the subunit, thus generating additional conflict. Not all such

[13] For a sophisticated elaboration and defense of this theoretical perspective, see Francesca Cancian, "Functional Analysis of Change," *American Sociological Review,* vol. 25 (December 1960), pp. 818–827. See also Talcott Parsons, "Some Considerations on the Theory of Social Change," *Rural Sociology,* vol. 26 (1961), pp. 219–239.

conflict necessarily produces soci:.l change, but change is one frequent outcome. More specifically, *relatively permanent change in or of the larger organization results from the use of social power by subunits attempting to gain their own goals.* Partially autonomous subunits must exercise power in relation to other subunits and the larger organization if they are to succeed in these endeavors. Necessary resources must be procured, existing relationships with other subunits must be altered and new ones created, and the encompassing organization must be induced to meet the demands of these self-acting units. As power is successfully employed by subunits in these directions, both they and the larger organization are very likely to change.

The power explanation of conflict and change places special emphasis on the actions of those subunits which wield predominant amounts of power over all other subunits and even the whole organization. The exercise of power by such elites will normally result in opposition and alterations throughout the entire organization. In effect, then, social conflict and change in organizations are often consequences of actions and activities by powerful elite subunits. Regardless of whether or not such elites purposefully attempt to influence other subunits or the larger organization, their activities will necessarily have ramifications throughout the entire organization of which they are a part. In short, *social conflict and change result from the exercise of social power by subunits of an organization acting as partially independent elements in pursuit of their own goals.* From this perspective, conflict and change represent a perpetual process of social disruption.[14]

At first glance, the adjustment and power conceptions of conflict and change may appear wholly contradictory. Further examination, however, reveals that although they do offer quite divergent explanations of how and why conflict and change occur, they are in fact largely complementary. Each simply orients the observer to different aspects of the broader processes of conflict and change. The fundamental distinction lies in the focus of one's analysis. The adjustment perspective focuses on a given organization as a single entity, assumes that its subunits are at least temporarily acting as institutionalized parts, and then attempts to explain how this organization reacts to external stresses and internal strains. The power perspective focuses on the various organizational subunits, assumes that they are at least temporarily acting as functionally autonomous elements, and attempts to explain how their actions influence the rest of the organization.

---

[14] The major source of this perspective is the writings of Karl Marx, in Bottomore and Rubel, *Karl Marx: Selected Writings.* A leading contemporary spokesman for this position is Ralf Dahrendorf, *Class and Class Conflict in Industrial Society* (Stanford, Calif.: Stanford University Press, 1959), chap. 5.

Partial convergence of the two perspectives is readily apparent once we remember that any given organization can be viewed and analyzed either as a separate entity or as a subunit of a larger whole. The threatening stresses and strains that the adjustment perspective takes as given phenomena are frequently power demands of other related organizations, more encompassing entities, or component subunits. And the independent goal-seeking actions of subunits that the power perspective takes as given phenomena are frequently these units' attempts to protect their own key features through adjustive measures. Quite obviously, a more comprehensive theory of social conflict and change must somehow synthesize these two viewpoints by explaining when and how both adjustment and power activities contribute to social organization.[15]

Management of Conflict and Change

As social organizations experience conflict and change resulting from either adjustive or power processes, they react to these phenomena in various ways. Some organizations view conflict and change as essentially undesirable because of the resulting disruptions or alterations in established social practices, and hence they seek to prevent or suppress these processes whenever possible. Other organizations remain basically neutral in their responses to conflict and change, neither discouraging nor encouraging them, but simply accepting them as they happen to occur and letting them resolve themselves. Still other organizations view conflict and change as essentially desirable as long as they can be kept within broad limits and can be constructively utilized, which necessitates developing procedures for managing these processes. What we are here describing is a continuum along which all social organizations can be classified, depending on the degree to which they purposefully promote, manage, and utilize social conflict and change. The principal means of promoting or encouraging these processes in an organization is to grant all subunits some amount of functional autonomy—or conversely, to refrain from totally institutionalizing all subunits. Several ways in which conflict and change can be used to benefit an organization are discussed in the next chapter. The idea of managing conflict and change requires further elaboration, however.

As ongoing social processes, *conflict and change can often be ordered, so that they follow fairly regular and predictable patterns.* To accomplish this, organizations must create numerous means of effectively managing

---

[15] A number of suggestive ideas along these lines are given in Pierre van den Berghe, "Dialectic and Functionalism," *American Sociological Review*, vol. 27 (October 1963), pp. 695–705.

and resolving conflict and change whenever they occur. Typical management techniques include established procedures for bringing together opposing sides of a conflict, for promoting full communication among them, for achieving mutually satisfactory compromises or other solutions to conflicts, for developing compensatory mechanisms to deal with threatening stresses and strains, for enabling all actors or subunits affected by a change to make necessary adjustments in their own activities, and for limiting the amount of power that any actor or subunit can exercise over the rest of the organization. Labor-management negotiations, as currently practiced in many industries in the United States, provide an example of the application of such management techniques to one type of conflict. They constitute an organized means whereby the contending parties can peacefully resolve their differences and achieve changes that often benefit all parties involved.

The extent and success of these management procedures largely determine what kinds of conflict and change occur in an organization. For analytical purposes, social conflict and change are sometimes described as either sporadic or continuous, although there are innumerable intermediate combinations. *If an organization suppresses conflict and resists change, these processes will occur only sporadically.* They cannot be totally eliminated, however, since stresses and strains never cease acting upon an organization. If the pressures they generate are not brought into the open in some manner, tensions will continue to build up within the organization. Eventually they may become uncontainable and will erupt into sharp conflicts and abrupt changes, which then seriously disrupt, alter, or even destroy the entire organization. Strikes, divorces, race riots, and political revolutions are common manifestations of this kind of drastic conflict and change.

In contrast, *if an organization encourages the expression of conflict through established procedures and allows as much change as possible, these processes will then occur relatively continuously.* No single conflict or change will be very disruptive or extensive—indeed, they may often go largely unnoticed—but over time the cumulative effects of many minor alterations will produce widespread social change and continued organizational stability. Such organizations are spared the throes of violent conflict and abrupt change, since stresses and strains are resolved as they arise rather than being allowed to mount up over time. Continuous conflict and change is achieved through the use of such techniques as labor-management grievance committees, marital counseling, community human relations commissions, and political elections.

Organizations falling at the former pole of this theoretical continuum are frequently described as rigid, whereas those at the latter pole are flexible.[16] *A rigid organization suppresses conflict and resists change as much as possible.* Such tactics will frequently enable it to survive for some time. But because it cannot resolve stresses and strains and adjust to new conditions, these disruptive forces are likely sooner or later to overcome their bonds and explode in rapid and often violent social conflict and change. Nevertheless, in some organizations at some times, relative rigidity may be the most effective means of preserving crucial values or other organizational characteristics.

At the other end of the scale, *a flexible organization allows and even encourages conflict and change that follow established procedures.* Because of its ceaseless activity, such an organization appears at any given time to be rather unstable. But because it resolves stresses and strains as they arise and is capable of adjusting to new conditions, the resulting gradual but continual conflict and change may give this organization great stability in the long run. In some cases, though, flexibility may purchase organizational stability at the price of sacrificing traditional practices and beliefs.

In final summary, the main point of this chapter has been that conflict and change are ubiquitous throughout organized social life, as a result of numerous stresses and strains that perpetually act upon all organizations. These phenomena are inherent aspects of social organization and do not negate this overall process, though they often disrupt or alter it. Conflict and change often display considerable patterning, and hence can be studied as ordered social processes. The ways in which an organization responds to and manages conflict and change nevertheless have broad consequences for the overall functioning and structure of that organization.

The process of social integration, to be examined in the next chapter, is often thought of as the opposite of conflict and change. As we shall presently see, though, these phenomena can in fact reinforce rather than contradict each other.

[16] For a more extensive discussion of these concepts, see Lewis A. Coser, "Social Conflict and the Theory of Social Change," *British Journal of Sociology,* vol. 8 (September 1957), pp. 197–207.

RECOMMENDED READING

COLEMAN, JAMES, *Community Conflict* (New York: The Free Press, a division of The Macmillan Company, 1957).
    An exploration and analysis of the process of social conflict as it occurs in communities.

Coser, Lewis A., "Social Conflict and the Theory of Social Change," *The British Journal of Sociology*, vol. 8 (September 1957), pp. 197–207. (Also Bobbs-Merrill reprint S-51.)
Discusses the phenomena of social conflict and change, suggests several beneficial consequences of conflict, presents the concepts of rigid and flexible organizations, and sketches the relationship between conflict and integration.

Dahrendorf, Ralf, "Toward a Theory of Social Conflict," *Journal of Conflict Resolution*, vol. 2 (1958), pp. 170–183.
Presents a view of social organization that stresses ubiquitous social conflict, together with a sketch of the power theory of social change.

Mack, Raymond W., and Richard C. Snyder, "The Analysis of Social Conflict—Toward an Overview and Synthesis," *Journal of Conflict Resolution*, vol. 1 (June 1957), pp. 212–248. (Also Bobbs-Merrill reprint PS-177.)
Summarizes and evaluates much of the literature on social conflict and attempts to clarify various aspects of this phenomenon.

Moore, Wilbert E., *Social Change*, chaps. 1, 2, 5 (Englewood Cliffs, N.J.: Prentice-Hall, Inc., 1963).
An introductory presentation of the major concepts, causes, processes, and trends of social change.

Thompson, James D., "Organizational Management of Conflict," *Administrative Science Quarterly*, vol. 4 (March 1960), pp. 389–409. (Also Bobbs-Merrill reprint PS-282.)
Outlines several ways in which organizations seek to manage and control social conflict.

van den Berghe, Pierre, "Dialectic and Functionalism," *American Sociological Review*, vol. 28 (October 1963), pp. 695–705.
Contrasts and compares the "adjustment" and "power" theoretical perspectives on social change and suggests several lines of convergence between them.

CHAPTER 11

The Process of Social Integration

Conflict and change pervade all social organization, but equally fundamental is the process of social integration. As delineated social entities are created through the process of social organization, they must develop some degree of unity or integration if they are to survive or function effectively. An organization lacking such unity can be destroyed by the slightest disruption. Rudimentary social organization exists whenever social interactions become patterned, recurrent, and meaningful, but the social entities resulting from this process will constitute viable organizations only to the extent that they become integrated. This process gives an organization strength to handle stresses and strains, stability through time, and operational effectiveness.

Nature of Social Integration

Through the process of social integration the subunits of an organization become bound together, so that the organization acquires a wholeness greater than the sum of its parts. A relatively integrated organization has solidarity or cohesion; it ceases to be a mere collection of diverse activities, but rather can act as a single unified entity. Formally defined, *social integration is the process in which the component parts of an or-*

ganization become united so as to give unity to the total organization.[1] Virtually all organizations possess some degree of integration, but its quality and quantity vary widely. In other words, social integration is not a single or fixed condition, but rather a variable phenomenon with several dimensions.[2]

Thus conceived, social integration is always a property of an organization as a whole, not of its subunits or of its individual members. We must, then, distinguish integration from two other related but different phenomena. First, subunits vary in the extent to which they are dependent upon the total organization. The poles of this continuum, which we have already examined, are institutionalization and segmentation. Second, individual members vary in the strength of their ties to the organization and its subunits. One person might be intensely involved, while for another person the organization might be of marginal significance. The degree to which the total organization is integrated remains a separate question, however. Failure to distinguish between organizational integration and individuals' ties to the organization can produce much analytical confusion. Too often, for instance, we speak first of a community as being highly unified, and then of the strong bonds or ties that individuals feel toward the community, without distinguishing between these two meanings of social integration. This latter process of binding or linking individuals into organizations might more properly be called assimilation—as it is in ethnic relations theory. The three phenomena of organizational integration, institutionalization, and assimilation are interrelated, in that it is virtually impossible for an organization to be highly unified if its subunits are relatively segmented and its members are only weakly assimilated. For conceptual and analytical clarity, however, it is necessary to distinguish among these processes. Our concern in this chapter is solely with organizational integration.

We must also avoid confusing social integration with social organization. Integration is a more limited phenomenon, which occurs within the broader process of social organization. Patterns of social order and shared cultural ideas can be created without integration of the resulting organizational entities. Put differently, the actions that create social order and culture are not the ones that produce social integration. Hence all degrees

---

[1] Although in the United States today "integration" often means "racial integration," the unifying of diverse ethnic populations into a single society is only one instance of the generic process of social integration.

[2] For a summary of current theories and research on social integration see Robert C. Angell, "Social Integration," to be published in the forthcoming new edition of the *International Encyclopedia of the Social Sciences* (New York, The Macmillan Company). Many of the ideas presented in the present discussion were sketched in Marvin E. Olsen, "Durkheim's Two Concepts of Anomie," *The Sociological Quarterly*, vol. 6 (April 1965), pp. 37–44.

of integration can occur within any given organization. The importance of this distinction is particularly evident in the case of organizations created through the use of force. The application of force—from either external or internal sources—can produce a certain amount of social order, and in some cases is the main or only factor sustaining an organization. By itself, though, force does not appear to be an adequate basis for organizational integration. If a nonintegrated organization is being maintained solely by the exercise of force—or more generally, by social power of any type—its ability to survive through time and to achieve goals will remain highly precarious. The organization will lack inner unity and stability, it will probably not possess any single set of pervasive values and norms, its component parts will be in constant conflict with each other, it will be quite vulnerable to disruptive stresses and strains, and it will operate effectively only to the extent that power is applied directly to it. In short, social power often creates social ordering, and it is a vital factor in the activities of virtually all organizations, but it cannot integrate diverse social relationships, patterns of social order, and cultural ideas into a single, unified organizational entity. (Power can be used, of course, to generate the conditions that in turn lead to integration, but this is a two-step process.) For these reasons, most sociological writings on social integration have excluded the use of force as a means of unifying organizations.

Theories of Social Integration

Two basic theories of social integration have pervaded social thought since ancient times. These two explanations of how all social organizations achieve and maintain unity are usually called normative and functional integration, although the terms "consensual" and "symbiotic" integration are also used, while Robert Angell has proposed calling them the "common orientation" and "interdependence" theories.[3]

[3] Angell, "Social Integration." A third distinct type of social cohesion—affective integration, or what Angell calls the "interpersonal" theory—has also been identified. It is based on personal attraction, friendship, and other emotional ties among all the members of a group. Shared affectivity is obviously extremely important in holding together families and some small groups, but it cannot have significant effects for larger organizations in which the members do not know each other personally. Because of its limited applicability, affectual integration is not included in the present discussion. Werner Landecker ["Types of Integration and Their Measurement," *American Journal of Sociology*, vol. 56 (January 1951), pp. 332–340] once proposed a fourth type of social integration, based on the extent and effectiveness of the communications within an organization. As Angell points out, however, adequate communication is a necessary requirement for any kind of integration, rather than being a distinct type itself.

The theory of *normative integration,* which has tended to dominate contemporary sociology, has been stressed in the writings of Talcott Parsons and several of his colleagues.[4] This explanation of social integration begins with the assumption of a number of basic values that are shared by a population as a result of a common or similar cultural heritage. These values are expressed more specifically and applied to actual social situations through a set of shared moral norms, which may or may not be codified as laws. To preserve their values and attain common goals, the people then establish social organizations that are infused with these values and that operate in accordance with accepted norms. Such organizations in turn shape individuals—through role acting and norm internalization—who cherish the fundamental values and seek to perpetuate them through their actions as responsible members of the organization. In sum, *a social organization becomes normatively integrated as norms based on common values are imbedded within it and internalized by its members.*

The degree of normative integration in any social organization thus depends on such factors as (a) extent of consensus on basic values and absence of any antithetical values, (b) development of an adequate and internally consistent set of norms (that is, lack of anomie[5]), (c) relative congruence between values and norms, so that adherence to norms leads to realization of goals derived from the values, (d) degree to which common norms are infused into specific organizations, so as to keep organizational activities in line with basic values, and (e) effectiveness of role training and norm internalization procedures for individuals.

The theory of *functional integration* is closely associated with the work of Amos Hawley[6] and other social ecologists. The initial assumption of this explanation of social integration is the existence of some division of labor among a number of social actors. As these differentiated actors become specialized in their activities, they lose self-sufficiency and grow increasingly interdependent upon each other. Interdependence necessitates the formation of complementary exchange relationships among these specialized units. The creation of such interdependent relationships unites the actors into an organization. To promote and maintain their relation-

---

[4] See especially his "An Outline of the Social System," in Talcott Parsons, *et al.,* eds., *Theories of Society* (New York: The Free Press, a division of The Macmillan Company, 1961), pp. 30–79.

[5] Anomie is a condition within social organizations in which the social norms are inadequate to guide and direct the actions of individuals and subparts in the interests of the total organization. See Émile Durkheim, *Suicide,* trans. John Spaulding and George Simpson (New York: The Free Press, a division of The Macmillan Company, 1951), pp. 246–258.

[6] See especially his "Human Ecology," to be published in the forthcoming new edition of the *International Encyclopedia of the Social Sciences* (New York: The Macmillan Company).

ships, furthermore, procedural rules must be formulated and some kind of administrative unit must be established to coordinate and regulate all activities within the total organization. In sum, *a social organization becomes functionally integrated as complementary relationships among specialized and interdependent subparts are established and maintained through unified coordination.*

The degree of functional integration existing in any social organization is thus determined by such factors as (a) extent of specialization or division of labor among its component parts, (b) establishment and maintenance of complementary relationships among these interdependent parts, (c) presence of adequate and internally consistent procedural rules to guide these relationships (that is, lack of discordance[7]), (d) effectiveness of the overall coordinating unit, and (e) operation of communication channels to make rules known and to report back problems to the administrative unit.

The classic formulation and comparison of these two theories of social integration is Émile Durkheim's discussion of the effects of growing division of labor in society.[8] He argued that "mechanical solidarity" (normative integration) tends to predominate in small, primitive, homogeneous societies, because of their strong common values and norms and relative lack of division of labor. As societies grow in size and density of interaction, however, division of labor increases and "organic solidarity" (functional integration) becomes progressively dominant. He carefully pointed out that a certain amount of consensus on norms and rules is still vital in these societies to ensure the establishment and fulfillment of contractual relationships—which he referred to as "the noncontractual elements of contracts." But the primary source of unification in these complex societies is functional interdependence.

Durkheim's evolutionary thesis, as an attempt to explain the effects of growing size and complexity of social organization on the process of integration, has proved stimulating to two generations of sociologists. Nevertheless, many social theorists today argue that *both functional and normative integration occur together as complementary processes in virtually all societies.* Their relative strengths, as well as the specific activities through which they occur, vary widely from one society to another, but neither process can operate effectively without the other. Each source of

---

[7] Discordance is a condition within social organizations in which the existing procedural rules are inadequate to regulate complementary relationships among interdependent subparts in the interests of the total organization. See Olsen, "Durkheim's Two Concepts of Anomie."

[8] Émile Durkheim, *The Division of Labor in Society,* trans. George Simpson (New York: The Free Press, a division of The Macmillan Company, 1951).

integration has several weaknesses that are complemented by the other type. As a consequence, neither theory is adequate by itself to explain social integration.

To criticize normative integration theory first: What basis is there for its initial assumption of consensus on basic values? Shared social values can arise only out of common social experiences; social life creates shared social values, not vice versa. Hence a certain amount of unified social organization must already exist before the processes of normative integration can begin. To carry this line of reasoning further, the two requirements comprising the core of the theory—normative consistency and infusion of norms into organizations—also cannot occur until social organization has already been created and at least partially solidified. In short, it can be argued that a certain amount of functional unification must take place before effective normative integration can begin.

Functional integration theory, on the other hand, does not explain why the component parts of an emerging organization trust each other enough to surrender self-sufficiency and become dependent on each other in symbiotic relationships, if they do not share some common norms or if there is at first no encompassing organization capable of assuring social order. Nor does it explain why the subunits of an organization adhere to common procedural rules instead of seeking to exploit each other for their own self-interests—unless one also includes in the theory either an assumption of total rationality or an ultimate reliance on the use of force. In short, what is the "invisible hand" that turns self orientations into collectivity orientations, if it is not shared social values and norms?

Quite clearly, the process of unifying social organization ordinarily has both normative and functional aspects. No one has yet succeeded in weaving both normative and functional processes into a single, composite theory of social integration,[9] although one possible starting point for such an attempt can be identified. The climate of mutual trust necessary to initiate complementary exchange relationships before a common set of values and norms has emerged might be provided by what Alvin Gouldner calls "the norm of reciprocity."[10] The essence of this norm is that social actors are obligated to return benefits to those from whom they have pre-

---

[9] An effort in this direction has been made by Talcott Parsons, but it strongly reflects his own emphasis on normative phenomena: "Durkheim's Contribution to the Theory of Integration of Social Systems," in Kurt H. Wolfe, ed., Émile Durkheim, 1858–1917 (Columbus, Ohio: The Ohio State University Press, 1960), pp. 118–153.

[10] Alvin W. Gouldner, "The Norm of Reciprocity," American Sociological Review, vol. 25 (April 1960), pp. 161–178. Peter Blau has argued, however, that simple exchange relationships can be initiated without the existence of even this minimal norm of reciprocity, through a cumulative series of conditional actions: P. Blau, Exchange and Power in Social Life (New York: John Wiley & Sons, Inc., 1964), pp. 92–95.

viously received benefits—although the norm may not require equality in these exchanges. If this single norm is shared by actors starting an exchange relationship, it provides minimal grounds for confidence and thus promotes a willingness to initiate action. Gouldner points out that to the best of our knowledge this moral norm of reciprocity is universal (although this fact does not explain its ultimate origin), so that a potential foundation exists among all peoples on which to base complementary relationships and begin the process of creating unified social organization.

Lest this discussion of normative and functional integration appear solely academic and of no practical use, let us briefly apply these two theories to the process of creating viable international organization. Throughout the twentieth century mankind has been attempting to erect some kind of international organization to prevent war. To our dismay, however, neither the League of Nations nor the United Nations has proved capable of meeting this challenge. Perhaps the underlying reason for the failure of these organizations to unify the world is that both of them have relied primarily on normative integration. More specifically, both the League and the U.N. were founded on the assumption that all participating nations shared a common set of basic values, which were elaborately spelled out in a Covenant and a Charter. It is readily apparent at this point in history that neither of these assumptions was well founded.

In marked contrast, the European Economic Community (the "Common Market") has achieved spectacular success in unifying the economies of its member nations, despite several sharp value conflicts. Perhaps the crucial difference here is that the EEC is based largely on functional integration. It has sought to create mutual interdependence and solidarity among its members through the gradual establishment of complementary exchange relationships. Value consensus, especially in politics, is expected as an outgrowth of these mutually beneficial relationships, rather than being a necessary precondition for unity. Whether or not this experiment in economic functional integration will eventually lead to political and other forms of international unification remains to be seen.

Integration of Complex Societies

Large, complex societies cannot achieve strong normative or functional integration unless several supporting social conditions also exist.

Normative integration is most effectively developed in relatively small and homogeneous social groups. Common values and norms are easily shared and maintained, they can become deeply imbedded within the organization, and they are always immanent in the lives of individual members. Within contemporary complex nations these social conditions are not met by the total society itself. For normative integration to occur in such societies, therefore, a series of social links must exist between the individual and the society, in the form of multitudinous groups, associations, communities, and other types of "intermediate" organizations. (The nuclear family is often excluded as being too small to serve as a link to the society, while the mass media are usually held to be too large and impersonal.) These "mediating" organizations provide the setting in which normative integration of the total society actually occurs. To the extent that these organizations are institutionalized parts of the larger society, they will embody basic societal values, support societal norms, and provide roles for individuals that benefit the whole society.

The mere existence of intermediate organizations within a society does not guarantee normative integration, however. These societal subunits are rarely, if ever, full institutionalized. Rather, they usually have some degree of functional autonomy and hence can at times act counter to the interests of the larger society. Moreover, subcultures usually differ somewhat from the culture of the entire society and often directly conflict with it. Thus individuals frequently find themselves caught between the values, norms, activities, and demands of their society and those of other organizations to which they belong. Because these latter organizations are usually more immediate and important in most people's lives than is the total society, persons caught in such a dilemma will commonly give their first allegiance to the local community, groups, and associations to which they belong. As a result, the society suffers normative disintegration.

In a totalitarian nation, adequate normative integration is achieved by establishing a proliferation of intermediate organizations throughout the society, all of which are directly controlled by the government or the official party. In this way the elites can be sure that the only values and norms being expressed in the society are those which they provide. *It is fully possible, however, to obtain a high level of societal normative integration while at the same time maintaining a considerable amount of functional and cultural autonomy among component subunits.* Partially autonomous intermediate organizations can perform the mediating actions necessary for normative integration if they are themselves normatively integrated, if they present their particular values and norms as supplements to the societal culture rather than as alternatives to it, if they have overlapping memberships (especially of leaders) that tie them together, if they interact with each other and in the process influence and limit each other's activities, and if there is a common socialization or educational process for the entire society that cuts across all subunits and subcultures.[11] When these conditions are met, a partially segmented society can achieve as much normative integration as the most tightly controlled totalitarian society.

Strong functional integration, in contrast to normative integration, is not likely to develop in small, homogeneous organizations. Although even the most simply organized group often exhibits some task specialization (on the basis of age or sex, if nothing else), such a group lacks the elaborate division of labor necessary for full functional integration. Functional integration operates most effectively in complexly structured organizations with larger populations and high levels of material and social technology.

Extensive division of labor does not automatically ensure functional integration. The achievement of functional integration also requires such factors as a vast web of complementary exchange relationships, procedural rules (such as contract laws and a money economy) for carrying out these relationships, a communication network, overall coordination and regulation of exchange relationships to prevent disruptions and resolve operational problems, and control procedures to discourage extreme dominance of one subpart over the others or exploitation of a particularly vulnerable participant.

All of these requirements push in the direction of centralized administration of the total organization. Quite frequently, one or more administrative units are established to provide these overall communicative, coordinative, regulative, and control services, since none of the more specialized parts has a broad enough scope of power to deal with all activities throughout the entire organization. If this administrative unit also assumes the task of making and implementing decisions for the total organization, as often happens, it becomes a centralized government. The tendency toward increased centralization of administration and decision-making in all modern societies is so marked that social theorists sometimes state as a fundamental social "law" the proposition that growing functional specialization within an organization demands increased centralized control if the organization is to remain functionally integrated.

This apparently absolute requirement for overall coordination and regulation within complex societies does not imply any necessity for totalitarianism, however—although totalitarianism is one means of achieving it. More specifically, the necessity for centralized administration in modern societies does not dictate whether decisions are to be made democratically or autocratically, whether the society will be operated for the

---

[11] David Aberle has examined in some detail this phenomenon of "cultural unity within diversity." See his "Shared Values in Complex Societies," *American Sociological Review*, vol. 15 (1950), pp. 495–502.

benefit of all members or just the controlling elite, whether governmental positions will be filled through open achievement or closed ascription, the extent to which specialized subparts can influence collective decision-making and control societal activities, or whether coordination and regulation are to be exercised through voluntary compliance, overt coercion, or some other procedure. Most important, this demand for centralized administration does not indicate the degree of overall control required for adequate functional integration. In fact, the most effective situation is perhaps one of less than total power centralization, since completely centralized control often tends to make a society extremely rigid and incapable of adjusting to changing social conditions. As with normative integration, then, *a partially segmented society can maintain functional integration as long as adequate procedures are present for societywide coordination and regulation.*

Normative and functional integration are sometimes presented as antithetical processes for unifying complex social organization, since the demand of normative integration for networks of intermediate groups and associations seems to oppose the demand of functional integration for centralized administration. But the underlying social conditions required by these two types of integration are not incompatible. Both forms of unification depend upon the creation of viable relationships among partially autonomous subunits as well as procedures for overall organizational coordination. Furthermore, neither form necessitates complete institutionalization of all subunits. Extreme segmentation among component parts can, of course, destroy the unity of any social organization, but total institutionalization often provokes consequences that are in the long run equally disastrous.

Complementarity of Conflict and Integration

At first glance, conflict and integration appear to be contradictory social processes. Conflict disrupts social organization while integration strengthens it. But in fact this need not occur. Under certain conditions the two processes can not only coexist but can directly complement and reinforce each other. The basic proposition underlying this argument is that *the amounts of conflict and integration existing in any social organization are interrelated, so that the greater the unity of an organization, the more conflict it can tolerate and utilize constructively without disintegrating.* Although extensive conflict may destroy a weakly integrated organization, it can benefit a strongly unified organization. *Integration thus enables an organization to encourage conflict and change, thereby increasing its flexibility and stability.* Extensive conflict throughout an organization does not necessarily indicate disintegration, nor does absence of conflict indicate integration—in reality the situation may be just the opposite.

Lewis Coser has described a number of beneficial consequences that conflict can have for organizations,[12] of which the most important are the following: (a) establishing and maintaining organizational boundaries; (b) strengthening members' identification with the organization; (c) creating awareness of organization stresses, strains, and problems; (d) stimulating activity to deal with these problems and maintain and improve the organization; (e) breaking down old rituals and routines and thus encouraging innovative and creative actions; (f) promoting clarification or formation of organizational norms and rules; (g) developing social relationships and "antagonistic cooperation" among previously isolated actors; and, most crucial of all, (h) stimulating organizational change.

Not all conflict provides such benefits for organizations, however, and Coser lists several conditions that must be met if conflict is to have useful social consequences:[13] (a) conflict must be practical, centering on operational issues, not ideological positions or individual personalities; (b) it must be instrumental rather than expressive in nature, so that it is not valued for its own sake; (c) it must be limited to specific areas and manifested through prescribed channels; (d) it must be managed or resolved within a reasonable length of time, so that it does not become too prolonged or overly disruptive; (e) it must be sequential and intermittent, so that several related conflicts do not occur at the same time; (f) conflicts must be crosscutting rather than cumulative or superimposed, so that various disruptions will cut across the organization in different ways rather than all reinforcing the same entrenched cleavages; (g) conflict must not threaten to destroy the basic values of the organization; and (h) the culture of the organization must contain a certain amount of normative diversity, as well as a norm of tolerance for social and cultural differences. We can summarize all of these requirements by saying that the organization must possess established social procedures for effectively managing—that is, limiting, directing, controlling, and resolving—social conflicts. The development of such conflict-management procedures depends, however, on fairly high levels of both normative and functional integration within the organization.

If an organization is only weakly unified and lacks procedures for managing conflict, it cannot tolerate extensive disruptions without being destroyed. Hence it must seek to suppress and resist social conflict and

---

[12] Lewis A. Coser, *The Functions of Social Conflict* (New York: The Free Press, a division of The Macmillan Company, 1962).

[13] This topic is also discussed by Ralf Dahrendorf in *Class and Class Conflict in Industrial Society* (Stanford, Calif.: Stanford University Press, 1959), chap. 6.

change in order to survive and retain at least short-run stability. It thus becomes extremely rigid. On the other hand, if an organization is strongly integrated and has established procedures for effectively managing disruptions, it can reap the benefits of ordered social conflict. Indeed, it can actively encourage and promote a considerable amount of conflict and change. We are therefore led to conclude that *an optimum condition for social organization is not some sort of balance or compromise between conflict and integration, but rather simultaneous growth in both areas.*

To the extent that many social organizations throughout human history have tended to discourage conflict and change, the reason may be that they have lacked viable normative and functional integration. Their only recourse has been to suppress conflict, maintain order through the overt or covert use of force, and resist pressures for social change until they became too strong to be contained, at which point abrupt, far-reaching, and often violent change has frequently erupted. Perhaps, though, if social organizations can slowly increase both their normative and functional integration and also develop effective procedures for conflict management, they can then expand their capacity to tolerate conflict and benefit from it. The result would be greater flexibility in social organization, continuous instead of sporadic change, and long-term social stability.

In contrast to this complementary relationship between conflict and integration, the phenomena of segmentation and institutionalization are mutually exclusive, so that the optimum condition on this dimension is a compromise between the two extremes. Extensive segmentation, in which the subunits of an organization possess almost complete functional autonomy, often promotes ideological conflict among organizational parts, prohibits effective normative or functional integration, makes it virtually impossible for the organization to fulfill its survival and operational requirements, and prohibits the development of conflict-management techniques. At the other end of this continuum, extreme institutionalization, in which the organizational parts possess no functional autonomy, usually discourages social innovation and change, makes cultural diversity impossible, produces a totally centralized organization, and leaves the organization highly vulnerable to external stresses that threaten key activities such as resource procurement. As yet, sociology cannot specify the most effective balance between segmentation and institutionalization, although this point probably varies with different organizations and under diverse conditions.

Figure 11-1 shows these suggested relationships between the processes of conflict and integration, the dimensions of rigidity-flexibility and segmentation-institutionalization, and the phenomena of sporadic versus continual social change.

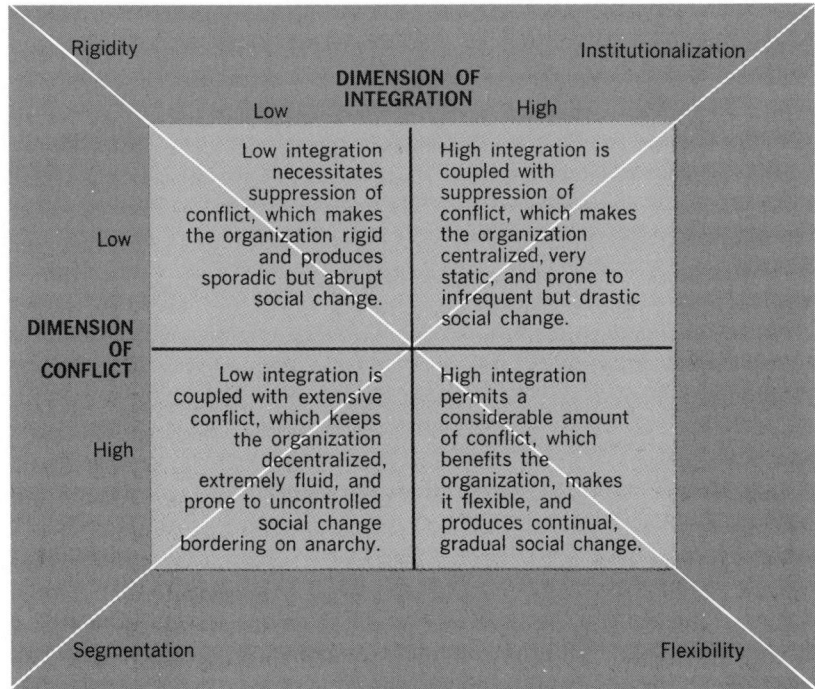

FIGURE 11-1. Relationships between the processes of conflict and integration, the dimensions of rigidity-flexibility and segmentation-institutionalization, and the phenomena of sporadic and continual change.

In this chapter we have examined the phenomena of normative and functional integration, viewing these both as theoretical explanations of organizational unity and as dynamic processes occurring in all social organizations. The point has been stressed that these two types of integration not only occur together in virtually every organization but are in fact highly interdependent. Each process supplements and reinforces the other. High levels of both normative and functional integration can be achieved in complex societies, provided that their subunits possess some degrees of functional autonomy and that effective procedures for overall administration have been developed. Furthermore, a highly integrated organization can frequently tolerate, encourage, and benefit from extensive social conflict and change without being destroyed.

An integrated but flexible organization will generate considerable amounts of social power as it operates through time. The exercise of power in social life becomes our concern in the next chapter.

RECOMMENDED READING

ANGELL, ROBERT C., "Social Integration," forthcoming in the new edition of the *International Encyclopedia of the Social Sciences* (New York: The Macmillan Company).
Summarizes and evaluates existing theoretical and empirical work on the phenomenon of social integration.
_____, "The Social Integration of American Cities of More Than 100,000 Population," *American Sociological Review,* vol. 12 (June 1947), pp. 335–342. (Also Bobbs-Merrill reprint S-3.)
An attempt to measure the degree of normative integration existing in all major American cities.
BACK, KURT W., "Influence Through Social Communication," in Eleanor Maccoby, Theodore M. Newcomb, and Eugene L. Hartley, eds., *Readings in Social Psychology*, pp. 183–197 (New York: Holt, Rinehart and Winston, Inc., 1958).
A report of one of the major laboratory studies of social cohesion in small groups.
DURKHEIM, ÉMILE, *The Division of Labor in Society,* trans. George Simpson, especially Book 1, chaps. 2, 3, and 7, and Book 2, chap. 2 (New York: The Free Press, a division of The Macmillan Company, 1951).
The classic discussion of the ideas of mechanical solidarity (normative integration) and organic solidarity (functional integration).
GOULDNER, ALVIN, "The Norm of Reciprocity," *American Sociological Review,* vol. 25 (April 1960), pp. 161–178.
A challenging, suggestive discussion of the phenomenon of reciprocity as a common link between functional and normative integration.
GROSS, EDWARD, "Symbiosis and Consensus as Integrative Factors in Small Groups," *American Sociological Review,* vol. 21 (April 1956), pp. 174–179.
Studies of several natural groups indicated that functional integration tended to produce greater group unity than did normative integration.
LANDECKER, WERNER S., "Type of Integration and Their Measurement," *The American Journal of Sociology,* vol. 55 (January 1951), pp. 332–340. (Also Bobbs-Merrill reprint S-158.)
Discusses four different types of integration and suggests procedures for measuring each type.

CHAPTER 12

The Process
of Social Power

An inevitable outcome of all social organization, whenever and wherever it occurs, is the creation of social power. By ordering their social interactions and infusing their relationships with common meanings, participants in social organizations collectively exercise power that none of them could exert individually. Whether these organizations be small groups, families, communities, formal associations, functional networks, or total societies, their actions and activities always involve the wielding of power in social life. Social power is generated through the process of social organization and is inseparable from it. As expressed by Amos Hawley: "Every social act is an exercise of power, every social relationship is a power equation and every social group or system is an organization of power. Accordingly, it is possible to transpose any system of social relationships into terms of potential or active power. Perhaps such a transposition is nothing more than the substitution of one terminology for another."[1]

Social activities that directly involve the use of power in social life are often called "politics," so that a more dynamic name for the phenomenon we are now examining might be "the process of social politics." In its broadest meaning, politics refers to the total process through which social power is distributed and exercised, with particular emphasis on the making of collective decisions. Political activities, in this generic sense,

[1] Amos H. Hawley, "Community Power and Urban Renewal Success," *The American Journal of Sociology*, vol. 68 (January 1963), pp. 422–431.

take place within all social organizations. A family conference or an executive board session or a labor union meeting can be just as political in nature as the United States Congress. In popular speech, however, the term politics is commonly associated only with the operations of local and national governments and related associations such as political parties. To avoid misunderstandings, therefore, we shall speak of "the process of social power" and shall refrain from using the term "politics" in this discussion.

Power is not only a direct consequence of social organization but also a causal factor contributing to the creation of additional organization. As power is generated through the process of social organization, it can then be used to impose further patterns of social order or cultural ideas upon either that particular area of social life or other areas. In other words, power can be employed to strengthen existing social organization or to create new organization. Although power will not directly increase the integration of an organization, it can be used to establish the social conditions and patterns of order that contribute to the process of social integration.

We shall focus our attention here on the fundamental nature of social power, the process of power exertion, various subtypes of power, two attempts to explain how power is created through social activities, and several uses of power in social life. An examination of the general theories of social organization that place particular emphasis on the exercise of power will be deferred until a later chapter.

Nature of Social Power

Power in social life is somewhat analogous to energy in the physical world: wherever we look we observe its effects, and all activities are in one sense an expression of it. We talk freely about the uses of energy and power, but when we attempt to specify more precisely what either of these phenomena is, we encounter difficulties. The main reason is that neither energy nor power can be directly observed or measured. Their existence, nature, and strength can only be inferred from their effects.

Rather than arbitrarily adopting one of the numerous ideas of social power offered by previous writers—most of which are limited in scope— we shall employ a conception of social power broad enough to include all previous definitions as special cases. For our purposes, *social power is the ability to affect social life (social actions, social order, or culture)*.[2]

[2] The only other definition of social power that approaches this one in scope is by Talcott Parsons: "Power . . . is the generalized capacity of a social system to get things done in the interest of collective goals." See his *Structure and Process in Mod-*

Whenever a social actor in any way affects the course of a social or cultural process or phenomenon, social power is being exercised.

Social power is a relational, not a psychological phenomenon. That is, *social power always exists within social relationships, never within individual persons.* Individuals may themselves possess a certain amount of physical strength, special knowledge or competence, strong personality qualities, or particular interaction abilities such as leadership skills, but none of these capabilities constitutes social power. One's personal characteristics can contribute to his power in a particular situation, but social power always resides within social relationships and patterns of social order. The chairman of a committee, for instance, might exercise power over the actions of the other members and over the activities of the committee as a whole, but this power lies in his relationships within the committee—in the roles he enacts and the position he occupies. Personal capabilities, such as skill in conducting meetings, can facilitate his acquiring and exercising of power, but they are not themselves social power. If he should be removed from office or leave the group, he will no longer wield the power created by the group, even though he retains his skill at conducting meetings.

The terms "influence" and "control" are frequently used as synonyms for social power, though they might more properly be thought of as special cases of power. *Social influence is an instance of power in which outcomes are not predetermined.* Influence can only be attempted, not enforced, and its results are always problematic. It follows, then, that the object of an attempt at influence can either accept or reject the influence. In contrast, *social control is an instance of power in which outcomes are largely or totally predetermined.* Control can be exercised regardless of the wishes of the recipient, with little or no doubt concerning its results. To mention one example, a railroad company might be able to exert only moderate influence over a large metropolis but be able to control the economic fate of a small business that relies on rail shipment of its products. Both influence and control are relative phenomena, depending on the amounts of power wielded by each actor in a given situation, and might perhaps be thought of as constituting the opposite ends of a continuum.

Although power always exists within social relationships, the actors

ern Societies (New York: The Free Press, a division of The Macmillan Company, 1960), pp. 180–183. Many definitions of social power include the idea of overcoming resistance, including both direct opposition and indirect limitations and scarcities. This phrase is redundant, however, since the ability to affect social life logically implies overcoming resistance. That is, if an actor cannot overcome whatever resistance he encounters in a particular situation, he has no power to affect that sphere of social life. Nevertheless, he might be able to exercise power in other situations that offer less resistance to his actions.

who exercise it can be either individuals or organizations. To distinguish between these two kinds of power phenomena we use the concepts of interpersonal and organizational power situations. *A social power relationship is interpersonal if the actors exercising power are individuals, and organizational if they are social organizations.* Real social life contains endless diverse combinations of interpersonal and organizational power. A husband who determines how much money his wife spends on household expenses each week is wielding interpersonal power; as a social unit his family exerts organizational power in relation to other social organizations with which it interacts, including local businesses, perhaps a church or school, and to some extent the entire community. The president of a corporation might personally influence the other executives (and secretaries) with whom he comes into daily contact, but the business as a whole rather than the president himself controls the work schedule (and hence influences the family routines) of its employees, and buys and sells goods with other organizations. Similarly, one member of a national legislature may wield interpersonal power over another member, while the legislature as a whole exercises organizational power over its component parts (such as committees) and over many other organizations within the society, as well as the entire nation.

The theoretical distinction between interpersonal and organizational power situations is fairly clear. In practice, however, it is often very difficult to separate these two phenomena. This problem arises because organizational power must be exerted by individuals acting as representatives of that organization, yet individuals often use their organizational roles and positions as resources for interpersonal power. In other words, how do we tell whether a person is acting as an involved part of some larger social entity and thus merely administering organizational power, or acting as an autonomous element and thus exercising interpersonal power? It is true that we frequently label our power acts as either personal ("do this for me") or organizational ("this church opposes . . ."), but our actions do not always substantiate our words. The conceptions of interpersonal and organizational power, therefore, remain only heuristic analytical tools rather than empirical variables.

The exercise of social power can also be classified along several other analytical dimensions, including the following four:

(1) Purposeful versus nonpurposeful power. If a social actor intentionally affects other actors, patterns of social order, or cultural ideas, his exertion of social power is clearly purposeful. In other cases, though, his actions might have the same social effects even though he had no intention of wielding power. Often an action has both intended and unintended power consequences, as when a newspaper union calls a strike to

gain higher wages for its members, and the strike has extensive side effects on stores, theatres, voluntary associations, and other community organizations.

(2) Positive versus negative power. Positive power is the ability to accomplish something that otherwise would not occur, while negative power is the ability to prevent something that otherwise would occur.[3] Any given exercise of social power can operate positively or negatively or both ways simultaneously.

(3) Internal versus external power. Internal power is exerted by an organization over its own members or subunits. External power is wielded by an individual or an organization over some other actor in the social environment. By definition, internal power can be exerted only by organizations, since only they contain partially autonomous subunits. External power, though, might be exercised by individuals or organizations.

(4) Direct versus indirect power. The exercise of social power is direct when it flows from the power wielder straight to the power recipient. It becomes indirect when it passes through one or more intermediate stages before reaching its ultimate destination.[4] Indirect social power frequently takes the form of ordering social situations in particular ways, which in turn produce certain specific actions or activities. Much of any organization's power, for instance, lies in its ability to shape the social context in which its members act and the social environment in which other organizations exist.

Exercise of Social Power

To exert power in a social relationship, an actor must have resources upon which he can draw. *A resource is anything that an actor can use to produce social power.* The most obvious resources for social power are possessions, such as goods, money, or knowledge. Resources can also take the form of occupancy of vital organizational roles and positions, grants of legitimacy to the actor by others, communicative and persuasive skills, and special qualities of the actor that others find attractive. In addition, if the actor is an organization, its available resources might include the size and quality of its population, the strength of its integration, the degree of

---

[3] The only major discussion of social power that treats it solely as a negative phenomenon (in the form of either blocking actions or withdrawing benefits) is Peter M. Blau, *Exchange and Power in Social Life* (New York: John Wiley & Sons, Inc., 1964), chap. 5.

[4] Other terms for this distinction might be "one-step" and "multistep" exercise of power.

its stability and flexibility, its overall operational effectiveness, and various customs and traditions contained in its culture. Whatever the specific resources employed in a given situation, it is by using them (or threatening to use them) that an actor gains social power. The main distinction between resources and power is that resources are possessed by an actor himself, whereas power is only exercised by an actor in a social relationship.

Some writers speak of the existence of "potential power" whenever an actor possesses resources and is capable of employing them if and when desired.[5] Power then becomes "active" as these resources are utilized—either to back up verbal threats or in overt actions. The main points of this "potential-active" distinction are (a) that resources must be readily available for use before they become relevant for the creation of social power, and (b) that an actor can be seen to possess the potentiality for wielding power even though he never overtly uses his resources. The difference between potential and active power becomes exceedingly cloudy, however, when we realize that if others perceive an actor as having resources for potential power, they may act in accordance with this perception, thus giving him active power over them, regardless of whether or not he ever makes use of his resources. Where does one draw the line between potential and active power? Moreover, potential power (in contrast to resources) does not even exist until it is actually expressed (at least symbolically) in a social relationship. In short, upon closer examination the idea of "potential power" dissolves into either resources possessed by the actor or power exercised by him. We shall therefore discard the idea of "potential power" and simply distinguish between available resources and effective social power.

Resources provide a person or organization with a basis for generating social power. However, if the use of these resources is prevented or if they are inadequate to overcome whatever resistance exists, the actor cannot realistically be said to exert any power in this situation. Resistance can take many forms, including direct opposition by a counterpower, indirect limitations or scarcities inherent in the situation, avoidance of the relationship through alternative courses of action, or indifference to the effects of the power. In general, the amount of power one actor exercises over others in a given relationship is a resultant of the extent and adequacy of the resources actually used (sometimes called inducements) minus the degree of resistance encountered.

[5] Robert Bierstedt ["An Analysis of Social Power," *American Sociological Review*, vol. 15 (December 1950), pp. 730–738] prefers to restrict the meaning of social power to potential power, and to describe active power in terms of the specific form its assumes, such as force or authority. For terminological convenience, though, many sociologists retain "social power" as a generic term referring to all instances of social power.

Given a relationship in which social power is actively being exercised, the sociologist's next concern is to describe and analyze this situation. Two main approaches are commonly used: distributive and developmental analysis. These approaches are in no way incompatible, but they do involve different questions and perspectives. *Distributive analysis examines the way in which the total amount of power being exerted at any one time within a given situation is divided among the participating actors.* Is power shared relatively equally by all actors, is it wielded almost exclusively by a single actor, or does some intermediate condition prevail? The usual result of distributive analysis is a structural description of the distribution of power among the actors at one particular time. In contrast, *developmental analysis investigates increases and decreases through time in the total amount of power being exercised within a given relationship or organization.* To what extent has the creation of social organization and the accumulation of resources over time augmented the total amount of power being employed by all participants? Or, conversely, has the disintegration of social organization or the depletion of available resources reduced the amount of power they can exert? The usual outcome of developmental analysis is an explanation of changes that have occurred through time in dynamic power processes. For example, a study showing that businessmen presently have more influence on community decisions than do politicians would be distributive in nature, while a study of growth in the effectiveness of community decision-making during the past twenty years would be developmental in nature.

Both of these approaches to power analysis are equally valid and productive of scientific knowledge, but serious problems arise if one's conception of social power is not appropriate for the kind of analysis being performed. For distributive analysis we must temporarily assume a *zero-sum conception* of social power, which sees the total amount of power being exercised at any specific time as fixed or finite. Developmental analysis, on the other hand, requires the temporary assumption of a *positive-sum conception* of social power, which sees the total amount of power being exerted through time as varying or infinite. These are simply heuristic conceptions of the nature of power which the analyst temporarily accepts as a basis for performing either distributive or developmental analysis. They are in no way contradictory, as long as one keeps the time factor clearly in mind. Unfortunately, not all writers have done so. For instance, if we demonstrate that large businesses, the executive branch of the federal government, and the military have all grown in power in the United States during the past thirty years,[6] this is clearly developmental analysis. On the basis of this information alone, however, we cannot simply assume

[6] This illustration is drawn from C. Wright Mills, *The Power Elite* (New York: Oxford University Press, 1956).

that other parts of the society—such as Congress, state and community governments, schools, churches, labor unions, political parties, and voluntary associations—have necessarily all lost power. If such a conclusion were reached without additional information concerning these other realms of society, we would be assuming a zero-sum conception of social power when our developmental analysis requires a positive-sum conception. The total amount of social power being exerted in the United States might have increased considerably during this period, so that these other unexamined parts of the society could have grown in power at equal or even faster rates than businesses, government, and the military.

Types of Social Power

As a fundamental social process, the exercise of social power occurs whenever a social actor affects social life. This process can take many different forms. We shall now attempt to clarify and interrelate what appear to be the four major types of social power: force, dominance, attraction, and authority.[7] These four types are analytically distinct, although any particular power phenomenon might include several or all of them.

In its broadest meaning, *force is the application of pressures as a means of gaining results.* These pressures range from subtle hints to monetary payments to physical punishments. Although we commonly equate the idea of force with overt coercion or violence, the sociological meaning of this concept is considerably more inclusive, covering all forms of social pressures. The resource base for the exercise of force thus consists of all actual or threatened pressures that one actor can bring to bear upon others.

More specifically, three identifiable subtypes of force are (a) compensation, or providing desired objects or conditions in return for compliance, (b) deprivation, or administering punishments or withholding expected benefits as a consequence of noncompliance, and (c) persua-

---

[7] Whatever usefulness this typology has over previous efforts probably lies in its inclusiveness, since it draws from several different schools of thought that have not before been combined. The major, though not the only, sources of the ideas presented here are Bierstedt, "An Analysis of Social Power"; John R. P. French, Jr., and Bertram Raven, "The Bases of Social Power," in Dorwin Cartwright, ed., *Studies in Social Power* (Ann Arbor, Mich.: The University of Michigan Institute for Social Research, 1959), chap. 9; Seymour Martin Lipset, *Political Man* (New York: Doubleday & Company, Inc., 1960), chap. 3; Robert E. Park, *Human Communities* (New York: The Free Press, a division of The Macmillan Company, 1952), chap. 13; and Max Weber, *The Theory of Social and Economic Organization*, trans. A. M. Henderson and Talcott Parsons (New York: The Free Press, a division of The Macmillan Company, 1947), pp. 324–363.

sion, or the manipulation of information, emotions, special knowledge, or social values. The use of force can thus be seen in the payment of wages for work, in the expulsion of a member from a professional association, and in newspaper editorials.

The exercise of force commonly occurs within exchange relationships, and in a very general sense the two phenomena of force and exchange are synonymous. That is, the exertion of force can be seen as the exchange of pressures for compliance, while exchange involves a committment of resources to elicit desired responses from other participants. In both everyday and sociological usage, however, the ideas of exchange and force are at least partially distinct. We generally think of exchange relationships as being relatively balanced, with all participants possessing roughly equal resources. Force relationships, on the other hand, are predominantly onesided or unbalanced, with the power wielder employing (or at least possessing) superior resources. This is a useful analytical distinction, but it leaves unanswered the basic question of how unbalanced a relationship must become before it shifts from a process of exchange to one of force. The apparent resolution is to conceive of exchange and force as the end points on a continuum, ranging from perfect balance among all actors to total control by one actor. Most actual situations then fall somewhere between these two extremes.[8]

Force can be an easily exercised and very powerful means of achieving desired ends, provided one can employ adequate resources. Nevertheless, because the exertion of force is especially likely to arouse opposition, it often remains a relatively unstable and unreliable type of social power.

Dominance is the ability to affect social processes because of an actor's roles or activities within a social organization. Functional specialization and interdependence among the members and subunits of an organization tend to make each part vulnerable to the actions of all the other parts with which it is functionally interrelated. Through the routine performance of its normal roles or activities, therefore, a given subpart often influences or controls the functioning of many other interdependent parts. Whatever it does has either direct or indirect effects on these other parts, and also on the entire organization. To the extent that a subpart of an organization wields this kind of functional influence or control, it exercises dominance over social processes within the organization. Hence the greater its functional effectiveness the stronger will be its dominance. The resource base for the exertion of dominance as a type of social power is therefore the roles or social functions that an actor performs within a larger organization.

[8] The differences between power and exchange relationships are extensively discussed in Blau, *Exchange and Power in Social Life,* chap. 5.

Dominance is perhaps most commonly observed in such realms as (a) economics, as when an industry, a university, a military installation, or some other large organization provides the primary economic foundation for an entire community, (b) information, as when a few radio, television, and newspaper chains supply most of the news reaching the population of a society, and (c) decision-making, as when the major policy decisions for a whole society are made by a single centralized government.

A social actor can use a position of dominance within an organizational structure as a basis for exerting force, by threatening to withhold services until certain demands are met. In practice, therefore, force and dominance are often very difficult to disentangle, but theoretically they remain distinct. Whereas force always requires the actual or threatened exertion of additional pressures, dominance flows from the routine performance of a subpart's activities within an organization. To the extent that an organization is unified and its subunits are institutionalized, dominance can obviously become an extremely stable and predictable type of social power.

Attraction is power based on the appeal that one social actor has for others. If people are for some reason attracted to an individual or an organization, he or it will be able to wield a certain amount of influence or even control over them. These persons will tend to shape their actions in accord with the ideas or activities of the actor to whom they are attracted, regardless of whether or not this actor exerts any pressures upon them or is functionally related to them. The resource base for the exercise of this type of social power therefore lies in psychological bonds among actors.

Three common sources of attraction are (a) cognitive identification by one person with another, or by individuals (either members or non-members) with an organization, (b) feelings of affectivity or "liking" toward an individual or an organization, and (c) charisma, or the attributing of "superhuman" or "divine" qualities to a person or an organization.[9] Thus individuals might submit to the dictates of a political party because they identified with its policies, because it had always been their family's party, or because they believed that the party or its leaders were carrying out some "ultimate" mission.

In these ways attraction provides a basis for social power, but the recipient of this attraction is never directly assured that his lead will be

[9] Charismatic appeal, which is clearly the strongest form of attraction, is in no way limited to religion. A military officer may have charismatic influence over his soldiers, a political ruler may be literally worshipped by his subjects, and the leader of a social movement may be seen as a hero by his followers. Although charisma is most often attached to a single individual, there is no reason why it cannot also be given to an organization such as a government or a church.

followed by others. The strength of his power is determined by the amount of attraction others feel toward him, not strictly by his own actions. Consequently, power based on attraction tends to be unstable and unreliable, though at times it can become extremely strong. In practice, attractive power often shades into force, as the recipient of attraction seeks to manipulate or utilize these feelings as a means of exerting pressures upon the attracted individuals.

Very briefly, *authority can be described as the exercise of legitimacy within a social organization.* If a social actor is granted the legitimate right to make decisions, direct activities, or otherwise exert influence and control, we say that this individual or organization exercises authoritative power. Authoritative dictates are voluntarily complied with because they are seen as legitimate. To understand authority, we must therefore clarify the idea of legitimacy. *Legitimacy is the right to exercise power within and for an organization,* as voluntarily granted to an actor by other members of that organization. To the extent that legitimacy is granted, a government has authority to wield power over all other parts of a society, the personnel office of a company has authority to hire and fire workers, and a committee chairman has authority to conduct meetings. The other subparts and members of these organizations recognize the right of their leaders to exercise power over them as agents of the total organization. Grants of legitimacy thus provide the resource base for the wielding of authoritative power.

Legitimacy is sometimes granted through formal procedures, such as elections or vows of obedience, but more commonly it is informally expressed through a decision to remain a member of an organization or by failure to oppose the demands of leaders who claim legitimacy. Although the leaders of many organizations commonly employ force, dominance, and attraction to supplement and support their formal authority, in a theoretical sense the exercise of authority is always based on voluntary grants of legitimacy.[10]

Three significant grounds on which legitimacy and authority often rest are (a) traditional values, as well as related beliefs, norms, and customs, (b) legal prerogatives established through agreements among many

---

[10] In addition to being granted "upward" by members, legitimacy can also be granted "downward" by some larger organization, as when a society authorizes an army to make war, a business to retain part of its profits, a prison to restrain its inmates, or a family to control its children. Such "authorization" legitimates the activities of an organization in the eyes of the other organizations in its social environment, but it does not legitimate its actions to its own members. If they do not also grant legtimacy "upward" to the organization and its leaders, the organization must rely on some other type of power—usually force—in its internal operations.

or most members of the organization, and (c) rational expertise or technical knowledge relevant to organizational activities that is possessed by particular actors. Legitimacy is especially strong when these are combined, as when a government supports traditional societal values, is legally selected through popular elections, and operates on the basis of rational knowledge. In addition, exercise of any of the other three types of social power—force, dominance, or attraction—can also lead to the granting of legitimacy. If a social actor wields extensive force long enough, effectively performs vital functions for an encompassing social organization, or is attractive to others, any or all of these factors can serve as further grounds for legitimacy.

Because authority is by far the most stable and reliable type of social power, leaders of organizations almost invariably seek at least a minimum amount of legitimacy, regardless of how they first acquired power. Even if a government comes to power through violent revolution and controls its society with rigid totalitarian practices, it will still seek to create an image of legitimacy among its subjects through such devices as plebiscites and mass communications. Indeed, it can hardly afford to do otherwise, since until it gains the use of authority it must rely largely on force to maintain its own position, as well as order throughout society.

If we now stop to compare these four major types of social power, we note that two separate analytical dimensions cut through them. First, both force and dominance rely ultimately on the performance of overt social activities, and hence in a broad sense may be described as operational or "functional power." Attraction and authority, meanwhile, both rely fundamentally on the acceptance of normative ideas, and hence might loosely be described as "normative power." Second, when individuals or organizations exercise either force or attraction in social interaction, they are at least temporarily acting as relatively independent elements, since their power does not depend on their being parts of any larger social entities.[11] To exert either dominance or authority, though, a social actor must be a relatively integral part of some encompassing organization, since these types of power are derived solely from the larger organization.

When these two analytical dimensions—functional versus normative power, and power wielding by independent elements versus organizational parts—are cross-classified, they produce a chart into which the four types of social power can be fitted. This chart (Figure 12-1) provides an analytical scheme for comparing and relating force, dominance, attraction, and authority as distinct but interrelated types of social power.

[11] Although the wielders of force and attraction may in fact be subunits of larger organizations, they are presently acting as social elements, even when their power is directed toward other parts of the same organization.

Power-wielder acts as an

Independent element   Organizational part

Functional power	**FORCE** (compensation, deprivation, and persuasion)	**DOMINANCE** (over the economy, information, or decision-making)
Normative power	**ATTRACTION** (identification, affectivity, and charisma)	**AUTHORITY** (traditional, rational, and legal)

FIGURE 12–1.   Cross-classification of four types of social power.

Theories of Power Creation

Sociologists have made few efforts to explain theoretically the process through which social power is created, although two noteworthy exceptions are the "dependency" theory of Richard Emerson and the "trust" theory of Talcott Parsons. The dependency theory applies most directly to the creation of force, while the trust theory is most applicable to legitimate authority.

The *dependency theory of social power* begins with the assumption that power is always a property of social relationships among two or more actors. Most social relationships entail at least some ties of mutual interdependence among the participants, and this interdependency provides a basis for social power. One actor (A) exercises power over another actor (B) to the extent that B depends upon A for some goal he seeks, and vice versa. This power becomes manifest as A uses B's dependency to make demands upon B that result in changes in B's actions despite his resistance. More formally, the theory states that the dependency of B on A is directly proportional to B's motivational investment in goals mediated by A, and inversely proportional to the availability of those goals to B outside of this relationship. In turn, the power of A over B is determined by the degree of B's dependency on A and by the amount of resistance by B that A can overcome. In short, "the power of A over B is equal to, and based upon, the dependence of B upon A: $P_{AB} = D_{BA}$.[12]

The *trust theory* also begins with the assumption that the basis of social power is interdependence. From this theoretical perspective, however, the essence of interdependence is men's investment of trust in others and in social organizations. This investment of trust occurs when an individual believes that the other persons or the organization will act in ways that are beneficial for him. In relatively small and intimate organizations, the existence of shared common values is enough to assure the individual that an investment of trust will benefit him. In more complex and formal organizations, though, the individual often requires some kind of guaranteed protection—such as a legal contract or established control procedures —before he will render himself vulnerable by investing trust in the organization. In either case, this investment of trust in an organization by its members gives the organization power and enables it to obtain goals. As individuals commit themselves to an organization and act as responsible parts of it, both the organization as a whole and they as agents of the organization gain increased social power.[13]

Quite clearly, neither of these theories offers a complete explanation of all the ways in which social power is created, but they do offer numerous promising ideas for further work. In particular, the theme of social interdependence which they share appears to be a fundamental starting point from which to explore the creation of social power. Given the existence of interdependence, the next question is: how do the participating actors use this interdependence? Are they acting as relatively independent elements in pursuit of their own goals, or are they acting as relatively committed parts in a collective effort to obtain organizational goals? In the former case, we will tend to see an actor's exercise of influence and control as "power over others," and we may find Emerson's dependency

---

[12] Richard M. Emerson, "Power-Dependence Relations," *American Sociological Review*, vol. 27 (February 1962), pp. 31–41. For an elaboration of this thesis, see Blau, *Exchange and Power in Social Life.*

[13] Talcott Parsons, "On the Concept of Influence," *Public Opinion Quarterly* (Spring 1963), pp. 37–62. See also James Coleman, "Comment on 'On the Concept of Influence,'" *ibid.*, pp. 63–82. Parsons goes on to draw an analogy between organizational trust investment and banking: Banks create economic power by increasing the amount of money in circulation and by creating new money through the extension of credit. A similar process occurs when a person invests trust in an organization by joining it and giving it his support. The organization can transform this trust into influence or control, which it then uses either directly in goal attainment or indirectly in support of other organization or social activities. These economic and political actions (creation of economic, political, and social power) are ultimately limited not by the amount of the initial investment, but only by public confidence in the system.

theory particularly useful. In the latter case, we will see an actor's exercise of influence and control as "power to accomplish something with others," and we will probably find Parson's trust theory more fruitful. In the first case we are also more likely to take a zero-sum perspective on social power and to perform distributive analysis, while in the second case we will probably assume a positive-sum perspective and perform developmental analysis. Once again, our theoretical viewpoint hinges on whether we consider the actors in a given social situation to be acting primarily as independent elements or as involved organizational parts.

Uses of Social Power

Once social power has been created in a social relationship, what consequences does its exercise have for organizations? How do organizations use social powers? The major consequences of power exertion can be divided into four general categories: internal ordering, internal coordination, external procurement, and external attainment.[14] The first two processes occur among the subunits comprising the power-wielding organization; the last two involve its relationships with the natural and social environments.

The primary necessity of any social organization is survival. No organization will survive long if the stresses and strains that continually disrupt it are not dealt with. If an organization has achieved relatively high degrees of functional and normative integration and has also developed effective conflict-management techniques, it may be able to tolerate and even benefit from a considerable amount of social conflict. Lacking these characteristics, however, an organization must rely upon the use of power —especially force—as a means of maintaining social order. And even strongly integrated organizations frequently employ power to cope with disruptions that cannot be handled by other means. Thus *the most basic use of social power by organizations is for the protection and perpetuation of boundaries and patterns of social relationships—or the ensuring of internal order.*

Beyond mere survival, most organizations normally strive to increase the efficiency of their internal functioning, so as to satisfy more effectively their operational requirements. As the size and internal complexity of an organization increases, so does the functional specialization, or division of labor, among its subunits. This in turn requires a certain amount of cen-

---

[14] This suggested classification is in some ways analogous to Talcott Parsons' AGIL scheme, but it is not intended to be a direct application of that scheme and it was not derived from Parsons' writings.

tralized coordination, communication, regulation, and planning. It also requires overall direction of the internal allocation process, by which the benefits of collective action are distributed to the members of the organization. To establish and operate such centralized coordination and administration among its subparts, an organization must utilize power. Any (or all) of the four major types of power can be used, although authority is particularly advantageous because of its predictability and stability. In general, *the second way in which all organizations use power is for the promotion of overall operational efficiency through standardized administration—or the ensuring of internal coordination.*

Turning outward, all social organizations depend upon their natural and social environments for the procurement of resources necessary for their operation. Whether they be goods, people, services, or information, these vital resources are frequently acquired by using some type of power. Although organizations sometimes gain necessary resources solely through balanced exchange relationships, most of the time they must also seek to influence or control portions of the external world. This generalization holds whether the organization relies on forceful pressures, functional dominance, authority, or voluntary attraction to obtain its resources. We may say, therefore, that *the third way in which all organizations use social power is to procure necessary resources from the environment.*

Finally, to obtain whatever goals they seek, social organizations must further influence or control other organizations, individuals, or natural phenomena. Depending on the nature of the organization, goal attainment may involve selling goods and services (as in the case of business concerns), disseminating information (in the case of communication media), providing personal services (in the case of hospitals), educating and training individuals (in the case of schools,) gaining acceptance of values and beliefs (in the case of churches), providing public services (in the case of communities), or dealing with other societies (in the case of national governments). As in the process of resource procurement, organizations may employ force, exploit functional dominance, exercise authority, or make normative appeals in order to gain the goals they seek, but all such activities involve the exertion of power. Thus *the fourth use of social power by all organizations is to attain goals through activities in the environment.*

All four of these uses of social power have been described from the point of view of the organization exercising power—and hence appear to be beneficial for it. From the viewpoint of other organizations, however, this wielding of power can be quite detrimental. These other organizations may be forced to provide resources or benefits to the power-wielding organization against their "wishes" or best interests, they be restrained from influencing the powerful organization but may themselves be severely controlled by it, or they may even be totally destroyed by other organizations with superior power. In other words, "power serves him who holds it," but not necessarily others.

Our concern in this chapter has been to gain a basic understanding of social power and the ways in which it affects organized social life. Arising out of social interdependence among interrelated actors and being exerted through social relationships, social power—in its various forms of force, dominance, attraction, and authority—is employed by social organizations for a wide variety of purposes. The principal conclusion we might draw is that social power pervades virtually all social activities, so that we cannot fully understand the process of social organization without taking into account the ubiquitous exercise of power.

Closely related to the exertion of power in social life, and often a direct outgrowth of it, is the process of social allocation or stratification, to which we now turn.

RECOMMENDED READING

Bierstedt, Robert, "An Analysis of Social Power," *American Sociological Review*, vol. 15 (December 1950), pp. 730–738. (Also Bobbs-Merrill reprint S-343.)
A conceptual analysis of the phenomenon of social power.

_____, "The Problem of Authority," in Morroe Berger, Theodore Abel, and Charles H. Page, eds., *Freedom and Control in Modern Society*, pp. 76–81 (New York: Octagon Books, 1964).
Discusses the nature and use of authority in social life, and views authority as being ultimately derived from social organization and upheld by the use of force.

Emerson, Richard M., "Power-Dependence Relations," *American Sociological Review*, vol. 27 (February 1962), pp. 31–41.
A theoretical explanation of the creation of social power through differential dependence among interacting actors.

Hawley, Amos H., "Community and Urban Renewal Success," *The American Journal of Sociology*, vol. 68 (January 1953), pp. 422–432.
Conceives of social power as an organizational phenomenon, largely in the form of dominance, and relates the distribution of power in communities to their success in urban renewal programs.

Lipset, Seymour Martin, *Political Man*, chap. 3 (New York: Doubleday & Company, Inc., 1959). (Also Bobbs-Merrill reprint S-175, pp. 86–103 only.)
Analyzes the concept of legitimacy, and points out several social factors that promote and destroy it.

LYND, ROBERT S., "Power in American Society as Resource and Problem," in Arthur Kornhauser, ed., *Problems of Power in American Society*, pp. 1–45 (Detroit: Wayne State University Press, 1957).
Conceives of power as a social organizational process, and discusses its functioning in contemporary American society.

WEBER, MAX, *The Theory of Social and Economic Organization*, trans. A. M. Henderson and Talcott Parsons, pp. 324–363, "Types of Authority and Imperative Co-Ordination" (New York: The Free Press, a division of The Macmillan Company, 1961).
The classic discussion of traditional, rational-legal, and charismatic bases of authority.

CHAPTER 13

The Process of Social
Allocation or Stratification

To suggest that individuals differ widely in the power they wield, the privileges they enjoy, and the prestige they experience is to state the obvious. But to observe that these various types of human inequality are largely shaped by established social orders, and are in turn themselves forms of social organization, is to begin the sociological study of social stratification. Virtually all social organizations, from friendship cliques to modern nations, exhibit some amount of social stratification, and this pervasive phenomenon has been observed as far back in human history as written records take us. Yet, paradoxically, there is no imperative theoretical reason why stratification must exist within social life, in the same sense that conflict and change, integration, and power are inherent in the process of social organization. Social stratification, in other words, is a result of man's more-or-less purposeful strivings to gain social power, privilege, and prestige. The process of social organization does not require social stratification, although whenever stratification occurs it takes place within patterns of social order and culture.

Social stratification is an outgrowth—though not an imperative consequence—of the broader process of social allocation or distribution. This process, like the others we have previously examined, is inherent in all social organization, and hence provides a universal foundation for stratification. Strict conceptual rigor might demand that we discuss allocation and stratification as two separate social processes, since stratification need

189

not always accompany allocation. Because the two phenomena are so thoroughly interwoven in all social life, however, we treat them here as essentially a single process. Our primary emphasis will be on stratification, though we can never ignore the fact that underlying all stratification is the more fundamental process of social allocation.

In this chapter we shall focus upon the essential nature of social stratification, the concepts of class and strata, the phenomenon of social mobility, two competing explanatory theories of stratification, and a few broad consequences of this process.

Nature of Social Stratification

To understand social stratification, we must first briefly examine the underlying process of social allocation. Allocation occurs whenever social power is generated through the process of social organization and then used by the organization to acquire resources and attain collective goals. In one way or another, the benefits of organizational functioning—power, privilege, and prestige—become allocated or distributed among the component subparts and individual members of the organization. Various people or subunits within the organization will come to exercise the social power that is created, enjoy the privileges gained through collective activities, and be granted prestige by others. The specific manner in which this distributive process is accomplished—whether through coercion, bargaining, gifts, or any other technique—depends on the particular organization in question. In general, though, *social allocation is the process in which the benefits of organizational activities are distributed throughout that organization.* It occurs in some form in all social organizations.

Theoretically, these benefits could be distributed equally among all the parts and members of the organization, so that no stratification would result. Outside of some small friendship groups, however, this situation rarely occurs. Almost invariably, some subunits or individual members acquire more power, privileges, and prestige than do others, so that the resulting distribution is unequal. The polar opposite of total equality would be complete concentration of all power, privileges, and prestige in the hands of one or a very few elites. Within most organizations, however, the patterns of distribution fall somewhere between these two extremes of total equality and complete inequality. The various actors within the organization normally hold differing amounts of power, privilege, and prestige, and hence can be ranked on one or more vertical continuums, with many intermediate gradations. As these differences become perpetuated through time, social stratification emerges. More formally, *the process of social stratification involves perpetuated inequality in the allocation of power, privilege, and prestige within an organization.* As we have repeatedly mentioned, the major aspects of all social stratification are power, privilege, and prestige.[1] Social power has already been described as the ability to affect social life, but the ideas of privilege and prestige require elaboration.

Social privilege is access to desired goods, services, activities, or positions that is granted to an actor by others. Privileges can take unlimited specific forms, according to what is deemed desirable in a given situation —which is in turn largely shaped by cultural values. The most obvious privilege in contemporary societies is money, which in turn allows the holder to acquire a wide variety of other benefits. In addition, privileges often include selective admittance to certain social events or organizations, prerogatives to act in distinctive ways or to receive services from others, and special rights to enact specific roles or participate in certain social activities.

Social prestige is favorable evaluation that an actor receives from others. Whereas privileges are relatively tangible benefits or rewards, prestige is always an intangible evaluation. It also takes numerous forms, including recognition, esteem, honor, and fame. Prestige is usually expressed through deference on the part of others, ranging from casual remarks (such as compliments and praises) to symbolic gestures (differential modes of speech) to overt actions (saluting or remaining standing) to formal awards and honors (citations and memorials).

Power, privilege, and prestige are distinct social phenomena, but usually they become highly interrelated, so that the study of social stratification must include all of them. In fact, it is often possible for an actor to transform one of these phenomena into another, as when a person uses his "good name" to acquire special privileges or to influence a decision, or when membership on the executive committee of an organization brings a person both honor and control over organizational policy. And money can serve simultaneously as a prestige symbol (when it is given or displayed), as a means of gaining privileges (when it is spent for goods and services), and as a resource for power (when it is used to influence actions or decisions).

Privilege and prestige, like power, are created through the process of social organization, and can be expressed only within social relationships. Stratification is always a social phenomenon; it does not exist within a single personality. Robinson Crusoe alone on an island did not possess any

---

[1] The use of these three terms in relation to social stratification is taken from Gerhard E. Lenski, *Power and Privilege: A Theory of Social Stratification* (New York: McGraw-Hill, Inc., 1966), chaps. 3–4.

social power, privileges, or prestige. Not until Friday arrived did at least a minimum amount of stratification become possible. Privilege and prestige differ from power in one important respect, however. Both must be granted to the actor by others, whereas social power (especially force and dominance) can often be wielded regardless of the wishes of others. Furthermore, privilege and prestige are normally sought as ends in themselves, because of the benefits or satisfactions they give to their recipients. Power is sometimes sought as a goal for its own sake, but more commonly it is used as a means for shaping social organization or for acquiring privilege and prestige.

The basic units of social stratification, as of all social organization, are social roles. In the most fundamental sense, it is the various roles within an organization that acquire differential amounts of power, privilege, and prestige. However, most roles are rather closely associated with the individuals who enact them at any given time, so that studies of social stratification have usually taken individuals rather than roles as their units of analysis. In many social settings, moreover, it is possible to focus on the nuclear family as a single unit within a pattern of stratification, since both spouses (as well as minor children) tend to share similar power, privileges, and prestige in the community. Although it has not frequently been done, there is no theoretical reason why even larger social bodies could not be taken as the primary units of social stratification, as long as these organizations did in fact act as single entities. It should be possible, for instance, to investigate the differential power, privilege, and prestige of associations within a functional network, or communities within a society. Our discussion in this chapter will focus largely on roles and individuals as units of stratification—but we reiterate that social stratification occurs whenever social actors of any kind enjoy differential amounts of the benefits of organizational operations.

Closely related to this topic of units of stratification is the question of the organizational setting in which stratification takes place. Social stratification always occurs within some encompassing organization, as a result of unequal allocation of power, privilege, and prestige among the component units of that organization. Thus there would be a pattern of stratification within a small committee, which might or might not resemble the stratification structure of the larger "parent" association, which might or might not correspond to the distribution of power, privilege, and prestige in the entire community, which in turn might or might not reflect the national stratification pattern. The various patterns of stratification existing within different organizations commonly exhibit considerable similarity, but they are rarely identical. For example, as a lawyer employed by a large business corporation Mr. Smith might be the junior member of the executive policy committee, even though he rated V.I.P.

treatment in the company as a whole. Concurrently, his status in the community might be relatively low because of his short period of residency and his particular ethnic background, even though he enjoyed a national reputation within his profession. It is therefore a gross oversimplification to speak of social stratification in general terms, without specifying both the social units involved and the relevant organizational setting.

The larger and more complex a given social organization, the more extensive will be its allocation process, and the greater the likelihood that its patterns of stratification will be multidimensional rather than unidimensional. In other words, *an organization can contain a number of different stratification hierarchies or dimensions.* Although these various dimensions might in fact be highly interrelated, the sociologist must attempt to distinguish them analytically and to determine the degree of congruence among them. A given stratification dimension, in turn, can often be measured in terms of several empirical variables, which may be only partially intercorrelated.

In the contemporary United States, for instance, the major stratification dimensions and their empirical indicators include the following: (a) socioeconomic, as indicated by one's occupation, educational credentials, or income; (b) public influence, as measured by one's activities in party politics, community decision-making, or mass communications; (c) reputation, as shown by the recognition, esteem, or deference granted one by others; (d) ethnicity, as determined by one's race, religion, or national origin; (e) style of life, as demonstrated by one's neighborhood, housing, or other material possessions; and (f) intellectual level, as seen in one's social attitudes, tastes and preferences, or intellectual attainments.[2] The phenomena of power, privilege, and prestige cut across all of these dimensions and variables, and probably enter into each of them to some extent, although obviously some dimensions give more weight to power, others stress privileges, and still others are primarily expressions of prestige. As a general rule, the various dimensions and indicators of stratification within an organization are never totally unrelated, but in modern societies wide divergencies commonly occur among them.[3]

Each of the stratification hierarchies within an organization normally

[2] Of all the various empirical measures of stratification, a person's occupation is the single indicator most commonly employed in sociological studies, because of the crucial importance of one's occupational role in all industrialized societies, because occupational status serves as a general measure of power, privilege, and prestige, and because occupation is highly correlated with many other objective indicators. Education is the next most commonly used measure, for the same reasons.

[3] This conceptualization of social stratification as a multidimensional phenomenon is an expansion of ideas first suggested by Max Weber, "Class, Status, and Party," *From Max Weber: Essays in Sociology,* trans. H. H. Gerth and C. Wright Mills (New York: Oxford University Press, 1958), pp. 180–195.

consists of numerous gradations, or statuses. That is, *a social status is a specific position or level on a stratification dimension or variable.* The number of identifiable statuses contained within a given hierarchy depends partially upon the complexity of the organization, but also on the concerns and sophistication of the observer who designates them. For example, one study might lump together all persons with incomes between $5000 and $8000 as a "middle income level," while another study might separate these same people into several income categories. The distance from the top to the bottom statuses of a stratification hierarchy is sometimes spoken as "the range" of that dimension or variable.[4]

Most social actors normally hold several social statuses, according to the number of separate startification hierarchies on which they are located and the number of different social settings in which they act. A given social status, in other words, is specific to a particular dimension or variable and to a particular organization. Mr. Wilson might reside in a more desirable neighborhood of the community than Mr. Baker, even though Mr. Baker might be Mr. Wilson's supervisor at work. Some amount of congruence normally exists among an actor's various social statuses, since power, privilege, or prestige gained in one area can often be transferred into other related activities. But considerable disparity can develop among an actor's various statuses, at least in the short run. A high income, for instance, does not automatically bring one either public esteem or intellectual sophistication. The terms *status consistency* or *status crystallization* (they are synonymous) are used by sociologists to describe the degree to which the diverse statuses of a given actor are equivalent.[5]

In general, the more complex the stratification process within an organization (in terms of the number of different status dimensions, plus the variety of subunits with dissimilar stratification patterns) and the faster the prevailing rate of social change, the more likely it is that many actors in the organization will experience status inconsistency. As a consequence, widespread status inconsistency is considerably more common in modern industrialized societies than in primitive agricultural societies, and more common in large metropolises than in small towns. Several empirical studies have suggested that marked inconsistency among an actor's various statuses may cause him to favor certain forms of social change, presumably as a means of redressing his disparate social conditions.[6]

---

[4] In popular speech, the term "status" often means only the top level of a stratification hierarchy, but technically these positions should be referred to as "high social statuses."

[5] The term "status crystallization" was first suggested by Gerhard E. Lenski, "Status Crystallization: A Non-Vertical Dimension of Social Status," *American Sociological Review,* vol. 19 (August 1954), pp. 405–413.

[6] For a review of this literature, see E. Dennis Kelly and William J. Chambliss, "Status Consistency and Political Attitudes," *American Sociological Review,* vol. 31 (June 1966), pp. 375–382.

Patterns of inequality in power, privilege, and prestige vary widely in their stability through time. If we are to observe and describe social stratification, ordered inequality must persist for some minimal period; random fluctuations in the allocation process are not usually spoken of as social stratification. But how long a given pattern of stratification will endure is always a problematic question.

Historically speaking, broad societal patterns of social stratification have commonly persisted through at least several generations, changing only slowly and gradually. Children have tended to assume approximately the same statuses in the society and the community as their parents, and in turn to pass on these same statuses to their offspring. This generalization holds equally for elites, "middle-status" artisans and merchants, and "lower-status" workers and peasants. To the extent that social roles and their accompanying social statuses are ascribed rather than achieved, an existing pattern of stratification is especially likely to continue with only minor changes for a long time.

One of the most striking characteristics of modern societies, however, is the opening of more and more roles to competition. There are many reasons for this trend, including the existence of more wealth to be distributed among all the members of the society, rapidly expanding public education facilities, and slowly emerging norms of rational efficiency and social equality. No existing society even approaches the ideal of total role achievement and completely open role competition—if that were ever possible—so that considerable grounds for the perpetuation of patterned stratification still exist everywhere. Nevertheless, social stratification in many contemporary societies is tending to become considerably more fluid than ever before.

Social Strata and Classes

In describing patterns of stratification, sociologists commonly speak of social strata and social classes. Both are outcomes of the process of social stratification, and both help us explain the effects of this process on other aspects of social life. There is a crucial distinction between them, however: social strata are designated by social scientists, whereas social classes are delineated by the participants themselves. Let us explore this idea.

Social strata are arbitrarily defined classifications imposed upon relatively continuous status hierarchies by social scientists for analytical purposes. A social stratum, in other words, is composed of a population of actors who hold roughly similar statuses on one or more of the major stratification dimensions and variables within an organization, and is separated from other strata only by "artificial" lines. It has no real social boundaries, hence it is always merely a population, never a social organization. There can be as many different social strata in an organization as a social scientist wishes to designate. In some cases he might be content to work with a simple dichotomy such as "manual" and "nonmanual" occupations, while at other times he might split the organization into a large number of arbitrary strata. The essential point is that social strata are defined only for research or theoretical purposes, as means of temporarily simplifying what are in reality relatively continuous status hierarchies.

In many social settings, though, differences in social status among actors give rise to the existence of real social entities, or classes. Social classes emerge as actors who share roughly similar statuses on one or more of the major stratification dimensions and variables within a larger organization become bounded and delineated as social units. The members of a class interact to create at least minimal patterns of social order and common cultural ideas, although the degree to which they are thus organized is always problematic. In short, *social classes are delineated, discrete social organizations composed of actors with approximately similar amounts of power, privilege, and prestige on one or more status dimensions.*[7] By definition, classes always exist within more encompassing organizations—such as associations, communities, or societies—and hence can be looked upon as subunits of these larger bodies. To the extent that a class possesses some degree of functional autonomy, however, it also constitutes an organization in its own right. The essential point is that social classes, in contrast to strata, are never arbitrarily defined by an outside observer; rather they are real social objects existing in social life.

It is often difficult for Americans to conceive of social classes as discrete entities, since class boundaries in this society are relatively vague, weak, blurred, and transitory. The United States shows a considerable amount of social stratification, but for the most part it takes the form of continuous hierarchies of power, privilege, and prestige, all containing innumerable status gradations. Yet even a brief glance into history or around the world at other contemporary societies reveals that discrete

---

[7] Some writers (see Lenski, *Power and Privilege*) conceive of social classes as existing on only one stratification dimension, so that "socioeconomic classes" are distinct from "public influence classes" or "ethnicity classes." They do this for conceptual clarity, reminding us that the various stratification dimensions are rarely perfectly correlated. In real life, however, most classes do cut across several, if not all, major stratification dimensions and variables, and hence become multidimensional phenomena. For this reason we have here described social classes as covering one or more status hierarchies, and have left as an empirical question the number of dimensions within a given class.

social classes are common phenomena. In fact, class boundaries can become so strong—as in the caste structure of India—that a person cannot
normally change social classes during his lifetime no matter what he does.
Nor should we too quickly conclude that class lines are absent in the
United States, simply because they are vague. Several writers have in fact
pointed to the recent emergence of new types of class boundaries in this
society, which could in time become quite marked.[8]

Class organization frequently develops around common concerns and
living conditions that actors share as a result of their similar amounts of
power, privilege, and prestige. As a class becomes delineated and acquires
organizational unity, stability, and effective power, it tends to come into
conflict with other classes and organizations. We must remember, though,
that the degree of class organization, as well as conflict, existing in any
given situation is always a problematic question, not a theoretical imperative. The occurrence of this process of class organization is commonly
affected by such factors as the degree of status homogeneity among class
members, strength of the class boundaries, and extensiveness of communication within the class. Nevertheless, whenever class organization
does occur it usually involves the creation of class consciousness, or awareness among the actors of their common social situation, as well as the
emergence of patterns of social order among class members and the creation of a shared class culture.

Social Mobility

Not only do total patterns of stratification within societies and other
organizations change through time, as a result of broad social trends such
as industrialization, urbanization, and bureaucratization, but social actors
within this process of stratification also frequently alter their statuses.
That is, they are socially mobile, in either an upward or downward
direction. *Social mobility occurs whenever a social actor changes one or
more of his/its statuses within a broader pattern of stratification.* The rate,
extent, and forms of social mobility are all open questions to be investigated in particular social settings, but the general phenomena of both
upward and downward social mobility occur quite frequently in almost
all organizations. Social mobility can be experienced by any kind of social
actor, but most theory and research has focused on individual mobility.

[8] Three such works are James Burnham, *The Managerial Revolution* (Bloomington, Ind.: Indiana University Press, 1960), Ralf Dahrendorf, *Class and Class Conflict
in Industrial Society* (Stanford, Calif.: Stanford University Press, 1959), and William
H. Whyte, Jr., *The Organization Man* (New York: Simon and Schuster, Inc., 1956).

Some amount of social mobility is virtually inevitable in any organization, as old members leave and others move in to fill their places. Several other social processes also contribute to the promotion of both upward and downward mobility, however. First, as the practice of role achievement (in contrast to role ascription) becomes increasingly prevalent in an organization, opportunities for mobility expand. Open competition for roles and positions enables actors to be upwardly mobile to the limit of their abilities and interests, forcing other, less competent actors to move downward. Second, broad changes in overall stratification processes and patterns normally produce considerable social mobility. If the major resource for power in a society shifts from control of money to possession of technical knowledge, for instance, many individuals will find themselves either gaining or losing both privileges and prestige. And third, extensive expansion or contraction in the size of an organization or its activities often leads to widespread mobility. If the organization is growing in size or activities, new roles and positions are continually being created, thus allowing many members to be upwardly mobile. In contrast, if the organization is declining in size or activities, numerous members may be pushed downward.

For any actor, social mobility is always relative to other actors; he moves upward or downward by comparison with them. From the perspective of the larger organizational setting, though, *social mobility can be either relative or absolute.* If the size and activities of the organization remain essentially unchanged through a given period, then any upward mobility that occurs must be balanced at least roughly by a corresponding amount of either downward mobility or withdrawal from the organization. There is only a limited amount of power and privileges to be allocated within the organization, so that if one member gains, another must lose. This is a condition of relative mobility. However, if the encompassing organization as a whole is growing in size and activities, then the amount of power and privileges to be allocated among the members will increase through time. Consequently, many members can be upwardly mobile without denying status to others. All gain in the long run, and at no one else's expense, though likely at somewhat different rates. (Conversely, if the total organization were declining, there would be much more downward than upward mobility.) This is a condition of absolute mobility.

The process of absolute upward mobility on a vast scale is a significant feature of most contemporary industrialized nations. Whereas some amount of relative mobility has undoubtedly always occurred in all societies, *extensive absolute mobility is a new phenomenon in social life.* As long as agriculture forms the primary economic base of a society, the amount of surplus resources and benefits available for allocation to members will remain relatively limited. Inequalities in power, privilege, and prestige will normally be quite marked, and most upward mobility (to the extent that any occurs) must be matched by corresponding downward mobility or withdrawal (through death or emigration). Although social reformers since antiquity have called for a more equitable distribution of power and wealth in society, their demands have largely gone unheeded—for a very simple reason. They were essentially calling for a redistribution of the existing benefits among the people, which would have required elites to relinquish considerable portions of their power and wealth. In effect, elites would have had to be somewhat downwardly mobile so that others might move upward. Elites have not usually taken kindly to such suggestions, and for the most part have successfully resisted all attempts to promote greater equality in preindustrial societies.

The whole situation is entirely different, though, if the primary economic base of the society is expanding rapidly through industrialization. Under these conditions of growth, the total volume of resources, power, and privileges in a society will be constantly increasing, so that large numbers of people can be upwardly mobile without denying benefits to others. In the simplest of terms, almost everyone becomes at least a little better off, in comparison with the past. Most significantly, elites are not forced to relinquish their superior statuses, and hence are not so likely to resist change. Absolute upward mobility by many or even all members of an organization does not necessarily eliminate social inequality, however. If everyone gains at the same proportional rate, patterns of inequality will remain unchanged, though they may be more tolerable to those at the bottom. If elites gain benefits at a faster rate than others, social inequality will actually increase. But if a reverse process occurs, so that those persons with lower statuses gain proportionately more than those with higher statuses, then overall patterns of inequality will tend to decrease. Everyone will be moving upward, but those with farther to go will be moving somewhat faster, thus decreasing the distance from the top to the bottom of the stratification pattern. In very broad terms, this is what has been happening in recent years in many industrialized nations throughout the world.

In more specific terms, as a society industrializes and thus expands its available resources, several interrelated trends begin to occur, all of which tend to promote considerable amounts of absolute upward mobility—though this is never inevitable. These social trends include: (a) a shift in the occupational distribution resulting from a decline in the number of unskilled manual jobs and a growth in the number of skilled and nonmanual jobs available, which forces many people to be upwardly mobile in order to find work; (b) an expansion in the number of goods and services available to all persons, as a consequence of continually rising economic productivity; (c) expanding educational opportunities of all kinds, which provide routes for upward mobility to many people; (d) declining birth rates, especially among higher-status families, which necessitates recruitment from below for many higher positions; and (e) creation of organizations such as labor unions through which less privileged persons can exert pressures upon elites to share the expanding benefits more equally among all persons. None of these trends is an imperative consequence of industrialization, but to the extent that they do occur, they make possible more extensive opportunities for social mobility than have ever existed in the past.

Finally, as social mobility occurs in an organization, it can take one of two basic forms: (a) career mobility, in which a person significantly changes one or more of his statuses during his own lifetime; and (b) generational mobility, in which a person's major statuses are noticeably different from those of his parents. Both kinds of mobility occur often in relatively "open" societies such as the United States, but generational mobility appears to be more frequent. It is not that individuals rarely change statuses during their lives, but rather that a person's occupational role is increasingly being determined by the amount and nature of his education, so that the most extensive shifts in status tend to occur between generations through formal education instead of during a person's occupational career. It is interesting to note, though, that most individual cases of mobility involve relatively short movements, whether upward or downward. Most persons, that is, tend to hold social statuses not too dissimilar from those of their parents, and to make only relatively minor shifts during their lifetimes. The Horatio Alger dream of "rags to riches in a lifetime" has always been more of a myth than a reality. Nevertheless, the cumulative effects of thousands or millions of small individual status changes upon a society's stratification pattern can become exceedingly significant.[9]

Theories of Social Stratification

Two general theories of the causes of social stratification are predominant in current sociological thinking. One of these, the "functional theory" of stratification, has been extensively debated in the literature for over twenty years but still lacks adequate supporting proof. The other,

[9] The reader wishing to explore recent studies of social mobility in greater detail is referred to Seymour Martin Lipset and Reinhard Bendix, *Social Mobility in Industrial Society* (Berkeley, Calif.: University of California Press, 1959).

which might be called the "power theory" of stratification, represents an ancient idea that has only recently been formulated as a general thesis. Let us examine and evaluate each of these theories.

In essence, *the power theory of social stratification suggests that stratification results from the differential exercise of power in social life.* As elaborated by Gerhard Lenski, the major propositions of this thesis state that:[10]

(1) Power determines the distribution of nearly all surpluses existing in any society beyond the bare subsistence level. Hence privilege is largely an outcome of the exercise of social power, and is only slightly a product of altruism.

(2) In turn, prestige is largely, though not solely, a resultant of the exertion of power and the enjoyment of privileges in all postsubsistence societies.

(3) In general, both privilege and prestige are ultimately derived from the exercise of social power. Privileges and prestige accrue to those who wield power in social life.

(4) Although power is sometimes sought as an end in itself, more commonly it is used to gain various forms of privilege and prestige valued by the actors. Hence social actors usually seek to exercise as much power as possible, and then to transform this power into privileges and prestige.

(5) Once the use of power has resulted in the acquisition of some forms of privilege and prestige, these benefits can in turn be utilized as resources for gaining additional power, privileges, and prestige. In other words, the phenomena of power, privilege, and prestige are all highly interrelated in social life, so that any one of these factors can eventually produce either of the other two in a circular process.

(6) Although it is conceivable that power, privilege, and prestige might be evenly distributed among all the members of an organization, in reality this rarely happens. Power, and hence privilege and prestige, tend to become unequally distributed among social actors for a variety of psychological, social, and cultural reasons, thus creating social stratification.

(7) Patterns of stratification are perpetuated through time because most forms of privilege and prestige are highly valued. Consequently, social actors normally attempt to retain whatever privileges and prestige they presently enjoy, to acquire more privileges or prestige through increased utilization of power, and to pass their power, privileges, and prestige on to their children or other heirs.

(8) As they employ power to attain and protect privileges and

---

[10] These propositions are derived from *Power and Privilege* and from personal conversations with Professor Lenski.

prestige, actors frequently come into conflict with each other. Such conflicts can be either distributive or developmental in nature—that is, aimed at either redistributing existing benefits or creating additional resources or benefits.

(9) Conflict and competition will lead social actors to devise and use whatever techniques they can to protect, increase, and perpetuate the social power, privileges, and prestige they presently enjoy. Such devises include restricting the ability of others to exercise power or to gain access to privileges, employing one's present resources to acquire additional power, creating ideologies to justify one's privileges and prestige, supporting traditional customs such as inheritance and nepotism, and using overt force to oppose competing actors.

(10) Of the three factors of power, privilege, and prestige, power is the most immediately dependent upon ongoing social relationships, and hence is the most fluid, while prestige is the most detachable from a given social context and hence is the most stable over time. At any given time, therefore, many discrepancies can exist among an actor's power, privileges, and prestige. In the long run, though, these three factors will tend to remain in approximate balance, so that a change in any one of them will eventually result in changes in the other two also.

In an entirely different vein, *the functional theory of social stratification argues that stratification exists because it is beneficial for social organization.* This thesis was originally proposed by Kingsley Davis and Wilbert Moore, although it has subsequently been elaborated and modified by several other writers.[11] The main ideas of this theory can also be expressed as a series of propositions:

(1) All organizations must satisfy numerous functional requirements if they are to survive or attain goals.

(2) The various roles in an organization contribute differentially to the fulfillment of these functional requirements. The roles that contribute most directly to the satisfaction of crucial organizational requirements are of the greatest functional importance to that organization.

(3) If the organization is to survive or attain goals, these functionally important roles must be enacted by qualified persons in an adequate manner.

(4) In general, however, these functionally crucial roles require

[11] Kingsley Davis and Wilbert E. Moore, "Some Principles of Stratification," *American Sociological Review,* vol. 10 (1945), pp. 242–249. See also Richard Simpson, "A Modification of the Functional Theory of Stratification," *Social Forces* (December 1956), pp. 132–137; Dennis H. Wrong, "The Functional Theory of Stratification: Some Neglected Considerations," *American Sociological Review,* vol. 24 (1959), pp. 772–782; and Wilbert E. Moore, "But Some are More Equal than Others," *American Sociological Review,* vol. 28 (February 1963), pp. 13–18.

higher qualifications and more extensive training than do other roles in the organization, and are also frequently quite demanding in terms of duties and responsibilities. Consequently, the supply of actors to fill these roles is normally limited in any organization.

(5) All organizations are thus faced, in varying degrees, with the twin functional problems of filling functionally important roles with the most capable actors available and of encouraging these actors to enact their roles to the best of their abilities.

(6) These problems are resolved by the organization through the differential awarding of privileges and prestige to various actors. That is, valued forms of privilege and prestige become incorporated into functionally necessary roles, as a means of inducing actors to acquire necessary training and adequately enact these roles.

(7) These inducements or rewards need not be directly proportional to the functional importance of each role, as long as they are sufficient to insure that the role will be filled and performed by qualified actors.

(8) Thus social privileges and prestige tend to accrue to those actors who perform necessary functions for an organization, in rough proportion to the difficulty of inducing actors to adequately fulfill these roles. "Social inequality is thus an unconsciously evolved device by which societies insure that the more important positions are conscientiously filled by the most qualified persons."

(9) In general, some degree of unequal privileges and prestige is a functional necessity if an organization is to survive and attain goals. The actual amount of inequality required in any situation depends on such factors as the nature of the organization's functional requirements, the supply of qualified actors, and the demands of the crucial roles to be enacted.

(10) The process of allocating differential awards to role actors is sometimes purposefully performed by organizational leaders, but more commonly it is an indirect result of the balancing of supply and demand in the labor market. In either case, though, the unequal distributions of privilege and prestige within an organization that result from this process constitute patterned social stratification.

Both the power and functional theories of social stratification are open to numerous criticisms, which indicates that neither theory is sufficient by itself. On the empirical level, for instance, the power theory has considerable trouble explaining why powerful actors such as leaders of criminal syndicates or political "machines," who may virtually dominate a community, nevertheless do not often enjoy public esteem, deference, and honor. Nor can it adequately deal with people such as Albert Schweitzer, Tom Dooley, and Eleanor Roosevelt, who exercise little or no power in society and yet are revered by others.[12] On the other hand, the functional theory is contradicted by professional baseball players, nightclub singers, and similar individuals who presumably are not fulfilling functionally crucial roles but who nevertheless reap fame and fortune. Nor does it tell why teachers, who supposedly are performing a vital function for society, receive relatively small incomes and little public respect.

Both of these explanations of stratification also contain several theoretical weaknesses. The power theory is perhaps the logically "tighter" argument, since if one makes certain assumptions about the nature of man, its component propositions do logically fit together. But if we should accept this theory of social stratification, what would be the implications for any broader theory of the general process of social organization? For instance, how are functional requirements satisfied according to this theory, except by pure chance, since presumably every social actor is basically self-oriented and without serious concern for larger collectivities? Or how is the process of functional integration to be explained if all actors continually strive to maximize their functional autonomy? Furthermore, the theory gives little consideration to normative influences on stratification patterns, as seen in contemporary ideals of social equality, "protection of the inept," and public responsibility for promoting the welfare of all persons.[13] These questions do not deny the usefulness of the power theory in explaining many facets of stratification, but they do raise doubts concerning its broader theoretical implications. Internally, the weakest point in the theory is perhaps the link between the exercise of power and the acquiring of privilege and prestige. Through what mechanisms does this process typically occur in various settings?

The functional theory has been criticized on several grounds, only some of which are noted here.[14] First, how do the members of an organization discover what its crucial survival or operational requirements are, or determine which roles satisfy these requirements? And on what grounds do they rank these roles into hierarchies of social importance, or decide

---

[12] Lenski leaves room in his theory for such variables as social altruism, but he does not deal with them.

[13] Lenski notes the presence of these normative factors in modern societies but does not fully incorporate them within his theory. The growing importance of these phenomena has been stressed by William J. Goode, "The Protection of the Inept," *American Sociological Review*, vol. 32 (February 1967), pp. 5–19.

[14] These criticisms are drawn from several sources: Melvin Tumin, "Some Principles of Stratification: A Critical Review," *American Sociological Review*, vol. 18 (1953), pp. 387–394; Simpson, "A Modification of the Functional Theory of Stratification"; Walter Buckley, "Social Stratification and the Functional Theory of Social Differentiation," *American Sociological Review*, vol. 23 (August 1958), pp. 369–375; and George Huaco, "A Logical Analysis of the Davis-Moore Theory of Stratification," *American Sociological Review*, vol. 28 (October 1963), pp. 801–804.

how many and what kinds of privileges and prestige are necessary to induce individuals to train for and enact them? All of these tasks are largely beyond the capability of contemporary social science, and obviously they could not be accomplished in most organizations except through mere happenstance or shrewd guessing. Second, the theory assumes that all roles are acquired through open achievement, when in fact the majority of functionally necessary roles in most societies have historically been filled through closed ascription.[15] Third, to what extent do roles that carry heavy public responsibilities require "external" inducements to attract capable individuals or to encourage maximum performance? Do not most such roles carry their own "intrinsic" rewards, such as a sense of accomplishment or creativity, so that in many cases they would be filled regardless of whatever privilege or prestige was attached to them? In other words, cannot there be functional alternatives to inequality that would also insure the satisfaction of necessary requirements?

Fourth, the functional theory entirely ignores classes as established social organizations, as well as the perpetuation of patterned stratification through time. It attempts to show that status inequality is functionally necessary, but it does not apply this argument to organized, perpetuated social classes. In this light, the theory is perhaps more accurately an explanation of division of labor than of social stratification. Fifth, social inequality can have many dysfunctional consequences for an organization as well as the beneficial effects described by the theory. Under various conditions it can impede vital communications and coordination, promote unnecessary social conflict, restrict social change, and weaken the integration of an organization. And sixth, this theory at times anthropomorphizes social organization, when it claims that "society unconsciously insures" that socially important roles will be carried out. Individuals within organizations may sometimes purposefully take such a course of action—as when an employer decides to offer a high salary for a job in order to attract "the best man available"—but society has no mind and cannot engage in this kind of teleological action. We are thus led to the conclusion that although the functional theory is applicable within limited social settings, it cannot by itself offer an adequate explanation of social stratification.

Despite all these criticisms, both the power and functional theories are nevertheless partially supported by empirical observations. In almost all societies it does happen that those persons who exercise social power also tend to receive at least some forms of privilege and prestige.[16] At the

[15] Davis and Moore note that under conditions of closed role ascription their theory explains only role performance, not recruitment or training.

[16] Lenski has amassed a considerable amount of data from many types of societies to support this generalization.

same time, it has been repeatedly demonstrated that a substantial correspondence exists in most societies between the perceived functional importance of a job and the privilege and prestige afforded to those who perform it.[17] Because both of these empirical relationships are far from perfect, additional evidence must be gathered to test the intriguing hypothesis that those actors who enact functionally roles also normally wield social power. The existing data do suggest, however, that both theories can be useful in explaining some aspects of the total process of social stratification.

Any complete theory of stratification will undoubtedly incorporate at least portions of both the power and functional theses. Perhaps such a composite stratification theory might follow the outline sketched below:

(1) Social actors tend to seek power, privilege, and prestige, because of the benefits these phenomena give them. Although power may not be sought as an end in itself, under most conditions actors must first gain the use of social power if they are to acquire valued privileges and prestige.

(2) One means of acquiring power—though not the only means—is to become qualified for, or otherwise gain access to, social roles that control resources. Adequate enactment of such roles will then enable the actor to exercise power for the attainment of privileges and prestige.

(3) Considerable power inheres in the enactment of functionally necessary roles. To the extent that a role contributes to the satisfaction of organizational requirements, its incumbent will wield dominance over other related roles and actors. Functionally important roles are also likely to provide additional types of power, including access to resources with which to exercise force, a basis for gaining legitimacy and hence authority, and even attraction through public visibility.

(4) Hence the power-wielding roles that actors seek and enact, as a means of gaining desired privileges and prestige, are also quite likely to contribute to the fulfillment of organizational requirements. However, the fact that an actor's roles may be functionally important for some larger social organization is often unknown to him, or if known, is usually incidental to his interests. An exception is the special case of social altruism. Thus the satisfaction of organizational survival and operational requirements is largely an unintended, or at least secondary, consequence of the enactment of power-wielding roles by actors seeking to gain privileges and prestige.

---

[17] Alex Inkeles and Peter A. Rossi, "National Comparisons of Occupational Prestige," *The American Journal of Sociology*, vol. 56 (January 1956), pp. 329–339. See also Archibald O. Haller and David M. Lewis, "The Hypothesis of Intersocietal Similarity in Occupational Prestige Hierarchies," *The American Journal of Sociology*, vol. 72 (September 1966), pp. 210–216.

(5) Elites who occupy powerful organizational roles frequently reward other less powerful role actors in proportion to the services they render to these elites. That is, differential distribution of privilege and prestige is utilized by elites to promote role enactment that is functional for them in the attainment of their particular goals. Some of these roles may also have beneficial consequences for the total organization; others will not.

(6) Actors who occupy power-wielding roles will normally attempt to protect and enhance their power, privileges, and prestige through such techniques as limiting the access of others to the roles, making themselves functionally indispensable, using their roles to gain additional power, and legitimizing their activities in the eyes of others.

(7) Because these powerful roles frequently do have functional consequences for other actors and for organizations, pressures will be exerted on the incumbents to perform the roles in an adequate and responsible manner. If these pressures do not produce minimally acceptable role performance, the incumbent is likely to lose his role sooner or later, unless he can marshall enough power to resist all such pressures.

(8) The patterns of social inequality that emerge and are perpetuated through this process constitute social stratification. The fundamental causal factor in this process is the seeking by social actors of power, privilege, and prestige, but as a consequence of their role activities, organizational functional requirements do tend to be satisfied, at least in the long run.

(9) In general, the more complex an organization, the greater the number of its roles possessing some functional importance, and hence dominance and other types of power. As a result, growing complexity of social organization provides a basis for—though does not guarantee—increased diversification in the distribution of power, privilege, and prestige among all participants.

(10) As the overall functional effectiveness of an organization increases, there is also a tendency for a norm of equality to develop, since enough resources and power are now being generated to give all participants at least minimally acceptable privileges and prestige. As this norm gains support, the organization will tend to create various procedures for more equitable distribution of privileges (if not always prestige) and for protection of the incapable and inept.

Consequences of Social Stratification

As a means of emphasizing the significance of social stratification throughout social life, we shall now mention a few of the innumerable consequences of this process for both individuals and organizations.

The social statuses that an individual occupies in various stratification dimensions have been shown by many studies to affect a wide range of his actions and attitudes. Strictly speaking, these relationships are only statistical correlations, not statements of causation, but they do indicate that much of what a person thinks and does is directly associated with his particular social statuses.

In the area of health and welfare, the higher an individual's socio-economic and other statuses, the longer his life expectancy, the less likely he is to become psychotic, and the better the medical care he receives. In regard to participation in organized social life, the higher a person's statuses, the more likely he will be to have several close personal friends, to belong to one or more special-interest voluntary associations, to vote in elections, to take part in civic activities, and to attend church fairly regularly. Finally, in reference to sociopolitical attitudes, higher-status people are more prone to hold "conservative" opinions on many economic questions and hence to vote Republican, but at the same time they tend to give much stronger support than do lower-status people to "liberal" positions on civil liberties, civil rights, and international cooperation. As stated here, these extremely crude generalizations gloss over the many qualifications and exceptions that researchers have carefully specified, but they do illustrate the pervasive effects of social stratification upon all individuals.

On a broader scale, the extent and nature of social stratification occurring within an organization can also have numerous consequences for that entire organization. Notwithstanding the debate over the functional benefits of stratification in satisfying organizational requirements, it is clear that gross inequalities in the distributions of power, privilege, and prestige have underlain a considerable proportion of all social strife and conflict throughout human history. This is particularly true when the process of stratification gives rise to relatively delineated and closed social classes. Privileged classes have traditionally sought to protect and expand their benefits, while relatively deprived classes have periodically—though often not too successfully—sought to gain more for themselves. Whether the immediate issue be a local zoning ordinance, industrial wages, control of the national government, or the present worldwide "revolution of rising expectations," some kind of inequality will almost inevitably be a crucial, if not the basic, factor in any social dispute.

The most critical problems for social organizations arising from the existence of social stratification center on the use of power by elites. To the extent that power in a society or other organization is centralized within an elite class (or classes), it becomes increasingly difficult for other members to affect or limit the ways in which these elites exercise their

power. If an elite class chooses to wield power primarily for its own benefit rather than for the welfare of the whole organization—as has frequently occurred throughout history—other classes may be incapable of
exerting enough pressures on the elites to make them act in socially responsible ways. Under such conditions, unless some external agent forces
the elites to alter their actions, the organization may experience serious
operational problems if not total destruction. This predicament is all too
evident in many "underdeveloped" nations around the world today.

This chapter completes our survey of the basic processes occuring
throughout all organizations: conflict and change, integration, power, and
allocation/stratification. As a general conclusion, it may be well to re-
emphasize that all these social processes occur only within patterned
social relationships and shared cultures, and hence must be understood
and explained as aspects of the broader process of social organization. Although they are distinct social phenomena, these processes of conflict,
change, integration, and stratification frequently become thoroughly intertwined in actual social life. Hence no one of them can be thoroughly
studied unless all the others are also taken into account.

The next two chapters are somewhat more abstract and demanding
than the preceding discussions. They deal first with several types of analysis and an analytical model that are often used in sociological studies of
social organization, and second with six different schools of theoretical
thought that have developed in sociology as explanations of the general
process of social organization. The beginning student may wish to skip
over them and go on to the topic of social evolution in Chapter 16, which
can be done without seriously disrupting our train of thought. The more
advanced or ambitious reader, meanwhile, will hopefully discover in these
chapters a challenging introduction to the fundamental analytical techniques and theoretical ideas of contemporary sociology.

RECOMMENDED READING

CHINOY, ELY, "Social Mobility Trends in the United States," *American Sociological Review*, vol. 20 (April 1955), pp. 180–186. (Also Bobbs-Merrill
reprint S-40.)
    Draws on historical and survey data to point out a number of factors that
    both limit and encourage upward social mobility.
COREY, LEWIS, "The Middle Class," *The Antioch Review*, Spring 1945, pp. 1–
20. Reprinted in Reinhard Bendix and Seymour Martin Lipset, eds.,

Class, Status, and Power, pp. 371–380 (New York: The Free Press, a division of The Macmillan Company, 1953).
Discusses the changing nature of the middle class in the United States, comparing the "old middle class" of entrepreneurs to the "new middle class" of bureaucratic employees.

DAVIS, KINGSLEY, AND WILBERT E. MOORE, "Some Principles of Stratification," *American Sociological Review,* vol. 10 (1945), pp. 242–249. MELVIN TUMIN, "Some Principles of Stratification: A Critical Review," *American Sociological Review,* vol. 18 (1953), pp. 387–394. (These two articles are bound together in Bobbs-Merrill reprint S-69.) GEORGE HUACO, "A Logical Analysis of the Davis-Moore Theory of Stratification," *American Sociological Review,* vol. 28 (October 1963), pp. 801–804.
The major presentation and two critiques of the functional theory of social stratification.

INKELES, ALEX, AND PETER A. ROSSI, "National Comparisons of Occupational Prestige," *The American Journal of Sociology,* vol. 56 (January 1956), pp. 329–339. (Also Bobbs-Merrill reprint S-425.)
Summarizes and compares occupational prestige rankings in six different industrialized societies, pointing out the high degree of similarity existing among all these societies.

LANDECKER, WERNER, "Class Boundaries," *American Sociological Review,* vol. 25 (December 1960), pp. 868–877.
Reviews the distinction between discrete social classes and continuous social strata, and suggests a procedure for objectively delineating class boundaries.

LENSKI, GERHARD E., "American Social Classes: Statistical Strata or Social Groups?," *The American Journal of Sociology,* vol. 58 (September 1952), pp. 139–144.
Demonstrates that, in at least one American community, considerable social stratification occurs in the form of several continuous status hierarchies, but not as discrete social classes.

_____, *Power and Privilege: A Theory of Social Stratification,* chaps. 3–4 (New York: McGraw-Hill, Inc., 1966).
The major presentation of the power theory of social stratification.

CHAPTER 14

Analysis
of Social Organization

As they seek to describe and explain the process of social organization and the many diverse forms this process assumes, social scientists employ a variety of different analytical techniques. These various types of scientific analysis are not mutually exclusive, and many studies utilize several of them simultaneously. Nevertheless, each raises distinctive questions about social life and leads to particular kinds of insights and understandings. In addition, social scientists also construct broad analytical frameworks, or models, as a means of maintaining analytical coherence in their research and theorizing.

Our concern in this chapter is to explore a few of these analytical tools currently being used in sociology. We shall not deal with any specific substantive phenomena, although we shall draw upon several empirical studies as examples of various analytical techniques. A basic understanding of the process of sociological analysis should in turn provide a foundation for our examination in the following chapter of the major schools of general sociological theory.

The four analytical approaches most commonly used by sociologists are structural, process, causal, and functional analysis. Table 14-1 briefly summarizes these four types of analysis, and in the following sections we shall first illustrate and then explain each approach. These discussions are all quite cursory, not definitive or exhaustive; our purpose here is only to introduce the major features of sociological analysis.

TABLE 14–1
Four Types of Sociological Analysis

Type	Key Question	Essential Feature
Structural	What is it like?	Describe the structural characteristics of a social phenomenon
Process	How does it occur?	Investigate the social processes through which a social phenomenon occurs
Causal	What caused it?	Determine the social factors that produce a social phenomenon
Functional	What are its social consequences?	Discover the consequence of a social phenomenon for the organization in which it occurs

In the final section of the chapter we shall explore the main characteristics of the analytical model most widely used in contemporary sociology: the social system model.

Structural Analysis

A well-known example of sociological research that is primarily (though not totally) structural in nature is Floyd Hunter's study of the community power structure in Atlanta, Georgia.[1] The principal thesis Hunter attempted to document in his work was that most of the effective power in this community—and presumably in all large metropolises—is concentrated in the hands of a very small number of individuals. More specifically, he hypothesized that behind the officially elected government of Atlanta stand a few unofficial but extremely powerful elites who actually "run" the community. Through their control of vital resources, major businesses and industries, communication facilities, banking and other monetary activities, and the reigning political party, these elites supposedly dominate all major community decisions and programs. The corollary of this thesis is that no one outside the highly centralized power structure—and least of all the voting public—actually has much control over community affairs.

Hunter asked "judges" who were knowledgeable about community activities to select the "top men" from a previously compiled list of prominent citizens. The names picked were then compared for similarities. A relatively few persons—Hunter somewhat arbitrarily limited the number

[1] Floyd Hunter, *Community Power Structure* (Chapel Hill, N. C.: The University of North Carolina Press, 1953).

to forty—were repeatedly nominated as dominant power-wielders, while other prominent members of the community received only scattered or no votes. Furthermore, these elites formed a relatively closed class, in that they themselves tended to nominate only each other as "top men," although within this class some individuals were said to be considerably more influential than others. The majority of these community elites were businessmen, not politicians, and they exercised their power through informal pressures rather than by official decision-making, but their power over the community was nevertheless very real and quite extensive. Hunter's work has since been criticized on many grounds—theoretical, methodological, and analytical—but nevertheless it did generate a host of further studies of community power structures.

As this illustration suggests, structural analysis tends to be relatively descriptive in nature. Some amount of straightforward description enters into most sociological analysis, since the usual first step in studying any social phenomenon is to describe its major characteristics. The distinctive feature of structural analysis, however, is that it seeks only to answer such question as: "What patterns of social ordering does it display?" or "How are its parts interconnected?" or "In what ways is it related to other social phenomena?" In purely structural analysis, no attempt is made to deal with the further questions: "Through what processes does this organization operate or this phenomenon take place?" or "What factor or factors caused it?" or "What are its consequences for the larger organization(s) of which it is a part?"

Besides describing the distribution of power within an organization, structural analysis might be used in studying the web of friendships occurring within a group, the paths of communication among the various departments of a university, the location of social class boundaries in a society, the extensiveness of the division of labor within an industry, the patterns of relationships occurring within a political network, or the different positions existing in a sports team.

Descriptive structural analysis is sometimes likened to journalistic reporting, in which the sociologist supposedly only records whatever he observes—though perhaps in a more thorough fashion than does the nonscientist. There is a crucial difference between journalistic reporting and social science, however. The sophisticated social scientist, unlike the typical journalist, gathers information as a means of formulating valid empirical generalizations or testing a theory, not just to inform his readers of certain facts.[2] Thus both a reporter and a sociologist might investigate

---

[2] There are exceptions, of course: some sociological work is nothing but social reporting, while some sophisticated journalists do link their findings to more fundamental social generalizations or theories.

the incidence of crime in various neighborhoods of a community, but only the sociologist would be seeking to throw empirical light on the hypothesis that certain kinds of crimes and other indicators of social disorganization are most common in deteriorated and transitional areas immediately surrounding the central business district.

As a means of generalizing structural analysis beyond mere description, sociologists often construct typologies, or sets of categories into which many diverse social phenomena can be classified. Typologies vary considerably in the degree to which they are abstracted from immediate observations, and hence in their analytical depth:

(1) Descriptive types are merely logically derived divisions into which the observed phenomena are placed—such as "no-party," "one-party," "one-and-a-half-party," "two-party," and "multiparty" governmental structures.

(2) Composite types are constructed by abstracting from many different observed situations the characteristics that are common to most or all of these phenomena, as in the "folk" and "feudal" societal models to be described in Chapter 16.

(3) Ideal types are obtained by combining several variables or dimensions into a single abstract conception and then extending this conception to its logical extreme, as in Max Weber's account of a totally rational bureaucracy which we shall examine in Chapter 17.[3]

There are many analytical limitations to the use of typologies, since (a) types only classify phenomena and do not relate them to other situations as either causes or consequences; (b) there are no standardized procedures for the construction of descriptive, composite, or ideal types; and (c) types are only "sensitizing" devices, not measurement tools, since they contain only the selected information we build into them. Nevertheless, when appropriately employed, typologies enable us to carry structural analysis considerably beyond sheer description.

In summary, *the purpose of structural analysis is to describe and classify structural patterns of observed social phenomena.* When performing this kind of analysis, the social scientist attempts to explore and record the significant structural characteristics of the interactions, relationships, social ordering, or cultural ideas he is studying. Structural analysis is thus a fundamental first step in the total process of scientifically analyzing the process of social organization.

---

[3] *From Max Weber: Essays in Sociology,* trans. and ed. H. H. Gerth and C. Wright Mills (New York: Oxford University Press, 1946), chap. 8.

Process Analysis

As an illustration of process analysis we summarize a discussion of goal formation by James Thompson and William McEwen.[4] These writers argue that organizational goals are never static, but rather are fluctuating outcomes of interaction within the organization and between the organization and its social environment. The setting of organizational goals must therefore be viewed, they suggest, as a continual process that is always sensitive to impinging social forces. An organization must constantly be alert to, and take account of, changing circumstances in its social environment as it formulates its goals.

Thompson and McEwen then analyze four alternative strategies organizations can use in their dealings with other organizations, arranged in order of increasing environmental control over organizational goal-setting processes: (a) competition, or rivalry between two or more organizations as mediated by neutral third parties—which prevents unilateral or arbitrary goal choices by the competing organizations; (b) bargaining, or negotiation between two or more organizations for the establishment of exchange relationships—which limits an organization's goal-setting activities by committing some of its resources to situations over which it does not have complete control; (c) cooptation, or the absorption of threatening outside elements into the leadership ranks of an organization in order to blunt their attacks—which further diminishes organizational autonomy in goal-setting as "outsiders" are given a direct voice in the process, and as organizations become tied together through overlapping memberships; and (d) coalition, or the formation of temporary working partnerships between two or more organizations—which eliminates autonomous organizational control over goal-setting, since all decisions must now be made jointly with the coalition partners.

Process analysis, like structural analysis, can be largely descriptive in nature, as in a recording of a religious ritual or a group discussion. But this technique may go beyond sheer description as it seeks to generalize about social processes occurring through time and to interpret these processes in terms of organizational functioning. In any case, process analysis is always concerned with ongoing, dynamic activities, in contrast to the static patterns described by structural analysis.

Besides examining relationships between an organization and its social environment, process analysis might also be employed to investigate

[4] James D. Thompson and William J. McEwen, "Organizational Goals and Environment: Goal-Setting as an Interaction Process," *American Sociological Review*, vol. 23 (February 1958), pp. 23–31.

such questions as how elite social classes use their power to maintain their privileges and gain social prestige, how governmental agencies coerce or cooperate with private business firms to keep the economy stable, how sporadic protest actions become organized into sweeping social movements, how new families in a community become assimilated into neighborhood and community activities, how peasant societies become "modernized" through such processes as industrialization and urbanization, or how mass-communication networks unify a society.

Sociologists as yet have not made extensive use of process analysis in their studies of social organizations, although a number of techniques have been devised by social psychologists to study the process of social interaction within small groups. By far the most widely used is Robert Bales' procedure of "interaction process analysis," which enables observers to record and evaluate everything that happens during a group discussion.[5] Part of this technique involves the classification of all communications into one of twelve categories: "shows solidarity" or "shows antagonism," "shows tension" or "shows tension release," "shows agreement" or "shows disagreement," "gives suggestions" or "asks for suggestions," "gives opinions" or "asks for opinions," "gives information" or "asks for information." In addition, a count is kept of the number of times each participant speaks or otherwise communicates information, the length of each communication, and the person or persons to whom his remarks are directed. This technique has been used to study such processes as task differentiation, the emergence of leadership roles, group problem-solving, and the development of group solidarity.

Although process analysis sometimes employs typologies for classification purposes, the usefulness of static typologies is in this case quite limited. One common means of exploring dynamic processes is a "variable" or "multivariate" approach, in which we: (a) examine separately the various dimensions of a given phenomenon, measuring each of them with one or more empirical variables; (b) investigate the dynamic relationships found among the variables and dimensions; and (c) look for and study changes occurring through time in these relationships. The difference between "typological" and "variable" process analysis is evident in two contrasting ways of studying industrialization. A typological approach would classify societies into a number of discrete categories, such as "preindustrial," "early industrial," "advanced industrial," and "postindustrial," on the basis of whatever relevant information was available. A variable approach, in contrast, would isolate a number of factors thought to be crucial for the process of industrialization, such as energy production and

---

[5] Robert F. Bales, *Interaction Process Analysis: A Method for the Study of Small Groups* (Reading, Mass.: Addison-Wesley Publishing Company, Inc., 1949).

consumption, agricultural productivity, transportation facilities, and labor organization, and then measure these variables through time and examine their effects upon one another. As social scientists become increasingly adept at the use of computers for data manipulation, the employment of complex multivariate techniques should expand considerably.

In summary, *the purpose of process analysis is to inquire into the ongoing processes that constitute social reality.* In this case, the social scientist attempts to examine and explain the dynamic social processes through which social organization is created and through which existing organizations operate to handle conflict and change, achieve unity and stability, employ power to attain goals, and allocate benefits to participants. Process analysis is thus a necessary complement to structural analysis in all studies of social organization.

Causal Analysis

To illustrate causal analysis in sociology, let us examine a study by Nancy Morse and Everett Reimer that fairly closely approximated an ideal research design.[6] Their research was an empirical test of the hypothesis that decentralization of decision-making within an organization tends to increase both the satisfactions of individual members and the productivity of the entire organization. As a setting for the research, they used four clerical divisions in the main office of a large insurance company. All four divisions were fairly similar in size, kind of work performed, types of personnel, operating procedures, supervisory structure, and other relevant factors. In two of these divisions, decision-making was decentralized by giving the clerks a great deal of freedom to decide among themselves how their offices should be run. In the other two divisions, decision-making was centralized by giving the supervisors and higher management sole authority for determining all activities.

The experiment continued for over a year, during which time both individual satisfaction and division productivity were repeatedly measured. People working in the decentralized divisions consistently expressed much greater satisfaction with the company, their supervisors, and their working conditions than did those in the centralized divisions. The data on productivity were less decisive, however. The decentralized divisions at first experienced many operational difficulties because of their unfamiliarity with the new procedure of group decision-making, and because

---

[6] Nancy Morse and Everett Reimer, "The Experimental Change of a Major Organizational Variable," *Journal of Abnormal and Social Psychology*, vol. 52 (1956), pp. 120–129.

of initial hostility to this practice among the supervisors. In contrast, the centralized divisions quickly increased their operating efficiency (measured in terms of number of clerks required to process a given work load) by simply firing several dispensable clerks. Over time, though, the production rate of the decentralized divisions began to rise markedly as the workers agreed not to replace individuals who left through normal attrition, and as the suspicions of the supervisors were slowly overcome. Although at the end of the experiment the centralized divisions were still slightly more efficient, several trends indicated that this superiority would not last indefinitely. Morse and Reimer concluded that decentralization of decision-making in an organization definitely improves member satisfaction, and may in the long run also increase organizational productivity.

Causal analysis is aimed at the discovery of those factors and conditions which are both necessary and sufficient to produce a given social phenomenon. Any existent social situation or process may be causally investigated: racial segregation, organized religion, the formation of friendship cliques in formal associations, changes in the family, growth of centralized national government, development of class consciousness, or suburbanization. The word "may" must be stressed, however, since whether or not we actually can discover all the causes of such phenomena remains an unresolved question. Of the four types of social analysis discussed here, causal analysis is perhaps the easiest to describe and yet the most difficult to perform adequately. In our everyday affairs we all think in cause-and-effect terms, but conclusively demonstrating the existence of causal links among phenomena is a formidable task in social science.

To understand sociological causal analysis, we must first distinguish it from both psychological and historical causal explanations. The psychologist seeks to learn why particular individuals behave in certain ways, whereas the sociologist is concerned with patterns of activity shared by two or more persons. For instance, the sociologist studying causes of suburbanization would not be directly concerned with why the Thompson family decided to move from their city apartment out to "Park View," or why Mr. Carson is willing to ride the subway for two hours every day in order to live in a suburban housing development. The sociologist would instead examine broad social and cultural forces operating in society to produce suburbanization, such as "middle-class" values on home ownership, migration of ethnic populations into central cities and resulting patterns of segregation, urban zoning ordinances, use of houses as status symbols, and land values and other economic considerations that force contractors to build new houses on the periphery of the community. The actions and attitudes of the Thompsons and the Carsons would thus constitute for him only sources of data, not phenomena to be explained in and of themselves.

The historian, meanwhile, might be interested in the process of suburbanization as it occurred in a particular historical location, such as New York City during the nineteenth century. He would look for specific factors operating in that setting at that time, and from them he would draw a causal explanation of that one historical event, not of the total process of suburbanization. In practice, historical and social causal analyses tend to merge, as when a historian broadens his scope to cover a certain process whenever and wherever it occurs, or when a sociologist attempts to generalize from a study performed at one place and time. Sociologists and social historians have not in the past cooperated anywhere nearly as extensively as they might, but today these two fields are slowly converging.

Causal analysis can never be purely descriptive in nature, since a cause-and-effect relationship cannot be directly observed. What we observe in our studies, as in all daily life, is a temporal sequence of specific events. Our research can show these events to be interrelated to some measurable extent, but on the basis of this evidence we must then infer a causal relationship. The certainty with which the social scientist can make such an inference depends on both the nature of the phenomenon being studied and the adequacy of his research design. Consider first the nature of many social phenomena:

(1) Few aspects of social life are caused by a single factor; complex multiple causation is the normal situation.

(2) Causation is rarely completely linear in social life; many social situations involve "feedback" from their effects to their causes, which makes the total process reciprocal or spiral.

(3) Although in an ultimate sense all social phenomena are caused, in an immediate sense many social events are more directly the result of random "conjuncture" than ordered causation.[7]

(4) The factors that initially cause a social phenomenon are often not those which perpetuate it through time.

All four of these situations tend to weaken—though they do not destroy—the credibility of sociological causal inferences.

Consider now the design of much sociological research. The ideal research design for performing causal analysis is the controlled laboratory experiment, in which all relevant factors affecting a given phenomenon are held constant, except for the experimental variable being manipulated

---

[7] For a discussion of the distinction between causality and conjuncture as well as many other logical problems inherent in sociological causal analysis, see N. S. Timasheff, "Order Causality, and Conjecture." in Llewellyn Gross, ed., *Symposium on Sociological Theory* (New York: Harper & Row, Publishers, 1959), pp. 145–164.

by the researcher. Since this one variable is then the only possible source of variation, the researcher can infer with considerable certainty that whatever changes occur in the situation are caused by the experimental variable. Finally, to complete this design the researcher must also have a control situation identical to the experimental one, except that no variation is introduced into it. It serves as a check on the thoroughness with which he has controlled the experimental situation, since his causal inference is considered valid only if no changes occur in this control situation during the course of the experiment.

A moment's thought should convince us that these ideal experimental conditions are extremely difficult, if not completely impossible, to achieve in sociology. Apart from the ethical considerations involved in purposefully manipulating individuals and organizations, social reality is far too complex and multidimensional to allow us to hold constant all relevant factors in an experiment. These problems are encountered in even the simplest small-group studies, and they become virtually overwhelming in research at the community or societal levels.

In an effort to surmount some of these difficulties, social scientists have devised several different partial approximations to the ideal experimental design. All of them provide some basis for inferring the existence of causal relationships in social life, although none is as conclusive as the controlled laboratory experiment. A few of these procedures are the following:

(1) "Partial experiments," containing some but not all of the features of the ideal design, as when a control situation cannot be established.

(2) "Natural experiments," or real situations that "accidentally" evidence at least some of the characteristics of a laboratory experiment, and which the social scientist studies while they are occurring.

(3) "Statistical controls," which the researcher imposes by performing various statistical operations on the data after they have been obtained, rather than in the course of an experiment.

(4) "Correlational inference," in which matrices of correlations among variables are manipulated to discover possible causal relationships.[8]

(5) "Historical evaluation," or the examination of numerous historical cases to determine whether they support a proposed causal theory.

In general, the more closely the research design of a sociological study approximates the ideal experimental method through the use of one or

---

[8] See H. M. Blalock, Jr., *Causal Inferences in Nonexperimental Research* (Chapel Hill, N. C.: University of North Carolina Press, 1964). It must be kept in mind, though, that single correlations taken by themselves are only measures of covariance, and never indicate causation.

more of these techniques, the greater the confidence we can have in the causal inferences it suggests.

In summary, *the purpose of causal analysis is to construct and verify inferences about cause-and-effect relationships among social phenomena.* In causal analysis, the social scientist attempts to discover temporal relationships among variables, and then to identify the factors or conditions that are necessary and sufficient to produce the situation he is studying. Causal analysis of the forces producing social phenomena is thus a demanding but imperative third step in the study of social organization.

Functional Analysis

Functional analysis is one of the most frequently discussed, and yet least fully used, analytical techniques in sociology. We shall begin with two brief examples of functional analysis, and then specify in greater detail what this analytical approach entails. The first of these examples pertains to religion, the second to the family.

Untold numbers of writers have concerned themselves with the consequences of religion for individual believers, but Émile Durkheim asked and attempted to answer a different kind of question: What functions does religion perform for society?[9] He was particularly interested in the processes through which societies and other social organizations maintain solidarity or unity, and he saw religion as a fundamental means of satisfying this critical organizational requirement. Through its public services, rituals, and ceremonies, religion strengthens the solidarity of society in four different ways, according to Durkheim. These four social functions of religion are (a) disciplinary, or teaching people self-discipline and willingness to accept social responsibilities; (b) cohesive, or bringing people together to reaffirm their common social bonds and values; (c) revitalizing, or teaching and perpetuating the social heritage and traditions of a society; and (d) euphoric, or building up a reserve of public acceptance of the social order, which can be used in times of crisis. In general, Durkheim saw these social functions of religion as being more important in simple, primitive, sacred societies than in modern, complex, secular nations, but nevertheless they can be observed to be operating in virtually all societies.

William Ogburn has written extensively about changing functions of

[9] Émile Durkheim, *The Elementary Forms of the Religious Life,* trans. Joseph Ward Swain (New York: The Free Press, a division of The Macmillan Company, 1947).

the family in contemporary industrialized-urbanized societies.[10] In prein-dustrial societies, most economic production centers in the family, as peasants work their fields in family units and artisans create their hand-made goods in home workshops. Families in "modernized" nations rarely perform these kinds of economic functions. Most economic production in these societies occurs outside the home, in factories, offices, and stores. People now participate in economic activities as individuals, not as fami-lies, so that the family as a social unit makes little contribution to the production of goods and services. (Some writers have pointed out that the family is still a very important unit in the consumption of goods and services, but this is a quite different phenomenon.) Along with the loss of its economic-production functions, the family in modern society has also slowly surrendered many of its other traditional functions to outside specialized organizations. Whereas the family was once the center of most educational, religious, recreational, health, and welfare activities for its members, these social functions are now usually performed by separate types of organizations—or more precisely, by dozens of different kinds of associations—each of which specializes in providing only certain limited services. In short, the family has lost most of its traditional functions to other organizations, with the exception of its primary responsibilities for rearing and socializing children and providing society with productive individuals through the satisfaction of personal socio-emotional needs. These appear to be the remaining major functions of the family in con-temporary society.

In its broadest sense, functional analysis involves simply looking for the consequences of a given activity or phenomenon for the organization in which it occurs, the actors involved, or other related social phenom-ena.[11] Viewed in this light, however, functional analysis tends to shade into process analysis on the one hand, as we examine the effects of certain activities upon ongoing social processes, while on the other hand it can also shade into causal analysis, depending on the perspective of the researcher. That is, the same study might be interpreted as showing either that A causes B, or that B is a consequence of A. Morse and Reimer, for example, conceived of their research as causal analysis, but it might

[10] His latest writing in this area was William F. Ogburn and Meyer F. Nimkoff, *Technology and the Changing Family* (Boston: Houghton Mifflin Company, 1955).
[11] This interpretation is close to Merton's description of functional analysis, except that he refers only to the consequences of an activity for larger organizations in which they occur. See Robert K. Merton, *Social Theory and Social Structure*, rev. ed. (New York: The Free Press, a division of The Macmillan Company, 1957), pp. 46–47. Functional analysis is sometimes referred to as "structural-functional analysis," although the term can be misleading, since this analytical approach does not attempt to describe or account for the social structures of particular organizations. We shall therefore employ the less ambiguous terms "functional analysis" or simply "functionalism."

also be described as an investigation of the consequences of decentralization of authority upon work output.

Many sociologists prefer to restrict the meaning of functional analysis, bringing it closer to the functionalism of biology and psychology. In this narrower sense, functional analysis is concerned with determining how given activities affect organizational survival and operational requirements.[12] How and to what extent does a given phenomenon either satisfy or hinder the fulfillment of one or more functional requirements of some social organization? Both Durkheim's and Ogburn's writings illustrate this limited conception of functional analysis.

Early efforts at functional analysis in anthropology and sociology frequently assumed that all social relationships and patterns of social order within a society contributed in some way to the satisfaction of organizational requirements. These studies began with an existing social phenomenon and proceeded to inquire into its beneficial consequences for society. Attempts were made to describe the positive "functions" performed by everything from crime to magic. Robert Merton has spoken of this idea that all activities have beneficial functions for society as an assumption of "universal functionalism."[13] More recently, social scientists have come to realize that many social phenomena actually hinder the fulfillment of organizational requirements, while others have no significant consequences at all for social organizations. This observation led Merton to suggest that any given activity can have functional, dysfunctional, or nonfunctional social consequences.

Merton has also described two other unwarranted assumptions that plagued most early attempts at functional analysis.[14] One was an assumption of "functional unity," which held that any activity performs functions for the entire society and all organizations within it. This assumption not only denies any degree of autonomy to the component units of society, but also overlooks the possibility that a phenomenon which is functional for one organizational requirement or one subunit of the organization may be dysfunctional or nonfunctional for other requirements or subunits. A rigid authoritarian decision-making procedure might temporarily increase the operating efficiency of a business, for instance, but at the price of stifling initiative and innovation and thus limiting the ability of the business to adapt to changing economic conditions.

The last of these unwarranted assumptions was that of "functional

[12] Bronislaw Malinowski and other early anthropologists who used functional analysis tended to stress individual needs, such as for food, shelter, safety, and health, rather than organizational requirements, but this concern is no longer dominant in sociological functionalism. See his "The Group and the Individual in Functional Analysis," *The American Journal of Sociology*, vol. 44 (1939), pp. 938–964.

[13] Merton, chap. 1.

[14] Merton, chap. 1.

indispensability," or the idea that any given functional requirement can only be satisfied in one particular manner. To refute this notion, Merton introduced the ideas of functional equivalents, alternatives, and substitutes, which we encountered in Chapter 6.

One other conceptual distinction drawn by Merton is also important for an understanding of contemporary functional analysis. He pointed out that while the functional consequences of some phenomena are manifest, many others remain latent.[15] The functions of an activity in satisfying organizational requirements are manifest if they are both intended and recognized by the participants, while latent functions are neither intended nor recognized. The efforts of a police department to control "deviant" behavior represent a relatively manifest function (although they may also produce several unrecognized consequences for the community), while the support that military contracts give to the economy of the society may remain a largely latent function. Most social activities have both types of effects, although it is probably safe to say that latent functions predominate in most types of social organization. On the other hand, a major trend in many contemporary societies is the application of rationality to social organization, which in part involves becoming aware of organizational requirements and the various possible ways in which they might be fulfilled.

Finally, although functional analysis is sometimes accused of promoting a "conservative" concern with order and stability in social life, any such bias that does occur is introduced by the researcher, and is not inherent in the technique itself. Since the promotion of conflict and change can be just as important for an organization as the protection of boundaries or the maintenance of integration, functional analysis is equally applicable to both "radical" and "conservative" activities.

As a result of growing sophistication among sociologists concerning the use of functionalism, the techniques employed in this type of analysis are slowly being modified. Instead of beginning with an activity and then looking for its effects on organizational requirements, several writers have suggested that functionalism should begin with one or more organizational requirements, and then attempt to discover the means through which these requirements are satisfied, as well as the problems typically encountered in this process. Merton summarizes this approach to functional analysis in the following passage:[16]

[15] Merton, chap. 1.

[16] Merton, p. 49. Merton uses the term "organism" rather than "organization," since he is borrowing this conception of functional analysis from physiology. He goes on to point out that sociology cannot yet perform such highly sophisticated analysis, and then offers his own paradigm as a compromise version of functional analysis that may be applicable to contemporary sociology.

First of all, certain functional requirements of the [organization] are established, requirements which must be satisfied if the [organization] is to survive, or to operate with some degree of effectiveness. Second, there is a concrete and detailed description of the arrangements (structures and processes) through which these requirements are typically met in "normal" cases. Third, if some of the typical mechanisms for meeting these requirements are destroyed, or are found to be functioning inadequately, the observer is sensitized to the need for detecting compensating mechanisms (if any) which fulfill the necessary function. Fourth, and implicit in all that precedes, there is a detailed account of the structure *for which* the functional requirements hold, as well as a detailed account of the arrangements *through which* the function is fulfilled.

Most functional analysis in sociology compromises with this ideal procedure in one way or another—as in Merton's own proposed paradigm for sociological functional analysis and in his famous discussion of the functions performed by urban political machines.[17] Nevertheless, this formulation remains a goal toward which sociologists strive in their use of functional analysis.

Much confusion has centered around the distinction between causal and functional analysis. Determining the social functions served by some phenomenon does not tell the social scientist what social factors originally produced that phenomenon. Functional analysis cannot be substituted for causal analysis, as Durkheim long ago pointed out: "When . . . the explanation of a social phenomenon is undertaken, it is necessary to seek separately the efficient cause which produces it and the function that it fulfills."[18] Yet periodically in sociology we encounter attempts to explain the existence of some social activity in terms of its consequences, as when the functional theory of social stratification asserts that inequality exists because it serves useful functions for society. A similar argument is seen in the following statement, which suggests that religion results from society's need to preserve basic values: "The reason why religion is necessary is apparently to be found in the fact that human society achieves its unity primarily through the possession by its members of certain ultimate values and ends in common."[19]

This kind of theorizing imputes teleological purposes and goals to society itself, which a nonminded social organization cannot possess. Individuals may, of course, consciously anticipate the possible consequences

[17] Merton, pp. 50–55 and 72–82.

[18] Émile Durkheim, *The Rules of Sociological Method*, trans. Sarah A. Solovay and John H. Mueller (New York: The Free Press, a division of The Macmillan Company, 1938), p. 95.

[19] Kingsley Davis and Wilbert E. Moore, "Some Principles of Stratification," *American Sociological Review*, vol. 10 (April 1945), pp. 242–249.

of organized activities and therefore seek to create certain kinds of social organization. The United Nations is a conspicuous example of this process. But such an explanation cannot account for the origins of the more fundamental types of social organization, such as families, communities, governments, and societies, without giving mankind credit for considerably more rationality and foresight than we have ever shown. Furthermore, the fact that so many social functions are latent, or unintended and unrecognized, totally invalidates most theories of this sort. To explain the origin of any social phenomenon, the sociologist must investigate specific historical events, trends, and situations that existed prior to the phenomenon in question and that in some way affected it.

A more difficult question involves the extent to which functional analysis can account for the persistence over time of the phenomenon in question. Does the fact that an activity has beneficial social consequences contribute to its perpetuation? This is an extremely involved theoretical issue, which we cannot thoroughly explore here. Two basic observations may be useful, however. First, this kind of theorizing may have some limited validity, in that the consequences of an activity can through time strengthen and preserve the social conditions that produce it. Also, people do tend to perpetuate through their cultures and socialization practices those social arrangements which they find useful. Nevertheless, and this is the second point, processes such as these cannot account for the persistence of all social phenomena unless one is willing to postulate the existence of several inherent, nonconscious tendencies within all social organizations[20] —assumptions that many sociologists are unwilling to make. Rigorous sociological analysis therefore demands that the question of persistence be examined separately from the question of social functions.[21]

In summary, *the purpose of functional analysis is to determine the consequences of social activities for the social settings in which they occur and, more precisely, for the fulfillment of organizational requirements.* In functional analysis, the social scientist seeks to discover and analyze the functions a given phenomenon performs for larger encompassing organizations or for other related organizations. Functional analysis thus represents the logical culminating step in the study of the process of social organization.

From this exploration of the various types of analysis—structural,

[20] Such as a tendency toward homeostasis, to be discussed later in this chapter.
[21] For more extended discussions of this problem, see the following articles: Harry Bredemeir, "The Methodology of Functionalism," *American Sociological Review*, vol. 20 (April 1955), pp. 173–180; Ronald Dore, "Function and Cause," *American Sociological Review*, vol. 26 (December 1961), pp. 843–853; and Carl Hempel, "The Logic of Functional Analysis," in Llewellyn Gross, ed., *Symposium on Sociological Theory*, pp. 271–307.

process, causal, and functional—commonly employed in sociology, we now move on to examine the nature, use, and different forms of the social system model.

Social System Model

Virtually all of the sciences—physical, biological, psychological, and social—find it useful to construct models as heuristic analytical tools. A model is neither a true description of reality nor a substantive theory nor an analytical procedure. Rather it is a conceptual device designed to facilitate the entire scientific process, from the formation of propositions to the design of research. Put differently, a model is an abstract but simplified representation of some real phenomenon, which is used to increase our understanding of that phenomenon. It rarely portrays all the features and details of the phenomenon being studied, since it selects only the aspects or characteristics that are crucial for the question under investigation, and omits many others. These selected features are combined into a unified conceptualization according to predetermined logical principles. A model therefore differs from reality precisely to the degree that we arbitrarily abstract it from real existence.

Although models cannot describe or directly explain empirical phenomena, they do have considerable scientific usefulness. First, a model can help us gain insight into the essential nature of a real phenomenon, by overemphasizing significant features and ignoring nonessential ones. Second, use of a model facilitates scientific analysis because the abstract concepts and symbols that comprise it are easier to manipulate than is the phenomenon they represent, and also because a model is usually more internally consistent than our observations of reality. Finally, a model can alert us to similarities existing among several seemingly different phenomena.[22]

Nonetheless, when we use a scientific model we must remember that it is only a conceptual and analytical tool, and cannot be substituted for either theory or research. Models can be evaluated only in terms of utility, never of validity. As summarized by Theodore Caplow:[23]

> The study of a model should not be confused with the study of the real world. Predictions derived from the study of the real world are more or less *probable*, but predictions derived from analysis of the model are either *correct*

[22] May Brodbeck, "Models, Meaning, and Theories," in Llewellyn Gross, ed., *Symposium on Sociological Theory*, pp. 373–403.

[23] Theodore Caplow, *Principles of Organization* (New York: Harcourt, Brace & World, Inc., 1964), pp. 90–91.

or *incorrect.* The model contains only what we put into it. The real world contains more than we can ever get out of it. No model is an exact replica of its subject, but a useful model identifies and simplifies strategic variables so as to produce a fairly good—never a perfect—fit between effects in the arena of observation and effects obtained by manipulating symbols. The tests of an analytic model are its internal consistency, the amount of simplification achieved, and whether it can be used to predict real events.

By far the most widely used analytical model in contemporary sociology is that of a social system. System models of various kinds are used in many fields besides sociology, so a social system can be thought of as a special case of a more general system model. A social system is not, however, a particular kind of social organization. It is an analytical model that can be applied to any instance of the process of social organization, from families to nations.[24] To the extent that the process of social organization is complete, so that the resulting organizational entities have a unity greater than the sum of their constituent parts, these organizations may approximate the social system model. But we must always distinguish carefullly between real organizations and analytical models. Nor is the social system model a substantive theory—though it is sometimes spoken of as a theory in sociological literature. This model is a highly general, content-free conceptual framework within which any number of different substantive theories of social organization can be constructed. As an example, the two theories of normative and functional integration, although widely divergent in specific content, both employ a social system perspective.

In practice, there is considerable variation in the extent to which the social system model is abstracted from reality and logically formalized. We shall first describe the most general features of all social systems, and then briefly examine two specialized and more abstract forms of this model: process systems and formal systems. Most sociologists today use relatively nonabstract versions of the social system model, which is perhaps one reason why we sometimes confuse our models with real social phenomena. As a science becomes more mature, however, its models tend to become more abstract and formalized, so that social scientists may in the future make increased use of process and formal system models.

Very briefly, a social system is a model of a social organization that possesses a distinctive total unity beyond its component parts, that is distinguished from its environment by a clearly defined boundary, and whose subunits are at least partially interrelated within relatively stable patterns

[24] In some fields of science real phenomena are sometimes said to constitute systems, such as the solar system or the structure of an atom. Regardless of the validity of this assumption in physics, social scientists are generally agreed that social systems are only conceptual or analytical models.

of social order. Put even more simply, *a social system is a bounded set of interrelated activities that together constitute a single social entity.*[25] Let us examine these ideas in greater detail.

The most distinctive feature of the social system model is its primary emphasis on the totality of the whole system. A system is seen as possessing distinctive properties and a unity of its own, so that it is more than just the sum of its component parts. Emphasis on the totality of a system does not preclude examination of the structure or dynamics of system parts, or imply that they have no functional autonomy. It does suggest, though, that the parts of a system can be thoroughly understood only in relation to the larger whole that they constitute. Viewing these parts as completely separate entities negates the social system model. In short, a social system is an emergent whole that cannot be reduced to its component parts without destroying the entire system. Use of the social system model is therefore appropriate whenever a sociologist wishes to focus on any type of social organization as an entity in and of itself.[26] In fact, many social scientists, when discussing real social organizations, call them social systems to emphasize their overall totality or unity. This practice entails no serious difficulties as long as we remember that in using systemic terminology we are viewing social organization from an abstract analytical perspective and are not directly describing social reality.

Two other basic characteristics of the social system model, in addition to its overall unity, are its open boundaries and internal ordering. *To define a given social system, it must first of all be bounded in some manner, so as to separate it from its environment.* Since a social system is analytically constructed rather than being observed in reality, its boundaries are always arbitrarily defined by the social scientist. Often he attempts to draw his system boundaries so that they coincide with real organizational boundaries, but sometimes he finds it useful to temporarily establish entirely "artificial" boundaries. Because the boundaries of real social organizations are always at least partially open to the natural and social en-

---

[25] A. D. Hall and R. E. Fagen, "Definition of a System," *General Systems*, vol. 1 (1956), pp. 18–28. As described here the social system model is neither mechanistic nor organistic.

[26] The social system model is sometimes contrasted with a coercive model, as in Ralf Dahrendorf's *Class and Class Conflict in Industrial Society* (Stanford, Calif.: Stanford University Press, 1959), chap. 5. It may be argued, however, that the coercive model can be incorporated within the social system model as long as one allows for some functional autonomy among the component parts. See Alvin Gouldner, "Reciprocity and Autonomy in Functional Analysis," in Llewellyn Gross, ed., *Symposium on Sociological Theory*. Use of the social system model is inappropriate only when one employs a completely behavioristic or psychological reductionist perspective, as in George Homans' *Social Behavior: Its Elementary Form* (New York: Harcourt, Brace & World, Inc., 1961).

vironments, in that they exchange individuals, materials, energy, or information with other social actors, social system boundaries are normally also conceptualized as more or less open.

Social systems are therefore often described as "open systems"—as are also cultural, psychological, and biological systems. Open boundaries are not an analytical imperative for social systems, however. The degree to which real organizational boundaries are open or closed to the environment is always a problematic question, but the social scientist constructing a social system model is free to give his model whatever degree of openness or closure he thinks most useful for the problem at hand. As we shall see later, extremely formalized social systems temporarily assume totally closed boundaries. As long as the boundaries of a system are left at least partially open, however, the model must take account of exchanges between the system and its environment.

Once the boundaries of a social system have been defined, the analyst must then determine its component parts and specify the relationships among them. Since by definition the subparts of any system are parts of a larger whole, they will always be interrelated to some extent. Hence the actions of any one part will either directly or indirectly affect many other parts, if not the entire system. When dealing with real organizations, the sociologist must always empirically investigate patterns and degrees of interdependence and interrelatedness among subunits. When constructing a social system model, though, he can arbitrarily specify the nature of the relationships occurring among component subparts.[27] He could, for instance, choose to have every part interrelated with every other part, or to have all the parts connected only through their common ties to a central unit. Depending on the purposes for which the model is being constructed, these patterns of relationships might coincide with those of a real organization or they might be wholly "artificial." Total interdependence and interrelatedness among the parts of a social system is not mandatory, so that the analyst can allow the parts considerable amounts of functional autonomy if he wishes, as long as they retain some minimal ties to the whole system. In short, *there must be some degree of internal ordering among the component parts of a social system, but the patterns and degrees of this ordering can vary.*[28]

[27] After the model has been constructed and "set in motion," the analyst can no longer determine the relationships among parts. His analysis then focuses on the patterns of relationships that develop through time, given the initial conditions that he established and the forces acting on the model.

[28] Sociologists often construct social system models in which the patterns of internal ordering are balanced in some manner, depending on the intended use of the model. For example, it is frequently convenient to balance population input with output, so that the size of the population remains constant. This balancing procedure

To the extent that any given system overlaps and interlocks with other systems, it can be viewed as part of a larger and more inclusive system. At the same time, as long as its subparts possess some amount of functional autonomy, they can be analyzed either as systems in their own rights or as subsystems of the original system. In turn, these subsystems are often composed of many subsubsystems, and so on. Furthermore, any given subsystem may simultaneously be a part of two or more overlapping systems, so that a "total social system" can become an extremely complex model. This interrelatedness of social systems at varying levels of complexity and inclusiveness does not negate the essential unity of any given system, however.

If these features of social systems appear to be mere repetitions of the main characteristics of real social organizations, the reason is that the model is abstracted from observations of organizations. Hence most organizations approximate the social system model to some degree. Nevertheless, since a social system is a theoretically constructed model, the extent of correspondence between the model and any real social organization must always remain a problematic question.

As described thus far, the social system model is essentially static or structural in nature, although this does not preclude its application to specific instances of ongoing processes. However, we must build additional characteristics into the model if we wish to analyze dynamic social processes as they occur through time. We thus create what might be called a "process social system model." The two processes that sociologists most commonly assume to be operating within social systems are homeostasis and morphogenesis.[29] An inherent tendency toward one or both of these processes is postulated to exist within a particular social system, and the model is then manipulated to discover how either or both actually take place. Though few sociologists work with both of these processes at the same time, they are not incompatible and may in fact be complementary.

A social system is homeostatic (or self-maintaining) if it acts to coun-

---

can be quite useful, but it is not necessary, so that we must not arbitrarily assume that social systems are always in balance. This error is compounded when a writer not only makes such an unwarranted assumption, but also speaks of "equilibrium" rather than balance. As we shall see later, equilibrium has a very precise, technical meaning, and cannot be included within a social system model unless several other special conditions are also met.

[29] The following discussions of both homeostatic and morphogenic processes are drawn largely from Ludwig von Bertalanffy, "General Systems Theory," *General Systems*, vol. 1 (1956), pp. 1–10; and from Walter Buckley, *Sociology and Modern Systems Theory* (Englewood Cliffs, N.J.: Prentice-Hall, Inc., 1967). See also Robert Chin, "The Utility of System Models and Developmental Models for Practitioners," in Warren G. Bennis, et al., eds., *The Planning of Change* (New York: Holt, Rinehart, and Winston, Inc., 1961), pp. 201–214.

ter disruptive forces from the environment or its subsystems, as a means of maintaining some crucial system feature(s). Only certain key features are protected in this process, not the entire system. These key features might be any characteristics of the system that are important for its survival, although the most common foci of homeostatic activities are boundaries, patterns of internal order, decision-making procedures, communication channels, and power centers. As the system experiences threatening stresses and strains, it takes whatever actions are necessary to maintain these key features. The process of homeostasis thus necessitates considerable activity and change throughout many or all parts of the system not being protected. But there is no single or preordained manner in which the system must operate to maintain any given key feature. A homeostatic system has equifinality of functioning, which means that its initial conditions do not fully determine its activities or final state, so that many different courses of action can lead to the same outcome.

This process of homeostatic depends upon a continual supplementary flow of information into the system. Part of the output of the system's operations (whatever results from its functioning) must be returned to the system as feedback information, which can be used to guide and control future system activities. For instance, if an environmental stress that threatens the system's boundaries is countered with a defensive action, the system must then receive information concerning the effectiveness of its maneuver so that it "knows" whether to continue this action or to try some other tactic. The language used to describe these information processes often appears to impute teleology, or minded purpose, to the social system, but such an inference is not warranted. One of the most common illustrations of a homeostatic system, in fact, is a furnace controlled by a thermostat—and thermostats clearly do not think. A drop in room temperature is registered by the thermostat, which in turn activates the furnace, which then provides heat so as to keep the room at a constant temperature.

Effective homeostatic actions operate to maintain a system in a "steady state." By protecting its crucial features against disruptive threats, the system preserves its overall stability and unity. If a homeostatic process is not successful, the key features being maintained will be changed or destroyed. Pressures will then be generated for further changes throughout many other parts of the system, which can ultimately result in radical alteration or even total destruction of the entire system. Homeostasis thus is basically a means of providing for system survival, so that a homeostatic social system is sometimes referred to as a survival model.

A social system is morphogenic (or developing) if the system as a whole moves toward increased order, complexity, adaptability, unity, or operational effectiveness. It need not move in all these directions at once, and development in one area does not automatically produce growth in all other respects. In general, though, a morphogenic system shows increasing ability to deal effectively with its environment and its own subsystems. As a consequence it grows both structurally, in terms of complexity and internal ordering, and functionally, in terms of its ability to control its activities and attain goals. Hence a morphogenic social system is sometimes called a growth or operational model.

System development is made possible by the conservation of a favorable ratio of input over output, which gives the system a surplus of resources to devote to its own growth. The actual process of development can occur in countless different ways, ranging from sporadic but extensive jumps that shift the system from one stage to another, to continuous but minute changes whose cumulative effects are observable only over a long span of time. In any case, the principle of equifinality of functioning applies to morphogenic as well as homeostatic models, so that the initial conditions from which a system begins do not determine (although they may affect) the final state of growth attained.

Feedback, or flow of information from the environment back into the system, is as imperative for morphogenesis as for homeostasis. If the system is to increase its functional effectiveness, create more complex patterns of internal ordering, gain greater unity, adjust to a changing environment, or develop in any other manner, it must constantly receive information concerning its present state, the consequences of its activities, and actions directed toward it by other systems. Informational feedback—or more generally, cybernetic processes of all kinds—thus constitute the vital "heart" of morphogenesis.

The process of morphogenesis does not necessarily involve rational thought or purposeful goal-striving, any more than does homeostasis. Much system growth is undoubtedly similar to the biological process of natural selection, in which random occurrences that prove beneficial to the system are incorporated and retained, while nonbeneficial occurrences are discarded.[30] Growth can also take place through manipulation of the system, even though the actors involved in these processes are not aware of the consequences of their activities for system development. For example, participants in a social system might for some reason increase the

[30] This "natural selection" thesis is based on the following line of reasoning: In order to counteract previously unexperienced disruptive forces, either internal or external, a social system must create and implement some new activities or parts. If these additions to the system succeed in maintaining crucial system properties, they will normally be incorporated within the system and retained for subsequent use when these same disruptive forces are again encountered. In short, system growth is in this case the end product of effective homeostatic activities.

flow of resources into the system, improve intrasystem communication, create new subsystems, or strengthen existing relationships among system parts—all without any conscious awareness that these activities were increasing the complexity or functional effectiveness of the total system.

A question often confronted by users of process system models—both homeostatic and morphogenic—is the extent to which either or both of these processes actually occur in real social organizations. Inherent tendencies toward homeostasis or morphogenesis exist in process system models because the analyst puts them there. For analytical purposes he constructs a system that contains one or both of these processes; they are postulates or assumptions of his system model. But are these assumptions valid for real organizations? Although this is a topic of considerable debate, most sociologists would probably answer in the negative. It is certainly true that actions by members and subunits of organizations sometimes do produce homeostasis or morphogenesis. In fact, since individuals are capable of purposeful social actions, they may intentionally seek to promote organizational maintenance or growth. (Such collectively oriented perspectives and actions are often mentioned as qualities of effective organizational leaders.) Nevertheless, the fact that homeostatic and morphogenic activities occur within real social organizations, either intentionally or unintentionally, does not warrant the blanket assumption that these processes are inherent in all organizations. Instead, the degree to which homeostasis or morphogenesis actually occurs in a specific organization should always be a problematic concern for sociological theory and research.[31]

The most highly abstract and logically precise level at which the social system model is presently used in sociology might be termed a "formal system model." This kind of social system is a purely contrived model in which all component parts are precisely specified and all relationships among these parts are expressed in mathematical terms. Such a model is not intended to describe social reality in any direct sense. It is solely a heuristic tool with which to analyze relationships among system parts under extensively controlled conditions. The model must bear some resemblance to social reality if the results are to have scientific applicability, but the system itself is totally artificial.

Most formal system models postulate an inherent tendency toward equilibrium among all the parts of the system, although this assumption is not imperative for analytical purposes. *Equilibrium exists in a social*

---

[31] A detailed examination of the possible uses of homeostatic and morphogenic process models in sociological analysis is beyond the scope of this discussion. The interested reader will find many such illustrations (on both the interpersonal and organizational levels) in Walter Buckley, *Sociology and Modern Systems Theory.*

system when all the parts maintain a constant relationship to each other, so that no part changes its position or relation with respect to all the other parts.[32] Dynamic processes such as homeostasis or morphogenesis can operate within the system, but the basic pattern of relationships among the constituent parts does not change through time. Disruptive stresses and strains may upset this equilibrium, creating temporary periods of disequilibrium, but eventually the system conquers, neutralizes, or destroys whatever disruptive forces impinge upon it. Over time, system equilibrium is thus always restored—or else the entire system is destroyed. At first glance, equilibrium often appears to be just another name for homeostasis, but there is a critical difference between these two processes. In homeostasis, only one or a few selected features of the system are protected through the actions of other parts of the system, while in equilibrium every part is preserved in a constant relation to the total system. Because all the parts of an equilibrium system are interrelated in some manner, a change in any one part will necessarily produce a corresponding change in every other part. In this way complete equilibrium is maintained throughout the system.

When he uses a formal equilibrium model for analytical purposes, the analyst must completely close its boundaries so that it cannot interact with its environment, and must also deprive its parts of all functional autonomy. No uncontrolled external stresses and internal strains can then affect the system. Since no social organization ever fully meets either of these requirements, equilibrium analysis cannot be performed with real organizations. Its use is limited to highly formalized social system models. Given these necessary conditions, the analyst then opens the boundaries of the system in a carefully controlled manner and interjects a precisely defined and measured disruptive force, which creates disequilibrium. After reclosing the boundaries, he observes and records whatever activity occurs in the system as it acts to reassert equilibrium. To enable him to measure this activity and determine when equilibrium is restored, all variables in the system must be mathematically quantified. Because at present we cannot quantify many important sociological variables, sophisticated analysis with equilibrium system models is extremely difficult, although the use of simulation techniques on electronic computers offers considerable promise for the future.

Equilibrium social systems are commonly divided into two basic

---

[32] This definition, as well as the following discussion of equilibrium, is drawn primarily from two sources: David Easton, "Limits of the Equilibrium Model in Social Research," *Behavioral Science*, vol. 1 (1956), pp. 96–104; and Everett Hagen, "Analytic Models in the Study of Social Systems," *American Journal of Sociology*, vol. 67 (September 1961), pp. 144–151.

types: stationary and dynamic. A system in stationary equilibrium will always return to its initial state after disruptive forces have been dispelled. A system in dynamic equilibrium, in contrast, may assume new forms as the result of its reequilibrating activities. In both cases, though, the overall pattern of relationships among all parts of the system remains constant. The point around which equilibrium centers can either remain at rest or move, but the basic form of the system never changes. Finally, stationary and dynamic equilibrium should not be confused with stable, neutral, and unstable equilibrium, which are simply three ways of describing the strength of the disruptive force that must be introduced before system equilibrium is upset. If the equilibrium of a system is unstable, the slightest disruption will upset whatever equilibrium exists; if the equilibrium is stable, a considerable amount of force is required to initiate reequilibrating activities; and if the equilibrium is neutral, nothing will disturb it.

One final point about the social system model remains to be noted. In recent years a number of scholars have been engaged in creating what they call "general systems theory." The fundamental principle of this body of theory is that the system model can fruitfully be applied to all human phenomena—biological, psychological, social, and cultural. These theorists have attempted to set forth a number of basic concepts and general propositions that pertain to organic systems, personality systems, social systems, and cultural systems.[33] General systems theory is not a substitute for more specialized kinds of system models, but it does offer a challenging and exciting foundation for interdisciplinary work, and possibly for the creation of general theories that apply to all human life.

In this chapter we have outlined the major analytical procedures used by contemporary sociologists in their attempts to study the process of social organization. Structural, process, causal, and functional analysis are four distinct but interconnected ways of examining social life. Each raises different questions and provides particular kinds of information for the analyst, but we must use all four approaches to gain complete understanding of social organization. The various forms of the social system model, finally, are abstract conceptualizations that sociologists find useful as analytical tools in the study of organized social life. None of these procedures, however, offers a substantive theoretical explanation of the process of social organization. An exploration of various theories of social organization is our concern in the next chapter.

---

[33] For a brief but inclusive introduction to this work, see James G. Miller, "Toward a General Theory for the Behavioral Sciences," *American Psychologist*, vol. 10 (September 1955), pp. 513–531.

RECOMMENDED READING

BERTALANFFY, LUDWIG VON, "General Systems Theory," *General Systems,* vol. 1 (1956), pp. 1–10.
A broad description of the system model, outlining its major characteristics and distinctive features.

BREDEMEIR, HARRY, "The Methodology of Functionalism," *American Sociological Review,* vol. 20 (April 1955), pp. 173–180.
Distinguishes among the three separate questions of the initial causation of a social phenomenon, its persistence through time, and its consequences for other phenomena, and evaluates the relevance of functional analysis for each of these questions.

DURKHEIM, ÉMILE, *The Rules of Sociological Method,* trans. Sarah A. Solovay and John H. Mueller, chap. 5 (New York: The Free Press, a division of The Macmillan Company, 1938).
The classical presentation of functional analysis as a theoretical approach in sociology.

EASTON, DAVID, "Limits of the Equilibrium Model in Social Research," *Behavioral Science,* vol. 1 (1956), pp. 96–104.
Argues that the equilibrium concept is not a necessary part of the system model, and questions the usefulness of the idea of equilibrium in social science.

ETZIONI, AMITAI, "Two Approaches to Organizational Analysis: A Critique and a Suggestion," *Administrative Science Quarterly,* vol. 5 (September 1960), pp. 257–278. (Also Bobbs-Merrill reprint S-80.)
Compares a "system" model with a "goal" model for the analysis of social organizations, emphasizing the advantages and drawbacks of the system model.

HEMPEL, CARL, "The Logic of Functional Analysis," in Llewellyn Gross, ed., *Symposium on Sociological Theory,* chap. 9 (New York: Harper & Row, Publishers, 1959).
Explores in considerable detail the logical assumptions and fallacies involved in the use of functional analysis in sociology.

MEADOWS, PAUL, "Models, Systems, and Science," *American Sociological Review,* vol. 22 (February 1957), pp. 3–9.
An argument that various kinds of system models pervade all sociological theory, and an outline of mechanistic and organistic system models.

MERTON, ROBERT K., *Social Theory and Social Structure,* rev. ed., chap. 1 (New York: The Free Press, a division of The Macmillan Company, 1957).
A comprehensive discussion of the use of functional analysis in sociology, pointing out many pitfalls encountered when functional analysis is used in an uncritical manner.

MILLER, JAMES G., "Toward a General Theory for the Behavioral Sciences," *The American Psychologist,* vol. 10 (September 1955), pp. 513–531. (Also Bobbs-Merrill reprint P-244.)
Presents the basic concepts of general systems theory and suggests nineteen propositions as being applicable to all living systems.

THEODORSON, GEORGE A., "The Use of Causation in Sociology," in Llewellyn Gross, ed., *Sociological Theory: Inquiries and Paradigms*, pp. 131–152 (New York: Harper & Row, Publishers, 1967).
Examines the meaning of causation in sociological analysis, contrasts causal analysis with strict empiricism and with functional analysis, and proposes a "limited conception of causation" in sociology.

CHAPTER 15

Theories
of Social Organization

Our objective in this chapter is broad in scope but quite limited in depth. We shall sketch in rough outline the six basic theoretical perspectives on social organization currently being used by sociologists. These are exchange theory, interaction theory, ecological theory, power theory, normative theory, and value theory. None of these actually constitutes a rigorous theory of social organization, in the sense of a set of logically interrelated propositions, but together they do represent the broad scope of theoretical thinking in sociology today.

We shall not exhaustively describe or extensively evaluate these various schools of social theorizing. Our concern here is only to become acquainted with the most fundamental ideas and views of each theory, so that we shall have a background with which to read the relevant sociological literature. In other words, the discussions in this chapter are merely brief introductions to these different theories of social organization. The fairly extensive list of recommended readings at the end of the chapter can then be used as a guide for further exploration of each type of theorizing.

Any classification of theoretical writings into "schools of thought," as done here, is somewhat arbitrary, and many sociologists might argue with one or more of these categories. Nevertheless, this approach does enable us to see more clearly the major strands of theoretical thinking that presently cut across sociology, and to appreciate the intellectual bonds uniting theorists working within each perspective. Our discussions in the following sections will focus on the ideas common to each school of thought, not on individual writers (with one exception). In all cases there are numerous differences—some of them critical—among the various representatives of each type of theorizing, which are readily apparent in their writings. For our present orientation purposes, however, the major ideas shared within a school of thought are more important than any internal inconsistencies.[1]

Finally, we shall make no attempt here to undertake what is undoubtedly the most pressing demand in contemporary sociological theorizing: to synthesize these diverse theoretical perspectives into a more complete and adequate theory of social organization. That task must await the future.

Exchange Theory

This theoretical perspective focuses on the basic social process of exchange among social actors. Although exchange theory does not attempt to explain all aspects of social organization, it does deal with what is perhaps the most fundamental feature of virtually all social relationships.

Exchange theory rests on several assumptions about social actors and activities: (a) social actors engage in activities as a means of obtaining desired goals; (b) all social activities entail some cost to the actor, such as time, energy, or resources expended; (c) social actors seek to economize their activities as much as possible, by keeping costs below rewards; and (d) only those activities which are economical—that is, which produce "payoffs"—tend to be perpetuated through time.

Social interaction begins, this theory states, when a social actor—either an individual or an organization—attempts to gain some kind of benefit from another actor (or actors) by exchanging something with him. If the other actor also believes that he will benefit from such an exchange, interaction occurs. The basis of this mutual attraction, and hence the nature of the interaction, can take many forms: each has objects that the other desires, each can perform services for the other, they enjoy one another's company, or they share common goals. In any case, the resulting interaction is an exchange process.

Initially, the emerging relationship may be quite precarious. Unless the actors share a "norm of reciprocity" or are constrained by an external power, neither actor has any guarantee that his overtures will by recipro-

---

[1] None of the discussions of these theories is footnoted, but the recommended readings for each body of theory constitute the major (though not the only) references from which these discussions are drawn.

cated by the other. If they are not, no relationship will develop. But if the second actor fails to reciprocate, it will be extremely difficult for him to receive any future benefits from the first actor. To protect his own self-interests, therefore, he must return a compensatory benefit of some kind. Apart from purely economic transactions in a money market, this "payment" for benefits received need not be an exact equivalent, as long as it is appropriate to the situation and of real benefit to the other actor. In other words, most social exchanges involve imprecise and often unspecified reciprocal obligations, not stipulated contractual terms.

Once an exchange process is initiated in this manner, it will continue as long as it proves rewarding to all participants—that is, as long as each actor's benefits exceed his costs. The emergent social relationship, which binds the participants together through reciprocal expectations and obligations, has properties of its own distinct from those of its members, and hence must be viewed as a real phenomenon. It is not necessary, according to exchange theory, for the participating actors to share common norms. But to the extent that norms such as "fair exchange" or "distributive justice" do emerge from exchange transactions, they will tend to strengthen and perpetuate the relationship. These norms are consequences, not preconditions or initial causes, or social interaction, however.

More crucial than shared norms for the maintenance of exchange relationships is a climate of mutual trust among the participants. The actor who initially offers a benefit to another does so on purely speculative grounds, in hopes of receiving a desired return, but with no assurance that this will occur (again assuming that no external power is present to enforce reciprocity). After an exchange relationship has been established, though, the actors come to trust each other on the basis of past experience. As a consequence, they feel secure in committing an increasing amount of their available resources to exchange transactions, thus expanding the scope of the relationship. In short, *exchange processes utilize self-interests of actors who are seeking benefits through reciprocal exchanges with others, but over time these processes develop into stable patterns of social order and give rise to culture norms, toward which the participants are committed.*

Exchange theorists usually exclude certain types of actions from their considerations, admitting that this theory cannot explain all social acts. The most frequently omitted types of situations are overt coercion and love (or altruism), although even here some elements of exchange may enter the picture. These theorists also recognize that once stable patterns of social order have been established, exchange processes become exceedingly complex. First, exchange transactions between actors are often supported by an encompassing organization, which decreases the need for mutual trust but which also perpetuates the relationship in spite of unequal exchanges. Second, organizational values, norms, rules, and goals frequently influence or drastically alter the processes through which exchanges occur. Third, organizational demands upon actors often cause them to abandon their original exchange relationships and take part in new types of activities. And fourth, many exchange interactions in organizations cease to be direct reciprocal transactions between actors, and become instead indirect chains of actions in which a member may benefit one actor but be compensated by another. Nevertheless, many relationships within and between even the most complex organizations can be explained using principles of exchange.

If one seeks to expand the exchange perspective into a broader theory of social organization, there are several possible directions in which to go. Classical economics, with its conception of markets as relatively automatic or self-regulating processes, offers one possibility, though it must be expanded to take account of all types of social exchanges. The theory of functional integration, in which interdependent relationships are coordinated (but not necessarily controlled) by a centralized administrative unit, is another direction in which exchange theory might be elaborated. A third possibility is to merge exchange theory into power theory, since unbalanced but unavoidable exchange situations normally give rise to unequal distributions of power. A variation on this same theme stresses the granting of legitimate authority by some actors to others as a consequence of services rendered, which then provides a framework for social organization. Finally, one might focus on the norms that tend to develop as a result of reciprocated exchanges, and then use normative integration theory to explain organizational stability and unity. All of these possibilities have been discussed by exchange theorists, but none has yet been extensively explored, so that exchange theory presently remains primarily on the level of interpersonal interaction rather than dealing explicitly with social organization.

Interaction Theory

As discussed here, this school of theoretical thought combines "symbolic interaction theory" with Talcott Parsons' social action frame of reference, on the grounds that they share many ideas in common.

Interaction theory begins by focusing on individuals who are engaging in social interaction as relatively independent elements. The interactions might be exchange transactions or any other type, but in all cases the individuals are seeking goals through social interaction. That is, social action is always at least partially purposeful or voluntaristic.

A distinctive feature of interaction theory is its emphasis on the symbolic meanings that individuals give to their own and others' actions. A person does not respond to overt behaviors, but rather to the meanings that he and others attach to both acts and objects. As an individual engages in interaction, therefore, he is continually interpreting or defining everything that takes place in that situation, including many aspects of the surrounding environment. His subsequent actions are then primarily shaped by these interpretations. In short, *social action and interaction are constantly being created through a process of self-indication, in which the person pieces together and guides his actions by interpreting everything of relevance to him in terms of its significance for his goal-seeking activities.*

Social organization, from this theoretical perspective, consists of the collective actions of minded individuals who are attempting to achieve goals through cooperative actions in social situations that are constantly being interpreted by them. Social organization thus results from common understandings or definitions of how to act in a given situation, which produce similarity of action among individuals. But since social situations are never fully and permanently defined, social interactions and relationships are always being reinterpreted and reconstructed by the participants. Thus social organization is never static. Another way of describing social organization from this perspective is to say that it provides the stable settings in which persons act, but it never fully determines the course of social interaction.

Shared culture, consisting of ideas or meanings held in common by interacting individuals, is far more important to interaction theory than are patterns of social order. As persons interpret situations and interact in terms of these meanings, they tend to communicate their ideas to each other. Over time, a common culture develops that all members of the organization share. Thus culture—and especially social norms—becomes the vehicle through which social relationships are perpetuated.

Once a culture has arisen among a number of individuals, it influences and guides, but does not fully determine, their collective actions by providing them with interpretations of social life, role expectations, established definitions of social situations, and social norms. Furthermore, these norms and other cultural ideas become internalized into the personalities of the members through the process of socialization. To the extent that an organization possesses a viable culture, and provided that fundamental socialization processes in primary groups are fairly uniform throughout the organization, a common core of basic interaction patterns, role expectations, norms, and values will be shared by all members and incorporated within their personalities. (Earlier writers referred to this common "core" of all personalities in an organization as "human nature," but contemporary theorists prefer such terms as the "social self" or the "superego.") Through this process the organization gains normative integration. In addition, individual's personal goals for social action will not be idiosyncratic, but rather will reflect the common culture. As a result, social actions are simultaneously voluntaristic and normatively oriented, and organized social life becomes possible.

With some oversimplification, we can describe the picture of social organization given by interaction theory as consisting of minded, socialized individuals, plus shared normative culture. For the most part, however, this theory fails to account for the realm of social order, or patterned social relationships. It tends to jump directly from interacting individuals (who continually interpret situations and guide their actions by these meanings) to the level of culture (which is created through the sharing of meanings in symbolic communication). Although interaction theory does not deny the existence of social order, it largely ignores this phenomenon, or else incorporates it into the concept of culture.

In sum, interaction theory offers many useful ideas concerning the process of symbolized social interaction, the emergence of shared cultural ideas in social life, socialization of individuals, and normative controls on social action. It thus provides a necessary supplement to exchange theory in explaining social interaction. Whereas exchange theory usually treats actors as social elements, interaction theory focuses on the way in which individuals become organizational parts through the enactment of roles guided by cultural norms that have been internalized through socialization. But because of its failure to deal explicitly with patterns of social order, interaction theory does not give us a complete explanation of the total process of social organization.

Ecological Theory

Unlike most other theories of social organization, which have intellectual roots in philosophy, social (or human) ecology grew out of biology. The central concern of both biological and social ecology is the way in which organisms (including people) adapt to their environment. Even today, many sociologists still think of ecology solely as the study of spatial and temporal arrangements of individuals in the natural environment. In recent years, however, ecology has developed into a general theory of social organization.

Whereas both exchange and interaction theory deal primarily with relationships among actors, ecological theory focuses directly on broader patterns of social order. It begins with a set of basic factors that largely shape all social order: the natural and social environments, population size and quality (such as age and sex distributions), and level of technology (both material and social). *Social organization develops as populations attempt to deal with their environments using available technological knowledge to obtain resources necessary for realizing survival or other goals.*

The essence of organization is interdependence among the members of a population, which forces them to create social order to survive or achieve collective goals. Interdependence takes two forms, both of which give rise to patterns of social order: symbiotic interdependence, based on complementary differences among actors, which produces "corporate" relationships or units, and commensalistic interdependence, based on supplementary similarities, which produces "categoric" relationships or units. A factory exemplifies a corporate organization, while a church is a typical categoric organization. In either case, these organizations are properties of populations, not of individuals. Over time, they become unified and self-sustaining entities with characteristics of their own. This overall process of organization development through interaction between a population and its environment, as mediated by technology, is sometimes described as the functioning of an "ecosystem."

Social organizations vary extensively in their degree of completeness, or closure—that is, in the extents to which their boundaries are open or closed to interchanges with the environment, their internal activities are ordered, and their overall structure achieves stability. In a completely open organization, all subunits have direct access to the environment in some manner, although they must also be linked together through minimal patterns of internal ordering (or else no organization would exist). In a partially closed organization, some of the parts relate directly to the environment, while others maintain only internal linkages and must receive necessary resources through the parts that are in contact with the environment. Finally, in a fully closed organization (which can be approximated but never realized in reality), only one part would engage in transactions with the environment, while all other parts would be linked to it and dependent upon it for resources. Most real organizations fall somewhere between the extremes of total openness and total closure, although there is a tendency for organizations to move toward closure as they increase in functional effectiveness. As an organization achieves closure, it gains greater control over its dealings with the environment, so that it is less vulnerable to external stresses. A state of full closure therefore ensures maximum possible boundary maintenance. Nevertheless, since an organization must always obtain resources from the environment through at least one subpart, it can never become independent of the environment. At the same time, increasing closure makes internal relationships progressively more crucial for the organization. Overall, the process of closure tends to give an organization greater unity and stability through time.

Those parts of an organization which mediate the flow of necessary resources between it and the environment or among other subunits exercise dominance in the organization, since other parts are functionally dependent on them. In many, if not most organizations, these dominant parts perform some kind of economic activity, since the production, distribution, and consumption of goods and services are normally basic to all other activities. Thus the economy of an organization usually exerts considerable dominance over all other subunits. There is no theoretical reason, though, why functional dominance could not inhere in any type of activity, from scientific research to religion. The more efficient and effective these dominant units are in performing their vital functions, the greater the quantity of resources and power available to the organization for goal attainment, the more extensively differentiated the organizational parts, and the larger and more complex the organization is likely to become.

In a relatively open organization, in which most parts have direct access to environmental resources, all of these parts tend to exert relatively equal dominant power. With increasing closure, a few parts emerge as "key functionaries," since they have sole responsibility for resource procurement. (In a completely closed organization, there would be only one key functionary.) These key functionaries then exercise dominance throughout the whole organization. Many other parts of the organization may wield lesser amounts of dominance, in an inverse ratio to their structural distance from the key functionaries, but this power is always derived from the units that mediate between the organization and its environment. In short, key functionaries, because of their dominant power, tend to influence or control all other parts of the organization.

Because the crucial factors of environment, population, and technology are never static, all organizations are constantly subject to disruptions and change, either continual or sporadic. Relatively open organizations, with many direct ties to the environment, tend to experience frequent and extensive changes, and hence lack stability. As organizations approach closure, they are able to acquire considerable control over the processes of change, but they can never escape it. In a relatively closed organization all changes would be mediated through the few key functionaries and then would affect other units in successive steps according to their degree of removal from these dominant units.

Finally, the processes of boundary closure, emergence of key functionaries, growing operational effectiveness, and internal functional and structural differentiation in an organization are all highly interrelated, and together all push the organization toward increased centralization. A few dominant units tend to have large amounts of resources at their disposal and to wield power throughout the entire organization. At the same time, they become functionally indispensable because of the overall coordination and regulation they provide for this highly complex organization and because of their crucial role in promoting functional integration in the organization.

The most commonly expressed criticism of ecological theory is that it totally ignores norms, values, and other cultural ideas. Ecologists do not deny the existence of these phenomena, but argue that they usually exert very little independent influence on the process of social organization, and hence are not necessary to explain at least the major features of social life. Without minimizing the importance of basic ecological considerations, most other sociologists would insist that cultural phenomena must always be considered in the study of social organization. In this respect, ecological theory is deficient as a complete explanation of organized social life. There also appears to be a serious logical flaw within ecological theory in that portions of it involve circular reasoning. The theory argues that organizational growth and closure occur as key functionaries increase in operational effectiveness and dominant power, but for key functionaries to exist there must first be at least moderate closure. We can avoid this logical pitfall by incorporating into the theory other sources of power besides functional dominance. For an explanation of these additional sources of power in social life, we turn to power theory.

Power Theory

The school of power theory includes many diverse writers, who are united only by a common concern with the effects of power on social life. These writers are frequently classified as either "class" or "elite" theorists, but in this discussion we shall emphasize their similarities rather than their differences.[2]

Power theory is similar to ecology in that it focuses directly on patterns of social order, though it tends to be much broader in scope. In contrast to ecology, however, all of the major power theorists have been Europeans; this perspective on social life in relatively rare in American sociology.

[2] Karl Marx' class theory of social organization is sketched in more detail in Chapter 16.

The fundamental proposition of power theory is that social power in its various forms—force, authority, dominance, and attraction—is both a cause and a consequence of all social organization. Furthermore, the distribution and use of power within an organization largely determines its structure and functioning. More specifically, most power theorists have held that power is always unevenly distributed, and that those members or parts which exercise a preponderance of power in an organization will frequently affect or shape virtually all its activities.

Power theory contains several basic assumptions, although they are not always made explicit:

(1) Social power is created through the process of social organization, in that organization enables actors to accomplish things they could not do separately, and hence gives them collective power.

(2) Power therefore occurs within social relationships or organizational entities; it is never a property of any single actor.

(3) Power exists and can be exerted only as long as a social relationship or organization is maintained, so that power is inseparably linked with social interdependence.

(4) The social actors who exercise power within relationships or organizations may be acting as either independent elements or as committed parts, and may hold either self orientations or collective orientations.

(5) The amount of power exercised by an actor in a given situation is determined jointly by the resources he employs and by the resistance he encounters.

(6) Social power can be exercised toward any social object: "downward" toward component subunits (including individuals, or more properly, roles), "laterally" toward other equivalent actors (either individuals or organizations), or "upward" toward more inclusive organizational units.

(7) Once some amount of power has been generated through the process of social organization, it can in turn be used to create new social ordering or to expand existing patterns of social order, in a continual cycle.

In sum, power is an integral aspect of the total process of social organization, and the exercise of power enters into all instances of this process to some extent.

Working with these basic assumptions, power theorists then postulate that in all organizations more complex than a simple friendship group (and perhaps even in many of these), power tends to be unequally distributed among the members and parts, for a variety of possible reasons. These include such factors as: (a) differential control over the major sources or means of producing wealth, (b) occupancy of organizational positions with differential amounts of authority, (c) dominant control over the flow of necessary resources or information in the organization, (d) superior qualities possessed by certain individuals (such as intelligence, energy, motivation, or training), (e) representation or expression by power-wielders of the major interests of the whole organization or a majority of its members, (f) the tendency of powerful actors to be better organized or more cohesive than others, (g) the fact that many members of an organization may be apathetic toward collective responsibilities and quite willing to grant power to anyone willing to assume leadership tasks, (h) the functional necessity for centralized control in all complex organizations, (i) the creation and manipulation of ideologies or "myths" to support the legitimacy of rulers, and (j) the use of force or overt coercion by some members or parts of an organization. These various factors are not incompatible, and most power theorists have incorporated several of them in their writings.

Given an unequal distribution of power in a society or other organization, these theorists have been concerned primarily with explaining prevailing structural patterns of power and the ways in which elites or ruling classes use their power. For analytical purposes (but not for descriptive purposes) power theorists have frequently conceived of power structures as dichotomies of those who do and those who do not exercise power in social life. This perspective greatly simplifies the analysis of power, and it also reflects an empirical tendency for conflicting parties to polarize into two opposing factions. Other writers have argued, however, that such a perspective grossly oversimplifies reality, and have suggested that many organizations may contain "top elites," one or more sets of "subelites," competing groups of "counterelites," and frequently several levels of "semielites" located between the rulers and the "masses." More recently it has been argued that each sphere of activity within a society or other organization might have its own power structure, and that none of these need necessarily correspond to each other, thus giving the total organization an extremely complex pattern of power.

Despite these conceptual differences, virtually all power theorists have stressed the idea that the predominant flow of power in an organization is from elites or ruling classes to the other members and subunits. Hence these power-wielders can influence, if not completely control, most activities within the organization and most of its transactions with other organizations. To understand or explain social organization, therefore, one must focus on the composition and actions of powerful elites or classes. As a consequence of this situation, the "masses" of "ordinary" members—who often constitute a majority of the membership—exert little or no influence in the organization. Only as they become aware of their common interests and organize themselves to take collective action can they have any hope of exercising effective power in social life.

Power theory has been given quite diverse ideological overtones by its various proponents, ranging from "radical" demands that the "masses" must organize and overthrow the dominant class that is exploiting them, to "liberal" beliefs that no particular distribution of power is impervious to change, to "conservative" arguments that there will always be powerful elites, to "reactionary" insistence that the existing power structure is inevitable and that the present "ruling class" is inherently superior. The obvious conclusion to be drawn from these contrasting views is that power theory does not in itself contain any ideological bias, although it can certainly be used to buttress any shade of political opinion.

Social power theory cannot account for the initial instigation of interaction among actors who are not constrained by an encompassing organization, since power must first be created through social ordering. In such cases we must rely on either exchange or interaction theory. This is not a serious weakness, though, since in reality the process of social organization rarely begins among actors who share no social ties derived from other relationships. For practical purposes, almost any social relationship or organization can be viewed from a power perspective, so that this school of thought has vast potential as a theoretical explanation of most aspects of organized social life. Thus far, however, it has not been extensively developed. Most research and theorizing dealing with social power has focused largely on structural distributions of power within organizations, and to a lesser extent on techniques of power manipulation. There have been very few attempts to view the entire process of social organization in power terms or to use social power as a theoretical explanation of all organization.

Perhaps a profitable step in this direction would be to abandon rigid elitist-mass conceptions of power and to explore the ways in which power is created through, embodied in, and exerted by all social relationships. It might be possible with such a broad perspective to identify and study power-wielders in every social situation, and to determine how power contributes to all social organization. Under some conditions, a few actors or units might exercise controlling power over an entire organization, while under other conditions social power might be exerted relatively equally by all participants. Finally, this perspective would suggest that patterns of power distribution and use in organizations vary considerably through time, so that social power can be understood only as a dynamic, ongoing process.

Normative Theory

Normative and value theory are often combined under the heading of cultural "consensualism," but there is a crucial difference between these two schools of thought. As the names imply, normative theory gives primary emphasis to moral directives and imperatives that directly shape social life, whereas value theory gives first attention to basic values, which are in turn expressed in norms and rules. Taken together, however, these two forms of consensualism have largely dominated American sociology.

Normative theory views common norms as arising out of social life, as a number of individuals seek to attain collective goals under similar life conditions. As people discover beneficial patterns of social life and solutions to common problems, they tend to repeat these activities, to symbolize them, and to communicate their ideas to others. In most cases this is not a rational or even a conscious process, but rather a gradual development of standardized ways of dealing with basic life conditions.

Over time, two things happen to emergent norms. First, they become dissociated from the situations in which they first arose, and are generalized to cover broad areas of organized social life. They constitute, that is, the core elements of the culture of a society or other organization. As such, norms are seen by those persons subject to them as existing outside of oneself, and as binding on one's actions. They become not just useful suggestions of how one might act, but moral directives or imperatives defining how one must act in a given situation. Adherence to most norms is not left up to individual choice and discretion but is a social obligation enforced by collective sanctions. Although social control over individuals' actions often seems quite arbitrary—and at times may in fact be so—in the long run it usually proves beneficial to all concerned because of the order and predictability it gives to social life. Without moral norms to guide people's actions, social relationships would quickly disintegrate, collective activities would be impossible, and anarchy would soon prevail.

The second alteration that occurs in norms over time is that they become differentiated according to their importance for organized social life. (1) Those norms which are of only limited significance for collective life remain at the level of mere customs. Most people tend to follow them out of tradition or habit, but few or no sanctions are applied if one chooses to ignore prevailing customs. Moreover, the culture often provides alternative customs for a given situation, any one of which is considered appropriate. (2) The norms that are of somewhat greater importance for social life are viewed as definitive standards of how one ought to act under particular conditions. They become infused with conceptions of morality, and deviant actions are sanctioned. Unless extenuating circumstances happen to prevail, an individual is expected to conform to these "folkways." However, a norm of this type is usually limited to a certain kind of social situation, and some departure or innovation may be tolerated under unusual or changing conditions. (3) Finally, norms that are crucial for the welfare or survival of an organization become moral imperatives, which everyone must obey without question. Severe sanctions will be applied to anyone who violates one of these "mores," for his act is seen as threatening not just himself or his role partners, but the entire organization.

Any of these three types of norms can be codified as a law and enforced by the power of the state. Although there is no necessary correspondence between the social importance of a norm and the likelihood that it will become a formal law, the severity of the sanctions applied when the law is broken does give a rough indication of the significance attached to the underlying norm. If the laws of a community or a society conflict sharply with more basic folkways and mores, the law will tend to be either ignored or changed. If authorities should continue to enforce it rigidly, severe strains will be generated.

The culture of an organization serves as a vehicle for preserving its norms, but culture does not automatically perpetuate itself. It must be passed on from person to person in either verbal or written form, and it must be taught to each new member of the organization. For this reason normative theory places considerable emphasis on the process of socialization, both of children and of adults. To the extent that norms become internalized within personalities, the necessity for external sanctioning decreases and the entire organization gains unity and stability. In short, *norms constitute the essence of social organization as a phenomenon distinct from its individual members, but these norms extensively influence individuals' actions as a result of both socialization and social control.*

Norms do not remain totally static, but change over time in response to alterations in the life conditions of an organization and its members. New situations and problems give rise to new norms, while old norms that are no longer useful are slowly discarded. In general, however, norms tend to change more slowly than do life conditions, so that organizations frequently experience strains between the normative demands of their culture and the problems they presently face. Some normative theorists postulate the existence of inherent tendencies within the norms of an organization toward improvement in relation to life conditions and toward internal consistency, but other theorists in this school argue that both phenomena are problematic in any given situation.

Finally, the fact that the norms are always contained in the culture of an organization does not preclude their being shared among many different organizations, or being part of the culture of a more encompassing organization. To the extent that a common set of norms is held in common throughout an entire society in this manner, the society acquires normative integration.

No sociologist would deny that norms exist and do affect social life. However, social theorists differ widely on the importance norms have for social organization. Some writers see them as being largely epiphenomena that reflect but do not significantly influence organized social life, while proponents of normative theory argue that they are the major factors shaping all social organization. Undoubtedly the truth lies somewhere between these extremes. Normative theory explains many aspects of social life, but by itself it does not constitute a complete theory of social organization.

Value Theory

There have been, and are today, many proponents of a value theory of social organization. Talcott Parsons nevertheless stands apart from all the others, because of his extensive contributions to this school of theoretical thought, and also because most other contemporary value theorists have been students of Parsons' or have been heavily influenced by him. For these reasons, our discussion here will be confined solely to Parsons' ideas. We shall draw only upon his most recent writings (those published since 1960), since they differ in several respects from his earlier work. Furthermore, we can do no more than briefly sketch the most significant of his thoughts on the structure of social systems and the essence of value theory.

For analytical purposes, Parsons suggests that the totality of human life (which he describes as constituting the "action frame of reference") can be divided into four types or levels of systems. Progressing downward, these are cultural, social, personality, and organistic systems. Each of these types of systems has distinct properties of its own, and hence cannot be explained in terms of "lower" levels of existence, yet at the same time they all thoroughly interpenetrate each other. Parsons distinguishes these levels of systems on the basis of the major type of function each one performs within the totality of human life. Cultural systems center around the function of pattern maintenance (abbreviated "L" for "latency"), or maintaining the major values of human existence. Social systems focus on the function of integration ("I"), or creating order in social life. Personality systems are concerned primarily with the function of goal attainment ("G"), or achieving goals in the social environment. Organistic systems deal with the function of adaptation ("A"), or adapting human life to the natural world. Sociology is concerned primarily with social systems, but must always take the other levels into consideration as environments within which social organization occurs.

Below organistic systems lies the natural environment, which is the source of all energy for human activities. Hence there is a continual upward flow of energy (or more broadly, of resources) from the natural environment, which he refers to as the "hierarchy of conditioning factors." Above cultural systems is the realm of "ultimate reality," which is the final source of all cybernetic control in human activities. Hence there is a continual downward flow of information and decisions from ultimate reality, which he calls the "hierarchy of controlling factors." As a consequence, social systems must always rely on lower levels (the personality and the organism, and ultimately the natural environment) for a constant supply of energy, while at the same time they are always controlled in a cybernetic sense by cultural systems.

Although any social entity can be described as a social system in this conceptual scheme, Parsons usually focuses on societies, since they are by definition the most inclusive and self-sufficient type of social system. All other organizations then become subsystems, subsubsystems, and so on of societies. All parts of a society are interdependent and interpenetrating, though they can also be analyzed as systems in their own right.

Parsons also uses the LIGA scheme of system functions to differentiate social systems into their major component parts, along both vertical and horizontal dimensions. Vertical differentiation of a social system, first of all, produces four structural components or levels, as follows (in a downward sequence): (a) the pattern maintenance or L level, composed of the values from the controlling cultural system that are relevant to this social system and that define its goals and norms; (b) the integrative or I level, composed of clusters of norms (or institutions—he uses the two terms almost interchangeably), each of which pertains to a functionally specialized but fairly broad sphere of social activities; (c) the goal-attainment or G level, composed of concrete collectivities, or bounded patterns of relationships among role actors; and (d) the adaptive or A level, composed of social roles (or sets of roles) that individuals enact as they participate in social life. Although any real social system (that is, organization) is always a combination of all four structural components, for analytical purposes it is useful to distinguish them, since each can be an independent source of variation.

The hierarchies of conditioning and controlling factors also operate within social systems, so that Parsons identifies a downward flow of cybernetic control throughout social life. Societal values legitimize, and hence ultimately shape, the clusters of norms constituting various institutional areas. The particular norms of each institution in turn give authority to the collectivities in that area, enabling them to take collective action for the attainment of goals in the public interest. Finally, each collectivity authorizes the incumbents of its component roles to make decisions and otherwise act for the whole collectivity. Concurrently, an upward flow of conditioning factors, or resources, moves from roles to collectivities to institutionalized norms to values.

Of the four types of system functions (LIGA), Parsons believes that integration is always the most important, since it is the locus of the distinctive properties and processes of the total system. "We contend, therefore, that the problems focusing about the integrative functions of social systems constitute the central core of the concerns of sociological theory."[3] As a result of this overriding concern with integrative functions, he gives most of his attention to the normative (or institutional) component in all social systems. The values that define and control these norms are usually taken as given phenomena, while collectivities and roles are seen as being largely shaped by norms.

Horizontal differentiation of social systems into functional subsystems, which also follows the LIGA scheme, occurs at each of the four structural levels, but Parsons speaks mainly of the integrative level of norms or institutions. The four subsystems of a society at the integrative structural level are (a) the pattern maintenance or L subsystem, composed of all institutions (such as religion, education, and the family) concerned with perserving and perpetuating the basic values of the total social system, as derived from the overriding cultural system; (b) the integrative or I subsystem, composed of the "societal community," which is the central institutional component of any social system; (c) the goal-attainment or G subsystem, which focuses on the polity as the institution through which personalities achieve goals; and (d) the adaptive or A subsystem, which centers on the economy as the institution through which acting organisms obtain necessary resources from the natural environment.

Because the integrative function is always the most crucial type of social phenomenon for Parsons, he suggests that sociology should focus first on the societal community subsystem of a society, and second on the pattern maintenance institutions that uphold the values which legitimize

---

[3] "An Outline of the Social System," in Parsons, et al., eds., Theories of Society (New York: The Free Press, a division of The Macmillan Company, 1961), pp. 40–41.

the norms of the societal community. The polity and economy subsystems he delegates to political science and economics, respectively, as objects of study. The societal community subsystem is not a geographical entity, but rather the "patterned normative order" around which a society is organized, and which gives the society unity. Furthermore, a societal community can for analytical purposes be conceptualized as a system in its own right, and then be further differentiated along both vertical and horizontal axes using the LIGA scheme. Thus a societal community consists, structurally speaking, of a set of general values (derived directly from the values of the encompassing society, and indirectly from a cultural system), clusters of more functionally specialized norms, certain collectivities (such as legal organizations), and the roles that individuals enact in these collectivities. It can also be divided into its own LIGA functional subsystems (or more properly, subsubsystems) on a horizontal plane.

Value theory, as proposed by Parsons, explains the functioning and overall unity of all social systems. The theory first assumes a set of common values contained within a cultural system, although their basic meanings are determined by perceptions of ultimate reality. Values can change over time (primarily as a result of changing perceptions of ultimate reality), but these alterations are normally so slow that for most analytical purposes values are considered to be constants. The values held in common by most or all the members of a given society (its L component) are extremely broad and nonspecific, but they serve to legitimize various clusters of norms (the I component of a society) which are specialized in terms of the four types of system functions. These legitimate norms in turn control the activities of the concrete collectivities within each subsystem, through the process of institutionalization. To the extent that a collectivity is institutionalized, it is organized around certain societal values and norms and operates to perform necessary functions for society. Finally, individual role actors are guided and controlled by the societal norms that have become internalized within their personalities through socialization. As these actors participate in social life by responsibly enacting their various roles, they obtain both material and nonmaterial rewards from their actions.

In a broad sense, then, *common values shape and control all social life as they are expressed through norms, which are institutionalized in collectivities and internalized within personalities.* According to Parsons, "That a system of value-orientations held in common by the members of a social system can serve as the main point of reference for analyzing structure and process in the social system itself may be regarded as a major tenet of modern sociological theory."[4] Parsons' value theory of social organization is in effect merely a restatement of the theory of normative integration—but this is not surprising given his overriding concern with the process of social integration.

Detailed evaluation of Parsons' value theory is beyond the scope of this discussion, but we can mention three of the criticisms most frequently made of it. First, what is the source of all values, and how do they change? Postulating the existence of a realm of "ultimate reality" that gives meaning to all values does not answer this question, since we are then left wondering, "What is ultimate reality?" Many critics suggest that Parsons' conception of social life comes close to pure philosophical idealism, in which values emanate downward from a realm of existence that is largely or wholly beyond human control. Second, why must the process of integration be taken as the most important function in any organization or social system? Does this perspective not lead us (either intentionally or unintentionally) to stress a "conservative" ideological view of organized social life, in which conflict and change are seen as unfortunate disruptions of social order which should be prevented or at least corrected if at all possible? Third, and most crucial, is this whole elaborate complex of ideas a theory at all, or is it merely a set of heuristic analytical concepts, which at best orients us toward various features of social organization? That is, has Parsons' work been actual theory construction, or simply "programming for theorizing?"[5] On balance, it would seem that Parsons has given sociology a wealth of stimulating analytical ideas, concepts, and insights, but has not yet developed a general theory of social organization.

In summary, this chapter has outlined the six major schools of theoretical thought—exchange theory, interaction theory, ecological theory, power theory, normative theory, and value theory—prevailing in sociology as explanations of social organization. Each offers valuable contributions toward increasing our understanding of organized social life, but none is adequate by itself. Sociology still awaits the development of a comprehensive and unified theory of the process of social organization.

In the next chapter we descend from this level of pure theory to explore the idea of social evolution—or the development of modernized societies—as it is being employed in contemporary sociology.

[4] Talcott Parsons, *Structure and Process in Modern Societies* (New York: The Free Press, a division of The Macmillan Company, 1960), p. 172.
[5] Austin T. Turk, "On the Parsonian Approach to Theory Construction," *Sociological Quarterly*, vol. 8 (Winter 1967), pp. 37–50.

RECOMMENDED READING

EXCHANGE THEORY

BLAU, PETER, Exchange and Power in Social Life, especially chaps. 1, 2, 4, 6, 10, and 12 (New York: John Wiley & Sons, Inc., 1964).
An elaborate, sophisticated discussion of exchange theory, emphasizing its application to social organization.

HOMANS, GEORGE C., "Social Behavior as Exchange," The American Journal of Sociology, vol. 62 (May 1958), pp. 597–606 (Bobbs-Merrill reprint S-122). See also his Social Behavior: Its Elementary Forms, especially chaps. 3, 4, and 18 (New York: Harcourt, Brace & World, Inc., 1961).
The article outlines, and the book elaborates, his conceptionalization of exchange theory on the individual behavioral level.

THIBAUT, JOHN W., AND HAROLD H. KELLEY, The Social Psychology of Groups (New York: John Wiley & Sons, Inc., 1959).
Uses an exchange perspective to analyze with considerable rigor processes of social interaction within small groups.

INTERACTION THEORY

BRYSON, GLADYS, Man and Society: The Scottish Inquiry of the Eighteenth Century, especially chaps. 1, 2, 6, and 9 (Princeton: Princeton University Press, 1945).
Examines the work of David Hume, Adam Smith, Adam Ferguson, and other Scottish writers of that time, viewing them as early proponents of this school of social theory.

BLUMER, HERBERT, "Society as Symbolic Interaction," in Arnold Rose, ed., Human Behavior and Social Processes, chap. 9, pp. 179–192 (Boston: Houghton Mifflin Company, 1962).
An attempt to expand symbolic interaction theory from the interpersonal to the organizational level.

COOLEY, CHARLES H., Social Organization, especially chaps. 1–5, and Human Nature and the Social Order, especially chap. 1 (New York: The Free Press, a division of The Macmillan Company, 1956).
Views social organization as an outgrowth of common human nature among all individuals, acquired through socialization in primary groups.

MEAD, GEORGE HERBERT, Mind, Self, and Society, especially pt. 4 (Chicago: The University of Chicago Press, 1934).
The classic discussion of symbolic interaction theory and its relevance for understanding social organization.

PARSONS, TALCOTT, The Structure of Social Action, especially chaps. 2 and 19 (New York: The Free Press, a division of The Macmillan Company, 1949).
Formulates a conceptualization of social interaction that unites ideas from utilitarianism, positivism, and idealism.

ECOLOGICAL THEORY

DUNCAN, OTIS DUDLEY, "Social Organization and the Ecosystem," in Robert E. L. Faris, ed., Handbook of Modern Sociology, chap. 2, pp. 36–82 (Skokie, Ill.: Rand McNally & Company, 1964).

Extensively discusses the bearing of ecological considerations on the study of social organization, with particular reference to social evolution.

_____, AND LEO F. SCHNORE, "Cultural, Behavioral, and Ecological Perspectives in the Study of Social Organization," *The American Journal of Sociology*, vol. 65 (September 1959, pp. 132–146. (Also Bobbs-Merrill reprint S-75.)

A brief presentation of the fundamental ideas of ecological theory, in comparison with two other theoretical perspectives.

HAWLEY, AMOS, *Human Ecology*, especially chaps. 10–12 (New York: The Ronald Press Company, 1950).

The first systematic statement of ecology as a theory of social organization rather than a description of spatial patterning.

_____, "Human Ecology," forthcoming in the second edition of the *International Encyclopedia of the Social Sciences* (New York: The Macmillan Company).

Summarizes the main ideas of ecological theory, and then expands and generalizes this approach to all social organizations.

MOTT, PAUL, *The Organization of Society*, chap. 3 (Englewood Cliffs, N.J.: Prentice-Hall, Inc., 1965).

An introductory explanation of ecological theory, using thirteen basic propositions concerning social organization.

POWER THEORY

BOTTOMORE, T. B., *Elites and Society*, especially chaps. 1–3 (New York: Basic Books, Inc., 1964).

Summarizes, contrasts, and compares the main ideas of Marx, the elitist theorists, and C. W. Mills, and suggests numerous questions for further work in this area.

_____, AND MAXIMILIEN RUBEL, *Karl Marx: Selected Writings in Sociology and Social Philosophy* (London: C. A. Watts & Co., Ltd., 1956). See also C. W. Mills, *The Marxists*, especially chaps. 2–6 (New York: Dell Publishing Co., 1962).

Bottomore and Rubel abstract from Marx' writings those passages which pertain directly to social organization and sociology. Mills summarizes and evaluates the major ideas of Marxian theory and includes selected portions of Marx' writings.

DAHRENDORF, RALF, *Class and Class Conflict in Industrial Society*, especially chap. 5 (Stanford, Calif.: Stanford University Press, 1959).

Sketches and then elaborates a "coericion-conflict" model of social organization, centering on the distribution of authority.

MICHELS, ROBERT, *Political Parties*, trans. Eden and Cedar Paul, especially pts. 1, 2, and 6 (New York: The Free Press, a division of The Macmillan Company, 1966).

The classic argument for the inevitability of oligarchy in all organizations.

MOSCA, GAETANO, *The Ruling Class*, ed. Arthur Livingston, trans. Hannah D. Kahn, especially chaps. 2, 3, 5, and 15 (New York: McGraw-Hill, Inc., 1939).

The most forthright statement in sociological literature of an elitist theory of social organization.

NORMATIVE THEORY

DURKHEIM, ÉMILE, *Moral Education,* trans. Everett K. Wilson and Herman Schnurer, chaps. 2–8 (New York: The Free Press, a division of The Macmillan Company, 1961).
Presents his conception of society as a normative (moral) reality outside of the individual, and stresses the importance of socialization in perpetuating social organization.

LINTON, RALPH, *The Study of Man,* especially chaps. 7, 15, 16, and 17 (New York: Appleton-Century-Crofts, 1936).
Views social organization as a population of individuals who share common normative ideals and pattern their interactions in terms of these ideals.

SUMNER, WILLIAM GRAHAM, *Folkways,* especially chaps. 1 and 2 (Boston: Ginn & Company, 1940).
Contains the main aspects of his conception of social organization as perpetuated patterns of folkways and mores.

VALUE THEORY

PARSONS, TALCOTT, "An Outline of the Social System," in Talcott Parsons, et al., eds., *Theories of Society,* pp. 30–79 (New York: The Free Press, a division of The Macmillan Company, 1961).
The most comprehensive statement of his overall theoretical approach to social organization.

_____, *Societies: Evolutionary and Comparative Perspectives,* chap. 2 (Englewood Cliffs, N.J.: Prentice-Hall, Inc., 1966).
Relates the major aspects of his social-systems analytical approach to his broader social-action scheme in a brief but inclusive manner.

_____, *Structure and Process in Modern Societies,* chap. 5 (New York: The Free Press, a division of The Macmillan Company, 1960).
Discusses a number of his fundamental theoretical conceptions in a very straightforward manner, with special reference to the use of authority in society.

CHAPTER 16

Evolution of Social Organization

Our discussions of social organization have thus far been ahistorical, in that they have not focused on any particular time periods or sequences of actual events. We have been concerned with the process and forms of social organization wherever and whenever they occur. Much sociological work, however, does in fact deal with historical phenomena. The sociologist must always gather his empirical data from specific spatial and temporal settings, and often he will attempt to explain broad historical trends and processes in sociological terms. As an illustration of this kind of sociological endeavor, and also to introduce what is rapidly becoming a dominant theme in current sociology, we explore in these next two chapters the process of social evolution. This present chapter very briefly discusses the meaning of social evolution, mentions several different theoretical perspectives on this phenomenon, and then sketches the main characteristics of two "simpler" types of societies as points of comparison from which to view contemporary evolutionary trends. Four major historical trends—industrialization, urbanization, bureaucratization, and centralization—will then be examined in Chapter 17.

Early sociological thinking was thoroughly infused with crude notions of social evolution, which were often coupled with ideas of either social progress or social degeneration. The French social philosopher Auguste Comte, who is sometimes called "the father of sociology," believed that all societies evolve through three cultural stages, which he

called theological, metaphysical, and positive (scientific). Herbert
Spencer, the first major English sociologist, wrote that sociology is "the
study of evolution in its most complex form."[1] The German theorist
Ferdinand Tönnies saw social evolution as movement from *gemeinschaft*
societies based on personal, communal relationships to modern *gesellschaft*
societies, in which social relationships are impersonal and contractual.
Émile Durkheim's thesis of the growing dominance of organic (functional) over mechanical (normative) solidarity in contemporary society
also expressed an evolutionary orientation. Willam Graham Sumner, an
early American sociologist, tried to apply Darwin's theory of biological
evolution through natural selection and survival of the fittest to the totality
of social life. And most important of all, Karl Marx' contention that social
dialectical processes might ultimately sweep all of mankind from feudalism through capitalism to socialism is thoroughly evolutionary in nature.

Although sociologists still study the grand evolutionary theories of
these "founding fathers," few serious attempts have been made to incorporate their emphasis on social evolution into current sociological
thought. In their wholehearted attempts, beginning about 1920, to make
sociology "scientific," an entire generation of sociologists (with a few
notable exceptions) conveniently "shelved" the whole question of social
evolution as too grandiose and empirically unverifiable for social science.

The Meaning of Social Evolution

Since World War II it has become painfully obvious that societies
around the world—both "primitive" and "modern"—are indeed "going
somewhere" with full deliberate speed. As a belated consequence, contemporary sociologists have recently awakened to the vast implications of
social evolution for contemporary social life.[2] In its current guise, the
thesis of social evolution is often called "modernization"—despite invidious overtones of enthnocentrism inherent in this word—but the fundamental conception remains the same. *From an evolutionary viewpoint,
social change is in the long run both linear and cumulative.*[3] Social change

[1] Herbert Spencer, *The Study of Sociology* (New York: D. Appleton, 1873),
p. 350.

[2] A parallel trend has also occurred in anthropology, as witnessed by such books
as Julian Steward, *Theory of Cultural Change: The Methodology of Multilinear Evolution* (Urbana, Ill.: University of Illinois Press, 1955), and Marshall D. Sahlins and
Elmar R. Service, eds., *Evolution and Culture* (Ann Arbor, Mich.: University of
Michigan Press, 1960).

[3] This discussion does not attempt to deal with the radically different thesis of
cyclical evolution, which sees a certain set of processes or series of stages as being
endlessly repeated throughout human history. Two leading proponents of this view

is linear if, over time, nonrepetitive trends run throughout many diverse events and alterations. Although short-term fluctuations may be observed, the broad patterns of change are neither random nor cyclical. The steady decline in the death rate that has been occurring around the world for the past century or more is an example of a fairly linear change, while periodic variations in dress style are not linear. Social change is cumulative if, again over time, it builds upon itself, so that prior changes are not only retained but also influence future changes. Although cumulative change can occur in a "downward" direction toward increasing disintegration of social organization, most such change throughout history has been "upward" growth or development of social organization toward increased size, scope, and complexity. The process of industrialization, for instance, tends to be relatively cumulative as well as linear, in that the more extensively a society is industrialized the more rapidly its economy can expand to encompass further industrial development.

More explicitly, contemporary students of social evolution or modernization point to a number of broad, long-range, nonrepetitive, cumulative changes in social organization that are becoming increasingly evident throughout the world. In analytical terms, these trends include such phenomena as (a) increasing size of organizational units, in terms of both population and geographic area; (b) growing functional interdependence among social organizations, with attendant diminishing of functional self-sufficiency; (c) shifting of many social activities and responsibilities from small organizations such as families and neighborhoods to large social networks, national governments, and even international confederations; (d) rising functional specialization, or division of labor, among both individuals and organizations; (e) emergence of extremely complex and formal organizations, composed of many levels of interrelated subparts; (f) increasing centralized coordination and control in many types of organizations; (g) spreading cultural secularism and universalism, so that social values and norms are seen as man-made, relative, open to change, and applicable to all people and organizations; and (h) growing application of scientific knowledge and rational thought to the organizing of social life. In more historical terms, social evolution or modernization can be seen in such processes as nationalization,[4] industrialization, urbanization, bureaucratization, secularization, centralization, and "internationalization."[5]

are Arnold Toynbee, *A Study of History*, one-volume edition (New York: Oxford University Press, 1953), and Pitirim A. Sorokin, *Social and Cultural Dynamics* (Boston: Porter Sargent, 1957).

[4] This phenomenon is also commonly spoken of as "nation building."

[5] This term refers to the creation of social relationships and organization among nations throughout the world.

In their attempts to free evolutionary theory from many of its older biases and limitations, sociologists today studiously avoid imputing to social evolution a number of corollary ideas that were once either implicitly or explicitly assumed. The process of social evolution, they argue, does not include or imply (a) progress, or any necessary betterment in human happiness or morality; (b) teleology, or ultimate plans, purposes, or goals; (c) fixed stages through which all societies or other organizations must successively pass; (d) unilinear change along any one particular path;[6] (e) social determinism, or the idea that development is somehow inherent in social life and hence beyond human control; or (f) universality of evolution in all social organization. By rejecting notions such as these, sociologists hope to find in the idea of social evolution a theoretical key with which to unlock part of the riddle of "How has social organization changed throughout history and where is it going in the future?"

In short, social evolution is seen as one particular kind of social change—or more accurately, as a theoretical and historical perspective on social change. Not all change is evolutionary in nature, but in the broad sweep of human history we can discern crucial social trends that are both linear and cumulative and that are slowly but radically transforming organized social life.

Theories of Social Evolution

Social change is always observed as a series of concrete historical events, so that any trends an observer sees running through a series of alterations, as well as the conceptual and theoretical framework he uses to analyze and explain these trends, are somewhat arbitrary. An artist, for instance, might not view human history in the same light as would a social scientist. Even among themselves, sociologists are far from agreement concerning the most useful or appropriate theoretical perspective from which to study the process of social evolution.

Four different theoretical perspectives on social evolution prevail in sociology today, each of which tries to explain the essential nature of this

[6] Nineteenth-century theorists frequently assumed that social evolution was not just linear, but unilinear, so that all change was seen as a single process leading to the same final conclusion. Today we are realizing, however, that modernization is in fact a complex multidimensional process involving many different aspects that are at best only partially interrelated. Modernization may follow any number of numerous paths leading in diverse directions, so that social evolution can be described only as a multilinear phenomenon.

process in terms of a few key ideas or variables. The most common names for these four perspectives are cultural accumulation, ecological development, structural and functional differentiation, and epigenesis. Let us examine each one.

The theory of cultural accumulation gained wide support among American sociologists during the 1930's and 40's, primarily through the writings of William Ogburn.[7] This thesis begins with the assumption that in literate societies cultural knowledge—especially material and social technology—is rarely permanently forgotten or ignored. Once man begins to record his hard-won knowledge concerning the world and himself, each new generation can in effect start out where the last generation left off. Since the technological knowledge of the past is already available, the new generation can learn it without having to rediscover it or repeat costly errors. Hence cultural knowledge tends to accumulate at an ever-increasing, or exponential, rate. Sooner or later this growing body of cultural knowledge influences and shapes social life, with a resulting evolutionary development of social organization. In short, *social evolution occurs as material and social technology is accumulated through time and applied to organized social life.*

This idea of cultural accumulation persists in current sociological writings, though it is now commonly incorporated within one of the other theoretical perspectives. It is also being employed by several anthropologists who stress man's increasing ability to harness and utilize sources of energy.[8] As a descriptive generalization of an empirical phenomenon, the thesis of cultural accumulation has considerable validity. Mankind's stockpile of technological knowledge has in fact tended to grow at an increasing rate. But as a general explanation of the process of social evolution, the theory contains several weaknesses. The most serious is that it does not specify how cultural accumulation becomes transformed into broader processes of social evolution—that is, how technological knowledge affects social organization. Nor does it deal with the question of how developing social organization influences the invention or discovery of new knowledge. For these reasons, the cultural accumulation thesis is perhaps most useful as an ancillary part of other, more inclusive theories.

A relatively new, and quite distinct, sociological perspective on social

[7] Ogburn's classic statement of this theory was his *Social Change* (New York: The Viking Press, Inc., 1922). For a more recent presentation, see W. F. Ogburn and M. F. Nimkoff, *Sociologically*, 4th ed. (Boston: Houghton Mifflin Company, 1964), chaps. 23 and 24.

[8] The best known of these writers is Leslie A. White, *The Science of Culture* (New York: Farrar Straus & Giroux, Inc., 1949). See also Fred Cottrell, *Energy and Society* (New York: McGraw-Hill, Inc., 1955).

evolution is provided by social ecology.[9] The major themes of this school of thought were sketched in the previous chapter, and we shall only briefly review them here. Ecological theorists focus on the functional means through which a society, community, or other organization satisfies basic organizational and individual requirements, especially those involving survival in the natural environment. They include technology as a factor of crucial importance in this process, but add the additional variables of population and the environment as major determinants of social organization.[10] Growth in population size and density, increased abundance of resources from the natural or social environments, and accumulation of technological knowledge all act singly and in combination to produce evolution of social organization, while the level of organizational development in turn influences each of these other three factors. Population, environmental, and technological forces act upon a society primarily through its economy, and especially through its key sources of wealth and power (such as farming in an agricultural society or major industries in an industrialized society). The more effective the economy in satisfying basic sustenance requirements of the population, the greater the extent to which collective efforts can be diverted away from survival problems toward other activities and goals, and hence the more complex the resulting societal organization. *Thus social evolution occurs as a society, acting through its economy, effectively copes with the task of surviving in its environment and therefore acquires surplus resources for population growth and organizational development.*

Ecological theory, like the other three perspectives, has several weak points. Most important is its treatment of changes in population size, the environment, and technology as essentially random—except to the extent that these factors influence each other, or when Ogburn's idea of technological accumulation is employed. Furthermore, this thesis has thus far shown only limited ability to specify the processes or forms of social organization that will develop once survival problems have been mastered. Nevertheless, it does stress a concern with the "hard facts" of physical reality that is rather lacking in the other theories.

By far the most popular theoretical perspective on social evolution in contemporary sociology is that of structural and functional differentia-

[9] The first systematic statement of social (as opposed to spatial) ecological theory was by Amos H. Hawley, *Human Ecology* (New York: The Ronald Press Company, 1950), especially chaps. 10–12. An introductory explanation of the theory as it applies to social change is given by Paul E. Mott, *The Organization of Society* (Englewood Cliffs, N.J.: Prentice-Hall, Inc., 1965), chap. 3.

[10] The letters P, E, and T, standing for population, environment, and technology, plus O for organization, together form the convenient mnemonic label "POET."

tion.[11] In simply organized societies, most social activities take place within a few basic types of organization (such as the extended family or a small community). All functions necessary to satisfy individual and social requirements are performed by these "multipurpose" organizations. Such functionally unspecialized organizations tend to be rather inefficient in carrying out their diverse activities, however, since they cannot commit all of their resources and efforts to any one type of problem. With growing population size, cultural knowledge, and common desires for more effective operational procedures, it becomes impossible to confine all social life to a few organizations. Through a process of trial and error, an ever increasing number and variety of new organizations is created, each of which specializes in a rather narrowly defined sphere of activity. The more extensive the web of diversified organizations within the society, the more complex it becomes. However, these emerging specialized organizations must be at least partially institutionalized if the society is not to become totally segmented and eventually disintegrate. In sum, *social evolution occurs as a few original multipurpose organizations become structurally differentiated into many functionally specialized organization each of which effectively performs its particular activities as an instit tionalized part of the total society.*

Considerable evidence has been compiled to support this thesis that social evolution does in fact frequently take place through structural and functional differentiation, but this statement is only an empirical generalization, not a causal explanation. What social forces, other than public dissatisfaction with existing procedures or rational social planning, operate to initiate this process of differentiation? In what ways are functionally ineffective organizational innovations discarded and satisfactory ones retained? And what factors determine the lines along which "fused" activities become functionally specialized, or the particular forms that structurally differentiated organizations will assume? Finally, how does a society remain integrated while undergoing structural and functional differentiation? In brief, this thesis describes a general process through which social evolution frequently occurs, but it does not explain this process—it tells us what happens, but not how or why it happens.

A fourth perspective on social evolution is provided by Amitai

---

[11] For a representative sampling of this literature, see the following: S. N. Eisenstadt, "Social Change, Differentiation, and Evolution," *American Sociological Review*, vol. 29 (June 1964), pp. 375–386; Talcott Parsons, "Evolutionary Universals in Society," *American Sociological Review*, vol. 29 (June 1964), pp. 339–357; Neal J. Smelser, *Social Change in the Industrial Revolution* (Chicago: The University of Chicago Press, 1959); and Winston White, *Beyond Conformity* (New York: The Free Press, a division of The Macmillan Company, 1961), chap. 6.

Etzioni's concept of epigenesis, which is essentially a theoretical formalization and expansion of traditional political thought.[12] This thesis begins with the assumption that individuals frequently propose, and societies or other organizations adopt, goals for collective social life. As a means of achieving these goals, existing organizations are expanded or new ones are established. Workers form a labor union through which to bargain with their employer, an association is begun to promote the game of golf, or a community is founded to take advantage of nearby natural resources. New organizations can be started from "scratch," but more commonly they emerge as several existing organizations merge to form a larger and more inclusive social entity. Etzioni has used this theoretical perspective to study the growth of international confederations, but it obviously has many other applications.

A major difference between the ideas of differentiation and epigenesis is that the former thesis stresses only the development of new ways of carrying out old activities, whereas the latter thesis emphasizes the creation of totally new social activities. According to the differentiation theory, all basic social functions are performed in even the most primitive society (though perhaps not very efficiently), so that evolution involves merely the splitting up of these functions among separate organizations. The epigenesis theory, in contrast, argues that through the collective seeking of new goals, mankind establishes both new organizations and new activities. Social evolution is not just a matter of learning how to perform social functions more effectively and efficiently; it also adds totally new activities and dimensions to organized social life. Although the process of epigenesis may at first appear to be overly rationalistic, the theory largely escapes this pitfall by emphasizing the actions of organizational elites, who use their power to influence, shape, and direct the process of social organization toward the attainment of whatever goals they seek for themselves or for their organizations. In other words, *social evolution occurs as social actors, especially powerful elites, more or less purposefully expand existing organizations and activities or create new ones to achieve goals through collective action.*

This theory does not attempt to explain all aspects of social evolution, and hence leaves many crucial questions unanswered. For instance, from what sources can leaders derive the power with which to carry out the process of organizational expansion or creation, or how do such organizations become integrated and functionally effective, or what happens when the masses of the people involved disagree with the elites? Nevertheless,

---

[12] Amitai Etzioni, "The Epigenesis of Political Communities at the International Level," *The American Journal of Sociology*, vol. 68 (1963), pp. 407–421.

epigenesis does offer a relatively straightforward explanation of at least some of the forces involved in the evolution of social organization.

None of these four competing theoretical perspectives on social evolution is necessarily incompatible with any of the others, although they do stress different factors and processes. Each therefore has its particular sphere of usefulness as a way of analyzing the development of organized social life. But as in all areas of social theory, a complete explanation of the process of social evolution would undoubtedly incorporate features from all of these more limited theoretical viewpoints.

The Folk Society

To appreciate the magnitude of the changes introduced into a society through the process of modernization, we must have some familiarity with "premodern" societies. To provide such a comparative baseline, we shall examine in these next two sections the major characteristics of "folk" and "feudal" types of societies. Our concern is not to analyze these "simpler" forms of societal organization in any detail, but rather to understand the social conditions from which modernization begins. Neither of these sketches describes an actual society, past or present. As we noted in Chapter 14, folk and feudal societies are both composite analytical types, each of which has been constructed by combining the most significant features of a wide range of real societies. Hence no actual society will necessarily display all of the features of either type, although many of the characteristics comprising each type do tend to occur together. Examples of societies that more or less approximate the folk and feudal types can be found throughout human history, both in the past and the present, although these kinds of societies are slowly disappearing as modernization spreads around the world.

Two further words of caution are necessary before we examine each of these societal types. First, the sketches presented here are drawn exclusively from the "classic" discussions of folk and feudal societies.[13] Subsequent research has indicated that both of them are severely oversimplified. We are now realizing that even the "simplest" societies are far too complex to be easily classified under either of these headings. Consequently, neither type is particularly useful in precise empirical research or

[13] These are Robert Redfield, "The Folk Society," *The American Journal of Sociology*, vol. 52 (January 1947), pp. 293–308; and Gideon Sjoberg, "Folk and 'Feudal' Societies," *The American Journal of Sociology*, vol. 58 (November 1952), pp. 231–239. Similar but not identical typologies have been presented by other writers under such headings as "hunting and gathering" and "agrarian" societies, but the terms "folk" and "feudal" are still widely used.

theoretical analysis. For our present limited purposes, however, they remain adequate.

Second, we must avoid the simplistic assumption that folk societies are the most primitive forms of social life and that feudal societies represent a halfway point between primitive and modern societies. We have no way of knowing what the earliest or "most primitive" types of societies may have been like, but the folk society does not represent the beginning of organized social life. And although it is evident that feudal society is more "advanced" than folk society but less so than industrialized societies, we cannot place this type at any one precise point along the process of social evolution.

The primary theoretical perspective employed in these discussions is ecological theory, since both types of societies must continually grapple with pressing survival demands. To a lesser extent, the idea of cultural accumulation is also relevant, and some structural differentiation can be observed in the feudal type. Although the typical feudal society is thus more complex than the simpler folk societies, it should not be assumed that in the course of social evolution a society must necessarily move from a "folk" to a "feudal" to a "modern" stage. Many folklike societies in Africa, for instance, are now attempting to become industrialized and urbanized without first undergoing feudalism.

The key feature of folk society is a minimal amount of internal organization, with most social life centering in the extended family. A folk society barely survives on a subsistence economic level, and it has no surplus resources for further organizational development beyond "multipurpose" kinship units.

From an ecological viewpoint, the natural and social environments, the level of technology, and the population size of a folk society are all nonconducive to large and complex social organization. The people are immediately and totally dependent on the natural environment for food and other resources, but no matter how abundant the environment, resource procurement is always limited by a lack of material technology. Because of their primitive means of transportation and communication, such societies are usually rather isolated from one another, and cannot benefit from trade or the diffusion of new ideas. Communication is further hampered by the absence of a written language. Hence the level of material technology is quite low, consisting of only a few simple hand tools and depending on human and animal muscles as the major sources of energy. The society experiences a very high death rate, owing to famine and disease, and consequently must also have a high birth rate to maintain its population. Even so, because of limited resources the total population usually remains quite small (a few hundred people at most), and the society continually maintains a precarious balance between underpopulation (leading to extinction) and overpopulation (producing starvation).

The economy of a folk society is most commonly based on either hunting of wild animals and gathering of wild plants, or on simple "slash-and-burn" transitory agriculture. In either case, it operates at or just above the subsistence level—producing only enough food and other necessary goods to keep the small population alive, with little or no surplus beyond the bare necessities of life. Everyone past the age of six or seven is directly engaged in productive economic tasks, with only minimal division of labor along age and sex lines. There is no extensive economic specialization.

Social order in a folk society centers almost exclusively in the extended family, clan, or tribe. It is the only significant type of organization within the society, and it performs almost all major social functions: economic, governmental, educational, religious, recreational, welfare, and socialization. The lack of resources above the subsistence level, plus the absence of specialized roles, prohibits any functional or structural differentiation. Because of its functional dominance, the family exercises almost all of whatever social power exists in the society, and family social ties are exceptionally strong. Most social interaction is in fact guided by the participants' kinship relationships to each other.

The folk community is nothing more than one or a few extended families banded together. Communities are relatively isolated from each other and hence must be almost totally self-sufficient. With rare exceptions, they are not stationary, but are forced to move periodically in pursuit of new game, plants, or fertile land. Links between communities are thus weak and transitory, based largely on kinship ties rather than economic or cultural exchanges, so that each community is in effect a total society. The folk community and society are thus normally identical.

There is little in the way of additional organization within a typical folk society, for the simple reason that people cannot be spared from economic tasks to establish or operate other forms of social order. No formal government exists, although a "council of elders" may sometimes meet to discuss communal problems. Education, religion, and other such specialized activities take place almost entirely within the family, and hence have no separate organizations. The one nonproductive role in folk society is that of shaman, which combines religious, magical, medical, and educational duties. Small friendship cliques are common but must remain subordinate to the family. Associations based on age and sex, such as a "men's club," may sometimes be formed, but these bodies are concerned almost exclusively with special ceremonial or recreational activities. Because of the relative absence of functional and structural differentiation, there is no basis for social stratification, except in the form of prestige based on personal qualities such as hunting ability.

The cultural values, beliefs, and norms of a folk society are both traditional and sacred. They are derived from ancient customs, myths, and traditions and are observed primarily because "this is the way things have always been done." They are seen, furthermore, as having supernatural or divine origins, so that it is impossible to change them and unthinkable to question them. Strong social norms pervade all aspects of life and are strictly enforced through informal sanctions, thus allowing relatively little personal choice of action. Norms are also extremely homogeneous, so that elaborate subcultures cannot develop. Physical survival and maintenance of a minimal amount of social organization is too precarious in a folk society to allow much cultural variation or individual role selection. There is no "margin of safety" within which to experiment with new ideas and practices without endangering the entire society.

Overall, folk society is strongly integrated, but almost entirely on a normative basis, since there is little division of labor and hence no ground for extensive functional interdependence. The few organizational subunits that do exist are highly institutionalized. Because of its social isolation, simple organizational structure, and strict social control, the society experiences relatively few conflicts other than those arising from the natural environment, changes in population size, or sporadic clashes with other societies. When disruptions do occur, they are usually suppressed as quickly as possible so as to prevent social change, which cannot be tolerated because of its threat to the survival of the society. Although folk society is thus quite rigid, it may persist unchanged for long periods, until it encounters external stresses (such as natural catastrophes or contact with technologically advanced societies) with which it cannot cope. At this point the folk society is either radically altered or totally destroyed.

The Feudal Society

In comparison with folk society, the feudal type of society is quite complexly organized, although it has not yet begun to experience the growth and expansion that usually accompany modernization. To fully understand this kind of societal organization, we must supplement ecological theory with the ideas of differentiation and epigenesis, although the ecological perspective remains paramount.

The key features of feudal society are extreme status differences be-

tween a small elite class and the peasant masses, plus the beginnings of functional and structural differentiation. The elites expropriate for their own use whatever agricultural surpluses are produced, and employ these resources to support the activities and organizations through which they control the society.

Feudal society exists in somewhat more favorable ecological conditions than does folk society. Since most of the population is directly engaged in some form of agriculture, the society as a whole is still highly dependent on the natural environment. However, the people have acquired sufficient agricultural knowledge to enable them to remain settled in one place. Sporadic contacts take place among neighboring societies, but these are usually limited to either warfare or trade in scarce luxury items. Each society therefore remains largely self-sufficient, although there is some cultural diffusion via wandering merchants and military expeditions. A variety of hand tools are utilized, but little machinery, while the major sources of energy are domesticated animals and natural phenomena such as wind and flowing water. In general, therefore, material technology has considerably less impact on social life in a feudal society than in more modernized societies. Birth and death rates both remain high, but the more adequate and reliable food supply permits a much larger total population.

The economic base of feudal society is settled agriculture, including the raising of grains, vegetables, and domesticated animals. Some handicraft manufacturing is also carried on by skilled craftsmen, or artisans, although most of their products are consumed by the small elite class. Whatever limited trade occurs with other societies is not significant for the total economy. The agricultural economy of feudal society is adequate to produce some surplus of resources above bare sustenance needs, but this surplus is so small that the bulk of the population still lives close to the subsistence level. Economic division of labor must therefore be limited to the few sectors of the population that have been freed from agricultural labor.

Social order in a feudal society is highly influenced by the allocation of the available economic surplus. Since land is the ultimate basis of wealth and power, whoever owns it will determine the allocation process and exert dominant power in society. Through warfare, consolidation, and other forceful means, a small elite class acquires ownership of most of the arable land in the society, controls the peasants, and through rents and taxes expropriates surplus production for its own use. In addition to land ownership, elites also have several other bases of power over the peasants: (a) they control whatever military organization exists, and use it to coerce their serfs as well as to protect them from external conquest; (b) the societal government is created and employed by the elites as a means of preserving the existing social order; (c) being the only literate people in the society (other than possibly a few artisans), they have a monopoly on technological knowledge and communication; and (d) they use the established church to persuade the peasants to accept their assigned lot in life, as well as to convince them that they have a divine obligation to pay homage to the elites. Although the rule of the elites is thus ultimately based on force, they are often quite successful in achieving legitimate authority based on fealty obligations. Through long tradition, the serfs come to feel that they owe allegiance to their lord, in return for the military protection he affords them. In addition to the land-owning nobles, the elite class also contains priests, scholars, military leaders, and governmental officials, all of whom owe their positions to the nobility and are often related to them. Elite status is largely ascribed, so that normally it cannot be attained by either peasants or artisans.

The other distinct social classes in feudal society, besides the elites, are a "retainer" class composed of officials and administrators who serve the elites, a small "middle" class consisting mainly of artisans and small shopkeepers, the vast peasant class, and sometimes a slave class gained through military conquest. The retainer, middle, and slave classes are made possible by the production of an agricultural surplus that frees these people for other types of work, but they are allowed to exist only because they provide the elites with desired goods and services.

Although the peasants live primarily on the land or in tiny villages, there are normally a few larger towns within the fief or estate of each noble. These communities serve as residences of the elites and the retainer and the middle class, and as centers for whatever trade takes place. Although in the early stages of feudalism each fief may be largely self-sufficient and thus constitute a society in itself, it is not uncommon for one noble to gain ascendant power (through economic domination or warfare) over his neighbors, and thus consolidate many small fiefs into a loose alliance that gradually acquires societal characteristics. Subordinate elites retain considerable local autonomy, but owe allegiance to the dominant noble, or king, and are bound to support him, especially in case of war.

The extended family is no longer the major social unit in feudal society, but it is still extremely important within each social class. The peasant family works together as an economic unit, must satisfy most of its own daily needs, and still performs many educational, recreational, and welfare activities for its members. Artisans jealously guard their craft skills and seek to pass their trades on to their sons. And membership in the elite class is normally acquired only through family inheritance.

Feudal society contains an organized government with formal laws, though it is weak by contemporary standards and highly decentralized among many local and regional elites. Governmental activities are dispersed throughout the numerous manors and fiefs comprising a society, and the king or other societal leaders are extremely dependent for their power upon locally based nobility. Political power is exercised authoritatively, without any popular decision-making. Nevertheless, the establishment of permanent governmental units and administrative bodies is a significant organizational advancement.

The church is also a separate association under feudalism, with its own full-time specialized roles. Although it is highly influenced, if not controlled, by the nobility, it exerts considerable power throughout the society. Education, in contrast, is not extensively organized. Formal schooling, conducted by independent scholars or religious leaders, is normally reserved for children of the elites and their retainers, while artisans pass on their skills by training apprentices in their workshops. The most significant special-interest associations in feudal society are artisan guilds, which act as mutual protection organizations in setting workmanship standards, supervising apprentice training programs, determining wages for journeymen, and providing numerous welfare services.

As in folk societies, cutural values, beliefs, and norms under feudalism tend to be highly traditional and sacred, especially among the peasants. The middle and elite classes do have subcultures of their own, though, which are somewhat less traditional and considerably less sacred. Artisans and merchants begin to emphasize individual accomplishment and active manipulation rather than passive acceptance of the environment. Elites, meanwhile, develop their own codes of honor, beliefs, customs, and traditions, which they rigidly enforce upon each other. This unique subculture sets the elites apart from the rest of the society and reinforces their claims to power, privilege, and prestige.

From an overall viewpoint, feudal society is weakly integrated, since there are few common values and norms shared by the entire population, and only limited forms of functional interdependence. Social order in such a society is maintained primarily through the wielding of power (both force and authority) by elites. Some segments of the society (such as the government and the church) may be highly institutionalized, but most subunits (subordinate fiefs, artisan guilds, peasant families) are relatively segmented with considerable functional autonomy, except for the economic and military control of the elites. Numerous bases for internal strains as well as external stresses exist in feudal society, but in most cases the elites strongly and quite effectively suppress conflict and resist change, in fear of losing their power in society. Feudal society is thus quite rigid, despite the tensions and conflict inherent in extreme stratification, and will normally persist until some new source of power arises within the society (or is imposed upon it) to challenge and destroy the control of the landed nobility. When that happens, though, revolutionary social change is likely to erupt.

With these broad pictures of the folk and feudal types of society in mind, let us now move on to the major evolutionary processes of industrialization, urbanization, bureaucratization, and centralization.

RECOMMENDED READING

EISENSTADT, S. N., "Social Change, Differentiation, and Evolution," *American Sociological Review*, vol. 29 (June 1964), pp. 375–386.
Analyzes the process of social evolution as occurring through structural differentiation, together with the effects on society of differentiation.

ETZIONI, AMITAI, "The Epigenesis of Political Communities at the International Level," *The American Journal of Sociology*, vol. 68 (1963), pp. 407–421.
Describes the epigenesis perspective on evolutionary change, distinguishes it from structural differentiation, and applies it to the creation of international organization.

MOTT, PAUL, *The Organization of Society*, chap. 3 (Englewood Cliffs, N.J.: Prentice-Hall, Inc., 1965).
An introduction to ecological theory as applied to the evolution of social organization.

OGBURN, WILLIAM F., AND MEYER F. NIMKOFF, *Sociology*, 4th ed., chaps. 23 and 24 (Boston: Houghton Mifflin Company, 1964).
The most recent statement of the theory of cultural accumulation.

REDFIELD, ROBERT, "The Folk Society," *The American Journal of Sociology*, vol. 52 (January 1947), pp. 293–308.
The classic description of the folk society model.

SJOBERG, GIDEON, "Folk and 'Feudal' Societies," *The American Journal of Sociology*, vol. 58 (November 1952), pp. 231–239. (Also Bobbs-Merrill reprint S-270.)
A concise description of the feudal society model.

CHAPTER 17

Processes of Social Evolution

The development of contemporary "modernized" societies has involved four basic evolutionary trends or processes: industrialization, urbanization, bureaucratization, and centralization. Each is a distinct social phenomenon, but historically they have tended to become highly interrelated, so that growth in one area is extremely likely to produce concomitant changes in other directions also. Although they are certainly not the only significant social phenomena occurring in today's world, they do constitute the major dynamic trends underlying the evolutionary processes of modernization. These four developmental trends have largely shaped the contemporary "Western world," and are now slowly transforming most remaining "folk" and "feudal" societies. Each constitutes a prominent area of investigation within sociology, so that in this chapter we can do no more than sketch their highlights and suggest ways in which they become interrelated. Hopefully, though, these brief sketches will provide an introduction to further study in each area.

Industrialization

All four of these major evolutionary trends—industrialization, urbanization, bureaucratization, and centralization—are unquestionably of great significance in every modernized society. But we must look first at industrialization, for it is primarily this process that destroys feudalism.

Industrialization is often viewed as a purely technological development, in which the use of power-driven machinery for all kinds of economic production becomes widespread throughout a society. But the replacement of handicraft production by machinery and mass-production techniques ramifies through all aspects of social life. *With growing industrialization the economy of a society becomes increasingly effective in meeting basic organizational and individual survival requirements, so that considerable amounts of resources and effort can be directed toward other kinds of collective activities.* The social and cultural development of a society is therefore no longer limited by relentless survival demands.

Preindustrial societies frequently experience at least moderate social change through time, so that they are not totally static. But their overall patterns of social order and culture do tend to remain highly stable for long periods, providing they do not encounter severe disruptive stresses such as changes in the natural environment or military conquest. In analytical terms, there can be extensive change within the society without producing radical change of the society, so that the basic feudal pattern often survives for centuries—as seen in medieval Europe. The explanation of this phenomenon lies in the somewhat paradoxical facts of extensive elite control coupled with weakly organized governmental and other administrative units. On the one hand, feudal elites often maintain such pervasive control over their society that they can fairly effectively prevent any extensive social changes of the total society. Other segments of the society, such as peasants or artisans or merchants, are too weak to challenge or overthrow the rule of the landed nobility. On the other hand, there are few societywide organizations such as strong central governments, political parties, mass communications, or educational networks through which members of the society might work to promote social change.

As a broad generalization, therefore, it appears that feudal types of societies cannot usually be transformed into more modernized societies without external impetus from material technology or the social environment. The only segment of a feudal society capable of introducing sweeping social change is the landed nobility, but their vested interests lead them to perpetuate the *status quo* as long as possible. Only with the appearance of entirely new sources of social power not dependent on ownership of agricultural land, plus attendant patterns of social order and culture, can feudalism be destroyed and the processes of modernization begun.

Industrialization provides these new sources of power and social organization. With industrialization, wealth and other power resources accrue to those who own and operate machines rather than land, so that a new power elite emerges to challenge the control of the feudal nobility. As industrialists gain economic power in a society, they almost invariably seek to extend their influence to other realms such as politics, and hence sooner or later clash with the landed nobles. A prolonged period of extensive, violent, and even bloody conflict may ensue, but as industry grows in productivity so does the power of businessmen, until the nobility can no longer suppress or control them. Sooner or later the old elites will be either driven out or reduced to powerless symbolic figureheads, and radical transformations will ensue throughout the entire society.

Rather ironically, in many feudal societies the landed nobility have unwittingly hastened their own downfall. In order to expand and consolidate their power, feudal elites have sought to create large standing armies and navies. They have also felt compelled to maintain lavish courts and engage in elaborate conspicuous consumption as symbols of their status in society. But all this has required more revenues than could be squeezed out of the peasants. The nobles consequently began to tax and borrow from merchants and nascent industrialists, and thus over time became increasingly dependent upon these additional sources of income. As the old elites sought on the one side to gain power and prestige, on the other side they gradually but continually surrendered power (if not immediately prestige) to businessmen.

The development of extensive industrialization within a society requires at least five sets of preconditions: material technology, agricultural productivity, social technology, political unification, and entrepreneurial values.[1]

Widespread utilization of power-driven machinery depends on the acquisition and application of a vast amount of scientific and engineering knowledge. Until such technology becomes available, either through innovation or diffusion, industrialization cannot occur. Because England was the first society to become highly industrialized, much emphasis is often placed on the inventions in the textile industry (such as the spinning jenny and the power loom) that initiated the entire process. But the industrialization of a society does not have to begin with textile manufacturing, and in fact has not done so in any other major society. Economists are generally agreed that if any one sphere of production is particularly crucial for industrialization, it is undoubtedly the manufacturing of steel. All other industries depend on steel for their own machinery, and for many it is also a basic raw material. More important than any specific type of production, though, is knowledge about and development of

---

[1] A concise but highly insightful analysis of requirements for industrialization is given by W. W. Rostow, *The Stages of Economic Growth* (New York: Cambridge University Press, 1964).

sources of inanimate power. Machinery, after all, is useless without power. In this light, it can be argued that the steam engine was the single most important invention for early industrialization. Today many other sources of power are also available, including oil, electricity, and atomic fission, although their application often raises many problems for industrializing nations. Finally, industrialization cannot proceed far without the development of extensive transportation and communication facilities.

If people are to work in factories, agricultural productivity in a society must be high enough to free large segments of the population from subsistence farming. More food must be produced by fewer farmers. Mechanization of agricultural work will greatly raise productivity, but most societies in the early stages of industrialization lack the wealth to buy and operate such equipment even if it is available. They must rely instead upon the development of such practices as fertilization, crop rotation, and irrigation. Once again, though, feudal elites have frequently hurried their own downfall. In England and Europe, it was they, not the peasants, who first introduced improvements such as these into agriculture. Their clear intention was to increase their own wealth and social power as a means of combating the rising merchants and industrialists. In eighteenth-century England the nobility also passed the famous Enclosure Acts, which entitled them to fence off and cultivate land that previously had been used as communal livestock grazing pastures. Agricultural productivity was raised as a result of these various innovations, and for a time the elites benefited. But in the long run they merely succeeded in freeing more peasants for work in factories.

Handicraft production in feudal societies takes place primarily within an artisan's home or small shop, with one or a few persons performing the entire operation from beginning to end. The introduction of machinery into the productive process changes all this, however. The high cost of machinery, the space it requires, and the necessity for connecting many machines to a common power plant, call for the building of factories. A factory is much more than a building that houses machinery; it is also a complex social organization consisting of countless novel social relationships and patterns of social order. Practices must be initiated and problems solved in such areas as recruiting workers into the factory and hiring them on a cash basis to work during certain specified periods of the day, supervising and disciplining workers who may never before have worked in accordance with time schedules and fixed routines, providing for the safety and welfare of employees, coordinating the many diverse activities taking place within the different parts of the factory, anticipating demands and problems so as to plan for and guide factory production, disposing of the finished products on the outside market, and in general managing a huge and highly complex organization. In short, *industrial-*

ization depends as much on developments in social technology as in material technology.

Beyond these basic features of factory organization, many other forms of social technology are also involved in industrialization. Two examples are specialized mass production and the corporate form of organization. Short of complete automation, industrial production becomes most efficient when each machine (and hence also each worker) performs only one or a few specialized operations, over and over again. With the addition of a moving assembly line, vast quantities of goods can be cheaply produced in this manner. But extreme division of labor introduces numerous problems of coordination and regulation, not to mention the loss of creativity and satisfaction suffered by the individual worker who becomes a distinctly minor cog in the vast process of mass production. On a broader level, the corporate form of business organization has many advantages over individual ownership or partnerships. It enables the company to raise large amounts of capital through the sale of stock, it protects investors from unlimited financial liability for the business, and it gives the company legal stability despite changes in ownership or management.

The small and relatively autonomous political units characteristic of feudalism are not well suited to extensive manufacturing and trade. Hence *close ties of political cooperation, if not complete political unification, are another necessary requirement for the industrialization of a society.* As long as each feudal fief is more or less politically independent of its neighbors, businessmen face such problems as inadequate or nonexistent means of transportation between localities, toll charges every few miles as goods move from one principality to another, lack of a common currency with which to conduct sales, wide variations in laws and customs pertaining to manufacturing and business transactions, a limited pool of labor from which to hire workers, and severely restricted markets for sales. Political cooperation and unification on an increasingly broader scope alleviates all of these problems for manufacturers and traders, even though the ruling nobility may seek political consolidation largely for its own aggrandizement and without any necessary intention of furthering industrialization.

At the beginning of the twentieth century Max Weber argued that in addition to economic, social, and political requirements, *industrialization is always dependent on a set of cultural values and norms, which must be internalized by individuals so as to motivate their activities.*[2] These

---

[2] Max Weber, *The Protestant Ethic and the Spirit of Capitalism,* trans. Talcott Parsons (New York: Charles Scribner's Sons, 1958). Weber spoke only of privately owned businesses, but it can be argued that his basic thesis applies to all instances of industrialization regardless of formal ownership.

values and norms, which he called the "Protestant Ethic," stress the importance of hard work, self-denial, self-discipline, thrift, frugality, self-reliance, and individual initiative. Industrialization requires the investment of large sums of money, or capital, into machinery, buildings, raw materials, and trained manpower. Entrepreneurs must therefore be willing to forego immediate rewards and invest their savings and profits as capital that may not begin to produce wealth for many years. Furthermore, the creation of industry always involves financial risks and requires ceaseless efforts by its founders. Weber argued that without the values and norms of the Protestant Ethic, individuals lack the motivation and drive necessary to carry out the process of industrialization.

This ethic, Weber believed, was first stressed by Protestant reformers, especially John Calvin and his followers. It was for them a purely religious doctrine, and they had no intention of applying it to economic affairs. But by a chance historical accident, these religious beliefs were ideally suited to the emergence of industry and commerce, and hence provided the necessary cultural support of industrialization in Europe. Weber amassed vast quantities of data to support his thesis. He showed, for instance, that Protestant England, Germany, and Scandinavia industrialized earlier and more extensively than did Catholic France, Italy, or Spain. He also tried to prove that the lack of a "Protestant Ethic" was the primary factor that prevented China and India from becoming industrialized long before Europe. Numerous critics have since attacked Weber's thesis, and have rather conclusively demonstrated many logical and factual errors in his linkage between Protestantism and this set of cultural values and norms.[3] Rejection of Weber's causal argument does not diminish the importance of cultural ideas such as these for industrialization, however. Under the newer names of "entrepreneurial values" or the "work ethic," they are stressed by many contemporary social scientists as being a vital requirement for industrialization.

Turning from causes to consequences of industrialization, we now ask: what social effects does widespread industrialization have on a society? This question can be approached both theoretically and empirically. Undoubtedly the most influential theoretical discussion of the social consequences of industrialization lies in the writings of Karl Marx. A major empirical effect of industrialization, meanwhile, is seen in changing stratification patterns.

Besides being a revolutionary polemist, Karl Marx was also a profound social theorist who devoted his life to describing and analyzing

---

[3] The most recent and thorough criticism is by Kurt Samuelsson, *Religion and Economic Action: A Critique of Max Weber*, trans. E. Geoffrey French (New York: Harper & Row, Publishers, 1961).

the effects of industrialization on man and society.[4] Although Marx defies easy categorization, the single phrase most descriptive of his overriding concern might be "secular humanitarianism." Observing Europe at the middle of the nineteenth century, he was struck by the existence of a profound paradox. On the one hand, growing industrialization was creating more wealth than ever before experienced in any society. But on the other hand, he saw everywhere exploitation of workers, atrocious working conditions, pitifully low wages, extreme poverty, vast slums, multiplying crime rates, and general human misery. "Why?" he asked. What is wrong with the organization of a society that produces so much misery in the midst of hitherto undreamed of wealth? How must society be changed to correct these evils and enable everyone to benefit from the productivity of industrialization? These were the questions his theory attempted to answer.

Marx' theory of social organization has three major components: a sociological perspective—economic-political dominance; a philosophy of history—dialectic social change; and a connecting thesis—social classes in continual conflict.

Underlying all of Marx' thought was the sociological proposition that *society rests on an economic foundation, so that whoever controls economic production can exert tremendous influence throughout organized social life.* He did not claim that all other sectors of a society—such as government, religion, education, or the family—are totally determined by the economy, but he did believe that they are highly shaped and constrained by more basic economic forces. Not all aspects of the economy are equally important for social organization, however. The fundamental factor in his theory was control over the major means of economic production within a society. Whoever controls the basic sources of wealth will determine how much wealth is produced and how it is distributed and used, and hence will hold dominant power in the society. Under feudalism these economic elites are the landed nobility; with industrialization they become the owners of factories and related business concerns. Relationship to (or control over) the means of production, which is as much a political as an economic phenomenon, is thus the fundamental factor in all social organization.

[4] The following discussion of Marx is based on several sources: T. B. Bottomore and Maximilien Rubel, *Karl Marx: Selected Writings in Sociology and Social Philosophy* (London: C. A. Watts & Co., Ltd., 1956); Ralf Dahrendorf, *Class and Class Conflict in Industrial Society* (Stanford, Calif.: Stanford University Press, 1959); C. Wright Mills, *The Marxists* (New York: Dell Publishing Co., 1962); Joseph Schumpeter, *Capitalism, Socialism, and Democracy* (New York: Harper & Row, Publishers, 1962); and Irving M. Zeitlin, *Marxism: A Re-Interpretation* (Princeton, N. J.: D. Van Nostrand Company, Inc., 1967).

This theoretical perspective was for Marx a key to understanding the dynamics of all societies, but his overall view of human history was shaped by the idea of dialectic social change. *He applied Hegel's philosophical dialectic of thesis, antithesis, and synthesis to European history as an analytical tool with which to explain societal change.* In a broad sense, feudalism was taken as the original thesis, capitalism was seen as its antithesis, and socialism became the emerging synthesis of these two previous societal forms. Capitalism was necessary to destroy feudalism, but should sooner or later give way to socialism.

Because the various subunits in a society are in continual conflict for control over the means of economic production, all societies contain within themselves potential "seeds" of change. Whether these "seeds" actually "blossom" into radical social change remains a problematic question in any given society, however. Marx used the dialectic as a heuristic analytical tool, not as an imperative blueprint for all history. Although theoretically all societies should develop from feudalism through capitalism to socialism, empirically this process is contingent on many interrelated factors, including the strength of the existing elites, the degree of organization among the masses, and the effectiveness of the spokesmen and leaders advocating social change. To the extent that the broad sweep of history does follow a dialectic pattern, however, societies will inexorably move toward socialism, or the "classless society."

To merge his sociological perspective with his philosophy of history, Marx formulated his well-known thesis of conflicting social classes. By defining social classes in terms of their relationship to the major means of production, and assuming that less powerful classes will inevitably be exploited by the dominant class that controls the means of economic production and hence rules the society, Marx neatly joined his sociological and historical interpretations into a single theory. In brief, he argued that *all societies past the simple folk type are composed of two or more social classes, which are identified on the basis of their relationship to the means of production and which are locked in continual power conflicts.*

For analytical purposes, industrial societies (at least in Europe) can be described in terms of two major social classes: the bourgeoisie who own the factories, and the proletariat who are forced to sell their labor to the industrialists. (Marx recognized the existence of other classes, such as peasants, small merchants, and intellectuals, but felt that they were not theoretically important because they were either rapidly disappearing or being incorporated into the proletariat.) The dominant bourgeoisie, Marx insisted, are not necessarily evil persons, but they are forced by the intrinsic laws of capitalism to exploit their workers, regardless of whether or not they want to. If they do not exploit, they soon go out of business.

Hence the inherent economic injustice of industrial capitalism. To support his criticisms of capitalism, Marx drew on current nineteenth-century economic theory, most of which has since been rejected by economists. Nevertheless, there is still abundant historical evidence that early industrialists did in fact severely exploit their workers, whatever the underlying reasons.

The proletariat in industrial society is a social class with boundaries determined by its subordinate relation to the means of economic production, but the members of the proletariat often remain largely unaware of their common interests. Before this population can take collective action, its members must develop class consciousness, or become aware of their common social fate, and must become strongly organized. The bourgeoisie make their fatal mistake, Marx contended, when they drive the small middle class, especially intellectuals, into the industrial proletariat. These intellectuals provide the leadership the industrial workers had lacked, promote proletarian class consciousness and class organization, and set the stage for revolutionary social change.

Theoretically, societal change might be gradual and continual, but in practice this rarely occurs, according to Marx. Rather, the dialectical process of social change usually occurs through the vehicle of class conflict. Drawing on his observations of feudalism, Marx concluded that powerful elite classes will never voluntarily surrender or share power, but instead will use whatever means are available to retain power as long as possible. The most important tool at the disposal of the bourgeoisie is the state and its military forces, which they control. Hence, if the proletariat is ever to gain power and give birth to socialism, it must organize and forcibly take control of the means of production from the bourgeoisie. Socialism can be created only through revolution. "The proletarians have nothing to lose but their chains. They have a world to win."[5]

As a result of this proletarian revolution the bourgeois class will be destroyed, but the "classless society" will not yet exist. Still remaining is the staggering task of completely reordering society by putting all means of production under public ownership and control, as well as teaching the people to assume the social responsibilities now being thrust upon them. To achieve these goals, it is necessary to create a temporary "dictatorship of the proletariat," during which time the revolutionary leaders act as agents of the people to prepare them and society for the future. Marx firmly believed, though, that eventually complete communism could be achieved, the "classless society" would become a reality, and the full possibilities of human life would finally be realized by all

[5] Karl Marx and Friedrich Engels, *The Communist Manifesto* (New York: International Publishers Co., Inc., 1948), p. 44.

persons. Because society would then be morally organized and all individuals would be socially responsible, the state as an enforcer of external social control would no longer be necessary, and would largely wither away. Under communism, control over the means of economic production would be shared by everyone, hence by definition there would be no more social classes, hence no more exploitation and human misery, hence no more class conflict, and hence no more dialectic social change. A morally perfect society will then have been attained on earth, in which all people participate and benefit on an equal basis. True social equality will prevail, while individual and collective social responsibility, not power and exploitation, will form the foundation of social life. No wonder that communism has such great appeal to deprived peoples around the world today!

As a theory of social organization, Marx' ideas have been severely criticized on many grounds. For instance, the following theoretical weaknesses are frequently cited by sociologists: First, he saw most social change as originating in internal strains, and largely ignored external forces and stresses such as international trade, war, or cultural diffusion. Second, he drew too heavily from the history of feudalism in assuming that class conflict is inevitable and that all social change must be revolutionary in nature. Third, he failed to realize that public ownership of industry requires larger and more complex governmental organization than does private ownership, which invariably leads to differences in power, privilege, and prestige, and hence makes a "classless society" impossible. Fourth, he did not offer an adequate theory of social integration, or the unification and persistence of social order, beyond the use of force and exploitation.

More devastating to Marxian theory than any amount of academic criticism, however, have been the economic and political developments of the twentieth century in the United States and Western Europe. Neither Marx nor anyone else in the nineteenth century could have begun to imagine the fantastic growth in productivity and wealth that would eventually result from full-scale industrialization. Manufacturing has become more efficient, profits more dependable, markets broader, personal incomes higher, and goods and services more readily available than could possibly have been foreseen a hundred years ago. As a consequence, owners and managers of industry have been willing (either voluntarily or under relatively mild pressure) to pass more and more of the profits of industrialization on to their workers. They could do this without feeling threatened or deprived because they themselves were also profiting so greatly from continued economic growth. And as Henry Ford argued, the more you pay your workers, the more they can buy from you, and the greater your profits. At the same time, industrial workers have come to value the existing economic order because of the benefits it gives them. They still seek gradual improvements in wages and working conditions, but they have no desire to destroy the entire economy. They have too much to lose and not much to gain through class revolution.

Along with these purely economic developments have come a host of related social and political changes that have further negated Marx' predictions: (a) the creation, public acceptance, and successful accomplishments of labor unions that are economically rather than politically oriented, and which therefore attempt to gain benefits for workers by operating within the established economic order rather than by destroying it; (b) extension of the franchise to all citizens rather than just property owners, which gives workers an advantage because of their larger numbers; (c) adoption of graduated income and inheritance taxes (as proposed by Marx) to curb the upper extremes of the income distribution; (d) intervention of government into private business as a regulator, coordinator, and spokesman for the public interest, but not necessarily as an outright owner or controller; and (e) development of public welfare programs designed to aid those individuals who are socially disadvantaged in one way or another.

The cumulative results of these trends have been so radical that the fundamental economic question for fully industrialized societies in the twentieth century is ceasing to be: "How should wealth and other benefits of industrialization be redistributed in society?" Instead, we are now beginning to ask: "What needs to be done to improve our society and how should we go about doing it?" We begin to envision programs of public betterment that benefit everyone without penalizing anyone, based on the phenomenon of continual economic growth. It is evident today that Marx' ideas appeal as a political goal primarily to classes and societies that have not yet attained the fruits of full industrialization or that are encountering grave difficulties in even initiating the process. For these peoples, the doctrine that economic and political power must be taken from traditional elites and used by new leaders for the benefit of everyone has immediate relevance and appeal.

The most noticeable empirical consequence of industrialization in all societies—capitalistic and communistic—is the growth of a large "middle class." Regardless of whether these people form a bounded class or are just an arbitrarily delineated stratum, they tend to share common social characteristics and to become increasingly numerous. Occupationally, they range from semiskilled machine operators to skilled craftsmen to clerical and sales workers to highly trained technicians and semiprofessionals. They are not, however, either "dominant bourgeois" owners and managers or "exploited proletarian" workers. They are relatively well educated, in that the majority of them have completed secondary schooling and many have additional technical or academic training. Annual incomes vary by several thousand dollars among the members of this "middle class," but they are all able to enjoy at least some material comforts beyond basic survival necessities. In other words, the bulk of the population in an industrialized society tends to fall near the middle of most stratification hierarchies, rather than at the bottom as in feudal societies. Several further social developments may in turn result from the growth of a large "middle class," including political stability, gradual social change, support for political democracy, increased secularism and sophistication in social values and norms, and growing urbanization and urban ways of living.

Urbanization

Although cities of at least moderate size have existed since antiquity, widespread urbanization is less than one hundred years old and has not yet reached three-fourths of the world's population. The explanation of this seeming paradox is that the existence of a few cities within a society does not render it urbanized. To mention one example, Rome under the Caesars is estimated to have achieved a population of over one-half million, while in the fifteenth century Florence and Venice both reached at least 100,000 population, but Italy never has been and is not now an extremely urbanized society.[6]

As a major evolutionary trend, *urbanization is the process in which communities within a society grow in size and power until they contain a large portion of the total population and exercise functional and cultural dominance over the entire society.* Even though we often use the number and size of cities in a society as an indicator of urbanization, this developmental process is actually societywide in scope. As urbanization progresses, the social life of an entire society is increasingly shaped by its urban communities.

Three aspects of this definition of urbanization require additional exploration. First, what is an "urban community"? The most commonly

[6] A concise review of the historical development of urbanization is given by Kingsley Davis, "The Origin and Growth of Urbanization in the World," *The American Journal of Sociology,* vol. 60 (March 1955), pp. 429–437. For data on world urbanization, see Jack P. Gibbs and Kingsley Davis, "Conventional vs. Metropolitan Data in the International Study of Urbanization," *American Sociological Review,* vol. 23 (October 1958), pp. 504–514.

used criteria are a large and dense population. But when is a population "large" and when is it "dense"? The United States Census Bureau defines as "urban" any community with at least 2,500 people, while some international studies have employed criteria of 50,000 or even 100,000 population. Any minimum population size for "urban communities" is thus entirely arbitrary, and the meaning of various population sizes varies from one society to another. A community of 3,000 persons might be looked upon as only a rural village in the United States but as a moderate-sized town in Africa, even though the American community might exhibit a much more urbanized "way of life" than the African community. The definition of density is only slightly less arbitrary. In most locations today there is still a fairly clear distinction between densely settled communities and sparsely settled countryside; so that "going to town" has an unambiguous meaning even if the boundaries of the community are not explicit. But with the growth of suburbanization and "urban sprawl," it becomes impossible in some areas to distinguish one community from another or from suburban "countryside."

In an attempt to meet these problems, demographers and urban sociologists in the United States have devised a set of concepts for describing various types of urban boundaries. Despite the Census Bureau, the minimum population for an urban community is frequently set at 10,000 or more.[7] The "legal city" or "central city" is that portion of the total community which is legally incorporated, has a single government, and lies within legally defined boundaries. The "functional city" or "urbanized area" is the total urban community, composed of the central city plus its immediately surrounding suburbs and other high-density residential and commercial sections. The "metropolitan area" or "Standard Metropolitan Statistical Area" is the entire territory that depends in its normal daily activities on a large urban community, including outlying suburbs, "satellite cities," and adjacent "truck gardening" farmland.[8] Finally, the "metropolitan region" is the whole area—usually several counties, and sometimes most of one or more states—over which a metropolis exercises considerable influence but not total dominance.

The second problem in the discussion of urbanization concerns the proportion of a society's population that must reside in urban communities before the society can be meaningfully described as urbanized. Again

---

[7] Gibbs and Davis, "Conventional versus Metropolitan Data in the International Study of Urbanization."

[8] The arbitrary Census Bureau definition of a Standard Metropolitan Statistical Area is one or more central cities with a total population of at least 50,000, the county (or counties) containing the city (or cities), and immediately surrounding counties if they meet certain requirements of functional dependence on the central city (or cities).

there is no standard criterion, but rather a scale along which societies are ranked, ranging from under 10 per cent in parts of Africa to over 80 per cent in Great Britain. (The United States is presently set at about 70 per cent urban.) These figures depend on one's definition of the minimum size of an urban community, and their significance varies from one society to another. At present a society might be considered relatively urbanized if at least 40 per cent of its population lived in urban communities (this would now include only twenty to twenty-five societies), but this criterion will undoubtedly rise as urbanization progresses around the world.

Third, what is meant by "functional and cultural dominance" of urban communities over a society? Sociologists have given considerably less attention to this phase of urbanization than to the more obvious population questions, even though urban dominance is the distinctive organizational feature of an urbanized society. No matter how large cities become, if they remain relatively isolated from the rest of the society—as in the case of ancient Rome—the society as a whole is not urbanized. Any city is always dependent upon the surrounding countryside for food and other raw materials, and will in turn exert some influence over its hinterland. But a nation does not become urbanized until these metropolitan influences are strong enough to affect most aspects of social life throughout the entire society. The situation is no longer one of reciprocal interdependence, but rather one-sided dominance.[9] Urban dominance can occur in numerous different activities, including politics, manufacturing and trade, education, recreation, transportation, communication, values, and "styles of life," although all such activities are usually interwoven to some extent. At the same time, the dominant urban communities become increasingly interdependent upon each other and less dependent on their immediately surrounding regions. The society can no longer be pictured as a series of relatively autonomous areas, each of which centers around its own urban center. Instead, we must now see the society as an ordered and interrelated network of urbanized communities and metropolises, all of which together draw on and dominate the nonurbanized portions of the society.

Given these difficulties in conceptualizing and measuring urbanization, it is not surprising that we have no reliable data on the extent of worldwide urbanization. It has been estimated, for instance, that between 20 and 25 per cent of the world's people now live in cities of at least

[9] A comprehensive analysis and investigation of urban dominance is given by Donald J. Bogue, *The Structure of the Metropolitan Community: A Study of Dominance and Subdominance* (Ann Arbor, Mich.: Horace H. Rockham School of Graduate Studies, The University of Michigan, 1950).

20,000 population, with about half of these persons residing in metropolises of 100,000 or more population.[10] But this tells us nothing about the extent of metropolitan dominance in various societies. Nevertheless, it is readily apparent that world urbanization is presently nowhere near its potential peak. The degree of urbanization around the world has been steadily rising since about 1800, but three-fourths of humanity still lives outside urban communities. If present rates continue, though, it is likely that close to half of the world's people will be urbanized by the year 2000.[11] We can only speculate as to how far this trend may go, although there is no reason why the world rate of urban dwelling could not exceed 90 per cent, since in the United States less than ten per cent of the population is directly engaged in agriculture, and that figure is steadily declining.

Several conditions must exist in a society before extensive urbanization can occur. The most important of these are high agricultural productivity, industrialization, development of transportation and communication facilities, and adoption of public sanitation practices.[12]

The necessity for rising agricultural productivity is obvious. As with industrialization, *people must be freed from agricultural work if they are to live in cities and engage in urban occupations.* This can occur only as farm operations are mechanized and techniques of scientific agriculture are discovered and applied. It has been estimated that in a typical feudal society at least twenty-five agricultural workers are required to support one town dweller, whereas in the United States one farmer can presently raise enough food for twenty-five or more urban residents. When agricultural productivity does increase to this extent, farm workers are not simply freed for urban occupations— they are forced by economic necessity to seek urban employment, since they are superfluous on the farm. The reverse side of this coin is the necessity in urbanized societies for the steady expansion of urban jobs in industrial, commercial, clerical, service, technical, and professional fields.

The growth of urbanization within a society is highly related to the development of industrialization. The reason is again readily apparent. The establishment of industrial and related business concerns provides work for those persons displaced from farms. In addition, the higher standards of living and new ways of life commonly found in industrialized communities attract increasing numbers of rural dwellers to the city, even when they are not forced to move by economic necessity. England

[10] Davis, pp. 429–437.

[11] Davis, pp. 429–437.

[12] Amos H. Hawley, "World Urbanization," in Ronald Freedman, ed. *Population: The Vital Revolution* (New York: Doubleday & Company, Inc., 1964), pp. 70–83.

was the first society to become fully industrialized, and since 1800 it has also continually led the world in rate of urbanization. Numerous studies have found correlations above .80 between the extents of industrialization and urbanization in societies around the world.[13] And of the seventeen most highly urbanized societies at the present time, all but two are also extensively industrialized.[14] Although in most societies the process of industrialization tends to precede urbanization by a slight margin, which suggests a causal link, this is not always the case. In several South American nations, for instance, the rate of urbanization is currently running ahead of industrial development, indicating that the attraction of city life may temporarily become greater than the opportunities for urban employment.[15]

Because of the extreme degree of economic and other functional specialization inherent in urban living, *extensive networks of communication and transportation facilities are also vital requirements for large-scale urbanization.* Individuals and organizations become highly interdependent in all areas of life, and must be able to interact with relative speed and convenience. Means of transportation between the city and its hinterland are of highest necessity, since the urban community must daily import food and other raw resources and export goods and services of all kinds. Transportation and communication between cities also become important as they develop interdependent links. Extensive internal communication and transportation facilities are not needed as long as towns remain fairly small and serve primarily as trading centers for the surrounding countryside. But large urban metropolises containing hundreds of thousands of people and countless specialized activities are absolutely dependent on such devices as automobiles, newspapers, and telephones. Even temporary loss of electric power, for example, can totally paralyze a modern city.

Plumbing may seem far removed from urban social organization, but *lack of adequate public sanitation has been a major hindrance to urbanization throughout history.* Medieval European towns, for example, were periodically swept by plagues, which often killed large portions of their

[13] Leo F. Schnore, "The Statistical Measurement of Urbanization and Economic Development," *Land Economics,* vol. 37 (1961), pp. 229–245. Thomas O. Wilkinson, "Urban Structure and Industrialization," *American Sociological Review,* vol. 25 (June 1960), pp. 356–363.

[14] The fifteen societies supporting the generalization are Great Britain, Israel, Germany, Australia, Denmark, United States, Belgium, Argentina, Canada, New Zealand, France, Netherlands, Japan, Austria, and Sweden. The two exceptions are Cuba and Venezuela. See Wilkinson, pp. 356–363.

[15] James R. Wood and Omer R. Galle, "Urbanization, Industrialization, and Modernization: The South American Experience," paper read at the 1965 annual meeting of the American Sociological Association.

entire populations. It would be virtually impossible for a million people to live together in close proximity without some procedures for ensuring a safe water supply, food preservation, and disposal of garbage and sewage. In addition, as cities become even larger and denser in population, public health measures to control communicable diseases become crucial.

From a geographical viewpoint, the process of urbanization is characterized by two distinct trends in population location: concentration and dispersion. Initially, *urbanization must consist of an inward flow of large numbers of people from scattered rural areas to urban communities.* Individuals and social organizations become highly concentrated within the small geographical area comprising a city, the center of which —"downtown"—is the scene of intense social activity. Because of this concentration, land values tend to be highest near the city center and to decline in a fairly steady ratio as one moves outward toward the periphery of the community. Land values in turn influence, but do not fully determine, the social uses to which various sections of the community will be devoted. The result is that patterns of social order within urban communities often assume identifiable spatial forms, as determined by such factors as distance from the city center, accessibility to transportation lines emanating from the downtown area, and proximity to industrial plants and other specialized activities. Urban sociologists have proposed several theories to explain the spatial patterning of urban communities, none of which is adequate by itself, but all of which when taken together do provide considerable insight into this phenomenon.[16]

Once highly concentrated urban communities have developed, the second geographic shift begins. *Individuals and organizations disperse outward from the "inner city" to the periphery of the urban community.* Dispersion does not negate concentration, since this type of movement remains within the metropolitan area and does not return people to rural locations. It does, however, profoundly affect both urban spatial patterns and urban ways of life. The predominant form of dispersion in the United States is suburbanization, in which families live in suburban communities on the outskirts of large metropolises but commute into the central city for work, shopping, and many other activities. Suburbanization is clearly dependent upon means of transportation in and out of the city, so that although a few "railroad suburbs" began to appear as early as the 1880's, the trend did not become widespread until the advent of the automobile

---

[16] The three major explanations of urban spatial patterning—the concentric-zone, the sector, and the multiple-nuclei theories—are summarized and compared in Chauncy D. Harris and Edward L. Ullman, "The Nature of Cities," in Paul K. Hatt and Albert J. Reiss, Jr., eds., *Cities and Society* (New York: The Free Press, a division of The Macmillan Company, 1957), pp. 237–247.

in the 1920's. Since then, however, the peripheries of most metropolitan areas have experienced two or three times as much population growth as have the central cities.[17] The mushrooming of suburbs in this society is primarily the result of our cultural emphasis on single-family dwellings and home ownership, people's desires to escape the congestion of city life and to find adequate schools for their children, and the economic fact that the only land available at a reasonable cost for large-scale housing developments is on the outskirts of cities.

Urban dispersion can take other forms besides suburbanization, two of which are "industrial scattering" and "urban sprawl." Instead of families moving outward, industrial plants and other businesses may locate in outlying areas, with individuals continuing to reside in or near the central city. This pattern is quite common in many European cities, which developed around feudal castles and trading centers long before industrialization began, so that when factories were built they had to be located on the periphery of the city. In recent years it has also become more common in the United States, as businessmen have discovered the economic benefits of inexpensive land and low taxes outside the legal city. Urban sprawl is the term frequently applied to the continual outward expansion of entire urban communities as they grow in size. Vertical expansion via skyscrapers has nowhere reached its possible limits, but it quickly becomes extremely expensive, and it cannot go on indefinitely. As urbanization proceeds, therefore, a metropolis must constantly expand outward, encompassing more and more territory. Not only families and/or businesses, but also retail stores, schools, churches, recreational facilities, and all other types of organizations relentlessly disperse over the countryside.

As a direct result of these various forms of dispersion, many urbanized areas in the United States presently face severe problems of political fragmentation. Although any metropolitan area is functionally and culturally a single community, in legal terms it may be divided into dozens of autonomous political units, including the legal central city, surrounding suburbs, satellite cities, specialized "authorities" for harbors, parks, water supplies, and transportation, one or more counties, and sometimes even two different states. The community faces countless problems in such areas as mass transportation, public utilities, public recreation facilities, school systems, crime, and housing, all of which can be solved only through unified communitywide programs. Yet concerted action of any kind is virtually impossible when numerous separate political units, each jealous of its own autonomy, must somehow reach mutual agreement

---

[17] Davis, "The Origin and Growth of Urbanization in the World," pp. 429–437.

before anything can be accomplished. The result in many cities is virtual stagnation; little or nothing is done to deal with pressing urban problems, and few attempts are made to plan for future community development.[18]

Finally, looking toward the future, *we can envision the emergence of giant "megalopolises," or "super metropolises," resulting from the expansion and merging of what were originally several separate cities.* The strips of land between these cities slowly become filled with urban or semiurban settlements, until each community merges imperceptibly with its neighbors. Ultimately there would be no particular areas of extremely dense population concentration, but neither would there be any open rural land. This trend is already evident on the American East Coast, extending for over four hundred miles from Boston to Washington, D.C. "One can travel from one end to the other of this super city without leaving territory that is predominantly urban in its land use, its occupations, and the way of life of its people. Within the area about 20 per cent of the nation's people are concentrated on less than 2 per cent of its land."[19] Similar trends can be seen in southern England, northwestern Europe, around Chicago, and in southern California. These are perhaps the prototype urban communities of tomorrow.

Urban life has been a major concern in American sociology since the 1920's, and literally hundreds of studies have been conducted in this area, but most of these have been concerned with urbanism rather than urbanization. There is a subtle difference between these two related phenomena. Urbanization, as we have seen, is the process of city growth, organization, and functioning in society. Urbanism refers to the kind of social life experienced by urban residents, including their values, norms, patterns of daily living, and modes of social interaction. In short, how does urban life differ from rural or small-town life?

Most early studies of urbanism—of which the majority were conducted in Chicago—stressed the relative impersonality of urban life.[20] Lacking the close interpersonal ties and strong traditional norms of rural and small-town living, urban life was seen as impersonal, segmented, isolated, pragmatically oriented, and only loosely controlled. These studies dealt with such topics as the disorganization of slum neighborhoods, social isolation of urban apartment dwellers, the growing prevalence of

[18] For a detailed discussion and analysis of this situation, see Scott Greer, *Governing the Metropolis* (New York: John Wiley & Sons, Inc., 1962).

[19] Leonard Broom and Philip Selznick, *Sociology*, 3rd ed. (New York: Harper & Row, Publishers, 1963), pp. 615–616.

[20] Many of these early studies of urbanism, both in Chicago and elsewhere, are summarized and evaluated in Maurice Stein, *The Eclipse of Community* (Princeton, N.J.: Princeton University Press, 1960).

"deviant behavior" due to the absence of effective social controls, special problems of ethnic neighborhoods, rising rates of mental illness among urbanites, and loss of traditional family functions. We realize today that much of this research reflected a biased concern with a presumed "loss of community" in large cities, but nevertheless it did give us valuable insight into urban social life and culture.

More recent studies have tended to correct many of these earlier biases, by showing that widespread social disorganization, isolation, impersonality, and deviant behavior are not necessarily inherent in urban living. Urban residents can and do form personal friendships and participate in voluntary interest associations, disadvantaged neighborhoods can be organized for collective social action, community programs can provide satisfying activities for both youth and adults, crime and juvenile delinquency can be effectively controlled, and the family is not in danger of disappearing. Numerous "social problems" do of course occur in all these areas in virtually every urban community, and we are still far from implementing adequate solutions to them. But the important point is that we no longer see them as inherent features of urbanism. We now realize that problems such as these are to a considerable extent a result of the rapid social changes that accompany urbanization, as individuals experience the shift from small-town to urban living and as we create radically new patterns of social organization. If we are to deal successfully with urban social problems, we cannot ignore them in hopes that they will eventually disappear, nor can we reestablish small-town life in urban metropolises. What is clearly called for is the creation, through rational planning, of new patterns of social life that are specifically designed for urban communities.[21]

Bureaucratization

Social organizations have been created throughout human history for many diverse reasons: to ensure survival in a harsh environment, to perpetuate traditional ways of life, to honor the gods, to facilitate exploitation of the masses by powerful elites, or to defend against alien peoples. Purposeful ordering of the actions of large numbers of people for the rational attainment of specified goals is certainly not unknown in "premodern" societies—armies have existed since antiquity—but this type of organization is of relatively minor importance in the daily routines of

[21] For a more extensive discussion of the thesis presented in this paragraph, see Harold L. Wilensky and Charles N. Lebeaux, *Industrial Society and Social Welfare* (New York: Russell Sage Foundation, 1958), chap. 5.

social life. One of the most distinctive features of modernized societies, however, is the widespread introduction of rationality into organized activities for more efficient and effective achievement of desired goals. Instead of doing things "the way they've always been done," we are asking, in effect, "Precisely what do we want to accomplish through social action, and what is the most expedient means of reaching this goal?"

To the extent that concerns such as this are acted upon in social life, we witness the process of bureaucratization, which is the third of the major historical trends comprising modernization. As we purposefully set goals for collective activities, establish organizations to attain these goals, and attempt to operate such organizations as efficiently as possible, we are bureaucratizing social life. In more formal terms, *bureaucratization is the process of rationalizing social organization, so as to improve operating efficiency and more effectively attain common goals.*

Several aspects of this definition require elaboration. First, bureaucratization is an ongoing social process, not a particular kind of organization, although we often apply the term "bureaucracy" to organizations that clearly manifest this trend. Second, "rationalization" is used here in a sociological, not a psychological, context. It refers to such activities as purposeful goal-setting, collection and utilization of all relevant information, objective evaluation and decision-making, and social planning. Ideally, there should be universal standards of social rationality that could be applied to all organizations, but we have not reached this level of sophistication, so that in practice we must rely upon judgments of presumed experts as to what is a rational social practice and what is not. Third, the criterion of rationality applies only to the ordered means employed by an organization to achieve its goals, not to the ends themselves. The ends or goals of collective social activities remain valuative in nature, while bureaucratization simply provides an efficient and effective organized means of achieving these goals. Thus it is fully possible to utilize highly rationalized procedures in pursuit of the most irrational ends—as in the "final solution" of the "Jewish problem" in Nazi Germany. Fourth, the process of bureaucratization occurs most frequently within relatively formal associations, such as businesses, governments, universities, hospitals, military units, labor unions, political parties, and special-interest organizations of all kinds, as well as in the social networks uniting such associations. To the extent that any other type of organization—from a family to a community to an entire society—attempts to rationalize its activities for the attainment of specific goals, however, it may also evidence bureaucratic characteristics. That is, there is no theoretical reason why the process of bureaucratization could not occur in any type of social organization.

In popular speech, "bureaucracy" is commonly equated with strict rigidity, "red tape," and general inefficiency, but sociology discards these connotations. All kinds of operational problems can and do arise in bureaucratic organizations, but they are normally due to inadequate or misdirected bureaucratization, not to its excess. In a more sophisticated but still imprecise sense, "bureaucratization" is sometimes used to mean simply the growth of numerous large and complex organizations throughout a society. In rough terms, that is the meaning sociologists give to the broader process of social evolution, of which bureaucratization is only one aspect. To repeat, bureaucratization technically refers to the rationalization of social organization for effective goal attainment. "Bureaucratic administration is, other things being equal, always, from a formal, technical point of view, the most rational type. For the needs of mass administration today, it is indispensable."[22]

Historically, the trend toward increasing bureaucratization has been an inevitable (though not fully predetermined) outgrowth of industrialization and urbanization. Both of these evolutionary developments in social organization bring large numbers of people together and demand that they cooperate to achieve common goals. Industrialization creates huge industrial and commercial enterprises that depend on broad-scale social coordination and that continually seek to improve their operations. Urbanization requires that thousands or even millions of individuals living together in a single community join forces to deal collectively and rationally with problems ranging from fire protection to education. Furthermore, as businesses and urban metropolises become linked together in interdependent networks, impetus is provided for bureaucratization of the national government and other societywide organizations to enable them to cope with the increasing complexity of organized social life. At the same time, though, a certain degree of bureaucratization is a mandatory requirement for the full development of industrialization and urbanization. The organization of businesses and communities must be rationalized if they are to handle adequately the countless demands impinging upon them. Once again we see the interweaving of all these developmental trends comprising modernization.

From a more analytical perspective, four organizational factors are particularly critical in producing bureaucratization: growth in the size of social organizations, formalization of social ordering, secularization of values, norms, and goals, and developments in social technology.[23] Each

---

[22] Max Weber, *The Theory of Social and Economic Organization*, trans. A. M. Henderson and Talcott Parsons (New York: The Free Press, a division of The Macmillan Company, 1947), p. 337.

[23] These factors are identified in Peter M. Blau, *Bureaucracy in Modern Society* (New York: Random House, Inc., 1956).

of these is a necessary component of the overall process of rationalizing social organization.

As long as organizations are relatively small, there is little need for bureaucratization. Families, friendship groups, artisan workshops, village communities, and similar small and intimate organizations can usually function fairly well without purposefully attempting to rationalize their activities. Whatever difficulties arise can be handled through face-to-face discussion. Larger organizations, in contrast, often find the establishment of rationalized operating and administrative procedures to be mandatory if collective goals are to be realized. A factory employing 10,000 persons to manufacture automobiles cannot even begin to operate, for instance, without first devising standardized means of ordering work activities and resolving countless operational problems. A certain amount of standardization and routinization is thus a functional imperative in all large organizations that seek to attain goals as effectively as possible.

It is difficult, if not impossible, to rationalize the activities of an organization unless its social ordering is relatively formalized. The structure of an organization is formalized to the extent that it meets such criteria as these: existence of clearly defined social positions and subunits; extensive task specialization, or division of labor, among positions and subunits within the organization; channeling of social interactions and communications among position incumbents and subunits into certain prescribed patterns; institutionalization of power within the organization as authority, which is located in certain specific positions and subunits; and overall coordination and regulation of organizational activities. Extensive formalization of patterns of social order does not obviate more personal or informal social relations among organizational members. Indeed, the reverse is often true; the more formal the social structure, the more extensive and viable the web of informal friendships is likely to be, as a "counterweight" to excessive formalism. But only as relationships within an organization become relatively formalized is there a basis or need for rationalization of organizational activities.

No matter how large and formal an organization, *rationality will not be extensively applied to collective activities until the prevailing values and norms, as well as goal-setting procedures, become secularized.* As long as patterns of social life are viewed as divinely inspired and impervious to human desires, people will make no attempt to change or improve existing activities or organizations. Only as goals for collective action become both purposefully formulated and realistically attainable will people seek to bureaucratize their social organizations. In addition, normative criteria of functional effectiveness and efficiency must predominate over traditional customs and folkways before individuals will willingly adhere to rationally derived procedural rules.

The fourth requirement for bureaucratization, social technology, can be illustrated by Max Weber's list of the major characteristics of bureaucratic organizations. Weber asked: "What would an organization be like if its operations were fully rationalized?" He then described an ideal type of a completely bureaucratized organization. That is, he attempted to specify all of the ways in which an organization might be rationalized, and then extended these features to their logical extremes. No real organization will necessarily ever correspond to an ideal type in all its details, but such a type does give us a picture of several of the major characteristics of totally rationalized organization. Weber's bureaucratic ideal type contained the following features, all of which can be viewed as developments in the technology of social organization:[24]

(1) Each role and position has clearly defined duties and responsibilities.

(2) All activities are guided by formally prescribed rules and regulations.

(3) All decisions are made on the basis of technical knowledge, not personal considerations.

(4) All activities are recorded on written documents, which are preserved in permanent files.

(5) Relationships among role incumbents are impersonal and limited to role obligations.

(6) Positions are filled on a contractual basis, with selection determined by fixed criteria of merit (training and/or experience).

(7) Role incumbents are judged solely on the basis of proficiency, and discipline is impartially enforced.

(8) An individual's work is his sole or primary occupation, and constitutes a career with opportunities for advancement.

(9) Individuals are given job security, in the form of fixed salaries, tenure, and retirement pensions.

If an organization is to be bureaucratized, Weber argued, it must establish operational procedures that at least approximate all of these characteristics.

Needless to say, the list above could be considerably extended, and many contemporary organizations have adopted numerous other practices aimed at furthering the rationalization of their activities. The more common of these include: cost accounting, inventory control, personnel training programs, information feedback, work simplification, flow process analysis, work inspection, management-worker conferences, and planning based on future projections.[25] These examples underscore the basic point that a bureaucracy is not a certain type of organization that meets fixed criteria. Bureaucratization is rather the process in which an organi-

---

[24] Weber, *The Theory of Social and Economic Organization*, pp. 329–341. *From Max Weber: Essays in Sociology*, trans. H. H. Gerth and C. Wright Mills (New York: Oxford University Press, 1946), chap. 8.

[25] For a more extensive discussion of contemporary techniques of social rationalization, see Robert A. Dahl and Charles E. Lindbloom, *Politics, Economics, and Welfare* (New York: Harper & Row, Publishers, 1953).

zation continually seeks to rationalize its functioning so as to achieve more effectively whatever goals it seeks.

In this discussion of bureaucratization we have not yet considered social power, especially as it is used to control activities and maintain order within organizations. Weber believed that power relations within a rationalized organization must be based primarily on authority derived from grants of legitimacy. He furthermore maintained that such authority must be rational-legal in nature. But what precisely is "rational-legal" authority? Several writers have pointed out that *Weber's conception of rational-legal authority actually contains two separate dimensions: expert (rational) and official (legal) authority.*[26] *Expert authority rests on technical knowledge and experience;* an actor is granted the legitimate right to exercise power within a defined set of activities because of his recognized competence and expertise. *Official authority inheres in organizational positions;* whoever occupies such a position in the structure of the organization is granted the legal or official right to exert power, by virtue of his office. Weber assumed that in a fully bureaucratized organization these two dimensions of expert and official authority would be identical, since according to his scheme officeholders were selected strictly according to technical merit. Both logically and empirically, however, these dimensions do not necessarily coincide. There can be either "knowledge without office," as in the case of the staff specialist who advises but never commands, or "office without knowledge," as in the case of a figurehead board chairman who wields no real power.[27] Strains and conflict often inhere in such situations, which thus become the foci of numerous organizational problems.

From this disparity between expert and official authority are derived a wide variety of different types of organizational structures, ranging from highly centralized to relatively decentralized organizations. Weber assumed that a fully bureaucratized organization must be completely centralized, but contemporary writers have suggested that operational rationality can be retained or even increased through decentralization.[28]

[26] This distinction was first made by Talcott Parsons in his introduction to Weber's *The Theory of Social and Economic Organization*, pp. 58–60, fn. 4. It has been extensively discussed by Alvin W. Gouldner, "Organizational Analysis," in Robert K. Merton, Leonard Broom, and Leonard S. Cottrell, Jr., eds., *Sociology Today* (New York: Basic Books, Inc., 1959), pp. 402–403 and 413–417; and by Victor Thompson, *Modern Organization* (New York: Alfred A. Knopf, 1961), chaps. 1–5. For two empirical studies of this phenomenon, see Stanley H. Udy, Jr., " 'Bureaucracy' and 'Rationality' in Weber's Organization Theory: An Empirical Study," *American Sociological Review*, vol. 24 (December 1959), pp. 791–795; and William M. Evan and Morris Zelditch, Jr., "A Laboratory Experiment on Bureaucratic Authority," *American Sociological Review*, vol. 26 (December 1961), pp. 883–893.

[27] These two phrases are taken from Evan and Zelditch, *ibid*.

[28] For a sampling of this literature, see the following: Rensis Likert, *New Patterns of Management* (New York: McGraw-Hill, Inc., 1961), chap. 8; Eugene

In a highly centralized organization, emphasis is placed on official authority that is exercised downward through a hierarchical pyramid of successively broader structural levels. Legitimacy is granted to the organization as a whole, not to any individual incumbents or subunits, and hence ultimately focuses on the single position at the apex of the structural hierarchy. (This position may be occupied by either one individual or a small group, but it must always speak with a single voice.) Authority is then delegated downward from the top position through a graded hierarchy of subordinate units and offices. Each position in the hierarchy derives its authority from the one immediately above it and is always responsible to this superior office. As a consequence, any given position normally exercises less power than those above it in the hierarchy, but more power than those below it. Furthermore, as we proceed down the hierarchy of authority, each successive structural layer usually contains more positions than does the level above it, giving the entire organization a pyramidal appearance. Overall, the subunits of the organization tend to be highly institutionalized, with relatively little functional autonomy.

Two major arguments are frequently given for the necessity of centralized official authority if organizational rationality is to be achieved. The first argument begins with the observation that many goal-oriented organizations are held together mainly through functional rather than normative integration. It is imperative, therefore, that a complex web of complementary exchange relationships be maintained among the specialized and mutually interdependent organizational units. This in turn requires centralized control to ensure overall communication, coordination, regulation, and planning. Without centralized control, the organization would likely drift or split apart, and common goals could not be attained. The second argument is based on the assumption that in most organizations operational rationality must be imposed upon the majority of the members and subparts. This argument assumes that if they are left on their own, individuals will tend to give more emphasis to interpersonal relationships than to impersonal rules, while subunits will tend to place their own requirements and goals above those of the larger organization. Discipline need not be harsh or autocratic—this is the main argument of "human relations management"—but it must originate from those positions at the top of the authority hierarchy which presumably represent the best interests of the entire organization.

Highly centralized authority tends to produce many serious opera-

Litwak, "Models of Bureaucracy Which Permit Conflict," *The American Journal of Sociology*, vol. 67 (September 1961), pp. 177–184; and Clagett Smith and Arnold Tannenbaum, "Organizational Control Structure," *Human Relations*, vol. 16 (1963), pp. 299–316.

tional problems, however. Three of these are stifling of initiative and creativity, organizational rigidity, and ineffective supervision. Individuals and groups at lower levels of the hierarchy are expected to perform their roles in accordance with the established rules and dictates of their superiors. Innovation is actively discouraged, unless it is first approved by higher authority. This procedure can work fairly well, despite the frustration and apathy it produces among workers, as long as tasks are uniform, routine, or repetitive. But it eliminates many opportunities for functional improvements, and it becomes totally inadequate when members are required to deal with tasks that are diverse, unique, or highly technical. A direct outgrowth of the stifling of initiative and creativity is organizational rigidity. The organization becomes incapable of continually and flexibly adjusting to changing external or internal situations. Over time, it will experience constantly declining functional efficiency and effectiveness, and it may eventually be overcome by conditions with which it cannot cope. Finally, adequate supervision becomes extremely difficult in a centralized organization as role requirements demand increased technical knowledge and skill. A supervisor cannot acquire or retain proficiency in all the intricate, technical aspects of his subordinates' work. He thus loses the ability to evaluate them, solve their problems, or promote coordination among them. This situation forces him to default on his supervisory responsibilities.

In a relatively decentralized organization, emphasis is placed on expert authority that is exercised in all directions throughout a horizontal structure according to functional requirements. Authority is vested in role incumbents according to their technical knowledge, experience, and ability, rather than in formally defined offices. A comptroller is given full responsibility for handling all organizational finances, for instance, but only after he has mastered extensive technical knowledge and skills, acquired many years of practical experience, and demonstrated his capabilities in less demanding positions. Each member or unit of the organization must earn authority; it is never simply delegated to the incumbent of a position. Structurally, the organization is divided into a number of semiautonomous units, each of which performs certain special activities for the entire organization. These functional subunits are arranged horizontally, not vertically, so that all units exercise relatively equal power, while each unit's authority is limited to its particular sphere of competence. Consequently, subunits of the organization are partially segmented, with considerable functional autonomy.

The two main arguments for centralization—the necessity for functional coordination and for discipline—are met in a decentralized organization through different procedures. The ensuring of overall communication, coordination, regulation, and planning is a critical problem in an organization with many semiautonomous specialized units. It is accomplished by establishing a specialized, nonelite administrative staff. Instead of occupying the upper levels of a hierarchical pyramid, the administration is simply another equally authoritative functional unit in the organization. Administrators are technical experts in their particular field of coordination and planning, but they exercise no authority outside their sphere of competence. They are relieved, that is, of the tasks of imposing discipline and evaluating technical performance throughout the organization, and hence can devote full attention to purely administrative responsibilities. Moreover, they do not make policy decisions for the entire organization.

Discipline over individuals and subunits within a decentralized organization, meanwhile, can be effectively maintained through professionalization. Within each functional area a code of professional ethics and norms is formulated, stressing the individual's responsibilities to his "clients," his colleagues, and the total organization—all of which take precedence over his own self-interests.[29] These standards are internalized by each member as part of his technical or professional training and his socialization in the organization, so that social control is for the most part entirely internal. If external enforcement should become necessary, appropriate sanctions are applied by one's colleagues, not by administrators.

A decentralized organization also faces distinctive functional problems. On the one hand, because administrators have close access to informational flows, resource procurement, and other organization-wide activities, there is always a possibility that their power will slowly expand beyond their prescribed area of authority. However, it is possible to build into an organization various safeguards against this tendency, as seen in the role of a hospital administrator who is prohibited from making any decisions pertaining to medical care of patients. On the other hand, there is always the additional possibility that professionals will begin to place the interests of their particular discipline above those of the total organization. Such conflicts of interest can also be controlled through appropriate procedural techniques, however, and can even be transformed into creative inducements for higher standards of performance.

As presented here, both centralized and decentralized organizations are solely analytical types. Almost all real organizations possess various

---

[29] Data supporting the proposition that centralization of authority is not necessary in an organization with a high level of professionalization among its members is given by Peter M. Blau, Wolf V. Hydebrand, and Robert E. Stauffer, "The Structure of Small Bureaucracies," *American Sociological Review*, vol. 31 (April 1966), pp. 179–191.

combinations of features from both types. Nevertheless, for analytical purposes we can describe most actual organizations as relatively centralized or decentralized, in varying degrees and dimensions. Historically, centralized authority has tended to predominate in most associations, probably because official authority is somewhat easier to establish and maintain than is expert authority, at least in the short run. Decentralization is constantly gaining more adherents, however, as its long-range benefits become apparent. Research laboratories and hospitals are examples of organizations that are currently moving toward decentralized structures based on expert authority and professionalization. And even such traditionally centralized organizations as business corporations and military units are now experimenting with different forms of decentralized authority. (At the same time, though, national political, economic, and other networks are simultaneously shifting toward increased centralization, as discussed in the next section.) Hopefully, social scientists and applied practitioners will eventually discover the unique combination of centralization and decentralization—that is, some blend of hierarchical and functional structures, official and expert authority, discipline and professionalization, and institutionalization versus segmentation—best suited for producing rationalization and effective goal attainment in each type of social organization.

Centralization

The last of our major evolutionary trends—centralization of power, and more generally, of all organized activities—has become prevalent only recently, and has not yet been extensively studied by social scientists. Indeed, it may prove to be more of a future development than a past or present trend, although its effects have been felt in the United States since at least the 1930's.

The process of centralization within a social organization involves the convergence of social power, and hence control over all collective activities, in a relatively small number of dominant elite positions. Centralization can and does occur in all kinds of organizations, although it is perhaps most evident in associations, networks, communities, and especially societies. We have spoken of centralized authority as a major characteristic of one analytical type of organization, but in a broader sense centralization is an ongoing dynamic social process. Thus we can identify trends toward increased centralization within any organization, regardless of its present social structure or distribution of power. Highly centralized power is by definition authoritarian, in that it is exercised downward through an organizational hierarchy from the ruling elites. These elites might be chosen by the rest of the members, so that centralization is not incompatible with representative democracy, but it does prohibit classical democracy in the sense of popular decision-making on all substantive issues. Authoritarian power must not be confused with autocracy, however. Centralized authority becomes autocratic only if it is used by elites solely for their own benefit, without any concern for the welfare of the whole organization—which need not occur. There is no inherent relationship between centralization and autocracy.

Centralized power within an organization frequently becomes focused within an institutionalized "governmental" unit whose primary functions are making decisions for the organization and controlling organizational activities. Such a unit might be referred to as "the executive committee," "top management," the "power elite," "central command," "the inner circle," "national headquarters," or "the federal government," but in any case it represents a fairly unified subunit that exerts influence and control throughout the entire organization. This institutionalization of power within "governmental" units does not always occur in simpler types of societies. Under feudalism, for instance, power is highly diffused among all land-owning nobles, so that the formal government is quite weak. During the early stages of industrialization, dominant power usually shifts to the owners and managers of industries, who frequently "employ" the societal government to protect their private interests.[30] With growing centralization of power, however, official authority transcends force and dominance based on economic or other similar activities. Hence, *the specialized wielder of official authority in an organization— its "government"—normally comes to predominate over all other subparts.*

Notice, however, that the convergence of official authority in a governmental unit is only the most obvious aspect of the much broader process of centralization. In addition, control over economic resources often becomes centralized in a relatively few functionally dominant units within the organization, regardless of whether this be a community, a voluntary association, a large corporation, a broad network, or a total society. The wielding of physical coercion is likely to become the special prerogative of highly centralized police and military units—either public or private. And given modern technology, the flow of information and cultural ideas throughout the organization also tends to be directed largely by centralized communication media. In short, *the process of*

---

[30] This generalization is less applicable when industry is entirely state-owned, although even here the industrial managers may wield at least as much power as the politicians who "supervise" them.

centralization may extend into all the activities occurring within an organization.

What factors produce this trend in a society? *The impetus toward centralization, if not the exact degree or forms it takes, is largely provided by the three trends of industrialization, urbanization, and bureaucratization.* First, the high levels of economic productivity generated by industrialization in turn create enormous amounts of new resources in a society, and enable people to attain goals that were once unimaginable. As a consequence, the exercise of power becomes an increasingly crucial social phenomenon. Furthermore, industrialization tends to concentrate economic power to an extent undreamed of in the days of skilled artisans in a handicraft economy. In a modern factory, incumbents of a relatively few positions effectively control the work of hundreds or thousands of people, as well as the economic resources of the entire organization. Hence industrialization both increases the total amount of power being exerted in a society and tends to centralize it in the hands of a few functionally dominant elites.

Second, urbanization brings together in a small area large numbers of people, and forces them to seek new, collective solutions to common problems. Activities that were once carried out primarily in the family or local neighborhood—such as fire and police protection, public transportation, food distribution, social welfare, education, public health measures, or determination of land usage—must now, for purely functional reasons, be turned over to specialized but also centralized agencies. Hence urbanization carries centralization beyond the economic sphere into numerous other areas of social life.

Third, the process of bureaucratization usually results in the growth of large, hierarchically structured, and predominantly centralized organizations. As we have already seen, the trend within organizations towards increased efficiency and effectiveness of goal attainment does not necessarily require the creation of centralized power hierarchies, but in practice this has usually been the outcome of bureaucratization. Until quite recently, we have tended to assume that rationalization of organizational functioning demanded power concentration, so that most highly bureaucratized organizations in all realms of social life have been structured in hierarchical patterns and operated in a centralized manner.

It is commonplace to think of organizational centralization and decentralization as opposing tendencies. But are they? If it is true that in the United States the national polity and other societywide networks are becoming increasingly centralized, while at the same time many smaller associations are experimenting with decentralization, these would appear to be divergent trends. From a broader perspective, though, the real negation of power centralization is anarchy, not decentralization. As random social actions become ordered into stable social organizations, it is perhaps inevitable that social power not only will be created but will be focused in dominant units or roles. The process of social organization, that is, creates centralized social power in the place of powerless anarchy. To take one simple example, eleven isolated individuals standing on a football field would be no match for any organized team. But as interactions among these individuals become patterned and recurrent in the form of a unified football team, the group as a whole gains the ability to do what no player could accomplish by himself—exert organizational power to score touchdowns. There can be only one signal-caller on the team if chaos is to be avoided, so that the power of the entire team is centralized in the authoritative position of quarterback. He then delegates responsibilities for specific plays to the other members as he (or his coach) sees fit.

Drawing an analogy from the successive stages of concentration and dispersion within urbanization, we might hypothesize that decentralization of an organization can occur only after some minimal centralization and unified power have been created through the process of social organization. Decentralization does not destroy the overall organization or its social power, but only distributes it among many subunits, each of which thus becomes capable of partially autonomous action. The presumed benefits of decentralization, despite its attendant problems of coordination, are stimulation of creativity, greater flexibility, functional efficiency, new opportunities for growth, and more effective goal attainment. Moreover, as various subunits acquire some latitude to develop their own special capabilities, the total power of the organization can be tremendously increased. To continue our football example, decentralization can occur only after the team has been organized to the point where it can be split into offensive and defensive units, each of which is given partial autonomy to perform certain specialized tasks and each of which now has a signal-caller.

One resolution of the apparent paradox of centralization on a national scale versus decentralization in smaller organizations, therefore, is that these two organizational levels are currently at different developmental stages. The process of creating associations with limited size, complexity, and goals has been carried on successfully in this society for numerous generations, so that many of these organizations are now well enough established and unified to be capable of experimenting with decentralization without threatening their own existence. In contrast, only recently have we begun to create social networks—most notably in the political and economic spheres, but to some extent in several other areas also—that are truly societywide in size and scope, that are fantastically complex, and whose goals are undefined except for vague conceptions of "public welfare." At this level of national organization, functional activities and social power may not yet be fully enough developed and centrally unified to allow extensive decentralization, especially when local organizations are frequently reluctant to assume responsibility for initiating new programs of collective social action. Societywide centralization of power might thus represent not so much a loss of power by local organizational units as the creation of new social activities and power on the societal level where none previously existed.

As an empirical fact, the United States is currently undergoing a noticeable trend toward increased centralization. C. Wright Mills has amassed considerable evidence that demonstrates growing power centralization within the executive branch of the federal government, gigantic business complexes, and the military, which he claims are the dominant spheres of organized power in today's society.[31] This trend can also be seen in labor unions, professional associations, mass communication and transportation, and several other areas. Mills then goes on to assert that the federal government, big business, and the military are not only becoming internally centralized, but concurrently are growing together in both functional and normative terms. As a consequence, he sees the emergence of a unified national "power elite," which increasingly dominates all major societal activities. His empirical evidence for this second thesis is not fully convincing to many critics, although even the most casual observation of American society suggests that the federal government, big industry, and the military are indeed becoming increasingly interwoven and functionally interdependent.[32] At the same time, we must also avoid the fallacy—which Mills fell into—of assuming that as the power of the polity or the economy expands, other organizations such as local communities must necessarily lose power. The creation of power through time is a positive-sum, not a zero-sum, phenomenon. For instance, if the federal government begins providing funds to cities for urban renewal, this also stimulates considerable community growth. Although the community may have only partial control over federally financed housing developments, it still gains many forms of new power that previously did not even exist.

[31] C. Wright Mills, *The Power Elite* (New York: Oxford University Press, 1956).
[32] See Fred J. Cook, *The Warfare State* (New York: The Macmillan Company, 1962); and Marc Pilisuk and Thomas Hayden, "Is There a Military Industrial Complex Which Prevents Peace?" *Journal of Social Issues*, vol. 21 (July 1956), pp. 67–117.

As a final aspect of this discussion of centralization, we note Robert Michels' insightful theory concerning an inherent tendency in all organizations toward oligarchical rule.[33] He argued that *oligarchy—the monopolizing of power by a small, self-perpetuating, elite group—is sooner or later inevitable in every organization.* He gave many reasons for this, including the following:

(1) Large size and an elaborate division of labor necessitate centralized coordination and regulation for effective action.

(2) Collective decisions on complex organizational matters can be made speedily and efficiently only by a few elites.

(3) Incumbents of leadership positions become indispensable as they develop special skills and experience in running the organization, so that other members cannot afford to deprive them of power.

(4) Over time, leaders build up a legitimate right to high office, as well as an extensive web of personal influence, which further increase their power.

(5) Leaders acquire dominant control over organizational finances, communications, disciplinary agencies, and so on, all of which they can use to their own advantage.

(6) Leaders are normally more unified than other members, and hence they can effectively thwart or absorb (coopt) potential challengers.

(7) Most rank-and-file members tend to be indifferent and apathetic toward the organization and its problems, and are only too happy to leave the problems of leadership to those who are willing to assume them.

Michels sought to test his thesis by studying European socialist political parties at the beginning of the twentieth century. He reasoned that if oligarchy existed in these associations, which were publicly dedicated to democracy, both internally and throughout society, then it must indeed be inevitable in social organization. He concluded that his research fully substantiated his predictions, from which he reasoned that "Who says organization, says oligarchy."[34]

This "iron law of oligarchy" may not be as inescapable as Michels presumed, but it is a serious problem with which all organizations must contend if they wish to preserve any aspects of democracy. It is perhaps most critical in highly centralized organizations, but it also plagues those with decentralized authority structures if the power of administrators is not strictly limited. We are therefore left with the fundamental question

---

[33] Robert Michels, *Political Parties,* trans. Eden and Cedar Paul (New York: The Free Press, a division of The Macmillan Company, 1966).

[34] Michels, p. 365.

of how to provide for necessary centralized leadership and overall functional effectiveness in social organizations, while maintaining democratic decision-making and ultimate control. As yet we have no adequate solution to this problem.

Two main themes have permeated our discussion of social evolution or modernization. First, the historical trends of industrialization, urbanization, bureaucratization, and centralization are all highly interrelated. Once the initial process of industrialization becomes established in a society, the other developments are almost inevitable. None of these phenomena is totally beyond human control, and we can at least partially plan and direct them if we so desire. But it would undoubtedly be impossible to reverse completely the process of modernization at this point in human history. Barring a total nuclear holocaust, it is extremely unlikely that mankind will ever revert to "premodern" societal organization.

The second theme has been the idea that the trends of industrialization, urbanization, bureaucratization, and centralization are largely responsible for most of the major changes that have been occurring in other areas of social life. Although we have not specifically examined such phenomena as the family, education, religion, social stratification, race relations, law, government, communication, transportation, or recreation, all of these social activities in contemporary modernized societies have been radically influenced or altered in recent years by the more fundamental evolutionary trends described here. The predominant thesis of the sociological literature in all these areas is that they are presently undergoing major changes in many societies as a direct result of the process of modernization.

If these trends of industrialization, urbanization, bureaucratization, and centralization have been primarily responsible for creating the kinds of modernized societies that are slowly emerging throughout the world today, what might be the course of future social evolution? In the next chapter we shall sketch several different models of possible future societies that may provide some answers to this question.

RECOMMENDED READING

BENDIX, REINHARD, "Bureaucracy: The Problem and its Setting," *American Sociological Review*, vol. 12 (October 1947), pp. 493–507. (Also Bobbs-Merrill reprint S-16.)
Bureaucratization is seen as a process involving both rationalization and

human relations, and containing both authoritarian and democratic power structures.

BIRNBAUM, N., "Conflicting Interpretations of the Rise of Capitalism: Marx and Weber," *The British Journal of Sociology*, vol. 4 (June 1953), pp. 125–141. (Also Bobbs-Merrill reprint S-26.)
Compares and contrasts the theories of Marx and Weber concerning social and cultural factors influencing the development of capitalistic industrialization.

BLAU, PETER M., *Bureaucracy in Modern Society* (New York: Random House, Inc., 1956).
An introduction to the phenomenon, development, and problems of bureaucratization.

DAVIS, KINGSLEY, "The Origin and Growth of Urbanization in the World," *The American Journal of Sociology*, vol. 60 (March 1955), pp. 429–437. (Also Bobbs-Merrill reprint S-66.)
Reviews the historical development of urbanization, its current extent and major trends, and its future possibilities.

EDITORS OF FORTUNE, *The Exploding Metropolis*, especially chaps. 4 and 5, "The Enduring Slums," by Donald Seligman, and "Urban Sprawl," by William H. Whyte, Jr. (New York: Doubleday & Company, Inc., 1957).
Critical analyses of the problems of urban slums and urban sprawl, including current and proposed attempts to solve these difficulties.

EVAN, WILLIAM M., AND MORRIS ZELDITCH, JR., "A Laboratory Experiment on Bureaucratic Authority," *American Sociological Review*, vol. 26 (December 1961), pp. 883–893.
Differentiates between official and expert authority, and attempts to measure experimentally the separate effects of each type.

GREER, SCOTT, *Governing the Metropolis* (New York: John Wiley & Sons, Inc., 1962).
A comprehensive discussion and analysis of the phenomenon and problems of urban political fragmentation.

HAWLEY, AMOS H., "World Urbanization," in Ronald Freedman, ed., *Population: The Vital Revolution*, pp. 70–83 (New York: Doubleday & Company, Inc., 1964).
A discussion of the historical development of world urbanization, with emphasis on social requirements for urbanization.

HARRIS, CHAUNCY, AND EDWARD ULLMAN, "The Nature of Cities," in Paul K. Hatt and Albert J. Reiss, Jr., eds., *Cities and Society*, pp. 237–247 (New York: The Free Press, a division of The Macmillan Company, 1957).
Discusses typical functions of cities for their societies, as well as three theories of the internal spatial patterning of urban communities.

LITWAK, EUGENE, "Models of Bureaucracy Which Permit Conflict," *The American Journal of Sociology*, vol. 67 (September 1961), pp. 177–181.
Presents and compares models of bureaucratic organizations based on centralized hierarchical control, human relations management, and professionalization.

MICHELS, ROBERT, *Political Parties*, trans. Eden and Cedar Paul, especially pt. one A, chaps. 1 and 2; pt. one B, chaps. 1 and 2; pt. two, chap. 1; and pt. six, chaps. 1, 2, and 4 (New York: The Free Press, a division of

The Macmillan Company, 1966). Highlights of this book are reprinted as "The Iron Law of Oligarchy," in C. Wright Mills, ed., *Images of Man*, pp. 233–261, (New York, George Braziller, Inc., 1960).
Michels' famous argument for the inevitability of oligarchy in social organization.

MILLS, C. WRIGHT, *The Marxists*, especially chaps. 2, 4, and 6 (New York: Dell Publishing Co., 1962).
A brief presentation, criticism, and evaluation of the major sociological ideas of Karl Marx.

————, *The Power Elite*, especially chaps. 1, 6, 9, 10, and 12 (New York: Oxford University Press, 1956).
An analysis of the growing centralization of power in the United States in the areas of government, business, and the military, leading to the emergence of a national "power elite."

MORSE, NANCY C., AND EVERETT REIMER, "The Experimental Change of a Major Organizational Variable," *Journal of Abnormal and Social Psychology*, vol. 52 (January 1956), pp. 120–129. (Also Bobbs-Merrill reprint S-206.)
Reports the results of a field experiment in which control within an organization was decentralized to the worker level.

ROGERS, DAVID, "Community Political Systems: A Framework and Hypothesis for Comparative Study," in Bert E. Swanson, ed., *Current Trends in Comparative Community Studies*, pp. 37–47 (Kansas City, Mo.: Community Studies, Inc., 1962). Reprinted as "Monolithic and Pluralistic Community Power Structures," in Richard L. Simpson and Ida H. Simpson, *Social Organization and Behavior*, pp. 400–405 (New York: John Wiley & Sons, Inc., 1964).
Summarizes several recent community power studies, and suggests that power tends to become decentralized as communities become industrialized and bureaucratized.

ROSE, ARNOLD M., "Automation and the Future Society," *Commentary*, vol. 21 (March 1956), pp. 274–280. Reprinted in Edgar A. Schuler, *et al.*, *Readings in Sociology*, pp. 428–436 (New York: Thomas Y. Crowell Company, 1960).
Sketches numerous social problems that may arise as industry and business become increasingly automated.

ROSTOW, W. W., *The Stages of Economic Growth*, chap. 3 (New York: Cambridge University Press, 1964).
Summarizes the major economic, social, and political conditions necessary for the beginning of sustained industrial development.

THEODORSON, GEORGE A., "Acceptance of Industrialization and Its Attendant Consequences for the Social Patterns of Non-Western Societies," *American Sociological Review*, vol. 18 (1953), pp. 477–484.
A discussion of the effects and problems created by the introduction of industrialization into nonindustrialized societies.

WEBER, MAX, *From Max Weber: Essays in Sociology*, chap. 8, trans. H. H. GERTH, AND C. WRIGHT MILLS, eds., (New York: Oxford University Press, 1946). Reprinted in H. Laurence Ross, *Perspectives on the Social Order*, pp. 249–255, New York, McGraw-Hill, Inc., 1963, and in Edgar

A. Schuler, *et al.*, *Readings in Sociology*, pp. 376–386 (New York, Thomas Y. Crowell Company, 1960).
Weber's classic description of the major features of a bureaucracy.
WILENSKY, HAROLD L., AND CHARLES N. LEBEAUX, *Industrial Society and Social Welfare*, chaps. 3–4 (New York: Russell Sage Foundation, 1958). Examines early and later effects of industrialization on society from a sociological point of view, then evaluates traditional thinking about urbanism.

CHAPTER 18

Models
of Future Societies

If industrialization, urbanization, bureaucratization and centralization have been the major historical trends producing contemporary "modernized" societies, what may future societies be like? In what directions may social organization develop in the future? When we preview the future, of course, we merely project from current trends, filling in details by imaginative speculation. Nevertheless, social scientists have been giving increasing attention to future possibilities for social life, as an important part of the process of rational social planning.

Models of five different types of possible future societies are briefly sketched in this chapter: pluralistic society, socialistic society, mass society, totalitarian society, and "systemic society."[1] As with folk and feudal societies, these are analytical constructs, not actual descriptions. Instead of being composite pictures of existing societies, though, they are "ideal types." In each case, an identifiable current tendency is expanded and carried to its logical conclusion, primarily for purposes of emphasis and contrast. No real society is ever likely to resemble any of these models in all respects, and features of all of the models will probably be visible in most actual situations, but some of the models may be more closely approximated than others.

[1] The latter term is my own, since no name for this type of societal model presently exists in sociology.

Theoretical Perspective

The basic theoretical perspective underlying all five of these projected societal models is epigenesis, or political development. It is assumed that social evolution toward more differentiated and complex social organization will continue, through expanding industrialization, urbanization, and bureaucratization. It is argued, however, that ecological considerations of survival in the natural environment will diminish in importance, provided that population growth is limited and controlled.[2] The economy of a society will necessarily provide a foundation on which all other patterns of social order must rest. But as economic production approaches the level at which all material needs and wants are supplied with a minimum of human effort, the economy will tend to lose its dominant power over the rest of society. Paradoxically, universal abundance destroys economic dominance based on scarcity. As economic productivity grows in both volume and efficiency, individuals and organizations are freed from basic sustenance and related economic concerns, and are then able to direct more attention and effort toward securing whatever other goals they choose to pursue. The primary basis of social power thus shifts from control over economic processes to political authority, so that political values and processes increasingly shape all social organization.[3] Only since World War II has complete opulence appeared to be even a remote possibility, and it will undoubtedly be a long time before anything approaching it becomes worldwide, but current economic trends in the United States and western Europe are beginning to offer the hope that some day material deprivation will be unknown.

Two additional themes pervade all five of these societal models, although in varying proportions: (a) a relative decline (but not total elimination) of traditional ways of social life based on kinship or personal ties and centering in small groups, families, neighborhoods, and local communities; and (b) growth in the size, scope, and especially the

[2] If population growth should continue unchecked at its present rate, the prediction of "standing room only"—one square foot of land per person—would be realized within two to three hundred years. The consequences for social organization are presently unimaginable.

[3] This general thesis is elaborated by W. W. Rostow in *The Stages of Economic Growth* (New York: Cambridge University Press, 1964), chaps. 8–10. Some writers have suggested that a further shift in the primary basis of social power may also occur, from political authority to technological knowledge, so that scientific values become predominant. See Piet Thoenes, *The Elite in the Welfare State*, trans. J. E. Bingham, ed. J. A. Banks (New York: The Free Press, a division of The Macmillan Company, 1966), ch. 8. This thesis is incorporated into the systemic societal model.

complexity of social organization, with concurrent creation of centralized social power. The crucial issue for future societies then appears to lie in the ordering and use of social power within complex, societywide patterns of social organization.

Pluralistic Society

A central concern of political philosophers since antiquity has been how to limit the powers of rulers so as to prevent tyranny. The idea of differentiating various governmental functions can be traced back at least as far as Aristotle, while the importance of embodying legislative, executive, and judicial powers in separate units was stressed by Montesquieu in the eighteenth century. Division of political power is also embedded in the federal type of government, in which the national state shares sovereignty with one or more levels of local government.

All of these forms of pluralism are limited to politics, however. Although a broader conception of pluralism can be seen in James Madison's *The Federalist, No. 10,* it was Alexis de Tocqueville who first gave clear expression to the idea of social pluralism as a model for an entire society.[4] He argued that social pluralism—including, but not limited to, political pluralism—is absolutely necessary for the realization of democracy. To counter the growing power of centralized government in modern societies, individuals of all ages and social conditions must constantly form, maintain, and act through private, voluntary, special-interest associations. These associations together provide a check against the power of government, and hence limit any tendencies toward despotism. "Amongst the laws which rule human societies there is one which seems to be more precise and clear than all others. If men are to remain civilized, or to become so, the art of associating together must grow and improve, in the same ratio to which the equality of conditions is increased."[5]

The importance of social pluralism for the preservation of highly complex societies was further stressed by Émile Durkheim: "Where the State is the only environment in which men can live communal lives, they inevitably lose contact, become detached, and thus society disintegrates. A nation can be maintained only if, between the State and the individual, there is intercalated a whole series of secondary groups near enough to the individuals to attract them strongly in their sphere of ac-

[4] Alexis de Tocqueville, *Democracy in America* (New York: Schocken Books, 1961).
[5] Tocqueville, vol. II, p. 133.

tion and drag them, in this way, into the general torrent of social life."[6] He suggested that occupational associations were particularly suited to this task in contemporary industrialized, urbanized societies.

A completely pluralistic society would contain a vast proliferation of groups, associations, and other organizations located between individuals and the national government (representing the total society). These intermediate organizations possess their own bases of power, and hence are relatively independent of the government. Some of them, such as political parties, may regularly function as parts of the polity, but most of them will be "parapolitical," entering the political arena only when their special concerns are involved. In addition to having political autonomy and voluntary membership, each intermediate association is limited in its sphere of actions, to prevent its becoming overly inclusive and powerful. Individuals will belong to several different associations according to their various interests and activities, so that memberships are overlapping and no one organization can demand total involvement and commitment from its members.[7]

To prevent a pluralistic society from disintegrating into a jumble of self-oriented competing organizations, several integrative conditions must exist in addition to crosscutting memberships. These include common societywide values and norms, general acceptance of the legitimacy of the existing political and legal orders, interlocking organizational activities and relationships, a mass communications network, a high level of public education and participation, and established procedures through which organizations can express their views and exert influence.

The intermediate organizations comprising the structure of a pluralistic society play a mediating role between individuals and the societal government.[8] On the one hand, they provide an institutionalized means by which individuals can gain access to and influence governmental elites without having to resort to mass demonstrations or revolution. By introducing flexibility into political processes, they promote gradual and continual rather than sporadic and violent social change. They also protect individuals from direct manipulation by elites through mass propaganda and mass movements. On the other hand, intermediate organizations also

[6] Émile Durkheim, *The Division of Labor in Society*, trans. by George Simpson (New York: The Free Press, a division of The Macmillan Company, 1933), Preface to the Second Edition, p. 28.

[7] The importance of these aspects of pluralism is stressed by Robert A. Nisbet, *Community and Power* (New York: Galaxy Books, 1962), chap. 10.

[8] These mediating functions are extensively discussed by William Kornhauser, *The Politics of Mass Society* (New York: The Free Press, a division of the Macmillan Company, 1959). See also Robert A. Dahl and Charles E. Lindblom, *Politics, Economics, and Welfare* (New York: Harper & Row, Publishers, 1953), chap. 11.

provide an effective means of social control through which leaders can maintain order and stability in society and can curb deviant actions. They also insulate governmental and legal officials from direct dependence on mass public opinion, enabling them to take socially necessary but unpopular actions without fear of riots or other uprisings. In short, the exercise of power by both elites and citizens is imbedded within an established web of social organization, so that no single small group or organization can dominate the total society.

If intermediate organizations are to perform these mediating political functions effectively, however, they must meet two criteria: (a) they must be small enough and close enough to their members so that individuals can influence organizational activities; and (b) at the same time, they must be large enough and well enough organized to be capable of generating and exerting social power within at least a limited sphere of activities. These apparently contradictory requirements are met in a complex society through the creation of several levels of organization. Individuals first form small clubs, committees, and similar groups, according to location, particular interests, or other factors. Several such groups in turn comprise associations concerned with particular types of social activities. Local associations then merge, successively, into nationally based organizations and functional networks. At this point, the organizational chain becomes powerful enough to influence the national government. Through the combined efforts of many such organizational webs, the power of the government can be controlled and continually directed toward the needs of the entire society.

Several theoretical criticisms are frequently made of the pluralistic model of society. First, it assumes a "natural harmony of interests" among all parts of the society, or wide consensus on basic values, lack of deep social cleavages, and absence of strong ideologies and extremist politics.[9] Only under such conditions will diverse actions by competing, self-oriented, special-interest organizations result in social unity and promotion of the general welfare. Lacking these conditions, pluralism can either paralyze or destroy a society, since attachment to intermediate associations does not by itself insure commitment to the total society. As society changes, some organizations are bound to feel adversely affected and deprived, while others will develop new aspirations and goals. In both cases, these organizations may decide that the existing social and political orders are not adequate, and reject them in favor of extremist ideologies, bitter intergroup conflict, and radical social change.

Second, to the extent that pluralism relies upon and promotes exten-

[9] Joseph Gusfield, "Mass Society and Extremist Politics," *American Sociological Review*, vol. 27 (February 1962), pp. 19–30.

sive functional specialization and structural differentiation, it increases the necessity for overall, centralized coordination and administration if the society is to remain integrated. It would thus appear that the inevitable result of pluralism is centralization—which is often seen as contradictory to many of the values on which pluralism rests. Following the argument of Robert Michels, this tendency might even lead to oligarchy.[10] Is it possible to have unified coordination, regulation, and planning, without also imposing centralized authoritarian control?

The third criticism of pluralism pertains to its practicability. In contemporary nations, in which the state predominates over all other parts of society, how effectively can private, limited-interest associations ever influence the government, no matter how well organized they may be? Are not all intermediate organizations relatively powerless on the societal level, acting only as peripheral spectators in the arena of national affairs? In short, it is sometimes argued that pluralism is unworkable in modern complex societies.[11]

Although pluralism is perhaps the unofficial sociopolitical philosophy of the United States, does this society today even approximate the pluralistic model? Two observers have recently claimed that the United States no longer resembles this model—if indeed it ever did—although they disagree in their descriptions of current conditions. C. Wright Mills has suggested that pluralism does continue to operate below the "power elite," in the "middle levels" of power: in Congress, state and local governments, political parties, labor unions, and other voluntary and occupational associations.[12] In reality, though, this middle level of power is largely controlled by the "power elite," he argues. Although these organizations do wield some power within their spheres of special concern, they rarely exercise much power over the total society. Instead, the "power elite" operate through them, using them as administrative vehicles for carrying out predetermined policies and as mechanisms for controlling the rest of the society. David Riesman disagrees sharply with Mills, in that he does not believe that any unified, national "power elite" actually exists in the United States.[13] He claims, instead, that power in this society

[10] Robert Michels, *Political Parties,* translated by Eden and Cedar Paul (New York: The Free Press, a division of The Macmillan Company, 1966).

[11] Nisbet, chap. 11.

[12] C. Wright Mills, *The Power Elite* (New York: Oxford University Press, 1956), chap. 11.

[13] David Riesman, *et al., The Lonely Crowd* (New York: Doubleday & Company, Inc., 1954), chap. 10. The observations of Mills and Riesman are compared and contrasted by William Kornhauser, " 'Power Elite' or 'Veto Groups?' " in Seymour Lipset and Leo Lowenthal, eds., *Culture and Social Character* (New York: The Free Press, a division of The Macmillan Company, 1961), pp. 252–267. The description of Chicago politics given by Edward C. Banfield in *Political Influence* (New York: The

is diffused throughout a vast number of separate "veto groups," each of which acts only when a public issue impinges upon its particular area of interest. Most significantly, though, this complex of veto groups—which corresponds rather closely to Mills' "middle level" of power—is not seen as wielding its power in a positive sense, seeking to impress its myriad concerns on the total society, as called for by the pluralist model. Rather, as Riesman's term implies, the power of veto groups is strictly negative in nature; the most these organizations can do is to block programs or activities that they oppose. There are, of course, other observers who maintain that the United States does in many ways approximate a pluralistic society, but Mills and Riesman have alerted us to the fallacy of blindly assuming that complete pluralism does exist in all areas of American life.

Numerous empirical studies have also investigated the extent to which the United States currently approximates the pluralistic model. The results reveal an interesting paradox. Early in the nineteenth century, Alexis de Tocqueville described America as a "land of joiners," and today there are estimated to be over 100,000 private voluntary associations in the United States. Nevertheless, large segments of the population do not participate in any such organizations.[14] If church membership is excluded, roughly one-third of the population belongs to no voluntary associations of any kind. Of the two-thirds of the people who do claim some kind of membership, many are only inactive members of a labor union. If labor unions are also excluded from the count of organizational memberships, only about two-fifths of the population comprise all other types of voluntary associations, and no more than half of these people belong to two or more different organizations, as called for by the pluralistic model. Furthermore, membership does not necessarily imply participation, so that active participants in voluntary associations are indeed a tiny minority of the total population. In other words, a very small number of extremely active people support most voluntary associations in the United States. One possibility for future change, though, lies in the fact that organizational involvement tends to increase with education, so that as the general level of education rises, so may membership and participation in voluntary associations.

Free Press, a division of The Macmillan Company, 1961) is quite similar to Riesman's conception of veto groups.

[14] Morris Axelrod, "Urban Structure and Social Participation," *American Sociological Review*, vol. 21 (February 1956), pp. 13–18. Charles R. Wright and Herbert Hyman, "Voluntary Association Memberships of American Adults: Evidence from National Sample Surveys," *American Sociological Review*, vol. 22 (June 1958), pp. 284–294.

If, as these criticisms and data suggest, pluralism is more of an ideal than a workable blueprint for the ordering of social power in contemporary societies, in what other directions might future societies develop? Socialism offers a markedly different goal for society, which its proponents insist is fully realizable.

Socialistic Society

Socialism means many things to many people, so that there are almost as many different conceptions of a socialistic society as there are writers on the subject. Nonetheless, *the ultimate goal of most forms of socialism is full enjoyment by all individuals of whatever benefits their society can provide.* Exploitation, deprivation, and human misery are to be eradicated as far as is humanly possible. A socialistic society, it is argued, will exist to serve all persons, not just a few privileged elites, so that everyone will be given the opportunity to maximize his life to the fullest possible extent. Individual and collective social responsibility will replace self-interest as the basis of social life.[15]

If exploitation and special privileges are to be eliminated, socialism must eventually come to grips with such "political" questions as centralization versus decentralization of collective decision-making, selection of public leaders, and methods of formulating common goals. At the present time, however, little consensus exists among proponents of socialism as to how these problems should be met. Presumably, a socialistic society would adopt whatever political arrangements most effectively promoted its overall goal of full individual and social development. But who can decisively determine what these specific arrangements might be in any given situation? As a consequence, we find socialistic thinkers arrayed across the entire spectrum of political philosophy, from "mass democracy" in which all issues are resolved by popular vote, to "paternalistic oligarchy" in which a small elite determines what is in the best interests of the entire society. In the contemporary world, Sweden has moved far toward socialism while retaining a high degree of political democracy, Russia combines socialism with a fairly totalitarian political structure, and many other nations occupy intermediate positions between these two extremes.

[15] For more extensive discussions of socialistic society, see Robert Heilbroner, *The Future as History* (New York: Grove Press, Inc., 1959), pt. II; Paul E. Mott, *The Organization of Society* (Englewood Cliffs, N.J.: Prentice-Hall, Inc., 1965), chap. 20; and Joseph Schumpeter, *Capitalism, Socialism, and Democracy* (New York: Harper & Row, Publishers, 1950).

Underlying this political diversity, though, is the common assumption that a fully socialistic society cannot be realized as long as economic injustice prevails. Since wealth is a primary resource for social power, its production, distribution, and use will inevitably influence most other aspects of social life. Socialists therefore argue that it is pointless to speak of political democracy if the economy benefits primarily a small elite sector of the population. Alternatively, given an economy that serves the welfare of the entire population, any form of government must of necessity operate for the most part in the public interest. Hence the immediate goal of all forms of socialism is economic reform and reorganization. *In a socialistic society, the economy is oriented toward public rather than private concerns, so that it benefits the entire society.* The antithesis of socialism is not necessarily capitalism, but rather private exploitation of the economy by a few economic dominants for their own selfish interests.

A wide diversity of specific procedures and social arrangements have been proposed as means of achieving the goal of a publicly oriented economy. Following Marx and other nineteenth-century writers, governmental ownership of all means of economic production has often been advocated as a mandatory requirement for reaching this goal. Governmental ownership is only one of many possible procedures, however, and a growing number of socialists today argue that it is not even necessary. Other proposals for achieving a socialistic society include the following:

(1) Governmental control of only certain key industries, such as steel mills, which dominate most other parts of the economy.

(2) Governmental regulation, but not control, of important economic activities, from banking to transportation.

(3) Societywide economic and social planning.

(4) Income, inheritance, and other graduated taxes.

(5) Promotion of full employment.

(6) Social welfare programs of all types, to protect individuals against poverty, unemployment, old age, serious medical crises, and similar problems.

(7) Establishment of producer and consumer cooperatives.

(8) Full opportunity for education and technical training to the limit of one's abilities.

(9) Abolition of all class, racial, religious, and other barriers to equal participation in the economy.

(10) A guaranteed minimum income for all individuals.

(11) Direct involvement of workers in the management of their employing organizations.

(12) Creation of occupational associations to protect the rights of all individuals engaged in each type of work.

(13) Formation of political parties to act as spokesmen for various categories or classes of individuals.

All of these proposals, it must be reiterated, are merely suggested means for attaining a socialistic society, and should not be viewed as ideological imperatives.

Although many people equate socialism with communism, for objective analysis we must distinguish between these two related but distinct philosophies. *Three critical differences between socialism and communism pertain to the distribution of wealth, governmental ownership of industry, and the nature of social change.* First, under socialism the benefits of the economy are to be used for the common welfare, but wealth need not be distributed equally among all individuals; a key phrase to describe the goal of socialism might be "economic justice for all." Each individual is to have full opportunity to enjoy the benefits of the economy, but each person will not necessarily receive the same income. Communism, in contrast, states that wealth must be shared among individuals strictly according to personal need; a key descriptive phrase for this idea is "economic equality for all." All significant economic differences among individuals are to be eliminated. Second, governmental control of all industry is for socialism only one possible means to a broader goal. For communism, though, it is an absolute requirement that must be realized before any other steps will become meaningful, since only in this way can classes and class conflict be eradicated. Third, socialism tends to be evolutionary in nature, seeking its goals through gradual social change within existing political frameworks. Communism, meanwhile, claims that economic, political, and social change are all inseparable, so that the entire society must be altered at once, often through revolution. Socialism thus provides the more general model of a possible future society, with communism being an extreme but not inherent version of this model.

Does contemporary United States at all approximate the socialistic model of society? We call our economy capitalistic, not socialistic, since its basic premise is private enterprise rather than collective welfare. In its pure form, this philosophy of private enterprise says that any person is free to engage in whatever economic activities he wishes (within the law), and to benefit from these efforts as fully as he can (again within the law). The private businessman is in business to make money for himself, and has no moral obligation to share the profits of his enterprise with the rest of society. Operating in an open market economy, he pays his employees whatever is necessary to secure their cooperation, sells his goods or services for whatever price the market will bear, and reaps the rewards (or suffers the consequences) of his efforts.

This ethic of unrestrained individual enterprise might have provided a fairly accurate description of much of the American economy during the latter decades of the nineteenth century, but it hardly fits contemporary economic practices in this society. Although we have retained the term capitalism, as well as many of the basic values of free enterprise, in practice our economy has in the twentieth century—and especially since the 1930's—moved far toward socialism. The basic socialistic goal of operating the economy for the benefit of the entire society—and especially the idea of abolishing poverty—has gained widespread public support, while most businessmen have themselves gradually come to accept a growing sense of public responsibility. It is now recognized that the government can be used to stimulate and guide the economy without directly controlling it, and that such action is necessary if the economy is to keep growing and serving the public interest. Even more striking is the extent to which the United States has instituted, if not fully realized, many of the socialistic proposals listed above. Although we do not accept outright public ownership of industry, the government does regulate the economy in numerous ways, and most of the other proposals have either been translated into operating programs or are at least being advocated. At present, no society even approaches complete fulfillment of the socialistic goal of economic justice for all citizens, but the United States and several western European nations are unquestionably moving in that direction, regardless of the terms used to describe their economies.

The major theoretical criticism of the socialistic model is that most of the specific measures it envisions—though not necessarily its overall goal—require action by a centralized national government. Does this not invite the danger of simply substituting one form of total dominance, if not exploitation, for another? If carried far enough, would not socialism place overwhelming power in the hands of the government, so that public control over the economy would be even more difficult than under any form of private enterprise? Political elites would then be in a position to direct the economy, through the government, in any direction they wished—including their own aggrandizement. At the very least, would not socialism increase the power of government in relation to other parts of the society, further the process of power centralization, and negate any attempts to create pluralism?

We are thus led back to the crucial problem of political organization, on which no clear agreement currently exists. Theoretically, it ought to be possible to devise a government capable of ensuring that the economy did operate for the welfare of the entire society, but whose powers would be so limited through decentralization and pluralistic sources of influence that it could not acquire total control over the society. In practice, no such ideal political state has yet been achieved—although many

Western nations are grappling with this question in various ways. Lacking such an ideal state, however, it can be argued that extensive economic socialism is only inviting governmental domination of society. This is precisely the possibility envisioned in either a mass or a totalitarian society.

Mass Society

No fully developed mass society exists anywhere in the world today, but the United States and other Western nations are frequently said to show tendencies in this direction. Unfortunately, many of the critics who make such claims do not agree on what they mean by a mass society. The model of mass society presented here is drawn largely from the writings of William Kornhauser.[16]

From the point of view of individuals, the chief characteristic of mass society is isolation or atomization. People are socially isolated from one another, and interact only as segmented and highly impersonal role actors. A dissolution of extended kinship and stable community ties destroys meaningful and binding social relationships among individuals, leaving them without secure "social roots" of any kind. "The chief characteristic of the mass . . . is isolation and amorphous social relationships. . . . Mass society is objectively the *atomized* society and subjectively the *alienated* population."[17] Each individual is adrift alone in a vast sea of anonymous humanity. The nuclear family may remain as a social unit in mass society, but it becomes isolated from all other social groups and cannot serve as a mediating bond between the individual and larger social organizations. The only viable social ties in a mass society are those which link each separate individual with the societal government. "Mass society is a situation in which the aggregate of individuals are related to one another only by way of their relations to a common authority, especially the state."[18]

From a broader structural point of view, the major feature of mass society is a relative absence of intermediate, mediating organizations between individuals and the larger society. Some groups—such as nuclear families, friendship cliques, or neighborhoods—are too small, weak, and transitory to have any important effects on the society. Other organizations—such as the government, huge business firms, or giant metropolises

[16] Kornhauser, *The Politics of Mass Society.* Other descriptions are given by Philip Selznick, "Institutional Vulnerability in Mass Society," *The American Journal of Sociology,* vol. 56 (1951), pp. 320–331; and by Mills, chap. 13.

[17] Kornhauser, pp. 31–33.

[18] Kornhauser, pp. 31–33.

—are too large, remote, and complex for individuals to exercise any influence over their activities. The proliferation of medium-sized, independent, special-interest voluntary associations that characterizes pluralistic society is largely missing in a mass society. The associations that do exist —such as political parties, labor unions, or professional organizations— either perform no important functions in society, or else lack the several levels of successively inclusive subunits necessary for effective individual participation. In sum, the social structure of a mass society contains essentially only two types of social ordering: (a) small, shifting groups, which provide no stable or meaningful ties among individuals, and which wield no power in society; and (b) huge, centralized organizations, which impersonally control virtually all societal activities, and over which individuals can exercise no influence.

Those few persons who occupy positions at the apexes of the dominant organizations in mass society, especially governmental leaders, form a small and relatively closed elite that authoritatively rules the society. Such elites are not particularly strong, however, for several reasons. First, they have no intermediate associations through which to reach the population. They cannot effectively control individual actions or mobilize and organize the population for collective activities. Their only means of access to the people is via mass communications, which may produce widespread conformity but will not lead to viable social relationships. Second, elites find it difficult to secure and maintain legitimacy, since they lack any organized support outside the government that would sustain them during periods of severe conflict or disruptive crises. Third, they have no established means by which potential new leaders in the population can be identified and gradually given positions of increasing responsibility as they gain administrative skills. By and large, all social positions are either "elite" or "nonelite," with few intermediate gradations. Fourth, elites cannot effectively deal with public dissatisfaction or disruptions of social order. There are no institutionalized "feedback" mechanisms to keep elites immediately informed of events and problems throughout society. Instead of dealing with stresses and strains continually as they occur, elites are periodically faced with intense social conflicts growing out of unresolved tensions. Fifth, elites are open to arbitrary and extreme popular pressures, in the form of mass movements and revolutions. Because they lack the social distance and insulation from the people that intermediate organizations would provide, elites have little freedom of operation. Before undertaking any activity, they must in effect ask themselves, "How likely is this to produce a demonstration or riot?" As a consequence, many necessary but unpopular actions are never attempted.

While elites in a mass society are overly accessible to popular pressures, the masses of people are also readily available for manipulation by elites and for conformity to the anonymous dictates of mass social movements. Lack of strong attachment to immediately relevant organizations leaves the masses open to whatever influences from the larger society happen to blow upon them. These inundating pressures may consist of either appeals by elites through the mass media, or popular demands for support of and participation in mass extremist movements. In neither case can the individual exercise control over his own social destiny, however. The relentless social forces confronting him are far superior to his lone powers of resistance—and the sources of these social pressures may be entirely anonymous. His social world is meaningless to him, and he is powerless to affect or alter it. Kornhauser's summary description of mass society is worthy of quotation at this point:

> Social groups larger than the family and smaller than the state operate to link elites and nonelites so that the nature of these groups shapes the political relation. Where intermediate groups do not exist or do not perform important social functions, elites and nonelites are directly dependent on one another; there is nonmediated access to elites and direct manipulation of nonelites. This kind of social arrangement leaves society vulnerable to antidemocratic movements based on mass support. Centralized national groups do not mitigate mass availability; neither do isolated primary groups. For the one relationship is too remote and the other is too weak to provide the individual with firm bases of attachment to society. This is the situation of mass society.[19]

Since no one has advocated "massification" as a desirable goal for society, in the same manner that pluralism and socialism are often proclaimed as ideals, there have been no corresponding theoretical criticisms of this model. On the contrary, the dissenter in this case is the writer who finds worthwhile features in the mass-society model. For instance, it has been suggested that some aspects of a mass society would tend to encourage continual (and presumably beneficial) social change, to inhibit extremist politics growing out of widely diffused social power, or to promote individual freedom of choice by providing a person with many different possible courses of action.[20] It is important to realize, though, that the conceptions of mass society held by these "critics" all differ

---

[19] Kornhauser, p. 100.

[20] These writings are, successively, Daniel Bell, "America as a Mass Society: A Critique," in his *The End of Ideology* (New York: The Free Press, a division of the Macmillan Company, 1960), chap. 1; Gusfield, "Mass Society and Extremist Politics"; and Edward Shils, "The Theory of Mass Society," in Philip Olson, ed., *America as a Mass Society* (New York: The Free Press, a division of the Macmillan Company, 1963), pp. 30–47.

markedly from the model proposed by Kornhauser. As sketched here, mass society remains largely a "negative utopia."

Are there any indications that societies such as the United States may be slowly drifting toward the mass model? In our discussion of the pluralistic model we saw that a vast number of Americans do not participate in, or even belong to, intermediate voluntary associations. At the same time, nevertheless, this society does contain thousands of such organizations, many of which do exercise considerable influence upon governmental decisions and actions. Nor are individuals becoming socially isolated from one another, even in the most highly urbanized communities. Kinship ties, personal friendships, and neighborhood activities are still extremely common occurrences in this society.[21] Informal social life in contemporary urbanized society differs in many ways from that experienced in small towns and rural areas, but it is by no means disappearing.

But do these bare facts tell the whole story? Numerous arguments have been put forth to support the thesis that pluralism eventually tends to give way to "massification" in contemporary societies, as a direct result of their growing size and complexity. Long ago, de Tocqueville warned that political equality inevitably gives preference to majority over minority views, which leads to a "tyranny of the majority" and mass conformity to perceived public opinion. More recently, sociologists have pointed out that (a) approximately 20 per cent of the American population moves every year, which makes the perpetuation of strong personal relationships quite difficult; and (b) intermediate organizations may not be disappearing in this society, but the more significant ones—such as labor unions, political parties, professional associations, and business organizations—are becoming so huge, formalized, and complex that ordinary members can exercise no more control over their activities than over the national government. On the national level, these kinds of organizations can and do influence the government and hence give the society a semblance of pluralism, but they do not provide an organized channel through which individuals can act collectively to make their interests felt on the societal level. Finally, some writers maintain that regardless of whether or not the structural forms of pluralism are retained in a society, the pervasive trend of power centralization leaves intermediate organizations as little more than administrative agents of the powerful national elites.

The major problem of a mass society, if one should ever be created,

[21] For a summary of much of the work, see Scott Greer, "Individual Participation in the Mass Society," in Roland Young, ed., *Approaches to the Study of Politics* (Evanston, Ill.; Northwestern University Press, 1958), pp. 329–342.

would probably be instability. The weakness of the elites, added to the volatility of the masses, gives mass society an inherent propensity to drastic social conflict and change. A likely direction that such change might take, as elites attempted to strengthen their power or to "rescue" society from "impending social anarchy," would be toward totalitarian society.

Totalitarian Society

Totalitarian society has come closer to actual realization in the twentieth century than any of the other societal models. This fact has both desirable and undesirable consequences for sociological analysis: we can describe and study most aspects of totalitarian society in considerable detail, but at the same time we may find it exceptionally difficult to maintain value neutrality. The two major prototype examples of totalitarianism—Germany under Hitler and Russia under Stalin—remind us, however, that this form of society can incorporate either a capitalistic or a socialistic economy. The distinctive feature of totalitarianism lies in its power structure, not in its economic order.

A totalitarian society differs markedly from a traditional dictatorship. In both types of regimes, power is highly centralized in a small governmental elite, which acts authoritatively—and often autocratically—without consulting the rest of the population. Traditional despots, however, have sought only to rule their society, not to control it totally. Their power has for the most part been limited to the formal government, plus its attendant legal and military networks, supplemented by a limited amount of influence over the economy. But the rest of society has usually been left alone. Most of these dictators have ultimately been concerned with promoting their own welfare, not that of the total society, and they have sought to exercise only enough power to expropriate the available benefits and resist all attempts at social change.

Not so in totalitarian society. Given the technological facilities and complex social organization of industrialized-urbanized-bureaucratized-centralized societies, *totalitarian elites attempt to extend their control over all parts of the society and all aspects of social life. They create a "total state," in which the government, acting through the political network, absolutely dominates the entire society.*[22] The state—or more pre-

---

[22] The major writings on totalitarian society, from which this discussion is largely drawn, are Hannah Arendt, *The Origins of Totalitarianism*, 2nd ed. (Cleveland: the World Publishing Company, 1958), chaps. 10–13; and Carl J. Friedrich and Zbigniew K. Brezezinski, *Totalitarian Dictatorship and Autocracy*, 2nd ed. (Cambridge, Mass.: Harvard University Press, 1965). See also Nisbet, *Power and Community*, chap. 8.

cisely, the elites who operate the government, which is the focus of the polity—control all subordinate governmental units, all social networks throughout the society (including the economy, education, communication, religion, socialization, medicine, and so on), all associations existing in the society (businesses, labor unions, political parties, occupational and professional organizations, special-interest associations, churches, youth clubs), and, as far as possible, all families and small groups. When carried to its extreme, total control by totalitarian elites would not even stop here, but would also influence or determine all individual behavior, and would ultimately employ socialization and propaganda techniques to mold the personalities of all members of the society. In short, totalitarian society is highly organized, integrated, and institutionalized, but it is also thoroughly dominated by the state, which is in turn completely controlled by a few elites.

These elites attempt to justify their total control of society on the grounds that they are in the process of constructing a totally new—and highly utopian—type of society that will eventually benefit everyone. Instead of just exploiting their society, totalitarian elites are presumably seeking to promote the common welfare. Hence instead of defending existing social conditions, they initiate radical social changes. Totalitarian elites may genuinely believe in the utopian ideals they propound, or they may simply be using these goals as a means of gaining legitimacy, but this factor is not crucially significant. Regardless of whether they are seeking personal gain or social betterment, the society is still totalitarian.

As a prelude to the massive social changes required for the creation of a totalitarian society, most existing social order and culture must be severely weakened or destroyed. Established relationships and organizations are subverted or eliminated, leaving the ground bare and fertile for the growth of totalitarianism. At this point coercion and violence may be used, although events such as wars and depressions might produce the same effects. "The political enslavement of man requires the emancipation of man from all the authorities and memberships . . . that serve, in one degree or another, to insulate an individual from external political power. . . . The monolithic case of the totalitarian State arises from the sterilization or destruction of all groups and statuses that, in any way, rival or detract from the allegiance of the masses to [the] State."[23] Thus it is that mass society, with its atomization of individuals and absence of intermediate associations, is often described as particularly ripe for the emergence of totalitarianism.

Destruction of the old order and creation of an organizational void

[23] Nisbet, pp. 202 and 205.

is only the first step on the road to totalitarianism, however. The controlling elites must now endeavor to create an entirely new structure of groups, associations, classes, networks, and other types of social organization throughout society. This elaborate set of organizations is established and thoroughly controlled by the state. The ruling elites determine what functions each organization is to perform, what its values, goals, and norms are to be, how it is to operate, whom its membership shall include, what power it is to wield, and which individuals shall act as its leaders. In short, *every organization within the society is merely an extension of the state, acting as its agent.* The society is pluralistic in outward form, but completely centralized in actual operation. All organizations comprising the society function solely for the benefit of the state, never for their individual members.

The unique characteristics of a totalitarian society can be briefly summarized under three headings: a monolithic political party, a pervasive ideology, and unlimited social control.[24] There is only one political party in totalitarian society, and it brooks no opposition. Although limited in size to a small percentage of the population, it is the single most powerful organization in the society. Party membership is the first requisite for all important social positions, and all members are expected to exhibit both loyal dedication and active participation. In its operation, the party is highly authoritarian, with all power exercised downward from a tiny inner circle through several successively broader but less influential levels of party membership and organization. The inner circle of elites that directs the party, and hence the entire society, may act as a collective unit or may select one or more of its members to be the head of state, but in either case the elite group as a whole remains the final seat of power. Totalitarian "supreme leaders" are always highly dependent upon their "coelites."

In practice, if not also in ideology, the party is superior to the formal government in totalitarian society. For all practical purposes, the party is the ruling political unit, which then acts through the formal government and other agencies of the state, which in turn pervades all organized social activities. The formal government is thus reduced to being largely an administrative organ, while all major policy formation and decision-making originates within the higher levels of the party. To maintain total control over the government as well as the rest of the society, the party assigns one or more of its members to every governmental bureau and office, and to every factory, business firm, military unit, youth organization, professional association, court, newspaper, broadcasting station, and other such organizations it considers important. This party agent does not

[24] For more extensive discussion of these various features, see Friedrich and Brezezinski, *Totalitarian Dictatorship and Autocracy.*

directly rule the organization or unit to which he is assigned, but rather acts as an observer and liaison to pass on party directives, to insure that party rules are enforced, and to report back to the party any problems or "deviations" that occur. Because of this intricate web of party observers, and also because of the fact that key governmental offices are often duplicated by parallel party units, totalitarian society is sometimes said to have a "dual social structure."

All societies have ideologies, or sets of interrelated values that explain, justify, and guide social activities. But totalitarian ideologies are distinctive in several ways: (a) they are proclaimed by the elites as the official values of the whole society; (b) they are utopian in nature, calling for complete reconstruction of the society along entirely new lines, and supposedly leading ultimately to an ideal way of life; (c) they are totally inclusive, pertaining to virtually all areas and aspects of human life; and (d) they are frequently universal in scope, appealing to all humanity. These ideologies serve primarily to legitimize the power of the elites and the totalitarian movement. By establishing goals for social action that are believed to be morally perfect, they justify all means required to achieve such ends. Their constant rejection of the present for the sake of grandiose schemes of social reconstruction and societal betterment provides the moral basis for the unlimited extension of totalitarian power to all parts of society. Totalitarian elites may not privately accept their ideologies at face value, but in public these ideas are incessantly preached to the people as ultimate truths to be accepted unquestioningly.

To propagate their ideologies and enforce their power, totalitarian elites use every available means of social control. They operate the educational and communications networks as vehicles for propaganda, allowing the public to receive only selected items of information. Teachers and writers must be approved by the party, their actions are continually monitored, and everything they present is censored. In addition, schools and youth organizations are used as socialization agents to mold each new generation into loyal supporters of the regime. There is an elaborate code of laws pertaining to every conceivable event, these laws are rigidly enforced, and the violators are judged by courts wholly controlled by the party. Besides the usual civil and criminal statutes, an extensive list of party rules and regulations is rigorously enforced, so that a majority of all "deviants" are classified as "political criminals." Public "show trials" and self-confessions are used as aids in sustaining the legitimacy of the state. And unlike traditional dictatorships, in which the military provides much of the backing for the political rulers and hence retains considerable autonomous power, totalitarianism regimes bring the military firmly under their control and employ military force as a coercive sanction.

Beyond all these pervasive techniques of social control, totalitarian elites also rely, in varying degrees, upon the exercise of terror by secret police. These police are responsible only to the party leaders, and their victims have no means of resistance or defense. Their terror tactics may include planting informants in private groups, electronic spying, arbitrary arrest and imprisonment, inquisitions to wring information or confessions from suspects, capricious harrassment of individuals, deportation to concentration or "work" camps, individual "liquidation," and mass "extermination." The main purpose of all such terror is to frighten the population into willingly obeying the dictates of the party and its leaders.

From a purely functional point of view, it is rather difficult to find fault with the totalitarian model. This type of society uses to the full all known techniques of sophisticated social organization on a vast, highly complex, and completely centralized basis. Overall, the resulting society may operate with relative efficiency in the attainment of whatever goals it seeks, may remain fairly well integrated, and may evidence considerable stability. Given enough time, a totalitarian regime might become overly rigid and incapable of adjusting to changing social conditions, but even this weakness is perhaps not inevitable. In any case, the elites' complete monopoly over all means of social control, including military coercion if necessary, makes popularly based resistance extremely difficult if not impossible. Only an organized counterelite within the party can realistically hope to succeed in overthrowing the ruling leaders, but such "palace revolutions" rarely produce major alterations in society.

Criticism of the totalitarian model must therefore be essentially valuative in nature. If we reject totalitarianism it is primarily because we dislike it, not because it will not work. And if we do reject this model on the grounds that it violates many values we hold to be crucial for social life, it becomes imperative that we develop alternative blueprints for future societies. Otherwise, totalitarianism is only too likely to emerge, as it has repeatedly in the twentieth century. Any such nontotalitarian model of society must incorporate some organized means of resolving the dilemma between the functional necessity for centralized coordination and regulation and the desire for the benefits of power decentralization through pluralism. This question remains largely unresolved, but the systemic model of society may offer some possibilities for its solution.

Systemic Society

This final model for future societies has not been thoroughly and explicitly formulated, although many of its features implicitly pervade much current social-scientific writing. Hence our present sketch of systemic society must be limited to suggesting some of its major characteristics, rather than specifying its total configuration.[25]

This model is in many ways merely an extension and fulfillment of pluralism throughout all parts of a society, and many sociologists would perhaps not distinguish it from the pluralistic model. There are, however, at least three crucial differences between the systemic and pluralistic models. First, the systemic model carries the idea of decentralization of power much further than does the pluralistic model. In the traditional conception of pluralism the power of the government is limited by an array of intermediate special-interest associations, but the polity remains the dominant arena of activity on the national level. In practice, this has meant that intermediate associations compete with each other in their attempts to influence public policy and decisions, but they do not compete directly with the government. They act only as pleaders for their special interests before the all-encompassing power of the state. In the systemic model, in contrast, power is decentralized to the point where the polity becomes only one among many equally powerful functional networks within a society, so that no single kind of organization dominates the entire society.

The second main difference between the systemic and pluralistic models is analogous to the distinction in economics between the classical competitive market and an organized market of countervailing forces. In the competitive-market scheme, as in the usual pluralistic model, power is controlled by competition among a large number of relatively small and independent units—such as producers of a certain commodity —all of which operate on the same side of the market. For example, if one manufacturer of shoes attempts to increase his profits by raising his price, he will be brought back into line by other shoe manufacturers who will undersell him. In the pluralistic model of society, if one voluntary association seeks to gain more than its "fair share" of benefits from the government, it will be undercut by other competing associations that demand less and offer more in return. The "countervailing-power" model has been specifically devised to fit the contemporary United States, in which many spheres of economic activity are largely dominated by a few

[25] A few of the recent writings that either implicitly or explicitly discuss various aspects of this model, and from which the present description of systemic society is largely drawn, are Robert A. Dahl, *A Preface to Democratic Theory* (Chicago: the University of Chicago Press, 1956); Robert A. Dahl and Charles E. Lindblom, *Politics, Economics, and Welfare* (New York: Harper & Row, Publishers, 1953); John Kenneth Galbraith, *American Capitalism* (Boston: Houghton Mifflin Company, 1956); Robert L. Heilbroner, *The Making of Economic Society* (Englewood Cliffs, N.J.: Prentice-Hall, Inc., 1962); Robert M. MacIver, *Power Transformed* (New York: The Macmillan Company, 1964); Rostow, *The Stages of Economic Growth;* and Thoenes, *The Elite in the Welfare State.*

huge corporations.[26] The power of such organizations tends to be limited not by their few competitors, but rather by organized forces operating on the opposite side of the market, such as labor unions, consumer-oriented chain stores (or consumer cooperatives in some societies), or governmental regulatory agencies. The systemic model generalizes this idea beyond the economy to all parts of society, so that each sphere of activity —whether it be education or religion or communication or medicine or the economy or government—is principally controlled by other organized functional networks exercising countervailing power against it, rather than by a proliferation of relatively small organizations operating within the same area.

The third major difference between these two societal models pertains to the traditional distinction between "public" and "private" organizations. In the pluralistic model, the multitude of intermediate organizations are entirely privately controlled and are essentially concerned only with their own particular interests and goals. The function of government is then to represent the broader public interests of the entire community or society, which it does by coordinating, mediating, and regulating the activities of the competing private organizations. In the systemic model, the line between public and private concerns becomes blurred or non-existent. Most of the various associations and functional networks comprising the society are simultaneously "public" and "private." They are public in that their primary orientation is toward promoting the general welfare of society, while their activities are guided by a strong norm of social responsibility. At the same time, they are private in that they are autonomously controlled by their members and are financially self-supporting. If such a fusion of public goals with private control sounds impossibly utopian, consider such phenomena in American society as the Tennessee Valley Authority or the Port of New York Authority (which are legally public bodies but which operate as relatively autonomous organizations) or Harvard University or many hospitals (which are legally private associations but which operate to serve the public welfare). These are tentative prototypes of the kinds of organizations comprising a systemic society.

As its name implies, a systemic society would first of all display the major characteristics of a social system. That is, it would contain (a) clearly delineated social boundaries, which nevertheless remain open to constant interchanges between the society and its environment (especially other societies); (b) numerous subunits, subsubunits, and so on,

[26] Galbraith.

all of which together give the society an extremely complex social structure; (c) interdependent and interrelated ties among all units of the society, though not necessarily between each unit and every other unit; (d) moderate, but never total, institutionalization of all component subunits, so that they are at least partially oriented toward the functional requirements and values of the total society; (e) considerable functional autonomy among most if not all of these component subunits, giving the society operational flexibility; and (f) a high degree of both functional and normative integration, resulting in relative stability of the society as an organization through time.

A systemic society would also exhibit many self-regulating (or homeostatic) processes, through which its crucial features—such as its boundaries, its major values, its government, its economy, or whatever other aspects its members believed to be especially vital—would be maintained despite disruptive stresses and strains. At the same time, the society would be constantly developing (through morphogenesis) toward more effective and complete realization of whatever social goals its members sought, which might include economic well being, scientific discovery, artistic creation, or constructive leisure.

The society would welcome social conflict and change, as long as they remained within established limits and did not threaten to destroy social order. Procedures and techniques for conflict management and resolution would be established, so that change resulting from stresses and strains might be continuous but gradual rather than sporadic and revolutionary. The society would thus become highly flexible and adaptable to changing conditions. Extreme segmentation of the component units would be avoided through limited institutionalization, but all subunits—and hence ultimately all individuals—would enjoy as much autonomy of operation and freedom of action as could be encouraged.

Departing from the systemic model back to empirical reality for a moment, it appears safe to predict that the trend toward centralization of power, especially on the societal level, will continue or even accelerate for some time to come. As more and more social activities are organized on a national rather than a local level, so that societies continue to grow in complexity, centralized societywide administration becomes imperative. But does this necessarily mean that the government—or more broadly, the political network—must assume increasing responsibility for managing and directing the entire society, as is now occurring in most modernized societies, so that it may eventually dominate all other spheres of social organization? Or can all the subunits comprising a society share power and responsibility on a relatively equal basis? Related to this question is the problem of how individuals are to participate in collective decision-making within highly complex societies. What is the future of political democracy?

The systemic model of society is an attempt to resolve these questions in the direction of power decentralization. As such, it provides an alternative to ultimate totalitarian state control of society. Power is decentralized in this model along functional, not geographic lines. *A systemic society would be composed of a series of highly complex but functionally specialized social networks, each containing numerous smaller organizations of all types.* Each network would be concerned only with a particular sphere of social activity, so that there might be separate networks for communication, transportation, education, medicine, law, science, religion, public safety, economic production, economic consumption, welfare services, housing, recreation, public administration, and foreign affairs. Each social network would itself display all the characteristics of a social system, except that it could not be self-sufficient because of its functional interdependence with all other networks. Each of these networks would assume primary responsibility for providing all necessary or desired services to the total society within its particular sphere of functional competence. Furthermore, to the extent that decisions could be made and problems handled within a single network on purely technical or professional grounds, that network would have full responsibility for handling the situation.

A specialized social network need not be a monolithic unit that authoritatively controls all organizations and activities comprising it; rather it would be essentially an administrative process for promoting communication, coordination, regulation, and planning among all its component parts. Operational power and responsibility could remain largely in the hands of smaller organizations, so that each network, as well as the total society, would be relatively decentralized. Social control by the network over its constituent parts and members would be provided primarily by a strong code of professional norms. When external control was required to augment self-discipline, it would normally be administered by colleagues within the network, not by the state.

Graphically, each functional network might be pictured as a large circle. Any individual or organization with an interest in its activities could voluntarily enter the network through participation in activities at its periphery. As this social actor increased its participation in network functions, gained necessary knowledge and skills, assumed broadening responsibilities, and exercised greater authority, it would in effect move closer to the middle of the circle. Such "inward" movement of actors within the network would be determined by the extent of their expertise in this area, by their willingness to assume more duties and social responsibilities, and by their commitment to the professional norms guiding network activities. Those actors occupying positions at the center—which together might perhaps constitute an executive council—would have primary responsibility and authority for coordinating the entire network. Their power would be severely checked, nevertheless, by the diverse influences exerted on them by all the partially autonomous organizations comprising the network. Each of these component subunits might in turn constitute a smaller circle, with individual members entering at its periphery and moving inward toward its center positions of organizational responsibility.

In this systemic model, the state loses its predominance over other sectors of the society and becomes merely another functional network. In fact, the powers and activities of government might be split, as the list above suggests, among several separate networks: public administration, foreign affairs, and the judiciary. Moreover, the "public administration" network would perform mainly administrative services for the society as a whole, and would not itself engage in operational programs. Its responsibility would be to provide coordination and planning among the other functional networks, but its activities would be limited to this area of special competence. The polity would not become engaged in highway construction, old-age pension programs, urban renewal, securities regulation, food and drug inspection, or any of the hundreds of other kinds of activities that governments presently perform.

In short, this model calls for decentralization of power in society along functional lines, with each social network exercising organized countervailing power in relation to all other networks. The main source of each network's—and ultimately each organization's—power in society would be functional dominance based on the vital services that only it could perform for the rest of the society. Effective performance of these functional responsibilities would in turn give a network or any smaller organization legitimate authority derived from rational expert competence. Yet because of functional specialization and interdependence among all networks, as well as their component organizations, no one network—such as the state—could wield overwhelming power throughout the entire society. *The fundamental theoretical assumption underlying this systemic model is that operating responsibilities, and hence power, can be decentralized within an organization—as long as it remains relatively unified—without sacrificing the desirable benefits of overall coordination, regulation, planning, and related administrative functions.* The twin keys to effective decentralization are self-regulation by semiautonomous functionally specialized subparts, and firmly established limits on the power of the unit providing administrative services for the entire society.

Still unresolved in this decentralized systemic model is the problem of providing for societywide goal determination, decision-making, and policy formation. With each of the major social networks focusing on its own specialized functions, who would maintain an overriding orientation toward the whole society and its overall problems? In short, who would perform legislative functions for the entire society? This problem is not as acute as it might appear, for two reasons: First, a moderate degree of institutionalization among all subunits of the society would sustain norms of social responsibility and prevent organizations from becoming extremely self-centered. Second, since most individuals would participate in several different organizations, and usually in more than one functional network, all of the units comprising a society would be interrelated by overlapping memberships as well as interdependent relationships. Nevertheless, this critical requirement for societywide leadership must somehow be met.

Although a totalitarian regime could not emerge in a decentralized systemic society, a political elite with certain special powers would undoubtedly be necessary. But how much power should this elite wield, and how should its members be selected? The resolution of these questions rests on basic political values, not on social theory. Depending on a society's values and the procedures it instituted to realize them, political elites might rule either autocratically or responsibly and might be either self-perpetuating or periodically chosen by the population. Their powers would always be severely limited, but that would not by itself prevent elites from attempting to act as dictators if the society would tolerate and legitimize them.

If a society did seek political democracy, however, some type of centralized legislative arrangement would be fully compatible with other features of systemic organization. For instance, some type of supreme council or congress—let us call it the "societal policy council"—might be selected through periodic elections, with members perhaps representing each of the functional networks in the society. In addition, there might be either a popularly elected chief of state or an executive cabinet chosen from among the members of the legislative body. Nor need voting be limited to selection of incumbents for elite positions; there might also be procedures whereby citizens could directly express their views concerning fundamental goals and substantive issues.

The forms of any such democratic political order would not be as important, however, as the functions the political elite would perform. A distinction must be drawn at this point between "technical" and "valuative" decisions. To the extent that any program or problem was purely technical in nature, it would be handled by the members of the network or networks concerned with that special area, on the basis of the best available technical knowledge and according to rational operational criteria. Political elites would deal only with matters that went beyond technical details, such as setting overall societal goals, formulating long-range policies, evaluating the desirability of various social programs, setting priorities and allocating resources among competing activities, resolving nontechnical conflicts among social networks, or suggesting guidelines for future societal development. In short, *the incompatibility between "official" and "expert" authority would be resolved on the societal level by assigning all technical operations to specialized experts, insofar as possible, and reserving for political officials only the questions that involved social values and hence required a nonspecialized, societal orientation and concern.* Individuals, furthermore, could effectively participate in societal affairs in two different ways: through voting, as citizens, on the selection of political elites and on basic value issues; and also through the enactment of all of their various roles within each of the functional networks to which they belonged.

By way of summary and conclusion, the point must be reiterated that this highly speculative model of systemic society is neither a description of any presently existing social arrangements nor an idiosyncratic value statement of what all societies should be like. It is intended, rather, as a rough blueprint for a fifth possible type of future societal organization, as an alternative or supplement to the pluralistic, socialistic, mass, and totalitarian models. This presentation of the systemic model has been predicated on several assumptions, however: (a) that the classic form of pluralism is a rather ineffective means of controlling power in highly complex, state-dominated societies; (b) that socialism has not, at least to date, dealt adequately with the persistent problem of the ordering of power in society, regardless of whatever we may think of its suggested economic goals; (c) that a mass society, if one should ever exist, would be inherently unstable and could not operate for long without either breaking down or drifting toward totalitarianism; and (d) that the totalitarian model, while theoretically fairly workable, violates many widespread and deeply held social values concerning freedom of action and political liberty.

With these assumptions in mind, an attempt has been made to sketch, as objectively as possible, some of the major characteristics of another societal model, which as yet has not been extensively developed by social scientists. The crux of the systemic model is the proposition that centralized administration is not necessarily incompatible with decentralized operational responsibility and power. A systemic model would bridge this paradox by creating many functional specialized social networks, of which administrative government would be only one among equals, all of which would comprise the major subunits of a unified but decentralized society.

The one aspect of the process of social organization remaining to be examined in the final chapter of this book is the topic of social planning. If mankind is to direct the future course of social organization toward any of these five societal models, or toward any other goals we might seek through collective action, it becomes imperative that we understand and practice rational social planning.

RECOMMENDED READING

BELL, DANIEL, "America as a Mass Society: A Critique," in his *The End of Ideology*, chap. 1 (New York: The Free Press, a division of The Macmillan Company, 1960). Reprinted in Edgar A. Schuler, *et al.*, eds., *Readings in Sociology*, pp. 195–202 (New York: Thomas Y. Crowell Company, 1960).
A critique and criticism of mass-society theory, suggesting that the main characteristic of a mass society is continual, orderly social change.

DEGRÉ, GERARD, "Freedom and Social Structure," *American Sociological Review*, vol. 11 (October 1946), pp. 529–536. (Also Bobbs-Merrill reprint S-70.)
Compares several different models of society, with emphasis on pluralism.

FRIEDRICH, CARL J., AND ZBIGNIEW K. BREZEZINSKI, *Totalitarian Dictatorship and Autocracy*, 2nd ed., especially chap. 2 (Cambridge, Mass.: Harvard University Press, 1965).
An overview of the major characteristics of totalitarian society, pointing out ways in which it differs from a traditional dictatorship.

HEILBRONER, ROBERT L., *The Future as History*, especially pts. II and III (New York: Grove Press, Inc., 1959).
Contemporary economic and social trends, in both emerging and modernized societies, are used as a basis from which to project future possible societal development under socialism and capitalism.

KORNHAUSER, WILLIAM, *The Politics of Mass Society*, especially chaps. 1–3 (New York: The Free Press, a division of The Macmillan Company, 1959).
A rigorous analytical discussion of the mass-society model.

———, " 'Power Elite' or 'Veto Groups'?" in Seymour Martin Lipset and Leo Lowenthal, eds., *Culture and Social Character*, pp. 252–267 (New York: The Free Press, a division of The Macmillan Company, 1961). Reprinted in Richard L. Simpson and Ida H. Simpson, eds., *Social Or-*

ganization and Behavior, pp. 199–208 (New York: John Wiley & Sons, Inc., 1964).

Contrasts and compares the patterns of power distribution in the United States as described by C. Wright Mills and David Riesman.

MARX, KARL, AND FRIEDRICH ENGELS, *The Communist Manifesto.* Bobbs-Merrill reprint S-455.

The classic statement of communist ideology.

NISBET, ROBERT A., *Community and Power,* especially chaps. 3, 8, and 11 (New York: Oxford University Press, 1962).

A penetrating analysis of the consequences for social life resulting from mass, totalitarian, and pluralistic social organizations.

OLSEN, MARVIN E., "The Mature Society: Personal Autonomy and Social Responsibility," *The Michigan Quarterly Review,* vol. 3 (July 1964), pp. 148–159.

An attempt to portray the main features of a societal model in which both personal autonomy and social responsibility would simultaneously be maximized.

WHITE, WINSTON, *Beyond Conformity* (New York: The Free Press, a division of The Macmillan Company, 1961).

Criticizes the view that the growing complexity of social life necessarily leads to mass conformity and cultural decline, and explores opportunities and challenges for individual freedom in contemporary society.

CHAPTER 19

Social Planning

Insofar as social organization is a dynamic process that is continually being created and recreated, it is always open to purposeful social planning. Planning is not necessary for the development or perpetuation of social organization, and much of organized social life has resulted from the actions of persons who "muddled along" from one day to the next, without much awareness of, or concern for, the broader social consequences of their actions. But it is also possible to establish purposeful goals for collective action, rationally plan organized activities that will effectively attain these goals, and then intentionally create social organization for this purpose. Purposeful planning of social organization and social change, especially on a societal scale, are still rather rare phenomena in today's world. Nevertheless, part of the overall process of social evolution has been a slow movement in many societies toward rational social planning. To what degree is it possible for mankind to willfully plan and direct the future course of social organization?[1]

---

[1] Much of the following discussion of social planning is adapted from Ronald Freedman, *et al., Principles of Sociology*, rev. ed. (New York: Holt, Rinehart and Winston, Inc., 1956), pp. 566–569.

344

Difficulties of Social Planning

Social planning cannot even be contemplated, let alone attempted, as long as cultural values and norms are viewed as sacred commandments. Only as culture becomes secularized and as conformity to ancient traditions ceases to be a moral virtue does rational social planning become credible. A strong impetus was given to social planning by the "rationalists" of the Enlightenment movement in Europe during the seventeenth and eighteenth centuries, although their ideas were in many ways oversimplistic. Reacting against the medieval view of social order as preordained and immutable, many writers of this period argued that social organization is created by man and hence can and should be altered as man sees fit. The naivety of this view lay not in its justification for rational social planning, but in the belief that, given a minimum of rationality and consensus, any desired change could easily be accomplished.

The Romantic movement of the nineteenth century arose as a direct challenge to these conceptions. A host of philosophers and social theorists insisted that the development of social organization is largely beyond man's control. Human societies may not be the direct expression of divine providence, but they are the results of imponderable natural or historical forces that are incomprehensible and unalterable. Mankind can have no more effect over the course of social evolution than over biological evolution. Hence social planning is futile.

Despite the calamities of the twentieth century, *contemporary social science holds that purposeful social planning is feasible, although we now have a more sophisticated realization of the limitations and enormous complexities of this process.* Men are not free to order social activities in whatever ways they might fancy. Historical trends and the ever-present weight of established social order and cultural ideas severely limit the extent to which any generation can alter the course of organizational development. We cannot today, for example, undo the effects of a century or more of expanding industrialization and urbanization. Nor can we, by simple fiat, change basic societal values and norms, as Prohibition dramatically illustrated. Within these broad limits, however, man can do much to affect, at least slowly and moderately, the social organizations within which he lives—provided that he has acquired the necessary scientific knowledge and social technology.

Present-day criticism of social planning tends to stress not its futility, but rather the argument that it restricts individual freedom of action. Collective planning, it is said, denies the individual control over his own life, and forces him to conform to the dictates of others. There is an undeniable kernel of truth in this proposition. Consider a few typical instances of social planning: city authorities set aside a plot of land for a park, and deny businessmen the right to construct a shopping center there; the national government institutes an old-age pension program, and requires all workers to contribute to it; because of the importance of education in contemporary society, a community provides public schools and forces all children to attend them until a certain age; a law is passed requiring stores to serve all customers, regardless of race or religion; to meet projected transportation demands, the government levies a gasoline tax on all motorists, the revenues from which are used to build new expressways. In all of these cases, individuals are denied certain "freedoms" their ancestors once enjoyed. But to focus exclusively on the negative side is to miss the point of social planning. *While restricting some individual rights, social planning can have the simultaneous benefit of greatly expanding the scope of activities open to all persons.* By surrendering certain small individual privileges, we can all gain vast new opportunities, as the examples above illustrate. In other words, we can gain much more than we lose through purposeful social planning.

Notice, though, the use of the provisional word "can" in the previous statements. Whether or not planning does result in expanded social freedoms depends on how that planning is carried out. Social planning is just as feasible in totalitarian as in democratic societies, but it will not have the same consequences for individuals. Democratic social planning, as opposed to autocratic dictates, is intended to promote the welfare of all people according to their own common wishes. But how are these wishes to be ascertained? The process of social planning is only a means of rationally and effectively directing social organization toward the attainment of whatever goals people desire. By itself, it says nothing about the nature or desirability of these goals; we could just as feasibly develop plans for the elimination of humanity from the face of the earth as for any type of human betterment. In short, *the process of goal setting for organized social life is distinct from the process of rational social planning.* To achieve democratic social planning, therefore, we must establish universal decision-making procedures through which common wishes can be determined and collective goals can be set. Only in this way can we ensure that planned social activities will benefit rather than restrict all persons.

Forms of Social Planning

Regardless of whether the decision-making procedures in a society are democratic or autocratic (or some of each), there remains the additional question of how the overall planning process will be organized. Few individuals or organizations in a modernized society would totally reject the idea of planning. Most current arguments about social planning are not over whether or not to plan but over who should do the planning.

In the traditional type of pluralistic society, social planning is carried out by the numerous independent, intermediate organizations comprising the society. Each of these organizations is concerned first of all with devising more effective ways of obtaining its own particular goals, and only secondarily (if at all) with the consequences of its activities for the total society. The national government is then responsible primarily for coordinating these diverse private plans and activities; it does not itself directly engage in social planning. The present trend toward centralized governmental planning in the United States results partly from the fact that private, pluralistic planning is proving inadequate in dealing with societywide problems of economic growth, urbanization, race relations, and international affairs. Needless to say, if a society should begin to approximate the mass model, even limited forms of pluralistic planning would be impossible.

Both the socialistic and totalitarian models escape the weaknesses of pluralistic planning by centering most or all social planning in the polity—either the formal government or the ruling party. Centralized society-wide planning has long been a major tenet of socialism, as a means of promoting economic justice for all. Although many socialists contend that such planning could be fully democratic in operation, it nevertheless would be largely or wholly centralized in the national government. This one network would perform most social planning throughout the society in all major spheres of activity. The totalitarian model, meanwhile, is explicitly designed to facilitate totally centralized societal planning, although in this case the party rather than the government would actually perform these activities.

The systemic-society model, in contrast, attempts to combine the best features of both private pluralistic and public centralized planning. Most planning activities in this type of society would take place within the various functional networks, according to their specific concerns. No one unit would perform all planning for the entire society, but the planning conducted within each network or smaller subsector would be oriented first of all toward promoting the general welfare of the entire society, and only secondarily toward more immediate interests. In other words, concerns of public responsibility would be infused into all realms of social activity, partially through strong professional norms and partially through the pervasive demands of functional interdependence. Finally, broad-scale planning for the entire society would be performed —but not implemented—by the "societal policy council." In short, society-wide social planning, like all other social activities, would be decentralized along functional lines but simultaneously highly oriented toward public rather than private concerns.

Social Science and Social Planning

What place is there in the process of social planning for the professional social scientist? How can his expert knowledge be used without infringing upon democratic decision-making and goal determination?

The distinction between the roles of expert and citizen is crucial for this question. The social scientist, in his role as a professional expert, has two responsibilities for social planning in a democratic society. First, he must seek as much knowledge as possible concerning social processes and problems, so as to increase our understanding of these phenomena. Second, he must use his expert knowledge to suggest various plans for achieving whatever social goals are being sought, and also to evaluate the advantages and disadvantages of each of these proposed courses of action. In sum, he must act as both a researcher and a planner. But his role as an expert ends there. The social scientist's special competence in technical matters does not qualify or authorize him to determine social values or formulate overall goals for society, although he may certainly participate in these activities in his role as a concerned citizen of his society. Final decisions concerning the ends toward which social planning will be directed—which ultimately rest on shared social values—must in a democratic society be made by all citizens. The category of "citizen" may be limited by such criteria as age, mental competency, or previous behavior, but it cannot be restricted to either a ruling elite or professional experts. *The role of the expert is to provide necessary scientific and technical information, on the basis of which all citizens determine basic goals for their society, which organizational leaders and experts then together translate into concrete programs of action.* This is the essence of democratic social planning and of democratically controlled social organization.

If democracy is to operate effectively in complex, modernized societies, all citizens must concern themselves about public issues and participate actively in public affairs. The process of social organization can be shaped by man—through rational social planning and purposefully created patterns of social order and cultural ideas—so as to lead us to the collective goals we seek through organized social activities. But this requires both scientific knowledge about social life and unending concerted effort by all citizens. The future of man's social organization is within our hands—if we rise to the challenges confronting us!

RECOMMENDED READING

HAUSER, PHILIP, "Social Science and Social Engineering," *Philosophy of Science,* vol. 16 (July 1949), pp. 209–218. (Also Bobbs-Merrill reprint S-114.)
Distinguishes between pure and applied social research, and between social science and social engineering, and then argues for the importance of both distinctions.

HIMES, JOSEPH S., *Social Planning in America* (New York: Doubleday & Company, Inc., 1954).
Describes and explains the relationship of social planning to social change, the nature of social planning, the method of social planning, and the enactment of social planning in the United States.

INDEX

INDEX

Index